WITHDRAWN

SOUTH AFRICAN HISTORY

THEMES IN EUROPEAN EXPANSION: EXPLORATION,
COLONIZATION, AND THE IMPACT OF EMPIRE
(General Editor: James A. Casada)
VOL. 5

GARLAND REFERENCE LIBRARY
OF SOCIAL SCIENCE
VOL. 153

THEMES IN EUROPEAN EXPANSION: EXPLORATION, COLONIZATION AND THE IMPACT OF EMPIRE
(General Editor: James A. Casada)

1. Robert Heussler, *British Malaya: A Bibliographical and Biographical Compendium.*
2. William J. Olson with the assistance of Addeane S. Caelleigh, *Britain's Elusive Empire in the Middle East: An Annotated Bibliography.*
3. Susan F. Bailey, *Women and the British Empire: An Annotated Guide to Sources.*
4. Edward J. Goodman, *The Exploration of South America: An Annotated Bibliography.*
5. Naomi Musiker with the assistance of Reuben Musiker, *South African History: A Bibliographical Guide with Special Reference to Territorial Expansion and Colonization.*

SOUTH AFRICAN HISTORY
*A Bibliographical Guide
with Special Reference to
Territorial Expansion and Colonization*

Naomi Musiker
*with the assistance of
Reuben Musiker*

GARLAND PUBLISHING, INC., • NEW YORK & LONDON
1984

© 1984 Naomi Musiker and Reuben Musiker
All rights reserved

Library of Congress Cataloging in Publication Data
Musiker, Naomi.
   South African History

(Themes in European expansion : exploration, colonization, and the impact of empire ; vol. 5)
(Garland reference library of social science : vol. 153)
   Includes indexes.
   1. South Africa—History—Bibliography.
I. Musiker, Reuben. II. Title. III. Series: Themes in European expansion ; v. 5. IV. Series: Garland reference library of social science ; v. 153.
Z3606.M84 1984 [DT766] 016.968   82-49171
ISBN 0-8240-9174-4 (alk. paper)

Printed on acid-free, 250-year-life paper
Manufactured in the United States of America

CONTENTS

Editor's Introduction		ix
Preface		xi
Introduction		xv
Chapter I:	General Histories	1
Chapter II:	Travel and Exploration	10
	Exploration and Early Colonial Policy to 1652	10
Chapter III:	Travellers	
	Seventeenth Century	16
	Eighteenth Century	18
	1800–1850	21
	1850–1900	25
Chapter IV:	Cape—General History	26
	Dutch East India Company, 1652–1795	28
	First British Occupation and Batavian Rule, 1795–1806	36
	1806–1836	41
	Settlers of British Origin, 1820 onwards	46
	The Great Trek, 1836–1854	53
	1836–1899	58
Chapter V:	Natal—History and Description	77
Chapter VI:	Zululand	89
	To 1879	89

	War of 1879	93
	After 1879	98
Chapter VII:	Orange Free State, 1854–1899	100
Chapter VIII:	Transvaal	105
	1852–1899	105
	Transvaal War of Independence, 1880–1881	118
	Discovery of Gold in the Transvaal, 1886–1899	121
	Jameson Raid, 1896	124
Chapter IX:	Political Aspects of Railway Development into the Interior	127
Chapter X:	Anglo-Boer War, 1899–1902	128
	General History	128
	Causes and Events	131
	Military Campaigns	134
	Concentration Camps	138
	International Diplomacy	139
	Reminiscences, Biographies	142
Chapter XI:	Peace Treaty and Settlement, 1902–1910	145
Chapter XII:	South Africa, 1910–1980	151
Chapter XIII:	British Colonial and Imperial Policy	159
Chapter XIV:	Political Parties	
	National Party	170
	Liberal Parties	172
	Black Sash	172
	Afrikaner Broederbond	173
Chapter XV:	Prime Ministers Since Union	
	Collective Studies	174
	Individual Prime Ministers	174
	Botha, L.	174
	Hertzog, J.B.M.	175
	Malan, D.F.	176
	Smuts, J.C.	176

Contents vii

	Strijdom, J.G.	179
	Verwoerd, H.F.	179
	Vorster, B.J.	180
Chapter XVI:	Race Contacts, Race Policy, Race Relations	181
Chapter XVII:	Missionaries	198
Chapter XVIII:	South African Population	
	Black Peoples	209
	Bushmen and Hottentots	220
	Chinese Peoples	222
	Coloured Peoples	223
	Indian Peoples	227
	White Peoples	
	Afrikaners	231
	Americans	236
	English	236
	Germans	237
	Huguenots	237
	Jews	238
	Scandinavians	239
Author/Title Index		240
Subject/Topographical Index		277

EDITOR'S INTRODUCTION

This work, the fifth to appear in the ongoing series "Themes in European Expansion: Exploration, Colonization, and the Impact of Empire," is a welcome and singularly appropriate addition to the reference collection of which it becomes a part. The product of an experienced husband-and-wife team of historical bibliographers, Reuben and Naomi Musiker, it deals with matters which have considerable interest to students of the current scene as well as those of the past. Like its predecessor volumes in the series, the central thrust of the present work is to provide in-depth reference coverage of the existing literature on its subject. In addition, it features a substantial introductory chapter delineating the current state of bibliographical endeavor in the field, careful indexing reflecting both subject coverage and authorship, and the other scholarly appurtenances needed to give a work of this genre the greatest possible utility. Of particular note are the exceptionally detailed annotations accompanying each individual entry.

South African History, in keeping with the overall scope of the series of which it is a part, attempts to provide representative coverage of the literature on all aspects of expansion, colonization, settlement, and development in the vast and diverse geographic region lying to the south of the Zambesi River. Today this is an important area buffeted by what former British Prime Minister Harold Macmillan called "the winds of change," and anyone who wishes to understand the complex forces producing these winds must first become familiar with the history underlying them. Surprisingly, given the region's historical importance in general and the acute historical consciousness of South Africans in particular, heretofore no extensive evaluative bibliography has existed treating European expansion into the continent's southernmost regions. Now Reuben and Naomi Musiker have pooled their talents in producing a major bibliography which fills a significant gap in reference literature.

Reuben Musiker, the book's editor, is today generally recognized as South Africa's premier bibliographer. He currently serves as University Librarian and Professor of Librarianship and Bibliography at the University of the Witwatersrand in Johannesburg, South Africa. The author of such works as *South African Bibliography* (the standard authority on the subject), the volume on South Africa in the World Bibliographies Series, and a *Guide to South African Reference Books*, he is an amazingly productive writer. In addition to these and other book-length efforts, Musiker is the author of upwards of one hundred and fifty articles on various specialized bibliographical topics and library themes. Presently he is particularly interested in the concept of bibliographical control and, in addition to his research and academic pursuits, he regularly serves as a consultant to bibliographers, historians, Africana collectors, and others working in his areas of expertise.

As regards the present work, Naomi Musiker's background and academic training nicely complement her husband's specialities. A graduate of the University of the Witwatersrand in History and French, she taught for a time in South African schools and subsequently qualified as a librarian. She and Professor Musiker have collaborated on previous projects, notably a number of entries in the *Dictionary of South African Biography*, and she is the compiler of a calendar of the papers of Sir Charles Crewe. In the present volume, she examined every book listed and prepared the accompanying annotations.

The finished product of the Musikers' efforts is a major reference work which promises to lend itself to the endeavors of students and specialists in a variety of fields and disciplines. Historians, geographers, anthropologists, linguists, sociologists, and others will find grist for their research mills in this book. It assesses, with detailed critical annotations, the major book-length publications on the southern African past. While it is a selective bibliography—the vast corpus of printed material on the subject dictates that such be the case—it nonetheless offers a comprehensive coverage of the variegated aspects of the history of the region and its peoples. As such, it is a reference tool which should find a home in all academic and larger public libraries.

James A. Casada
Series Editor

PREFACE

This bibliographical guide to South African history is not comprehensive, in that it does not purport to cover all South African subject fields. The work focuses on more than 1000 items which constitute the fabric of South African history as the term is generally understood.

A compiler in this area can be said to rush in where angels fear to tread, because the documentation is very extensive, so much so that it is an indisputable fact that South Africa is the best documented country on the continent of Africa. A bibliographer who has embarked on this course has the choice of one of two compilations. He can try to list every significant work in all fields, including all facets of knowledge and human development. Such a compilation will embrace also a wide variety of collateral fields, such as the social sciences (including sociology, politics, education, economics) as well as religion, fine arts, language and literature, science and technology, transportation, medicine and numerous specific topics spread across the entire spectrum of knowledge. This is the course four professors of history preferred when compiling their bibliography of South African history*. Their bibliography is not an effective guide to the literature of South African history because there are no annotations of a descriptive or informative type. It is in effect a nonevaluative bibliography, which would be more correctly described as a check-list.

The authors of the present guide adopted the opposite viewpoint. Having decided to confine their selection to the history of South Africa and not to delve into the great number of historical books in specific subject fields, they then felt obliged to person-

---

*Muller, C.F.J. and others, eds. *South African History and Historians* (Pretoria: University of South Africa, 1979).

ally examine and thoroughly describe each work listed. It was considered wiser not to serve as arbiters of what constitutes scholarship or to discriminate against popular or polemical works. In limiting the range of material, the compilers were able to apply themselves to the task of annotating the publications and guiding the research worker, who is often situated in a far-off land and does not have immediate access to the publication itself.

It was decided not to specify locations of the publications listed because the majority of the items listed are available in the Africana Collections of the University of the Witwatersrand Library, Johannesburg, as well as other major South African university libraries and Africana Collections. The immediate availability of all these books greatly facilitated the task of compilation.

A chronological arrangement is inevitable in a bibliography of this type, and the first ten sections follow this pattern. The last part of the compilation assumes a different form because this basic historical material does not lend itself to chronological treatment.

The emphasis throughout the compilation has been laid on the expansion of European peoples and influences into South Africa. The very nature of South African history involves a considerable incidence of expansion and penetration; this is apparent from even a cursory glance at the headings which comprise this bibliography. Furthermore, the concept of this expansionist tendency and the ensuing penetration is evident throughout the centuries. So much of what happened in South African history relates to this contact between Europe and South Africa. Beginning with the early explorers and travellers and progressing through the early Dutch and British occupations, the compilation proceeds to cover all the subsequent events involving further contact, expansion and penetration. The Great Trek of 1836–1854, the Zululand War of 1879, the Transvaal War of 1880–1881, and the Anglo-Boer War of 1899–1902 were some of the landmark events which shaped South Africa in the ensuing years.

Other relevant aspects of contact and penetration which receive detailed treatment in this bibliography are British colonial

Preface

and imperial policy, race contacts and policy, and the various European components of the South African population.

In order to keep the compilation in meaningful proportions, it was decided to exclude neighbouring territories, even though they form part of Southern Africa. Countries such as Botswana, Lesotho, Swaziland and Zimbabwe are all served by independent bibliographies of history (some annotated) appended to the relevant volumes in the African Historical Dictionary series, published by Scarecrow Press, as well as in the World Bibliographical Series published by Clio Press.

The present compilation is an analysis of published books; it would have swelled the work to unreasonable proportions had the decision been made to include periodical articles and theses (excepting those which formed part of the *Archives Yearbook for South African History*). It is possible that these will form the focus of a succeeding volume, Even so that decision is defended on the grounds that there are readily available comprehensive published lists of theses (See page xxiii) as well as indexes of periodical articles on South African topics (See page xxiv). Theses are also included in *South African History and Historians* (See page xxvi), where they are dispersed among the various chronological and subject sections. The majority of works dealing with the history of specific South African subject themes (e.g., education, religion, language and literature) can be readily pinpointed by consulting the relevant section of *South African History and Historians* and R. Musiker's *South Africa* in the World Bibliographical Series (Oxford: Clio Press, 1979). Biographies have on the whole been excluded, except where the subject has been a significant person in the charting of South African history.

The annotations of two categories of material are fuller than would normally have been the case: (1) Material in the Afrikaans language and (2) Monographs which were published in the *Archives Yearbook for South African History*. It was felt that research workers overseas would value the extra fullness because of language problems and also because the *Archives Yearbook* is not always readily accessible outside of South Africa.

The editor advised the compiler on the selection of material, edited the work as a whole, and was responsible for the bibliographical construction and final form of the work. The compiler and editor are most grateful to the Series Editor, Professor James Casada, for his painstaking help with many aspects of the book. The University of the Witwatersrand's Africana Librarian, Mrs. Beth Strachan, willingly and enthusiastically left no stone unturned in making readily available to the authors the books needed for this compilation. Mrs. V. Falk, who in her dedication as a typist has always been an inspiration to the editor, was responsible for typing a difficult manuscript.

> R. Musiker
> *The Library*
> *University of the Witwatersrand, Johannesburg*

INTRODUCTION

EARLY BIBLIOGRAPHICAL DEVELOPMENTS

The bibliographical tradition in South Africa, though sound, is of comparatively recent origin. The earliest bibliographical achievements date from the year 1821.[1] In this year the South African Library published its first library catalogue, just three years after the Library opened in March 1818. This catalogue, *Catalogue of the Dessinian Collection in the Public Library of Cape Town*, was compiled by two clergymen, the Rev. Messrs. H.W. von Manger and F.R. Kaufman. The Dessinian Collection was general in scope but contained a few rare items of Africana dating from the seventeenth and eighteenth centuries and was written in the Dutch language. Original copies of the catalogue are so rare as to be collector's items.

The first general printed catalogue of the South African Library appeared in 1825 and was followed by a fuller catalogue in 1834. Both were compiled by the Librarian, A.J. Jardine. Classified catalogues of the South African Library appeared periodically throughout the nineteenth century. By 1881, the catalogue had swelled to 646 pages.

By the middle of the nineteenth century published public library catalogues had made their appearance elsewhere in the Cape; notably Albany (Grahamstown) (1851) and Port Elizabeth (1854). Later catalogues included Lovedale (1879), Natal Society, Pietermaritzburg (1881), Kimberley (1884), Bloemfontein (1891), Queenstown (1893), Pretoria (1894) and Johannesburg (1896). The Library of Parliament's Catalogue of 1896 should also be noted. At first sight these published catalogues would appear to be too general to be of interest to the historian. However, R.F. Kennedy has very aptly remarked[2] that general collections are often strong in special topics or special material and sometimes stronger than the special collections. He goes on to quote as an example the Strange Collection of the Johannesburg Public Library which is very strong in maps, in Afrikaans and in vernacular languages and concentrates particularly on individuals such as Le Vaillant and Tachard.

THE PIONEER BIBLIOGRAPHERS

The first real South African bibliographies—as distinct from library catalogues—appeared in the second half of the nineteenth century. The first professional bibliographer in South African context was Wilhelm Heinrich Immanuel Bleek (1827–1875). In 1857 while engaged as an interpreter by the Governor of the Cape Colony, Sir George Grey, Bleek completed much of the first part of the Grey Library Catalogue. By May 1858 Bleek was at work on a descriptive catalogue of the African Library of Sir George Grey. Grey had accumulated a remarkable collection of manuscripts and books including incunabula, medieval illuminated manuscripts and early English printed books. Of great interest to South African philologists and historians are his collections of early Cape printing and South African philological material which contain the efforts of missionaries to document Bantu languages on small and primitive presses. The resulting catechisms and wordbooks now constitute the incunabula of South African printing history. Bleek recorded some 500 separate publications and manuscripts in, or relating to, no fewer than sixteen dialects in South Africa with brief and lucid annotations. Grey's library was presented to the South African Library in 1863. Bleek completed the catalogue of the Grey collection in 1867. The four volumes cover the entire collection and are still available for consultation in the Library. In 1884, T. Hahn compiled *An Index of the Grey Collection in the South African Library*.

In 1886, the catalogue of another private collector appeared—*Catalogue of Books Relating to South Africa*; and it was compiled by Charles Aiken Fairbridge (1824–1893) and John Noble (1837–1898).

Fairbridge was a parliamentarian from 1854 to 1879, a lawyer, a trustee of the Grey Library and a bibliophile with a library of 7,250 volumes, which subsequently passed to the South African Library through the benefaction of Sir Abe Bailey. In order to compile the catalogue for the Colonial and Indian Exhibition in London, Fairbridge and Noble, Clerk of the Legislative Assembly, listed not only Fairbridge's collection but also certain holdings of the South African Library. Some 600 works were listed but voyages, travels, government blue books, parliamentary papers and pamphlets were excluded. The value of the catalogue is that for the first time an attempt was made to enumerate books containing information regarding the Cape of Good Hope and Africa south of the Zambezi River. For each item the full name of the author, full title, size, place of publication and date are given. Although there are no annotations, it is a reasonable and acceptable pioneer effort. Its greatest weakness is lack of comprehensiveness; its contents represent less than a tenth of the items included in the two-volume Mendelssohn Bibliography of 1910 and no more than a third of the items found in Theal's Catalogue of 1912.

Sidney Mendelssohn remains the best-known name in South African bibliography, and his two-volume *South African Bibliography* is still the most familiar landmark among Africana bibliophiles and historians. Mendelssohn (1860–1917) was the son of a Bristol rabbi and prospered at the Kimberley diamond diggings. He was a director, later chairman, of the Bultfontein Mining Company in Kimberley and subsequently managing director of the Vaal River Diamond and Exploration Company. He returned to England in 1905 and began collecting, reading, and annotating books about South Africa. In searching for books he used as his major sources the Fairbridge/Noble catalogue and Theal histories. Encouraged by a remark made by Sir Percival Laurence at the first Conference of South African Librarians in 1904, Mendelssohn set about seriously compiling an exhaustive catalogue of works relating to South Africa. The *South African Bibliography* was not completed until 1910. The bibliography contained some 7,500 items consisting of annotated entries of his own collection with some entries for works he did not possess. In addition to the catalogue of books, there were also lists of South African imperial blue books, periodical articles relating to South Africa, autographed letters and signed documents, a list of maps and a chronological and topographical subject index. The work is arranged alphabetically by author or by title when the author is not known. The entries are very comprehensive with full author's name, title and descriptive annotations. Mendelssohn undoubtedly completed most of this mammoth task on his own although he did have four months assistance from P. Evans Lewin, Librarian of the Royal Colonial Institute. The introduction to the bibliography by Ian Colvin is in itself of great interest as it contains valuable bibliographical information and was reprinted by A.A. Balkema (Cape Town) in 1979. Evans Lewin, writing in *United Empire* in 1910, maintained that Mendelssohn's bibliography revealed "an historical and critical analysis that is not approached in any other colonial bibliography."[3]

R.F. Kennedy, the former Librarian of the Johannesburg Public Library and a noted expert on Africana, writing fifty-five years later, conceded that Mendelssohn's annotations contained a British bias and many inaccuracies. He maintained however that the work had proved invaluable to him for thirty years and was still more useful than any other bibliography of Africana.[4] In 1960 a revision project was launched to bring the *South African Bibliography* up to date. Financial support was obtained from the National Council for Social Research. The project was headed by A.M. Lewin Robinson, Director of the South African Library and supervised by an advisory committee. In March 1979, *A South African Bibliography to the Year 1925* was published.[5] It recorded omissions from, and corrections to the Mendelssohn bibliography, as well as additional material published up to 1925. The four-volume work contained 35,000 items drawn from twenty-nine South African libraries with major South African collections. Entries from the original bibliography were greatly abridged, thereby losing some of the unique appeal of Mendelssohn's annotations. The items were arranged alphabetically by author. Annotations were of the bibliographical variety and not descriptive or informative as they were in the original work. Maps, atlases, periodicals, newspapers, manuscripts, post-1854 government publications and works in African languages were omitted. The total absence of any form of subject approach is a

Introduction   *xix*

serious deficiency. The work covers the area south of the Limpopo River, South West Africa, Madagascar (to 1850), Mauritius (to 1850), Bechuanaland, Basutoland and Swaziland. Work has commenced on a supplement.

In 1912, two years after the publication of Mendelssohn's bibliography, there appeared a 408-page alphabetical bibliography listing some 2,000 books and pamphlets relating to Africana south of the Zambezi.[6] This work, *Catalogue of Books and Pamphlets Relating to Africa*, was compiled by George McCall Theal (1837–1919) who achieved fame as a chronicler of South African history. Canadian-born, Theal was successively teacher, journalist, public servant, Cape Colonial archivist and colonial historiographer. Theal is better known for his eight-volume *History of South Africa*, and his compilations: *Records of the Cape Colony* (35 vols.) and *Records of South East Africa* (9 vols). Theal based his bibliography not only on the works of his own collection but also on works in the South African Library and in the British Museum. His annotations, which are descriptive and often critical, helped to make his work very useful. The broad divisions in the subject section provided a retrieval facility complementary in a way to that given by Mendelssohn in his subject index, e.g., Bantu, Basutoland, Biography, German West Africa, Natal, Orange Free State, War of 1899/1902. Kennedy has made some interesting observations on Theal's *Catalogue*.[7] In spite of inaccuracies and technical effects, it is a valuable bibliography. Kennedy urges the reader to compare Theal's annotations with those of Mendelssohn. One becomes aware that Theal's annotations are those of an archivist and historian who has used the books in the writing of his histories. Theal's observations are often biased, but his facts, usually taken from primary archival sources, are accurate.

It is interesting to note in summing up this early period, that most of the bibliographers of the nineteenth and early twentieth centuries were not trained librarians or historians by profession. Fairbridge and Mendelssohn were wealthy bibliophiles with a consuming interest in their hobby while Bleek was a biblical scholar and philologist by profession. The first Librarian of the South African Public Library, A.J. Jardine, is described by A.M. Lewin Robinson as a man of good education and of literary merit but there is no evidence of bibliographic training.[8] Finally G. McCall Theal, one of the greatest of South Africa's early historians, appears to have acquired his archival training only after obtaining the post of Cape Archivist. The South African historian C.F.J. Muller has written of Theal as follows: "He had to work in his spare time under difficult circumstances. He was a self-trained historian and in many respects his work does not comply with the requirements of scientific archival sources, many of which were published by himself. Although they should be used with discretion, his documentary publications are still important keys to the original records in the archives."[9]

DEVELOPMENTS SINCE 1919

The period between the two world wars produced no major South African bibliographies of interest. The Mendelssohn and Theal bibliographies continued to be of great use but their alphabetical arrangement provided scholars with limited subject guidance. This deficiency made it necessary for historians to depend on the published catalogues of the Library of the Royal Commonwealth Society (formerly Royal Empire Society). Volume 1 (1930) of the four-volume set published between 1930 and 1937 included a South African component entitled *Subject Catalogue of the Library by P. Evans Lewin. Vol. 1. British Empire Generally and Africa*. A further volume published in 1961 was entitled *Biography Catalogue of the Library* by D.E. Simpson and included over 700 South African items. In 1971 a seven-volume subject sequel to the earlier catalogues of the Royal Empire Society was published.

From 1938 onwards there was a revival of interest in bibliographical production due to the influence of the newly established library school at the University of Cape Town. This was followed by library training courses at the University of Pretoria (also 1938), Potchefstroom University (1956), the Universities of the Witwatersrand and of Stellenbosch (1958), the University of South Africa (1955), the University of the Orange Free State (1964) and Rhodes University, Grahamstown (1966). Subject bibliographies were compiled as part of the course work for the

Introduction

diploma in librarianship at some of these universities. Many of these student bibliographies have been included in the present work under their relevant headings. The South African Library Association encouraged bibliographical projects through a specially appointed subcommittee. D.H. Varley, head of the South African Library, Cape Town from 1938 to 1961, played a great part in bibliographical development.

A contemporaneous development was taking place in the field of historical study at South African universities. Van Jaarsveld, in a penetrative study, estimates that scholarly history writing in South Africa dates from the third decade of the twentieth century.[10] History students were required to base their dissertations on archival research and source publications. Wide avenues of publication promoted historical writing. One of the most influential of these historical publications was *The Archives Year Book for South African History*, an official publication which first appeared in 1938. This contains research work done by history students at the various universities and is included in the present work.

It is interesting to note that at a congress held at the University of South Africa in March 1979, problems of the interpretation of history were discussed by a panel of specialists. Some traditional and almost sacrosanct beliefs concerning the events of the Battle of Blood River were challenged, resulting in considerable controversy.[11] Historiography in English was favoured by overseas contributions to Empire history and to that of the Commonwealth, for example, *The Cambridge History of the British Empire, Vol. 8: South Africa*, published in 1936. It was therefore inevitable that the renewed interest in bibliographical production and the increasing stream of scientific historical writing should result in the production of various bibliographies to assist the scholar.

ROLE OF THE NATIONAL LIBRARIES

Two of the national libraries of South Africa, the South African Library, Cape Town, and the State Library, Pretoria, were the first to play important roles in bibliographical development. The *Bibliography of African Bibliograhies Covering Territories South of the Sahara* was first compiled by P. Freer and D.H. Varley and published in *South African Libraries* for October 1942 and January 1943. It was subsequently expanded and revised by Lewin Robinson and published as no. 2 in the series of Grey Bibliographies (1948). A third, revised edition was published in 1955 and classified according to the Universal Decimal Classification. The fourth edition appeared in 1961, containing over 350 additional items and omitting a few superseded items. Entries were limited to bibliographies of some length and substance. When an item consisted of a self-contained booklist or bibliography, full pagination was given: otherwise the relevant pages only were indicated in the entry.

The *Bibliography of African Bibliographies* contained some 1,340 entries and never progressed beyond the 1961 edition. It became almost impossible to record all the subsequent bibliographical guides published overseas which included some reference to South Africa. R. Musiker has however attempted this task selectively since 1970.[12]

The South African Library also produced a national bibliography which commenced in September 1946 as a classified bibliography of material relating to South Africa in the *Quarterly Bulletin* of the South African Library. In 1958 this bibliography emerged as a separate publication entitled *Africiana Nova*. The first issue appeared in September 1958 and the last in December 1969. Publication was disbanded because the contents duplicated those of the *South African National Bibliography*. Items included works published in South Africa and abroad.

From 1959 onwards, the State Library commenced publication of the *South African National Bibliography* consisting of publications received under copyright legislation. This bibliography is a quarterly with annual cumulations. The arrangement is according to the Dewey Decimal Classification order, the entries in each broad group being subarranged alphabetically by author. Official publications, books in Bantu languages, and new periodicals are included. A cumulative volume of *South African National Bibliography* for 1968–1971 was published in 1972. The State Library aims to publish a retrospective bibliography to cover the period 1926 to 1958. The *South African National Bibliography* is limited to books bearing a South African imprint. To remedy this deficiency, the State Library has issued, from 1973 onwards a *Bibliography of Overseas Publications about South Africa*. The initial volume covers the years 1969 to 1971. Further volumes have appeared biennially.

THESES AND DISSERTATIONS

Mention should also be made of the documentation of work done as theses and dissertations in South Africa. The Union Catalogue of Theses and Dissertations of South African Universities, 1918–1977[13] supersedes previous lists compiled by A.M. Lewin Robinson (for 1918–1941) and S.I. Malan (for 1942–1958). The primary arrangement is by broad subject (e.g., history), and there is a detailed author sequence as well. The list is entitled Union Catalogue because it gives locations of all the theses listed in various South African libraries. The Catalogue was published on 116 microfiche and has been supplemented annually in hard copy. A comprehensive list of post-1918 South African theses in the field of history is being compiled by the Institute of Contemporary History at the University of the Orange Free State. Three overseas lists have South African relevance.[14] [15] [16]

ARCHIVES AND MANUSCRIPTS

The Government Archives in South Africa fulfill a valuable role in historical research and house primary source material. In South Africa the Archives are decentralised and there are six depots. In 1977 the Government Archives launched a project to compile a national register of manuscripts, using computer facilities (NAREM). The Register is a co-operative venture, with the Archives processing individual institutional guides to manuscript holdings. For each collection the Register gives such information as the donor, period covered and a summary of the contents.

The following collections are now available through NAREM;

Carnegie Library, University of Stellenbosch
Barlow Rand Archives, Johannesburg
National English Document Centre, Grahamstown
University of the Witwatersrand Library, Johannesburg
Merensky Library, University of Pretoria
Documentation Centre of African Studies, University of South Africa

There are now available several guides to overseas archives on South Africa.[17] The Archives have issued *List of Archives Publications Published Officially After 1925*. This is a full list of Archives publications giving author, title and price and including a full contents list of *Archives Year Book of South Africa* from volume one in 1938 onwards as well as a detailed list of *South African Archival Records* for each of the provinces.

INDEXES TO PERIODICALS

The *Index to South African Periodicals*,[18] which covers the period from 1940 to date, includes a considerable quantity of historical material. The *Index* covers 360 of the more important South African periodicals, and a good many of these are historical in scope. The series of volumes published so far include decennial cumulations for 1940/1949, 1950/1959, 1960/1969 as well as a quenquennial volume for 1970/1974 and annual volumes thereafter. The Johannesburg Public Library, which published this valuable research tool, has made considerable progress with an index to South African periodicals for the period 1900 to 1940.

Overseas indexes to periodicals have been listed by R. Musiker in his book *South African Bibliography*.

OFFICIAL PUBLICATIONS

The importance of government documents as sources for the study of a nation's history is too well known to warrant

Introduction

restatement here. The principal official South African publications have been described in R. Musiker's *South African Bibliography*.[20]

CONTRIBUTIONS OF THE HISTORIANS

The bibliographical work done by historians themselves should also be considered. Many of the general works on South African history contain excellent bibliographies. Some examples of these are as follows:

The Cambridge History of the British Empire, vol. VIII, edited by Eric Walker (1936) with a long bibliographic chapter by A. Taylor Milne and A. Lloyd, (Entry 004);

C.F.J. Muller has included a good bibliography in his work *500 Years—A History of South Africa* (Entry 028);

The Oxford History of South Africa edited by M. Wilson and L.M. Thompson (1966, 1969) contained a very extensive bibliography at the end of each of its two volumes. This bibliography included manuscript sources, government publications, printed books, and articles (Entry 041). In 1982, the first volume was republished in paperback form as *A History of South Africa to 1870*. The bibliography was omitted in favour of footnotes. The new preface contains a discussion of very recent historical works and is well worth attention.

T.R.H. Davenport, in his work *South Africa: A Modern History* (Entry 010), has provided informative bibliographical notes at the conclusion of the text. These notes are useful in supplying key publications for topics covered in the book but are arranged in a rather haphazard manner.

Thompson has provided some excellent bibliographical guides, including a useful guide to scholarly articles.[21] Although this is not annotated, it is arranged by subject headings. Thompson has also compiled an excellent critical survey of historical writing on South Africa from 1877 to 1965.[22]

Van Jaarsveld's work, *The Afrikaner's Interpretation of South African History*, contains the most sustained and objective evaluation of South African historical writing yet produced, particularly as regards the period prior to 1960. (Entry 1012). An evaluation of historical documentation on territorial penetration in South Africa was produced by D.M. Schreuder in *The Scramble for Southern Africa, 1877–1895: The Politics of Partition Reappraised* (Entry 727). Schreuder's bibliographical chapter at the conclusion of the book takes the form of an essay in which the most important books and periodicals are discussed. Schreuder has also offered a survey of the literature as of 1969 in a previous article.[23] The significant contributions of Thompson and Schreuder reaffirm that bibliographical guidance is sometimes offered in the form of valuable bibliographical essays, which give evaluative and critical information.

A study which covers new aspects of South African history is *The Frontier in History: North America and Southern Africa Compared* edited by H. Lamar and L. Thompson (Entry 820). The bibliographical chapter in this work is by George Miles and is a departure from the traditional insular listing of books dealing with the South African frontier as an isolated phenomenon.

The most comprehensive historical bibliography yet compiled in South Africa appeared in 1966 under the title *A Select Bibliography of South African History*. This work was undertaken by four history professors, C.F.J. Muller, F.A. van Jaarsveld, T. van Wijk and M. Boucher of the Universities of South Africa and Pretoria. A supplement was published in 1974. In 1979, a new edition appeared under the title *South African History and Historians*.[24] This bibliography contains 4,518 items and fulfils a definite need by listing extensively as many scholarly works as possible which could be of value to the historian. In addition, the bibliography is very logically arranged by period and by subject. There are certain drawbacks to the work. The first section, Aids to Research, contains certain omissions and is arranged alphabetically. The items contained in this section would have been more useful if arranged under their respective subject headings. In attempting to be comprehensive, the editors have intruded on other disciplines such as art, language and literature. There are no descriptive or informative annotations and the research worker is at a loss to understand the relevance of the above-mentioned inclusions. An even more serious criticism is that the total absence of annotations makes it impossible to discriminate between the large variety of publications which followed a major event such as the Anglo-Boer War, 1899/1902. The greater value of this compilation lies in its revelation of what still remains to be published. The omission of a title index is a further drawback when using this work. Despite all these faults, the work remains extremely valuable as a checklist and will no doubt be the forerunner of future historical bibliographies in South Africa.

Current annual reviews of South African historiography and of bibliographical development appear in each issue of the *Official South African Yearbook*[25] and in *African Research and Documentation*, respectively. The bibliography of history, in common with enumerative bibliography in other fields, can never reach finality. With the ever-increasing output of publications—which has attained flood-like proportions in the case of South Africa—it is necessary to revise those bibliographies and essays which have proved to be valuable research aids in the past. Surveys and assessments of historical literature date quickly after publication. Furthermore, the nature of historiography tends to change with the passage of time. For these reasons the authors of the present volume look forward to supplementing and revising their work from time to time.

REFERENCES

1. Musiker, R. "A Century of Bibliographical Achievement in South Africa." In: *Bibliophilia Africana IV*. Cape Town: South African Library, 1981. pp. 67–81.

2. Kennedy, R.F. *Africana Repository*. Cape Town: Juta, 1965 pp. 1–2.

3. Evans Lewin, P. "The Mendelssohn Library and Bibliography," *Africana Notes and News*, vol. 3, 1946, pp. 101–7.

4. Kennedy, R.F. *Africana Repository*. Johannesburg: Juta, 1965. p. 4.

5. *A South African Bibliography to the Year 1925*. London: Mansell, 1979. 4v.

6. Theal, G. McCall. *Catalogue of Books and Pamphlets Relating to Africa.* Cape Town: Maskew Miller, 1912. Facs. Repr. Cape Town: Struik, 1963.

7. Kennedy, R. F. ibid. pp. 9–10.

8. Robinson, A.M.L. "Alexander Johnstone Jardine," In: *Standard Encyclopaedia of Southern Africa.* Cape Town: Nasou, 1972, vol. 6, p. 186–187.

9. Muller, C.F.J. "George McCall Theal" In: *Standard Encyclopaedia of Southern Africa.* Cape Town: Nasou, 1974. vol. 10, pp. 468–470.

10. Van Jaarsveld, F.A. *The Afrikaner's Interpretation of South African History.* Cape Town: Simondium Publishers, 1964. pp. 116–165.

11. König. A. and H. Keane. "The Meaning of History: Problems in the Interpretation of History with Possible Reference to Examples from South African History such as the Battle of Blood River." Congress held at Unisa 28–30 March 1979. Pretoria: University of South Africa. 1980.

12. Musiker, R. *South African Bibliography.* London: Crosby Lockwood, 1970; 2nd ed. Cape Town: Philip, 1980.

13. *Union Catalogue of Theses and Dissertations of South African Universities, 1918–1977.* Potchefstroom: Ferdinand Postma Library, Potchefstroom University for Christian Higher Education, 1978. Cumulative Supplement, 1978–1981.

14. McIlwaine, J.H.St. J. *Theses on Africa, 1963–1975, Accepted by Universities in the United Kingdom and Ireland.* London: Mansell, 1978. A continuation of SCOLMA. *Theses on Africa, Accepted by Universities in the United Kingdom and Ireland, 1920–1962.* Cambridge: Heffer. 1964.

15. Pollak, O., and K. Pollak. *Theses and Dissertations on Southern Africa. [1884–1974].* Boston: Hall, 1976.

16. Sims, M., and A. Kagan. *American and Canadian Doctoral Dissertations and Master's Theses on Africa, 1886–1974.* Waltham, Mass.: African Studies Association, 1976.

17. For example: Matthews, N., and M.D. Wainwright. *A Guide to Manuscripts and Documents in the British Isles Relating to Africa*; ed. by J.D. Pearson. London: Oxford University Press, 1968. Supplement. 1971; Duignan, P. *Handbook of American Resources for African Studies.* Stanford: Hoover Institution on War, Revolution and Peace, Stanford University, 1967.

Introduction   xxix

18. *Index to South African Periodicals, 1940–*. Johannesburg: Public Library, 1942–.

19. Musiker, R. *South African Bibliography*; 2nd ed. Cape Town: Philip, 1980. p. 30.

20. Ibid., pp. 36–38.

21. Thompson, L.M., R. Elphick, and I. Jarrick, *Southern African History Before 1969: A Select Bibliography of Articles*. Stanford: Hoover Institution Press, 1971.

22. Thompson, L.M. "South Africa." In: *The Historiography of the British Empire-Commonwealth*. ed. by R.W. Winks. Durham, North Carolina: Duke University Press, 1966. pp. 212–236.

23. Schreuder, D. "History on the Veld—Towards a New Dawn." *African Affairs*. April 1969, pp. 149–159.

24. Muller, C.F.J., and others, eds. *South African History and Historians: A Bibliography*. Pretoria: University of South Africa, 1979.

25. South Africa: *Official Year Book of the Republic of South Africa*. Pretoria: Department of Information, 1974–.

SOUTH AFRICAN HISTORY

CHAPTER I
GENERAL HISTORIES

001. Agar-Hamilton, J.A.I. South Africa. London: Arrowsmith, 1934. x, 134pp. maps. bibl.

    Brief survey of important events in South African history written in an interesting and concise style comprehensible to scholars. This work is somewhat out of date.

002. Böeseken, A.J. and others. Drie Eeue: Die Verhaal van ons Vaderland. Cape Town: Nasionale Boekhandel, 1952. 5v. illus.

    A general history of South Africa written in a simple and interesting manner. Suitable for young people.

003. Cambridge History of Africa. Cambridge: University Press, 1975-. 8v. maps. bibl.

    The eight volumes are intended to cover the following periods in African history: (1) Earliest times to 500 B.C. (2) 500 B.C. to A.D. 1050. (3) 1050 to 1600. (4) 1600 to 1790. (5) 1790 to 1870. (6) 1870 to 1920. (7) 1920 to 1942. (8) 1943 to the 1970s. The complete series has not yet appeared. Each volume is divided into sections dealing with different regions of Africa. Very scholarly detailed treatment of African history with footnotes and extensive bibliographical essays and bibliographies at the end of each volume.

004. Cambridge History of the British Empire. Vol. VIII. South Africa, Rhodesia and the High Commission Territories; ed. by Eric A. Walker. Cambridge: University Press, 1963. xxviii, 1087pp. bibl.

    Part of a series of three 'dominion volumes' which aims at describing British expansionist and imperial policies. Divided into sections, each written by an expert in that particular field; e.g., I. Schapera on the native inhabitants, Sir George Cory on the British settlers, A.F. Hattersley on slavery at the Cape, W.M. Macmillan on coloured peoples at the

Cape, Sir Arnold Plant on the economic development of South
Africa. Very comprehensive and scholarly coverage of all
aspects of Southern African history. Very extensive bibliography.

005. Christopher, A.J. Southern Africa. London: Dawson; Hamden:
Archon Books, 1976. 292pp. illus. maps. bibl.

Attempts to show how white settlers, over a period of three
hundred years, have changed the landscape of Southern Africa.
This was done through the introduction of new crops and
animals, the creation of towns and industrial development.
Also discusses the results of European and African contact to
1960, and the effects of African tribes upon the landscape.

006. Cope, J. South Africa. London: Benn, 1965. xvii, 236pp.
maps. bibl.

Discusses historical events in South Africa which led to the
rise of Afrikaner republicanism and the policy of separate
development. Analyses the political scene in modern day South
Africa, political parties, African movements, and attitudes of
church leaders towards apartheid. Also discusses international
relationships.

007. Cory, G.E. The Rise of South Africa: A History of the Origin
of South African Colonisation and of Its Development Towards
the East from the Earliest Times to 1875. London: Longmans
Green, 1910. facs. repr. Cape Town: Struik, 1965. 6v.
illus.

Volumes 1 to 6 cover the history of South Africa from 1820
to 1856. Contains research based on archival material.
Particularly interested in the British settlers of the Eastern
Cape and much research and interviews with survivors of the
1820 settlement was carried out by the author. Like Theal,
his research and factual information still valuable, though
his judgements have been criticised.

008. Danziger, C. The Pioneers, B.C. - 1795: An Illustrated History of South Africa with Bibliographical Record. Cape
Town: Purnell, 1979. 100pp.

The first of a four-part history of South Africa, which
aims at presenting South African history from earliest times
and at describing customs and beliefs as well as historical
events. The first half of the book consists of a well-
illustrated survey of South African history. The second
section consists of an alphabetically arranged bibliographical
record of all persons mentioned in the volume. Useful series
for young people. Further titles in preparation are:
"Expanding Frontiers 1795-1854," "The Explosive Years 1854-
1910" and "A New Society 1910-1980."

General Histories 3

009. Davenport, T.R.H., and K.S. Hunt, eds. The Right to the Land: Documents on Southern African History. Cape Town: David Philip, 1974. 90pp. maps.

A collection of documents, chronologically arranged, to present in depth the recurrent problem in South African history --ownership and occupation of the land. Section 1 covers the manner in which European forms of land tenure were introduced into Southern Africa. Section 2 deals with the expansion of white settlement and establishment of reserves. Section 3 is devoted to the problems of tribal land tenure, traditional and transitional. Section 4 deals with documents illustrating ownership and occupation of land by Black peoples and Asians in urban areas.

010. Davenport, T.R.H. South Africa: A Modern History. 2nd ed. Johannesburg: Macmillan, 1978. xv, 432pp. illus. maps. bibl.

An attempt to study South African history from a modern "liberal Africanist" point of view; i.e., with emphasis on all the peoples of South Africa and their interaction rather than on Africa as a product of European colonisation. The analysis of South African history covers the period from the migrations of the various tribal peoples into Southern Africa to the present day. A scholarly work with an extensive bibliography.

011. De Kiewiet, C.W. A History of South Africa: Social and Economic. London: Oxford University Press, 1942. xii, 292pp. maps. bibl.

Attempts to set down succinctly the main social and economic developments in South African history from the seventeenth century to the 1920's. Written in a clear, lucid style. Presents a very effective summary, omitting details of political events.

012. Denoon, D. Southern Africa Since 1800. London: Longman, 1972. 242pp. illus. maps. bibl.

Consists of essays describing and analysing important social, political and economic changes which took place in Southern Africa from the nineteenth century onwards. The following aspects are discussed: The rise of the Zulu nation and the reaction of other Black communities to the threat of Zulu aggression, White penetration of the interior and the rise of the Afrikaner Republics; the conflict between White and Black peoples and between British and Afrikaners during the Anglo-Boer War; the economic conditions of the Southern African states before and after the discovery of precious minerals; parliamentary and labour struggles in the first half of the twentieth century; South Africa's neighbours; the growth of opposition to South African Nationalist government in the second half of the twentieth century; the decline of British, Portuguese and German Imperial control and African nationalism in the twentieth century.

General Histories

013. Elphick, R., and H. Giliomee, eds. The Shaping of South African Society, 1652-1820. Cape Town: Longman, 1979. xvi, 415pp. bibl.

Analyses the development of social and economic organisation at the Cape between 1652 and 1820. Part 1 deals with the major population groups: Khoikhoi, White settlers and Black peoples. Part 2 concerns relations between the governments and their subjects. Part 3 describes the expansion of the colony and development of its northern and eastern frontiers. Each section is written by a specialist. Bibliographies at the end of each chapter.

014. Eybers, G.W., ed. Select Constitutional Documents Illustrating South African History, 1795-1910. London: Routledge, 1918. xxxviii, 582pp.

Consists firstly of an introduction giving an outline of South African constitutional history between 1652 and 1910. The documents are arranged by province; viz., the Cape of Good Hope, Natal, Orange Free State and the South African Republic. The Cape and Natal documents are further subdivided into central government, local government and administration of justice. Documents are arranged in chronological order. The final chapter contains the South African Act of 1909.

015. Geen, M.S. The Making of South Africa. 7th ed. Cape Town: Maskew Miller, 1982. 355pp. bibl. First published in 1958.

Surveys South African history from 1652 to 1980. Fairly objective in approach. Suitable for high schools.

016. Gie, S.F.N. Geskiedenis van Suid Afrika. 2v. 4th ed. Stellenbosch: Pro-Ecclesia; 1942.

One of the earlier histories. Rather out of date.

017. Gordon, R.E., and C.J. Talbot, eds. From Dias to Vorster: Source Material on South African History, 1488-1975. Goodwood: Nasou, 1977. 464pp.

A chronologically arranged anthology of excerpts from journals, diaries, letters and despatches, newspaper material and official documents covering a period of three centuries. Intended for high school and university students. Each section concludes with a list of suggestions for further activity and learning and additional lists of books.

018. Hattersley, A.F. An Illustrated Social History of South Africa. Cape Town: Balkema, 1975. x, 261pp. illus. bibl.

Attempts to describe the social development of South Africa from 1652 to 1910. Descriptions are given of public life, the social scene, sport, houses, domestic life, religion, government, education, cultural activity, settlers and their problems and village life. Lavishly illustrated. The sport, pastimes and leisure activities of South Africans during the seventeenth, eighteenth and nineteenth centuries are also

General Histories 5

described in: De Kock V. The Fun They Had: The Pastimes of Our Forefathers. (Cape Town: Timmins, 1955). 194pp.

019. Hattersley, A.F. South Africa, 1652-1933. London: Thornton-Butterworth, 1933. 256pp. bibl.

Rather out of date history.

020. Hepple, A. South Africa: A Political and Economic History. London: Pall Mall, 1966. x, 282pp. map. bibl.

Aims at presenting an account of the historical background of South African society in order to explain racial policies applied in modern South Africa. Attempts to prove that racial discrimination is connected with the economic exploitation of non-white labour. Part 1 contains information about the various peoples and the economy. Part 2 is a survey of events relating to the acquisition of land by Whites and non-whites over three centuries. Part 3 traces political events leading to South Africa's emergence as an independent Republic. Part 4 deals with the labour question from the time of the slaves to the present day industrial colour bar and border industries.

021. Hofmeyr, J.H. South Africa. 2nd ed. rev. by J. Cope. London: Benn, 1952. x, 253pp. map.

First published in 1930. A history of South Africa which has become rather dated.

022. Houghton, D.H., and J. Dagut, eds. Source Material on the South African Economy, 1860-1970. Vol. 1: 1860-1899: Vol. 2: 1899-1919. Vol. 3: 1920-1970. London: Oxford University Press, 1972-1973. bibl.

Volume 1 is divided into two parts: The Economy in the 1860s and the Mining Revolution 1870-1899. Volume 2 consists of Part 3, entitled Wars, Reconstruction and Closure Union. Volume 3 is divided into three parts: Part 4 The Trough of the Twenties 1920-1923. Part 5 Industrial Breakthrough 1933-1945. Part 6 Growth and Economic Diversification 1945-1970. There is an introduction on secondary sources for the pre-1860 period and short notes on subsequent periods. Extracts are selected from a wide variety of sources and prefixed by a statement indicating its source. There is an index to the sources as well as a general index.

023. Keppel-Jones, A. South Africa: A Short History. 5th ed. London: Hutchinson, 1975. 251pp. map. bibl.

Brief survey of South African history based on essays revolving around selected topics such as the Dutch East India company's rule at the Cape, the Afrikaners, slaves and Hottentots, the frontier, the Great Trek, discovery of diamonds, the imperial factor, nationalism and race relations.

General Histories

024. Lacour-Gayet, R. A History of South Africa. Tr. from the French by S. Hardman. London: Cassell, 1977. ix, 387pp. maps. bibl.

Fragmentary survey of South African history from 1652 to the present day by an author who has not spent much time in South Africa.

025. Marks, S., and A. Atmore, eds. Economy and Society in Pre-Industrial South Africa. London: Longmans, 1980. 385pp.

Consists of essays presented at a seminar of the University of London's Institute of Commonwealth Studies. The object of the collection is to explore, through a series of case studies, three aspects of South Africa's nineteenth century history: the nature of precapitalist social formations; the ways in which these were affected by colonial penetration and mercantile capital; and the effect on Africans of the colonial experience.

The period covered in most cases is from 1800 to 1880. The regions which are analysed are Swaziland, Zululand, Pondoland, rural Natal and the Cape Colony. There is a concluding essay on economic wealth in the South African Republic.

026. Marquard, L. The Story of South Africa. 3rd ed. London: Faber, 1968. 272pp. illus. maps. 1st ed. 1955.

Attempts to trace the story of the various peoples who have contributed to the making of modern South Africa. Describes and discusses the main events in South African history. Provides a concise survey from the seventeenth century to the year 1967.

027. Millin, S.G. The People of South Africa. Johannesburg: Central News Agency, 1951. ix, 324pp. map.

Popular work on the origins of the various peoples who make up the South African nation. No bibliography.

028. Muller, C.F.J., ed. Five Hundred Years: A History of South Africa. 3rd ed. Pretoria: Academica, 1980. xiii, 467pp. maps. bibl. First published in 1969.

This comprehensive history of South Africa emphasizes the White man's role from the fifteenth to the twentieth century. The Black races are considered in an appendix written by D. Ziervogel. There are twelve contributors to this volume drawn from South African universities and colleges, and the text is a translation from the Afrikaans.

029. Perspectives on the Southern African Past. Cape Town: Centre for African Studies, University of Cape Town, 1979. 202pp. maps. bibl. (Occasional Papers No. 2).

Consists of a series of lectures delivered by various specialists, aimed at providing a historical foundation for an understanding of modern South Africa. The chapters are arranged in historical sequence and include discussion of

General Histories

pre-historic South Africa, San and Khoi people, Bantu-speaking people, the Mfecane, the extended frontier between Black and White, Boer-British conflict to 1910, English-speaking South Africans and Afrikaner nationalism.

030. South Africa's Yesterdays. Cape Town: Readers Digest Association, 1981. 344pp. illus. bibl.

A lavishly illustrated social history of South Africa, commencing at the year 1900. This book is intended for popular reading.

031. Theal, G. McCall. History of South Africa. London: Allen and Unwin, 1910. Facs. repr. Cape Town: Struik, 1964. 11v. illus.

A reprint of several independently published works by Theal. They have been consecutively numbered by Struik. Vol. 1: South African ethnography and conditions before 1505. Vols. 2-4: South African history before 1795. Vols. 5-9: 1795-1872. Vols. 10-11: 1873-1884. Theal's work is based on archival research and documentation. Still valuable, although many of his judgements and opinions are criticised by modern historians.

032. Troup, F. South Africa: An Historical Introduction. London: Methuen, 1972. xviii, 428pp. illus. bibl.

Survey of South African history up to modern times written from the 'liberal' point of view.

033. Van der Walt, A.J.H., and others, eds. Geskiedenis van Suid-Afrika. Rev. ed. in one volume by D.W. Kruger. Cape Town: Nasou, 1965. 620pp. bibl.

Revision of a standard work on South African history. Each section compiled by a specialist.

034. Van Jaarsveld, F.A. From Van Riebeeck to Vorster, 1652-1974: An Introduction to the History of the Republic of South Africa. Johannesburg: Voortrekkerpers, 1975. 484pp. illus. bibl.

Survey of South African history based on lectures delivered to first year university students. Attempts to provide an historical explanation for the existence of modern day social groupings and institutions.

035. Van Jaarsveld, F.A., and G.B. Scholtz, eds. Die Republiek van Suid-Afrika, Agtergrond, Ontstaan en Toekoms. Johannesburg: Voortrekkerpers, 1966. 307pp. illus. Published to commemorate Republic Day celebrations on 31 May 1966.

Contains contributions from various sources; viz., journalists, historians, political theorists and cultural leaders. Covers the establishment of the republican constitution and the struggle to uphold republican traditions in South Africa.

General Histories

036. Voigt, J.C. Fifty Years of the History of the Republic in South Africa, 1795-1845. London: Fisher Unwin, 1899. facs. repr. Cape Town: Struik, 1969. 2v. maps.

This work has severe limitations in that it is not documented, and it is written in rather a partisan style by the author whose sympathies are clearly on the side of the Boers. He expresses vehement anti-British sentiments and resentment against the philanthropic groups which advocate more favourable treatment for the Black people of South Africa. His descriptions contain long passages of invective regarding injustices suffered by the Boers at the hands of the Dutch East India Company and British colonial government. Volume 1 provides an account of the history of the Cape Colony from the time of the Dutch East India Company to the mid-nineteenth century, the causes of the Great Trek, the Treks of Trichardt, Potgieter and Maritz, the war with the Matabele, Retief's Trek and the Volksraad of Winburg. Volume 2 deals with Natal from the arrival of Retief to the annexation of Natal by Britain in 1844. This history is still of interest, although obviously biased in approach, as is evident from the appendix found in volume 2. Author greatly influenced by the writings and opinions of Theal.

037. Walker, E.A. A History of Southern Africa. 3rd rev. ed. London: Longmans Green, 1957. xxiv, 973pp. maps. bibl. First published 1928.

Standard history of Southern Africa covering the years 610 B.C. to 1955. Extensive bibliography and list of executive officers from 1652 to 1955. Author attempts to condense much detail into this one-volume work and descriptions are often difficult to follow.

038. Were, G.S. A History of South Africa. New York: Evans, 1974. xvi, 198pp. illus. maps. bibl.

Emphasizes the role of the African and Coloured societies in the history and development of South Africa, as the author is himself a Black historian.

039. Willcox, A.R. Southern Land: The Prehistory and History of Southern Africa. Cape Town: Purnell, 1976. xi, 274pp. illus. bibl.

Describes the history of Southern Africa from earliest geological times to the present day.

040. Wilson, D. A History of South and Central Africa. Cambridge: University Press, 1975. x, 342pp. illus.

Written from the point of view of the Black peoples of Southern Africa as a school text book for secondary school students of Kenya. Attempts to cover the history of Southern Africa from 1000 to 1965 A.D.

General Histories

041. Wilson, M., and L. Thompson, eds. Oxford History of South
     Africa. Oxford: Clarendon Press, 1969-1971. 2v. illus.
     maps. bibl. Vol.1. repr. Cape Town: David Philip, 1982.

   Attempts to study South African history as an interaction
between all its races of various origins, languages, tech-
nologies, ideologies and social systems. Volume 1 describes
firstly the pre-colonial history of African inhabitants, and
continues with the arrival of the Afrikaners and their expansion into the interior of the colony, the English settlements,
the rise of the Zulu kingdoms and the establishment of the
Afrikaner republics up to 1870. Volume 2 covers the period
1870-1966. Discusses economic, agricultural and urban growth
in South Africa, the subjection of the African chiefdoms,
Great Britain and the Afrikaner Republics, the creation of
Union and the growth of Afrikaner nationalism. Each section
written by a specialist in the particular field. Scholarly
work with an extensive bibliography.
   In the reprint of volume 1, a new preface has been introduced to outline developments in South African historiography
since first publication. The first chapter on archaeology has
been omitted. The bibliography is confined to footnotes.

CHAPTER II
TRAVEL AND EXPLORATION

Bibliographies

042. Cox, E.G. A Reference Guide to the Literature of Travel. Seattle: University of Washington, 1935-1938. Vol.1: The Old World. pp.354-401 : Africa.

043. Engels, L.J. Personal Accounts of the Cape of Good Hope written between 1652 and 1715. Africana Notes and News, vol. 8, no. 3, June 1951. pp.71-100.

044. Mackenzie, N.H. South African Travel Literature. Archives Year Book for South African History 1955, part 2. pp.1-112.

045. Schmidt, K.L.M. A Bibliography of Personal Accounts of the Cape of Good Hope in Printed Books, 1715-1850. Cape Town: University of Cape Town, School of Librarianship, 1956. ix, 109pp.

046. Stephen, R.G. Travellers in South Africa in the Eighteenth Century: A Bibliography. Cape Town: University of Cape Town, School of Librarianship, 1947. 21pp. Unpublished.

EXPLORATION AND EARLY COLONIAL POLICY TO 1652

Monographs

047. Axelson, E. Portuguese in South-East Africa, 1480-1600. Johannesburg: Witwatersrand University Press, 1960. x, 226pp. illus. bibl.

A revised and more detailed account of Portuguese exploration of the coasts of south and east Africa, first given in Axelson's South-East Africa, 1488-1530. (See entry 049). Discusses the Portuguese exploration of South-East Africa, the occupation of Sofala (1505-1506), and Mozambique and Cuama and subsequent history of these outposts to the end of the sixteenth century. Describes events on the Mombasa coast and the threat to Portuguese supremacy over the sea-route to India with the rise of the United Netherlands at the end of the sixteenth century.

048. Axelson, E. South African Explorers. London: Oxford University Press, 1954. 346pp. map. bibl. (World's Classics Series).

A selection of passages from the writings of nineteen explorers of South Africa describing their journeys. The explorers covered are: Da Gama, Dos Santos, Van der Stel, Brink, Sparrman, Barrow, Burchell, Campbell, Fynn, Gardiner, Moffat, Harris, Trichardt, Oswell, Chapman, Galton, Andersson, Livingstone and Selous.

049. Axelson, E. South-East Africa, 1488-1530. London: Longmans Green, 1940. xiv, 306pp. illus. maps.

Describes the early activities of Portuguese explorers in South Africa and analyses the reasons for the failure of a permanent Portuguese settlement. In Appendices 1 to 5, there is a discussion of "new material" drawn from the archives and libraries of Portugal, the British Museum, the Bibliotheque Nationale in Paris and the Vatican Archives and Library.

050. Beazley, R. Prince Henry the Navigator. New York: Putnam, 1895. Repr. London: Cass, 1968. xxvii, 326pp. illus. maps. bibl.

The introductory chapters deal with the influence of Greek and Arabic theories of the world and geographical knowledge and exploration during the Middle Ages of the fifteenth century. The life of Prince Henry, his ambitions, and his achievements are discussed in the following chapters. In conclusion, there is a summary of further achievements of Portuguese sailors after Henry's death.

051. Boxer, C.R. Four Centuries of Portuguese Expansion, 1415-1825: A Succinct Survey. Johannesburg: Witwatersrand University Press, 1961. ix, 102pp. illus. maps.

Based on four public lectures delivered at the University of the Witwatersrand during May and June 1960, dealing with the following themes: (1) From the Maghreb to the Moluccas, 1415-1521 (i.e., the first voyage of discovery). (2) The clash of colour, caste and creed in the sixteenth century (i.e., Portuguese versus Arab in Congo, Angola, Mozambique and the East). (3) The struggle for spices, sugar, slaves and souls in the seventeenth century. (4) The golden age of Brazil in the eighteenth century.

052. Boxer, C.R., ed. The Tragic History of the Sea, 1589-1622: Narratives of the Shipwrecks of the Portuguese East Indiaman 'Sao Thome' (1589), 'Santo Alberto (1593), 'Sao Joao Baptista' (1622) and the Journeys of the Survivors in South

East Africa. Cambridge: University Press, 1959. xiv, 297pp. illus. maps. bibl. (Hakluyt Society, Second Series, 112).

A translation of three extracts, from Historia Trágico-Marítima, published in Lisbon between 1729 and 1736 and edited by Bernardo Gomes de Brito.

053. Burman, J. Who Really Discovered South Africa? Cape Town: Struik, 1969. 170pp. illus. maps. bibl.

The author carefully distinguishes "discoveries" as opposed to "explorers". The discoverers discussed include Nuno Velho Pereira, Pieter van Meerhoff, Hieronymus Cruse, Willem van Dieden, William Christian, Jan Stefler, Hermanus Hubner, Jacobus Coetse and Pieter Pienaar.

054. Colvin, I.D. The Cape of Adventure: Being Strange and Notable Discoveries, Perils, Shipwrecks, Battles upon Sea and Land, Extracted from the Writings of the Early Travellers. London: Jack, 1912. xxxi, 459pp. illus. maps.

Extracts chosen from old writers by virtue of their interest rather than their historical importance and based upon Colvin's research in the archives of parliament and the library of Sidney Mendelssohn. The first group of extracts drawn from the account of Portuguese mariners of the fifteenth and sixteenth centuries. These are followed by Dutch and English travellers of the seventeenth and eighteenth century and followers of Rousseau e.g., Francois Le Vaillant. There is also an extract from Henry Lichtenstein's work: Travels in Southern Africa. Missionary accounts are not well represented.

055. Cope, J. King of the Hottentots. Cape Town: Timmins, 1967. 159pp. illus. map. bibl.

An account of an incident in the early seventeenth century when the English attempted to settle eight condemned men at Table Bay. These men later fled to Robben Island after a skirmish with the Hottentots, who were led by a chief called Xhoré. Xhoré had been a prisoner in England and acted as an interpreter after his return to the Cape.

056. De Castro e Almeida, V., ed. Conquests and Discoveries of Henry the Navigator, Being the Chronicles of Azurara. London: Allen & Unwin, 1936. 253pp.

This is based on a chronicle of the period of the fifteenth century and assumes the form of an epic narrative. The chronicle is preceded by introductory notes on the history of Portugal.

057. De Kock, V. By Strength of Heart. Cape Town: Timmins, 1953. 166pp. illus. bibl.

A readable and popular account of the exploration of the Cape from the time of Prince Henry, Diaz and Da Gama to the landing of Van Riebeeck (1652). The French and English explorers of the first half of the seventeenth century are described as well as various shipwrecks. Finally, the establishment of Dutch mercantile interest in the East is described, as is the growing importance of the Cape as a half-way house to India.

058. De Kock, W.J. Portugese Ontdekkers om die Kaap: Die Europese Aanraking met Suidelike Afrika, 1415-1600. Cape Town: Balkema, 1957. 308pp. illus. maps. bibl.

Deals with the history of exploration of Africa from the period of ancient Egypt and Phoenicia to the end of the sixteenth century. Each chapter concludes with numerous footnotes. Written in the manner of a textbook.

059. Hart, H.H. Sea Road to the Indies: An account of the Voyages and Exploits of the Portuguese Navigators, Together with the Life and Times of Dom Vasco da Gama. London: Hodge, 1952; New York: Macmillan, 1950. xii, 296pp. bibl.

The author aims at presenting a survey of the Portuguese contribution to the discovery of the East and supplying a fuller account of the life and achievements of Vasco da Gama. Information is based on documents, contemporary authors and chroniclers of the period.

060. Peringuey, L. Inscriptions left by Early European Navigators on their Way to the East. Cape Town: South African Museum, 1950. 47pp. illus.

The earliest relics left by Portuguese explorers were the padroes (stone crosses on pillars). In the sixteenth century, inscriptions were left on stones of which several examples are given. Relics of the days of the Dutch East India Company include tombstones, beacons and escutcheons.

061. Prestage, E. Alfonso de Albuquerque, Governor of India: His Life, Conquests and Administration. Watford: Voss & Michael Printers, 1929. 85pp. front. map.

Describes the life of Albuquerque, who left Lisbon for the East on April 6, 1506, became governor in November, 1509, and died on December 15, 1515. Albuquerque succeeded in the face of Arab opposition in establishing Portuguese control over an area which extended from Natal to the Moluccas.

062. Prestage, E. The Portuguese Pioneers. London: Black, 1933. xiv, 352pp. maps.

Deals with the history of Portuguese voyages of exploration from the twelfth century to the end of the fifteenth century. The concluding chapter deals with methods of navigation, cartography and ships used by seamen during the voyages of discovery.

063. Raven-Hart, R. Before Van Riebeeck: Callers at South Africa from 1488 to 1652. Cape Town: Struik, 1967. 216pp. illus. maps. bibl.

Covers over one hundred and fifty entries consisting of records of ships visiting the Cape. These entries are drawn from Dutch, German, Danish, French, English, Italian and Portuguese travel narratives, log-books and diaries.

064. Rego, A. Da Silva. Portuguese Colonization in the Sixteenth Century: A Study of the Royal Ordinances (Regimentos). Johannesburg: Witwatersrand University, 1959. viii, 116pp. bibl.

A study of Portuguese royal ordinances of the sixteenth century which were concerned with colonization in Africa, Brazil and India. Chapters 3, 4 and 6 concern Southern Africa. In each chapter the historical background of the particular exploratory period is given and the instructions issued by royal ordinance are then explained. Each chapter has a brief conclusion which analyses the success or failure of Portuguese policy in the respective colonies.

065. Robinson, E.F. With the Da Gamas in 1497: A Story of Adventure Told from the South African Point of View. Cape Town: Juta, 1922. x, 233pp. illus. map.

This work is intended as a school text book, and written in a style which the author feels will interest the average scholar. Attempts to portray Vasco da Gama's voyage as an event which the reader can picture as realistic.

066. Theal, G. McCall. The Portuguese in South Africa. 4th ed. London: Fisher Unwin, 1927; xvi, 324pp. maps. bibl. First published Cape Town: Juta, 1896.

An attempt to correct omissions in Theal's earlier work, the 'History of South Africa', which only dealt with Africa south of the Limpopo and commenced with the year 1652. This volume describes the native races south of the Zambezi and commences with the arrival of d'Anaya in Sofala in 1505. The account of Portuguese exploration in southern Africa in the sixteenth century is not based upon archival research, like Theal's history of the Dutch and English in South Africa, but upon secondary sources. The volume surveys the whole period of Portuguese colonization in southern Africa to the end of the nineteenth century. The bibliography takes the form of useful descriptive bibliographic notes.

067. Velho, A. A Journal of the First Voyage of Vasco da Gama, 1497-1499. Tr. and ed. by E.G. Ravenstein. London: Hakluyt Society, 1898. xxxvi, 250pp. illus. map. (Hakluyt Society Publications, First Series, 99).

Introduction consists of biographical details of da Gama's life and discussion of the authorship of the journal which is not attributed to da Gama himself. The translation of the journal is literal and various appendices have been added:

Travel and Exploration   15

viz., translations of the letters of King Manuel and Sernigi,
three Portuguese accounts of the voyage, descriptions of da
Gama's ships, equipment, members of his fleet and the voyage.
Includes early maps illustrating da Gama's first voyage.

068. Welch, S.R. Europe's Discovery of South Africa. Cape Town:
Juta, 1935. 365pp.

A history of Portuguese exploration of South Africa from
the period of Prince Henry to the end of the fifteenth century.

069. Welch, S.R. South Africa under King Manuel, 1495-1521. Cape
Town: Juta, 1946. 532pp.

The sequel to entry 068 covers South African history to the
year 1521. Tells of the foundation of the Portuguese Empire
in Southern Africa. Vasco da Gama's voyages to India,
Portuguese relations with the Arabs and Black people, the
settlement at Mozambique and Sofala and pioneering efforts
in Mashonaland are described in great detail.

070. Welch, S.R. South Africa under John III, 1521-1557. Cape
Town: Juta, 1948. 586pp.

Very detailed account of Portuguese exploration during this
period. Deals with the economic revolution in Europe resulting from the Cape Sea route to India, Mozambique's trade and
government and the conquest of Mombasa. Also discusses
missionary work in Mozambique and Abyssinia as well as the
exploration of the interior in Natal and Transkei.

071. Welch, S.R. South Africa under King Sebastian and the Cardinal,
1557-1580. Cape Town: Juta, 1949. 487pp.

The colonial aspect of Sebastian's reign is treated in great
detail. With the death of Sebastian at Alcazar, Portugal
passed to Philip of Spain. In 1576, Jan Huygen van Linschoten
sailed to India and this led to the formation of the Dutch
East India Company.

072. Welch, S.R. Portuguese Rule and Spanish Crown in South Africa,
1581-1640. Cape Town: Juta, 1950. 634pp.

This volume is a sequel to entry 071. It deals with Portuguese expansion into Mombasa and trade on the Zambezi.

CHAPTER III
TRAVELLERS

Seventeenth Century

073. Cortemunde, J. Adventure at the Cape of Good Hope in December 1672. ed. by N.H. Pietersz Hennings, D.H. Varley and V. Varley. Cape Town: Friends of the South African Public Library, 1962. 29pp. illus.

Extract from Cortemunde's diary written during a voyage on the ship "Oldenborg", travelling to the East Indies (1672-1675). Cortemunde acted as chief surgeon on board. Contains short descriptions of the Cape settlement and the Hottentots.

074. Hondius, J. A Clear Description of the Cape of Good Hope. (Klare Besgryving van Cabo de Bona Esperanca). ed. by L.C. Van Oordt and P. Serton. Facsimile of the text compiled by Jodocus Hondius and published by him at Amsterdam in 1652. Cape Town: Book Exhibition Committee Van Riebeeck Festival, 1952. 37pp. illus. map.

The Dutch publisher Hondius produced a pamphlet on the Cape, drawing his information from various travel accounts of the period; e.g., voyages of Houtman, Van Spilberger and various Dutch, Portuguese, French and Italian travellers. He also consulted the crew of the "Haarlem" who had been shipwrecked at the Cape. The description of the coast is better than that of the interior, where factual information was frequently lacking.

075. Mossop, E.E., ed. Journals of the Expeditions of the Honourable Ensign Olof Bergh (1682 and 1683) and the Ensign Isaq Schrijver (1689). Cape Town: Van Riebeeck Society, 1931. 270pp. maps. illus. (Van Riebeeck Society Publications, 12).

The book is divided into two parts. Forewords contain historical information of events leading to the expeditions of Bergh and Schrijver respectively. Each foreword is then followed by journal entries from the diaries of the two explorers. These entries are given in Dutch and English in the case of Bergh, and English only in the case of Schrijver.

076. Raven-Hart, R., ed. and tr. Cape of Good Hope, 1652-1702: The First 50 years of Dutch Colonization as Seen by Callers. Cape Town: Balkema, 1971. 2v. illus. maps.

Consists of extracts from the accounts of various travellers at the Cape. These extracts are arranged in chronological order and preceded by notes giving the historical background. The index in volume 2 has very full entries and is intended to replace footnotes in the actual text. Volume 1 covers the period to 1680, and volume 2 covers the period 1680-1702. All extracts are translated directly from original sources.

077. Strangman, E. Early French Callers at the Cape. Cape Town: Juta, 1936. v, 223pp. illus. map.

Consists of short biographical descriptions and extracts of the following travellers: Binot Paulmier de Gonneville, Jean Parmentier, Francois Pyrard, Jean Mocquet, Augustin de Beaulieu, Etienne de Flacourt, Jean Tavernier, Gui Tachard, Francois Timoléon de Choisy, Claude de Forbin, Chevalier de Chaumont and Francois Leguat. These journals cover the seventeenth century and all record travellers' impressions of brief stops at the Cape.

078. Van der Stel, S. Journal of His Expedition to Namaqualand, 1685-6; ed. from the manuscript in the library of Trinity College, Dublin, by Gilbert Waterhouse. London: Longmans Green, 1932. xxviii, 869pp. illus. map.

This journal was, in all probability, Van der Stel's official report to the Dutch East India Company and was preserved in the Company's archives until 1692. It was removed to England in 1794, when Holland was invaded by the French revolutionary army. The journal is reproduced in the original Dutch followed by an English translation. It is not certain whether the journal was written by Van der Stel himself, or an observer attached to the expedition.

079. Van der Stel, S. Simon van der Stel's Journey to Namaqualand in 1683; with a revised introduction by Gilbert Waterhouse; transcription of the original text by G.C. de Wet. English translation by R.H. Pheiffer. Cape Town: Human & Rousseau, 1979. 431pp. illus.

Consists of reproductions of seventy-one drawings accompanying the original manuscript and facsimile reproductions of the entire manuscript. Concludes with an English translation of the manuscript.

TRAVELLERS

Eighteenth Century

080. Brink, C.F., and J.T. Rhenius. The Journals of Brink and Rhenius, Being the Journal of Carel Frederick Brink of the Journey into Great Namaqualand (1761-1762) Made by Captain Hendrik Hop and the Journal of Ensign Johannes Tobias Rhenius (1724). ed. by E.E. Mossop. Cape Town: Van Riebeeck Society, 1947. xiv, 160pp. illus. maps. (Van Riebeeck Society Publications, 28).

    Introductory sections provide information on the authenticity of the journals and biographical information concerning the explorers. The journals of Brink and Rhenius are provided in Dutch and English on opposite pages. The journals are annotated.

081. De La Caille, N.L. Travels at the Cape, 1751-1753. An annotated translation of 'Journal historique du Voyage Fait au Cap de Bonne-Espérance,' into which has been interpolated relevant passages from 'Memoires de l'Académie Royale des Sciences.' ed. by R. Raven-Hart. Cape Town: Balkema, 1976. viii, 52pp. illus. map.

    De la Caille visited the Cape in 1751, in order to do astronomical observations of the southern stars, measure the length of a degree of longitude and collect botanical and zoological specimens. Extracts from de la Caille's diary are given for the years 1751 to 1754. There is also an essay on 'Customs of the Inhabitants of the Cape of Good Hope and of the Hottentots' and a section entitled 'Critical Notes and Reflections on the Description of the Cape of Good Hope by Pierre Kolbes.' A map is reproduced from the original in de la Caille's diary.

082. Forbes, V.S. Pioneer Travellers of South Africa. Cape Town: Balkema, 1965. 177pp. illus. maps.

    Attempts to provide a geographical interpretation of documents dealing with travel at the Cape during the later eighteenth century. These documents include travel books and journals, letters and maps. Historical events are also considered. The expeditions of some twelve travellers are analysed and discussed: viz., August Frederik Beutler, Carl Peter Thunberg, Francis Masson, Anders Sparrman, Hendrik Swellengrebel, William Paterson, Robert Jacob Gordon, Francois Le Vaillant, Count Louis Marie Degrandpré, John Barrow, Governor J. van Plettenberg and Jacob van Reenen.

083. Kirby, P.R. The True Story of the 'Grosvenor' East Indiaman Wrecked on the Coast of Pondoland, South Africa on 4 August 1782. Cape Town: Oxford University Press, 1960. xiii, 266pp.

Part 1 consists of a reconstruction of all events connected with the wreck of the 'Grosvenor' and the two expeditions which set out to rescue survivors. Part 2 is connected with legends and rumours which centred around the wreck of the 'Grosvenor'.

084. [Le Vaillant, F.] Meiring, J. The Truth in Masquerade: The Adventures of Francois le Vaillant. Cape Town: Juta, n.d. 242pp. illus. maps. bibl.

Popular account of the life of le Vaillant, who travelled into the interior of the eastern and north-western Cape between 1781 and 1784. The author has made use of le Vaillant's account entitled 'Travels from the Cape of Good Hope into the Interior parts of Africa' which was compiled originally in French from le Vaillant's journal and translated into English in 1790. This account has been paraphrased into a simple and readable narrative by the author.

085. Mentzel, O.F. A Geographical and Topographical Description of the Cape of Good Hope. Tr. by J.H. Mandelbrote. Cape Town: Van Riebeeck Society, 1921. 181pp. illus. map. (Van Riebeeck Society Publications, 4). Originally published Glocau: Gunther, 1785.

Describes the history of the Cape up to the time of its occupation by the Dutch East India Company. Discusses the administration of the Cape by the Company and notable features such as Table Mountain, boundaries and rivers, public buildings, the Castle and private residences and churches. Description based on Mentzel's stay at the Cape (1733-1741).

086. Paterson, W. Paterson's Cape Travels, 1777 to 1779. ed. by Vernon S. Forbes and John Rourke. Sandton: Brenthurst Press, 1980. 202pp.

First full-length account in English of four journeys into the interior of Southern Africa between 1777 to 1779 in search of botanical specimens. Paterson's travels covered a total of 9,000 kilometres and the work is accompanied by full-colour illustrations of plants, people, animals and scenery selected from Paterson's picture collection.

087. Somerville, W. William Somerville's Narrative of his Journeys to the Eastern Cape Frontier and to Lattakoe 1799-1802; with a bibliographical introduction and map and a historical introduction and notes by Edna and Frank Bradlow. Cape Town: Van Riebeeck Society, 1979. 255pp. illus. (Van Riebeeck Society Publications, 2nd Series, 10).

Contains interesting descriptions of the Tlhaping, a southern Tswana tribe, with whom Somerville's expedition attempted to barter cattle, it being the first official encounter between this tribe and Cape authorities.

088. Sparrman, A. A Voyage to the Cape of Good Hope Towards the Antarctic Polar Circle Round the World and to the Country of the Hottentots and the Caffres from the Year 1772-1776. ed. by V.S. Forbes. Cape Town: Van Riebeeck Society, 1975-1977. 2v. illus. map. (Van Riebeeck Society Publications, 2nd Series, 6, 7).

The first detailed account by a trained naturalist on the districts in the eastern parts of the Cape Colony. Hitherto travellers had personally visited only the districts around Cape Town. Interesting descriptions of Bushmen and Hottentots. Also discusses agricultural topics and fauna and flora of the Colony. Very few descriptions given of the White colonists at the Cape. The map of the Cape Colony drawn by Sparrman for the journal, although containing inaccuracies, is a great improvement on those previously published.

089. [Van Reenen, J.] Jacob van Reenen and the Grosvenor Expedition of 1790-1791. ed. by P.R. Kirby. Johannesburg: Witwatersrand University Press, 1958. viii, 142pp. illus. maps.

An attempt to find the solution to some questions which have arisen in connection with the expedition of 1790-1791. The first problem is to establish the identity of the organiser of the expedition. Secondly, the identity of the members of the expedition is clarified. The author also attempts to establish which member of the van Reenen family accompanied the expedition. There are four copies of van Reenen's journals, each one of which is critically examined by the author. The two English translations are also discussed. Finally, the letter of van Reenen to the governor and the maps of the route drawn up by Edward Riou are discussed.

090. Wikar, H.J. and others. The Journal of Hendrik Jacob Wikar (1779) ... and the Journals of Jacobus Coetsé Jansz (1760) and Willem van Reenen (1791). ed. by E.E. Mossop. Cape Town: Van Riebeeck Society, 1935. 327pp. maps. (Van Riebeeck Society Publications, 15).

Contains the account of three journeys which appeared originally in the second volume of Dr. Godée Molsbergen's 'Reizens in Zuid Afrika'. Wikar's report describes the travels of the first European who is known to have journeyed along the Orange River at the end of the eighteenth century. Jacobus Coetsé Jansz (1760) describes the first officially recorded crossing of the Orange River. Willem van Reenen (1791) journeyed from the Cape, across the Orange River to a mountain range in Damaraland and back.

TRAVELLERS

1800-1850

091. Alexander, J.E. An Expedition of Discovery into the Interior of Africa Through the Hitherto Undescribed Countries of the Great Namaquas, Boschmans and Hill Damaras. 2v. Cape Town: 1838. illus. map. Repr. Cape Town: Struik, 1967. (Africana Collectanea Series, 22-23).

    Describes the work of an expedition which took place in 1836-1837 under the auspices of the Royal Geographical Society. The aim of the expedition was to explore the country to the north of the Orange River. Gives interesting descriptions of various tribes encountered and of flora and fauna of the country.

092. Arbousset, T., and F. Daumas. Narrative of an exploratory tour to the North-East of the Colony of the Cape of Good Hope. Cape Town, 1846. facs. repr. Cape Town: Struik, 1968. vii, 330pp. illus. map.

    Describes a tour undertaken by Arbousset and Daumas on behalf of the Paris Missionary Society commencing in March, 1836. Observations made on the country, its flora and fauna and also on the various Black tribes, coloured peoples, Bushmen, Griquas and Koranas.

093. Bain, A.G. Journals of Andrew Geddes Bain, Trader, Explorer, Soldier, Road Engineer and Geologist (1826-1847). ed. by M.H. Lister. Cape Town: Van Riebeeck Society, 1949. xxxix, 264pp. illus. maps. (Van Riebeeck Society Publications, 30).

    There is an introductory biographical sketch of A.G. Bain, who was a self-taught road engineer and geologist. The accounts of Bain's journeys are taken from his journals and cover Bechuanaland (1826); journey to the Umzimvubu River (1829); hunting expedition to the Molopo River (1834); and his military journal (Fort Thomson 1836). There is a version of Bain's humorous poem "Kaatje Kekkelbek" and two of Bain's letters concerning roads and a section on the geology of the Eastern Province.

094. Baines, T. Journal of Residence in Africa, 1842-1853. ed. by R.F. Kennedy. Cape Town: Van Riebeeck Society, 1961-1964. 2v. illus. maps. bibl. (Van Riebeeck Society Publications, 42, 45).

    The first volume contains details of Baines' expedition to Port Elizabeth, Grahamstown, Shiloh, Burghersdorp, Colesberg and the Orange River as a member of the Liddle Expedition to the north east Cape. Baines then, on his own, toured King Williamstown, East London, Kafirland, Fort Cory, Pirie and other parts of the eastern Cape before returning to Grahamstown in October 1849. The second volume includes a description

of an 1850 expedition into the interior as far as the Vaal
River undertaken by Baines as a member of McCabe's party.
Baines' experiences in the Eighth Kafir War of 1850-1853 are
also covered. Baines painted interesting scenes of frontier
landscapes and events but his pictures of the Seventh Kafir
War were painted from descriptions given by various other
unknown individuals.

095. Burchell, W.J. Travels in the Interior of Southern Africa.
London: Batchworth Press, 1953. 2v. illus. map. Original
ed. London: Longman, Hurst, 1822-1824.

Valuable descriptions of various peoples, places and scenery
of South Africa. Burchell, a trained naturalist and collector,
created superb illustrations supplementing the information
given in the text. Shrewdly assesses the characters of peoples
encountered during his travels; e.g., Hottentots, Bathlaping,
Bushmen and White frontier farmers. His expeditions occurred
in 1811 and 1812, when he explored northwards as far as Takoon
and Heuning Vlei and eastwards as far as Graaff-Reinet and
Grahamstown. He discovered many new zoological and botanical
species.

096. Ewart, J. James Ewart's Journal Covering his Stay at the Cape
of Good Hope (1811-1814) and His Part in the Expedition to
Florida and New Orleans (1814-1815); with an introduction by
A. Gordon-Brown. Cape Town: Struik, 1970. xii, 137pp.
illus. map.

Personal narrative of a Scottish officer who spent the years
1811-1814 on garrison duties in Cape Town with the 93rd Highland Regiment of Foot. Valuable description of the country and
social life of the people at the time of the Governor Sir John
Cradock.

097. Krauss, F. Travel Journal/Cape to Zululand: Observations by a
Collector and Naturalist, 1838-1840. ed. by O.H. Spohr.
Cape Town: Balkema, 1973. 90pp. illus. map. bibl.

Consists of a travel journal copied by Krauss from diaries
which he kept on his journey from Cape Town to Uitenhage and
thence to Port Natal. Valuable information on flora, fauna
and natural features of the Cape.

098. [Krebs, L.] Ffolliott, P., and R. Liversidge. Ludwig Krebs:
Cape Naturalist to the King of Prussia, 1792-1844. Cape
Town: Balkema, 1971. xiii, 304pp. illus. map. bibl.

Consists of the correspondence of Krebs who penetrated the
interior of South Africa as far as the Makwassieberg between
the years 1820 to 1838, in order to collect botanical and
biological specimens for the Museum of the Humboldt University.

Travellers   23

099. Latrobe, C.I. Journal of a Visit to South Africa in 1815 and
      1816; with some Account of the Missionary Settlements of the
      United Brethren. London: Seeley, 1818. xii, 407pp. illus.
      map.

      Latrobe was sent by the Directors of the Church of the
      United Brethren to visit and report on mission stations at
      Genadendal and Groene Kloof. The journal covers the period
      from October, 1815 to October, 1816. Interesting descriptions
      of daily life at the mission stations, of the Eastern frontier
      and its inhabitants, and of flora and fauna. Illustrations
      done by Latrobe.

100. Lichtenstein, W.H.C. Foundation of the Cape. About the
      Bechuanas. tr. and ed. by O.H. Spohr. Cape Town: Balkema,
      1973. viii, 113pp. illus. map. bibl.

      The introduction consists of biographical details of
      Lichtenstein supplied by the editor. Lichtenstein provides
      an account of Cape history from the days of the Portuguese
      explorers to the year 1773. The account of the 'Bectjuanas'
      is based on Lichtenstein's observations made in 1805.
      Detailed description of appearance, customs, social life and
      government of the Bechuanas.

101. Lichtenstein, W.H.C. Travels in Southern Africa in the Years
      1803-1806. London: Henry Colburn, 1812. 2v. illus.

      The author accompanied de Mist on a tour of the Cape Colony
      in 1863, as medical superintendent and tutor to Henry Janssens.
      Explored the western, northern and eastern parts of the Cape,
      including Graaff-Reinet. The second volume describes the
      return from Graaff-Reinet, a botanical journey to Swellendam
      and a visit to the Bechuanas, Bushmen and Hottentots. Also
      discusses an excursion to the Roggeveld, the 'Bosjesveld' and
      Tulbagh. Gives information regarding the climate and geology
      of the country, flora, fauna, tribes, history, customs, form
      of government and importance of the Cape Colony.

102. Smith, Sir Andrew. Andrew Smith's Journal of His Expedition
      into the Interior of South Africa 1834-1836: An Authentic
      Narrative of Travels and Discoveries, the Manners and
      Customs of the Native Tribes and the Physical Nature of the
      Country. ed. by W.F. Lye. Cape Town: Balkema, 1975.
      323pp. illus. map.

      This expedition was undertaken on behalf of the Literary
      and Scientific Institution and entailed exploration of the
      ethnography, geology, botany and fauna of Africa South,
      covering Moshweshwe, the Sotho chief's domain, Philippolis,
      the country of Cornelius Kok beyond the Vaal River, Kuruman,
      the Kalahari, the Magaliesberg area, the Marico River as far
      as the Limpopo and beyond to the Tropic of Capricorn. The
      journal was published posthumously.

103. Smith, Sir Andrew. The Diary of Dr. Andrew Smith of the 'Expedition for Exploring Central Africa', 1834-1836. ed. by P.R. Kirby. Cape Town: Van Riebeeck Society, 1939-1940. (Van Riebeeck Society Publications, 20, 21). 2v. illus. map.

Introduction discusses the origin of Smith's diary and journals, provides a biography of Smith and analyses reasons for the 1834-1836 expedition into the interior. Smith's instructions were to explore Griqua territory, the Kalahari, and visit Moshesh, Sikonyela, Moroko and Mzilikazi, and go as far north as the Tropic of Capricorn. The diary does not contain a complete account of Smith's expedition, but includes valuable ornithological, zoological and ethnological information.

104. [Smith, Sir Andrew] Kirby, P.R. Sir Andrew Smith, M.D., K.C.B.: His Life, Letters and Works. Cape Town: Balkema, 1965. ix, 357pp. illus. map. bibl.

Biography of Smith in which emphasis is placed on Smith's anthropological studies among the Black peoples of South Africa in the first half of the nineteenth century, his expeditions to Namaqualand (1828-1829) and the North (1834-1836) and his scientific contributions.

105. Steedman, A. Wanderings and Adventures in the Interior of Southern Africa. London: Longman, 1835. facs. repr. Cape Town: Struik, 1966. 2v. illus. map.

An account of travels in South Africa undertaken over the course of ten years. Steedman explored a great part of the Cape Colony and Kaffraria and reached Griqualand West. He was extremely interested in the natural fauna of these regions. He also describes native races, their history and wars as well as the pioneers of Natal. The Appendices contain a letter and journal by A.G. Bain (see 093) who accompanied Dr. A. Smith's expedition as far as Philippolis, a narrative of the wreck of the Grosvenor, an account of the Kat River and other settlements in Kaffraria and a description of the Frontier Wars.

106. Thompson, G. Travels and Adventures in Southern Africa. ed. by V.S. Forbes. Cape Town: Van Riebeeck Society, 1967-1968. (Van Riebeeck Society Publications, 48, 49). 2v. illus. maps. bibl.

Part 1 contains a biographical sketch of Thompson as an introduction to the work. The first expedition is described as an excursion to the Eastern Cape frontier and to the country of the Bechuanas (1823-1824). Part 2 consists of a description of an expedition to the country of the Bushmen, Koranas and Namaquas (1824). Part 3 contains observations by the author on the inhabitants of the Colony and its possibilities for further colonization.

TRAVELLERS

1850-1900

107. Baldwin, W.C. African Hunting and Adventures from Natal to the Zambesi, Including Lake Ngami, the Kalahari Desert, etc., from 1852 to 1860. London: Richard Bentley, 1894. facs. repr. Cape Town: Struik, 1967. x, 428pp. illus. map.

    This work is written in the form of a diary covering expeditions made in the years 1852 to 1860. Contains descriptions of tribes, wild animals, scenery and adventures encountered in Zululand, Transvaal, at Lake Ngami and Zambesi.

108. Chapman, J. Travels in the Interior of South Africa. ed. by E.C. Tabler. Cape Town: Balkema, 1971. 2v. illus. maps. Originally published London: Bell & Daldy, 1868.

    A record of the author's travels from Natal to Walvisch Bay and visits to Lake Ngami and Victoria Falls in the course of hunting and trade expeditions from 1849 to 1863. Interesting descriptions of tribes encountered, and of flora and fauna of the various regions. Tabler worked from the original manuscript when editing the work.

109. Leighton, S. Notes on a Visit to South Africa, February-March-April, 1889. ed. by A.M. Lewin Robinson. Cape Town: Balkema, 1975. vii, 103pp. illus.

    Interesting descriptions of impressions on a journey from Cape Town, through Simons Bay, Paarl, Frenchhoek, Stellenbosch, then Knysna to Grahamstown and Kimberley. The author then travelled to Johannesburg and Pretoria and commented on coach travel in the Transvaal and Natal. After visiting Pietermaritzburg, Durban and Port Elizabeth, the author returned to Cape Town. Interesting pencil sketches accompany the text.

110. MacLeod, L. Travels in Eastern Africa; with the Narrative of a Residence in Mozambique. London: Hurst and Blackett, 1860. 2v. front.

    Describes the experiences of the author who in 1856 was appointed British Consul to Mozambique. Discusses his arrival at Cape Town, voyage along the coast of Kaffraria and arrival at Natal. Long descriptions are given of all these and other areas traversed on the journey to Mozambique. Volume 2 is mainly concerned with descriptions of the history of Mozambique; the problems connected with opposition from slave traders; experiences at Mauritius, Madagascar and the Seychelles and arrival at Aden.

CHAPTER IV
CAPE - GENERAL HISTORY

111. Botha, C.G. Collected Works. Cape Town: Struik, 1962. 3v. illus. bibl.

    The three volumes consist of articles, speeches and reports devoted to various topics of research done within the Cape Archives and intended to stimulate general public interest. Volume 1 is entitled 'General history and social life of the Cape of Good Hope', and contains little known information on seventeenth and eighteenth century history of general interest to the public. Volume 2 is devoted to the 'History of law, medicine and place names in the Cape of Good Hope'. Volume 3 concerns 'Cape Archives and Records' and discusses archival developments in Europe and America, the history of archival development in South Africa and extracts from the registers of births, marriages and deaths of the Cape during the nineteenth century.

112. Burman, J. So High the Road: Mountain Passes of the Western Cape. Cape Town: Human & Rousseau, 1963. 157pp. illus. maps.

    Discusses early pass builders and famous mountain passes of the Western Cape. Written for the general reader in an anecdotal style. The following four works also deal with early transportation and communication in the Cape.

113. Coates, P.R. Track and Trackless: Omnibuses and Trams in the Western Cape. Cape Town: Struik, 1976. 239pp. illus. maps.

    Traces the development of public transport from the establishment of the horse-drawn omnibus (c.1840) and horse-drawn trams (c.1880) to the electric tramcar of 1896 onward. The history of passenger wagons and early motor buses is also outlined up to 1930. The last chapter deals with the introduction of trolley buses.

Cape - General History 27

114. Mossop, E.E. Old Cape Highways. Cape Town: Maskew Miller, 1928. 202pp. illus. maps.

   Famous old western Cape highways are discussed, regarding appearance, historical significance and manner in which early exploration took place. The work of pioneers who opened up mountain passes is described. These highways include Tulbach Kloof, Hottentot Holland Pass, Bains Kloof, Piekenier's Kloof and the Olifants River.

115. Murray, M. Ships and South Africa: A Maritime Chronicle of the Cape with Particular Reference to Mail and Passenger Lines from the early days of Steam down to the present. London: Oxford University Press, 1933. 360pp. illus.

   Describes the development of steam navigation at the Cape from 1825 onwards, the establishment of the steamship lines and rivalries for the mail and passenger traffic. Three chapters are devoted to the effects of World War I on South Africa's shipping and the post-war period of 1919-1933. There is a section on shipwrecks and disasters and on voyages on early mail steamers and Cape liners. Part 2 provides a short history of every important South African liner since 1855 and is divided into British, foreign and local shipping companies.

116. Murray, M. Union-Castle Chronicle, 1853-1953. London: Longmans Green, 1953. xviii, 392pp. illus.

   A detailed history of the Union Castle shipping company, which resulted from an amalgamation in 1900 of the rival Union Castle Lines. The history is traced through the vicissitudes of the Anglo-Boer War and two World Wars. The Union Castle Company developed one of the finest merchant fleets of the period. The illustrations show almost every type of sailing vessel used from the middle of the nineteenth century onwards. An appendix lists the Company's ships, past and present, with brief notes on each.

117. De Villiers, S.A. Robben Island, Out of Reach, Out of Mind: A History of Robben Island. Cape Town: Struik, 1971. xv, 167pp. illus. bibl.

   A history of Robben Island from 1652 onwards, showing how the island was important to the Cape, firstly as a convict settlement, and subsequently as the site of an infirmary for lepers and lunatics (1844-1931). The parts played by various medical men, nurses and churchmen on the island, are discussed. The modern uses of Robben Island by the Navy and Prisons Departments are also discussed.

118. Gutsche, T. The Microcosm. Cape Town: Timmins, 1968. 217pp. illus. map.

   Consists of a history of the area on the Cape side of the Orange River known as the Toverberg, overlooking the Cis-Gariep and the town of Colesberg. The period covered is the late eighteenth century to the end of the nineteenth century.

Cape - General History

119. Kilpin, R. The Old Cape House, Being Passages from the History of a Legislative Assembly. Cape Town: Maskew Miller, 1918. xx, 200pp. bibl.

Describes the history of the Cape constitution from 1795 to 1872, the buildings occupied by the Cape parliament between 1854 and 1910 and speakers of the Cape House from 1854 to 1910. Annexures list ministers, executive councillors, constitutional legislation, duration of sessions and payment of members, 1854 to 1910.

120. Kilpin, R. The Romance of a Colonial Parliament: Being a Narrative of the Parliament and Councils of the Cape of Good Hope from the Founding of the Colony by van Riebeeck in 1652 to the Union of South Africa in 1910; to which is added a List of Governors from 1652 to 1910 and a Complete List of Governors from 1852 to 1910. London: Longmans, 1938. xiv, 175pp. illus.

Traces the history of Cape colonial government from 1652 to 1910. Annexures list Cape commanders, governors, ministers, parliamentarians and officials.

120a. Milton, J. The Edges of War: A History of Frontier Wars (1702-1878). Cape Town: Juta, 1983. 304pp. illus. maps. bibl.

A detailed narrative account of the frontier wars which took place along the eastern frontier of the Cape province between 1702 to 1878. Interesting descriptions are given of various governors, particularly Sir Harry Smith and of the events of the respective wars. The author is sympathetic towards the dispossessed Xhosa tribes. Comprehensive bibliography.

121. Picard, H. Cape Epic. Howick: Khenty Press, 1977. 184pp. illus. bibl.

Well-illustrated, brief survey of Cape history from the time of the early explorers to the present day.

CAPE - DUTCH EAST INDIA COMPANY, 1652-1795

Bibliography

122. Hopper, M.J. Slavery at the Cape 1652-1834. Cape Town: University of Cape Town School of Librarianship, 1964. iv, 47p. Unpublished bibliography.

CAPE - DUTCH EAST INDIA COMPANY, 1652-1795

Monographs

123. Beyers, C. Die Kaapse Patriotte Gedurende die Laaste Kwart van die Agtiende Eeu en die Voorlewing van hul Denkbeelde. 2nd ed. Pretoria: Van Schaik, 1967. 400pp. illus. bibl.

    A detailed study of the origins and nature of the movement at the Cape during the late seventeenth century led by certain burghers known as the Cape Patriots. The aims of this movement were embodied in a memorial of 1779 and 1782, presented firstly to the directors of the Dutch East India Company and finally to the States-General of Holland. The leaders of the Cape Patriots are mentioned and discussed and the economic grievances of the burghers outlined, particularly the resentment aroused by the appointment of certain autocratic government officials. The author investigates the possibility that the Cape Patriots were influenced by sentiments of nationalism gradually spreading throughout the Netherlands. In 1795, the Patriots of Graaff-Reinet and Swellendam revolted against their Landdrost, Maynier, and set up independent Republics. These Republics ended in 1799, when Britain occupied the Cape. The traditions established by the Patriots influenced the Great Trek and the establishment of Boer Republics in Natal and in the Transvaal.

124. Blommaert, W. Het Invoeren van die Slavernij aan de Kaap. Archives Yearbook for South African History. Vol. 1, part 1, 1938. Cape Town: Government Printer, 1938. 29pp.

    First chapter of Professor Blommaert's unfinished history of the slaves, entitled 'De Geschiedenis van de Slavernij aan de Kaap'. Describes the period 1652 to 1658, when the first slaves were introduced, and the economic effects the introduction of the slaves had at the Cape.

125. Böeseken, A.J. Die Nederlandse Kommissarisse en die 18de Eeuse Samelewing aan die Kaap. Archives Yearbook for South African History. Vol. 7. Cape Town: Government Printer, 1944. xv, 253pp. illus. bibl.

    Provides a comprehensive description of economic and social conditions at the Cape in the eighteenth century under the Dutch East India Company. Discusses the work of various commissioners who visited the Cape on behalf of the Company and the reports and recommendations made by these commissioners.

126. Böeseken, A.J. Slaves and Free Blacks at the Cape, 1658-1700. Cape Town: Tafelberg, 1977. 208pp. map. bibl.

    The introduction of slavery at the Cape occurred during van Riebeeck's time (c.1655). The company laid down certain regulations for their treatment which were comparatively humane.

The treatment of slaves during the administrations of Wagenaar, his successors and Simon van der Stel is discussed. The Dutch East India Company did not have slave markets in the Seven Provinces of Holland but only in the colonies. The legal position and rights of the 'Free Blacks' are discussed. There are two addenda of documents in the Cape Town Deeds Office pertaining to slaves.

127. Botha, C.G., ed. Collectanea ... Cape Town: Van Riebeeck Society, 1924. 141pp. (Van Riebeeck Society Publications, 5).

Consists of a collection of various documents relating to the Cape towards the end of the seventeenth and beginning of the eighteenth century. The first consists of instructions issued in 1699 by Simon van der Stel, as retiring governor, to his successor W.A. van der Stel. The next document is from the instructions of Commissioner C.J. Simons (1708) who visited and inspected the Cape. The third document is a copy of a letter written by John Maxwell, a traveller to the Cape, in 1707, containing a description of the Hottentots. The next two papers describe visits to the Hot Springs (now Caledon). The last four documents are extracts from the works of travellers who touched at the Cape; viz., William Dampier (1691), Ovington (1692) and Beeckman (1714).

128. Botha, C.G. Social Life in the Cape Colony in the 18th century. Cape Town: Juta, 1926. 109pp. illus. map.

Information for this book drawn from books of early travellers and from the Cape Archives. Part 1 deals with a description of Cape Town in the eighteenth century, the form of government, descriptions of houses and streets, order of precedence and military duty of the burger militia. Part 2 deals with social life in the towns. Part 3 is concerned with country life in villages and on farms.

129. Boxer, C.R. The Dutch Seaborne Empire, 1600-1800. London: Hutchinson, 1965. xxvi, 326pp. illus. maps. bibl.

A discussion of some factors which contributed to the rise of Holland as a seaborne empire. By 1648, Holland had become a great trading power. The various social classes which made up Dutch society are discussed; the burgher officials and merchant adventurers, industrial workers, farmers, craftsmen and sailors. The Dutch favoured free trade for their own ships but were monopolists regarding the area controlled by the Dutch East Company. The negative effect of Calvinism on the Islamic countries of the East is discussed as are Dutch culture and learning. The Dutch established forts and factories in the East to facilitate trade. The social attitudes of the Dutch towards the various coloured races and intermarriage with indigenous women is described. A chapter is devoted to the settlement at the Cape. During the eighteenth century Holland declined as an important power.

Cape - 1652-1795

130. Burman, J. The Cape of Good Intent. Cape Town: Human & Rousseau, 1969. 164pp. illus. map.

Written in a popular style, this book is divided into three sections covering the themes defence, mines and water. Under each heading the history of that particular aspect is given; viz., the construction of the Castle and blockhouses near Cape Town, the unsuccessful attempts at mining in the peninsular, and water supply problems of the Cape peninsula.

131. Chavonnes, M.P. de Reports of Chavonnes and His Council and of van Imhoff on the Cape. Cape Town: Van Riebeeck Society, 1918. 156pp. (Van Riebeeck Society Publications, 1).

The reports drawn up in 1716 by the Governor of the Cape, M.P. de Chavonnes and his Council discuss the economic and agricultural position of the Colony. The question of increasing the Colony's population was opposed by the Governor, who preferred slaves to free labourers. The brother of the Governor, D.M. Pasques de Chavonnes, differed in this respect. He advocated that more emigrants be sent to the Cape. He was the only member of Chavonnes' council to hold this view. In 1743, Governor-General van Imhoff toured the Cape and drew up a report on the orders of the company for the next governor's benefit. Comments on improvements needed for the economic and agricultural welfare of the colony.

132. De Kock, V. Those in Bondage: An Account of the Life of the Slaves at the Cape in the Days of the Dutch East India Company. 2nd ed. Pretoria: Union Booksellers, 1963. 240pp. illus. bibl.

This account is based on records kept by the Dutch East India Company at the Cape in the seventeenth and eighteenth centuries. Describes the circumstances under which slaves were first introduced at the Cape and the methods of transporting and disposing of them upon arrival. The work performed by the slaves, escape attempts, amusements, education, religion, superstitions and medicine are all comprehensively treated. The legal and judicial systems applicable to slaves and conditions of emancipation of slaves are also described.

133. Fairbridge, D. Historic Farms of South Africa: The Wool, the Wheat and the Wine of the 17th and 18th centuries. London: Oxford University Press, 1931. xii, 194pp. illus.

Describes the developments of farming methods at the Cape from the time of van Riebeeck to the end of the eighteenth century when Dominique de Chavonnes, Barrow and De Mist commented upon the Colony's agriculture, including the use of slave labour. The author is sympathetic towards the efforts of W.A. van der Stel at Vergelegen and depicts his agricultural policy in a far more favourable light than is the case with other historians.

134. Marais, J.S. Maynier and the First Boer Republic. Cape Town: Maskew Miller, 1944. xv, 161pp. map. bibl.

Deals with the history of the eastern frontier of the Cape Colony during the years 1778-1802. Describes the conflicts between the Boers, the Hottentots and Xhosa. Attempts to present a more impartial and favourable view of the landdrost of Graaff-Reinet, H.C.D. Maynier, who was much maligned by the historian, G.M. Theal.

135. Mentzel, O.F. Life at the Cape in Mid-eighteenth Century: Being the Biography of Rudolf Siegfried Allemann, Captain of the Military Forces and Commander of the Castle in the Service of the Dutch East India Company at the Cape of Good Hope. tr. by M. Greenlees. Cape Town: Van Riebeeck Society, 1919. vii, 170pp. front. (Van Riebeeck Society Publications, 2).

Mentzel acted as tutor to Allemann's children at the Cape during an eight-year period ending in 1741. Mentzel gives a detailed description of recruitment of soldiers for service at the Cape under the Dutch East India Company, of the administration of government at that period, of the career of Allemann and his promotion to Captain of the military forces at the Cape. Interesting description of a shipwreck which took place in 1740 (Dutch ship, 'De Vis'). Concludes with description of daily military routine carried out in the Castle and of the crew and cargo of an East Indiaman.

136. Neumark, S.D. Economic Influences on the South African Frontier, 1652-1836. Stanford: Stanford University Press, 1957. xiii, 196pp. maps. bibl.

Deals with the development of the frontier economy of the Cape Colony from the middle of the seventeenth to the early part of the nineteenth century. The frontier economy was one of exchange, with links to local and foreign markets. It was based partly on agriculture and stock-raising, on trading with the native tribes, on some processed foods such as butter, candles and soap and on hunting. Coastal trading centres grew up in Grahamstown, Graaff-Reinet and Port Elizabeth. The Great Trek has an economic basis, as cattle farmers sought better grazing in Transorangia, new sources of labour supply to replace slave labour and new tribes with whom to barter. The Voortrekkers did not venture into unknown land, as trading expeditions and trading centres in Natal and Delagoa Bay had established communication and trade before them.

137. Picard, H.W.J. Masters of the Castle: A Portrait Gallery of the Dutch Commanders and Governors of the Cape of Good Hope, 1652-1795; 1803-1806. Cape Town: Struik, 1972. 231pp. illus.

Popular, readable brief descriptions of Dutch commanders and governors of the Cape between 1652 and 1806.

Cape - 1652-1795

138. South Africa. State Archives. Kaapsche Archiefstukken ... 1718-1785. ed. by K.M. Jeffreys. Cape Town: Government Printer, 1926-1938. 7v.

Consists of important government documents in the original Dutch, including resolutions of the Dutch East India Company concerning the Cape, extracts from journals kept at the Castle, official correspondence, resolutions, reports and memoranda. Each volume carefully indexed. Other volumes of Cape Government documents for the seventeenth and eighteenth centuries are: (1) Suid-Afrikaanse Argiefstukke, Kaap, nos. I-V Resolusies van die Politieke Raad, 1651-1719. ed. by A.J. Böeseken. 5v. Cape Town: Government Printer, 1957-1964; (2) Suid-Afrikaanse Argiefstukke, Kaap; VI-VII -- Resolusies van die Politieke Raad, 1720-1728. 2v. ed. by G.C. de Wet. Cape Town: Government Printer, 1968-1971; (3) Kaapse Argiefstukke. Plakkaatboek, 1652-1795. ed. by K.M. Jeffreys and S.D. Naude. 2v. Cape Town: Government Printer, 1944-1949.

139. Spilhaus, M.W. Company's Men. Cape Town: John Malherbe, 1973. 247pp. illus. map. bibl.

An account of the achievements of three Dutch East India Governors at the Cape: Johan van Riebeeck, Simon van der Stel and Ryk Tulbagh. Suitable for non-specialist readers and schools.

140. Spilhaus, M.W. The First South Africans and the Laws Which Governed Them: To Which is Appended the Diary of Adam Tas. Cape Town: Juta, 1949. 284pp. illus. bibl.

A collection of essays in which the author discusses the 'plakkaaten' or laws which governed the Cape Colony from the time of Jan van Riebeeck's rule to the end of Willem Adriaan van der Stel's period of office (1652-1707). The resentment which the free burghers felt towards these laws culminated in the removal of van der Stel from office. The diary of Adam Tas, one of the leaders of the malcontents, voices these grievances and has been translated from the Dutch.

141. Spilhaus, M.W. South Africa in the Making, 1652-1806. Cape Town: Juta, 1966. 422pp. illus. maps. bibl.

The period of Jan van Riebeeck's rule as governor of the Cape station is firstly described. Van Riebeeck disliked the Cape intensely and the Dutch East India Company was dissatisfied with the low productivity of the Settlement. For twenty years after van Riebeeck's departure (1662) the freeburghers at the Cape made little headway, although from 1679 onwards they were permitted to establish farms outside the Cape peninsula. The governorships of Simon van der Stel and Willem Adriaan van der Stel are discussed. The charges against the latter are said to be exaggerated. From 1714 onwards, certain farmers were continually trekking northwards and eastwards in search of new grazing. A social distinction arose between frontier farmers and burgers of Cape Town. From 1775 onwards the Dutch East India Company's fortunes declined and the

Company was faced with demands from the Cape Town burghers for freedom of trade and by unrest on the frontier between farmers and tribesmen. The frontier problem was inherited by the British during their first occupation (1795-1802). The concluding section deals with the short period during which the Cape was under the rule of the Batavian Republic. Once again the frontier question remained a difficult problem (1802-1805).

142. Tas, A. The Diary of Adam Tas ... with an Enquiry into the Complaints of the Colonists Against the Governor, Willem Adriaan van der Stel. English translation by A.C. Paterson. ed. by L. Fouche. London: Longmans, 1914. 367pp. maps.

An account written in the original Dutch with English translation on opposite pages. Consists of an introduction giving biographical details of Adam Tas and description of the discovery and value of the diary. The diary itself follows. In conclusion, there are chapters devoted to discussion of the burghers' complaints against the governor and evidence for or against the validity of these complaints is presented.

143. Tas, A. The Diary of Adam Tas, 1705-1706. ed. by L. Fouche. Cape Town: Van Riebeeck Society, 1970. 430pp. map. (Van Riebeeck Society Publications, 2nd Series, no. 1).

The original diary of Tas has been lost, and the version reproduced in this volume is based on two copies, one in the Government Archives at the Hague and the second in the South African Library, Cape Town. The diary covers the period from June 13, 1705, to February, 1706. Some entries are missing, presumably deleted by government authorities. The diary is valuable in depicting social and economic conditions at the Cape during the time of Willem Adriaan van der Stel.

144. Theal, G.M. McCall. Chronicles of Cape Commanders, or an Abstract of Original Manuscripts in the Archives of the Cape Colony, Dating from 1651 to 1691, Compared with Printed Accounts of the Settlement by Various Visitors During that Time, also Four Short Papers upon Subjects Connected with the East India Company's Government at a Later Period, Reprinted from Colonial Periodicals, and notes on English, Dutch and French Books Published before 1796, Containing References to South Africa. Cape Town: W.A. Richards, 1882. xiv, 428pp. charts.

Covers the voyages of Portuguese discoverers of the sea route to India and the period of office of van Riebeeck, Zacharias Wagenaar, Cornelis van Quaelberg, Jacob Borghorst, Albert van Breugel, Isbrand Goske, Johan Bax and Simon van der Stel. These are described using various documents in the Archives which had hitherto been neglected. There is also discussion concerning Stellenbosch and Swellendam records of the eighteenth and nineteenth centuries, the rule of Ryk Tulbagh and description of events in 1781. Finally, there is a discussion of various Africana works.

Cape - 1652-1795

145. Valentyn, F. Descriptions of the Cape of Good Hope with the Matters Concerning It. ed. by P. Serton, and others. Amsterdam, 1726. Cape Town: Van Riebeeck Society, 1971, 1973. 2v. illus. map. (Van Riebeeck Society Publications, 2nd Series, nos. 2,4).

Valentyn visited the Cape in 1685, 1695, 1705 and 1714 for a total period of more than six months. He did not travel into the interior but relied on other writers such as Dapper, Bogaert, Kolbe and Grevenbroek for his descriptions of the interior. The 'Description of the Cape of Good Hope' forms part five of Valentyn's 'Oud en Nieuw Oost-Indiën'. Besides the description of the scenery, people, flora and fauna of the Colony, the volumes also contain an account of a journey made inland by Simon van der Stel in 1685 to visit the Amacquas, a journey of Landdrost Starrenburg (1705) and a summary of the discovery and colonization of the Cape by the Portuguese and Dutch, respectively.

146. Van der Stel, S. Simon van der Stel's Journal of his Expedition to Namaqualand, 1685-1686. ed. by G. Waterhouse. London: Longmans Green, 1932. xxvii, 193pp. illus. map. bibl. Supplement: Addenda and corrigenda. Dublin, 1953. iv, 19pp. illus. bibl. For description see entry no. 078.

147. Van Riebeeck, J. Journal of Jan van Riebeeck. ed. by H.B. Thom. Cape Town: Balkema, 1952-1958. 3v. illus. Volume 1. 1651-1655. Volume 2. 1656-1658. Volume 3. 1659-1662.

Volume 1 commences with an introduction giving biographical details of van Riebeeck's life and discussing authorship of the journal and various translations. The journal itself, contained in volumes 1 and 2, is annotated. Volume 3 contains an index to the three volumes.

148. [Van Riebeeck, J.] Leipoldt, C.L. Jan van Riebeeck: A Biographical Study. London: Longmans, Green, 1936. xi, 292pp. illus. bibl.

The first English biography of van Riebeeck is based upon material in the Cape Archives, mainly van Riebeeck's journal, letters dispatched from the Cape, letters and documents received and Council of Justice papers, all dealing with the years 1652 to 1662. This information has been included in an interesting narrative which covers van Riebeeck's life from the time of his childhood to his death in 1677. A more recent biographical study is: Böeseken, A.J. 'Jan van Riebeeck en sy Gesin'. Cape Town: Tafelberg, 1974. xviii, 285pp. illus. maps. bibl.

149. [Van Riebeeck, J.] Molsbergen, E.C. Godée. Jan van Riebeeck en sy Tyd. Pretoria: Van Schaik, 1968. 159pp. illus. bibl.

Authoritative biography of van Riebeeck translated from the Dutch into Afrikaans.

150. Wagner, Z. Zacharias Wagner: Second Commander of the Cape.
ed. by O.H. Spohr. Cape Town: Balkema, 1967. 103pp. illus.

Brief introduction giving events of Wagner's life. Description of the Wagner manuscripts including his brief journal and 'Animal Book' of sketches. The journal itself is well annotated by the editor.

151. Welch, S.R. Portuguese and Dutch in South Africa, 1641-1806. Cape Town: Juta, 1951. 944pp.

In 1641 Portugal re-established her independence of Spain and became a great trading power. This volume deals with the trade rivalry between Portugal and Holland, with England as a doubtful ally of Portugal. Portugal was entrenched in Mozambique and Angola while the Dutch established a settlement at the Cape. Events in these colonies were influenced by the Napoleonic Wars. England reoccupied the Cape in 1806 to safeguard the sea route to India.

CAPE - FIRST BRITISH OCCUPATION AND BATAVIAN RULE, 1795-1806

Bibliographies

152. Van Rensburg, E.E.J. The Cape of Good Hope under the Batavian Republic, 1803-1806. Cape Town: University of Cape Town School of Librarianship, 1966. v, 65pp.

153. Wagner, M. St. Clair. The First British Occupation of the Cape of Good Hope, 1795-1803: A Bibliography. Cape Town: University of Cape Town School of Librarianship, 1954. v, 38pp.

Monographs

154. Barnard, A. The Letters of Lady Anne Barnard to Henry Dundas from the Cape and Elsewhere, 1797-1803, Together with her Journal of a Tour to the Interior and Certain other Matters. ed. by A.M.L. Robinson. Cape Town: Balkema, 1973. xv, 303pp. illus.

These letters were first published in 1901 under the title 'South Africa a Century Ago'. (Entry No. 155). This early edition contained various errors and omissions which are rectified in the new edition. There are thirty-four letters in the collection -- twenty-one from the Cape and thirteen from England and Ireland.

155. Barnard, A. South Africa a Century Ago: Letters Written from the Cape of Good Hope (1797-1801). ed. by W.H. Wilkins. London: Smith Elder, 1901. x, 316pp. front.

An introductory memoir summarizing the events of Lade Anne Barnard's life is followed by a brief history of the Cape Colony up to 1797. The letters are from the private papers of Lord Melville and cover the period July 10, 1797, to February 16, 1801.

156. Barnard, A. South Africa a Century Ago (1797-1801): Part I. Letters written from the Cape of Good Hope: Part II. Extracts from a journal addressed to her sister in England; selected and edited by H.J. Anderson; with an introduction by A.C.G. Lloyd; and a memoir of the Lady Anne Barnard by W.H. Wilkins. Cape Town: Maskew Miller, 1924. 231pp. illus.

The introduction covers historical events at the Cape. The memoir contains biographical details of Lady Anne Barnard's life. The letters are addressed to Henry Dundas, Secretary of State. The journal deals with incidents related to Lady Anne's stay at the Cape and tour into the interior.

157. [Barnard, A.] Fairbridge, D., ed. Lady Anne Barnard at the Cape of Good Hope, 1797-1802. Oxford: Clarendon Press, 1924. xiii, 343pp. illus.

Biography of Lady Barnard's life which contains numerous excerpts from her letters from the Cape to the Earl of Macartney. Most of the biography deals with her life at the Cape. The period before and after this sojourn is summarized briefly.

158. Burchell, W.J. Travels in the Interior of Southern Africa. Reprinted from the original edition of 1822-1824, with some additional material. Edited by I. Schapera. London: Longman, 1953. 2v. illus. maps.

Describes an expedition undertaken during the years 1811 to 1815 which reached Litakun and returned via Graaff-Reinet, Grahamstown and coastal districts to Cape Town. Burchell made important botanical and zoological discoveries on this expedition. Includes interesting observations on the inhabitants of the Colony, both White and Black.

159. De Mist, A.U. Diary of a Journey to the Cape of Good Hope and the interior of Africa in 1802-1803. Introduction by E.H. Burrows. Cape Town: Balkema, 1954. 57pp. illus. map.

Diary of Julie Philippe Augusta Uitenhage de Mist who in 1803 accompanied her father Commissary J.A. de Mist on a tour of the Cape Colony as far as the eastern frontier.

160. De Mist, J.A. The Memorandum of Commissary J.A. de Mist, Containing Recommendations for the Form and Administration of Government at the Cape of Good Hope, 1802. ed. by S.F.N. Gie. Cape Town: Van Riebeeck Society, 1920. xiv, 290pp. illus. (Van Riebeeck Society Publications, 3).

Consists of the original Dutch version and English translation by Kathleen M. Jeffreys of de Mist's memorandum. This memorandum was drawn up on the instructions of the state government of the Batavian Republic. It contains a description of the administration, religion, economics, social conditions, population and financial conditions of the colony and is rather prejudiced against the former administration of the Dutch East India Company. It includes suggestions for the general improvement of the Cape Colony and ways in which these improvements should be carried out.

161. [De Mist, J.A.] Murray, A.H. The Political Philosophy of J.A. de Mist, Commissioner-General at the Cape 1803-1805: A Study in Political Pluralism. Cape Town: H.A.U.M., 1962. 150pp. bibl.

An in-depth study of the political philosophy of de Mist, and the way in which this philosophy influenced the establishment of new political, religious and educational systems at the Cape during the rule of the Batavian Republic (1802-1804). De Mist believed in the political theories of the sovereignty of corporations and the rights of groups within the state. He attempted to institute an administrative system in which the people would be represented; e.g., election of landdrosts and heemraden. He also treated the church and educational establishments as corporate bodies with certain rights subject to state control. The Black and Coloured peoples at the Cape were similarly considered corporate bodies. They were to be kept separated in reserves and contracts would be formed with them. Although de Mist's rule was very brief, his institutions profoundly influenced future developments at the Cape.

162. Duckitt, W. William Duckitt Diary. ed. by E.A. Nobbs. Archives Yearbook for South African History, 1942. Vol. 4, Part 2, 1942. Cape Town: Government Printer, 1943. pp.73-89.

Covers the period 1799 to 1800, when Duckitt was appointed as agricultural adviser to the Cape by the British government. Extracts are given from the diary describing the voyage of Duckitt and his party of skilled labourers to the Cape and the establishment of an agricultural experiment station at Klapmuts. They undertook an expedition through the western Cape and recorded impressions of the agricultural potential of the region. Duckitt later became a farmer in the Groenkloof at Klaver Valley and introduced improvements in horse breeding.

Cape - 1795-1806

163. Duminy, F.R. Duminy-dagboeke: Duminy Diaries. (1793, 1797, 1810). ed. by J.L.M. Franken. Cape Town: Van Riebeeck Society, 1938. 355pp. illus. maps. (Van Riebeeck Society Publications, 19).

Commences with a biographical account of the Duminy family who were originally of French extraction. The journal of 1793 was written by F.R. Duminy, a French naval captain who settled at the Cape and undertook an expedition to Walfish Bay (1793). This account is supplemented by extracts from the journal of S.V. van Reenen, another participant in the expedition. The 1797 journal was compiled by Johanna Margareta Duminy (née Nöthling) and relates the daily events of the family's life on holiday at 'Bokrivier'. The final journal of 1810-1811 is written by F.R. Duminy and describes a family visit to the Warmbaths at Swartberg and to Bokrivier. Interesting accounts of daily life of Cape burghers at the beginning of the nineteenth century.

164. Golovnin, V.M. Detained in Simon's Bay: The Story of the Detention of the Imperial Russian Sloop, 'Diana' from April 1808 to May 1809. tr. and ed. by O.H. Spohr. Cape Town: Friends of the South African Library, 1964. vi, 90pp. illus. map.

Very interesting description of conditions at the Cape, the appearance of Cape Town and the rest of the colony, daily life, trade and economic and social conditions under which the colonists lived, climate and products of the colony.

165. Idenburg, P.J. The Cape of Good Hope at the Turn of the Eighteenth Century. Leiden: University Press, 1963. 134pp. illus. maps. bibl. Originally published in Dutch.

Attempts to describe the opinions and way of life of the colonists of the Cape at the beginning of the nineteenth century. Special attention is paid to the problem of how far ideas of the Enlightenment affected political views at the Cape. Discusses the reorganization program of Commissioners-General S.C. Nederburgh and S.H. Frykenius (1792), A.J. Sluysken (1793-1795) and the Batavian administration as represented by J.A. de Mist and J.W. Janssens (1803-1806). Concludes with observations on cultural life at the Cape and on the struggle to maintain the Dutch language after the 1806 British annexation of the Cape.

166. Newton-King, S., and V.C. Malherbe. The Khoikhoi Rebellion in the Eastern Cape (1799-1803). Cape Town: Centre for African Studies, University of Cape Town, 1981. 136pp. illus. bibl. (Communications, No. 5).

The frontier war of 1799-1803 is described as the last attempt of the Khoikhoi to recover their lands and social and economic independence from the encroaching frontier farmers. Many of the Khoikhoi who took part in the uprising were former forced labourers of the frontier settlers who deserted and joined bands of Xhosa insurgents. The main centre of resistance was Graaff-Reinet. A description is given of Khoi captains.

167. Theal, G. McCall, ed. Records of the Cape Colony, 1793-1806. London: William Clowes, 1897-1900. 6v.

Consist of official correspondence, proclamations, instructions to officials, memoranda, orders-in-council and other official documents relating to the Cape copied by Theal for the Cape Government from the manuscript documents in the Public Record Office, London.

168. Van der Merwe, P.J. Die Kaffer Oorlog van 1793. Kaapstad: Nasionale Pers, 1940. 88pp. bibl.

Describes the Frontier War of 1793 as an example of the inefficiency of the Dutch East India Company in protecting the interests of frontier farmers against tribal raids. Denounces the efforts of the Landdrost of Graaff-Reinet, Maynier, who is alleged to have become sympathetic to the tribes and too inclined to blame the frontier farmers for unrest on the frontier.

169. Van der Merwe, J.P. Die Kaap onder die Bataafse Republiek, 1803-1806. Amsterdam: Swets and Zeitlinger, 1926. 384pp. illus. map. bibl.

The work and reforms of J.A. de Mist and J.W. Janssens are discussed in the areas of administration; education; religion; policy towards Blacks, Coloured peoples and slaves; economy; trade and monetary reforms.

170. Van Pallandt, A. General Remarks on the Cape of Good Hope (1803). Tr. from the French. Cape Town: South African Public Library, 1917. 39pp.

Van Pallandt acted as private secretary to General J.W. Janssens and accompanied him on his tour through the eastern Cape. The pamphlet was printed in 1803 and led to the dismissal of van Pallandt as it contained many critical remarks regarding treatment of Hottentots and Xhosa, economic conditions at the Cape, the military and strategic conditions of the settlement and trade and agriculture at the Cape. The Cape authorities destroyed as many copies of the brochure as they could find of what they considered a derogatory document.

171. Van Reenen, D.G. Die Joernaal van Dirk Gysbert van Reenen, 1803. ed. by W. Blommaert and J.A. Wiid. Cape Town: Van Riebeeck Society, 1937. viii, 322pp. map. (Van Riebeeck Society Publications, 18). (Eng. tr. by J.L.M. Franken and I.M. Murray).

Commences with a biographical sketch of Dirk Gysbert, a prominent burgher at the Cape at the beginning of the nineteenth century. The journal was compiled in 1803 when Dirk Gysbert accompanied General Janssens on an expedition into the interior. Gysbert assisted the Governor in negotiating with the Hottentots and Xhosa, and with the missionary van der Kemp. Describes the negotiations with the farmers and concludes with the economic prospects of the region.

CAPE - 1806-1836

172. Arkin, M. Storm in a Teacup: The Later years of John Company at the Cape, 1815-1836. Cape Town: Struik, 1973. xi, 258pp. illus. bibl.

    Primarily concerned with the English East India Company's monopoly of the tea trade at the Cape. This monopoly came to an end in 1835 after causing much resentment at the Cape. The Company also was engaged in other activities during this period and experienced remittance difficulties. The Company attempted to continue the indents of Bengal piece goods and export of Cape wines to Britain and India.

173. Bird, W. State of the Cape of Good Hope in 1822. London: John Murray, 1823. facs. repr. Cape Town: Struik, 1966. viii, 380pp. illus. maps.

    Author acted as 'Controller of Customs in Cape Town' and therefore makes reference in the text to Government papers, estimates and statistics to verify his observations. Describes in detail the Cape's administration, judicial system, banking system, agriculture, slave population, trade, manners and customs of the people and arrival and establishment of the 1820 settlers.

174. Campbell, C.T. British South Africa: A History of the Colony of the Cape of Good Hope from its Conquest 1795-1825. London: John Haddon, 1897. viii, 222pp. map. Cape Town: Juta, 1897.

    Attempts to give a full history of the British settlement at the Cape and describe the experiences of the 1820 British settlers and their setbacks as a result of the frontier wars. Gives biographical details of British settlers who achieved distinction and lists settlers who were elected to the Legislative Council and House of Assembly. Also gives lists of names of emigrating settlers of 1820 and names of leaders of various parties.

175. Cape of Good Hope. Archives. Documents relating to the Kaffir War of 1835. ed. by G.M. Theal. London: William Clowes for Government of Union of South Africa, 1912. xvi, 403pp.

    Consists mainly of correspondence of Governor Sir Benjamin D'Urban and Colonel Harry Smith relating to events on the frontier from January to September, 1835. This correspondence is addressed to various military officers on the border, including Colonel H. Somerset, Colonel John Bell, Colonel Cuyler, Commandant Stephanus van Wyk, Captain Armstrong, Captain Duncan Campbell, Major Cox and Lord Fitzroy Somerset. There are also letters to the Secretary of State; to various missionaries such as the Reverends W.J. Davis, J. Ayliff, W.B. Boyce, F.G. Kayser and W. Shepstone; and to various civil commissioners in frontier regions such as Uitenhage and George. Finally, there are copies of communications and treaties with the Xhosa chiefs Makoma, Tyali, Guanya, Kusia, Eno and Fadani.

176. Cape of Good Hope. Archives. The Rebellion of 1815, generally known as Slachters Nek. ed. by H.C.V. Leibbrandt. Cape Town: Juta, 1902. iv, 979pp. map.

A collection of all papers connected with the trial of the accused; viz., criminal records held at Uitenhage, 1815-1816; annexures to minutes of the special commission of justice in session at Uitenhage, 1815-1816; official correspondence regarding the case 1815-1816; and minutes of the Commission of Circuit, Drostdy, Graaff-Reinet, 1815.

177. Cape of Good Hope. Archives. Records of the Cape Colony. ed. by G.M. Theal. v. VI-XXXVI, 1806-1834. London: William Clowes for Government of Cape Colony, 1900-1905.

Consists of official documents and official correspondence copied by Theal from the manuscript documents in the Public Record Office, London, on behalf of the Cape Archives. Documents all arranged chronologically.

178. Chase, J.C. The Cape of Good Hope and the Eastern Province of Algoa Bay. London: Pelham Richardson, 1843. Facs. repr. Cape Town: Struik, 1967. xvi, 358pp. illus. maps.

This volume was written by an 1820 settler at the Cape for the information of the reading public of England. This history of the Cape Colony and particularly of the eastern province is outlined; the government, law, religion, education, press, agriculture, trade and commerce and amusements of the colony are described; and a plan made for more immigrant farmers to settle at the Cape.

179. [Cole, Sir Lowry] Cole, M.L., and G.S. Cole, eds. Memoirs of Sir Lowry Cole. London: Macmillan, 1934. viii, 262pp. illus.

Based on the private papers of Sir Lowry Cole. Chapter fourteen deals briefly with Cole's governorship at the Cape (1828-1833).

180. [Cole, Sir Lowry] Hunt, K.S. Sir Lowry Cole, Governor of Mauritius, 1823-1828; Governor of the Cape of Good Hope, 1828-1833; A Study in Colonial Administration. Durban: Butterworths, 1974. 191pp. maps. bibl.

Well-documented biography of Cole. Describes the British colonial form of government which Cole maintained in Mauritius and at the Cape and also the judicial reforms introduced by a Charter of Justice (1827). Also discusses the problems Cole encountered from slave-owners at the Cape in passing ordinances for the amelioration of the condition of the slaves between 1828 and 1833. Cole was unable to solve the frontier conflicts which existed between colonists and Xhosa on the northern and eastern boundaries. He advocated written treaties with chiefs and was in favour of the commando system. During Cole's period

of office, the British government attempted to remove the
restrictions on free trade. The wine trade at the Cape
improved as did other agricultural exports. However, the Cape
Government was financially embarrassed and administrative costs
had to be pruned.

181. Cunynghame, A.T. My Command in South Africa, 1874-1878.
London: Macmillan, 1879. xx, 376pp. maps.

An account of Cunynghame's experiences in South Africa as
commander of the British troops stationed there. The book is
divided into five parts. Part 1 deals with the Cape Colony
and contains descriptions of the inhabitants, Black and White,
and of their customs. Part 2 is a description of a tour of
military inspection of Kaffraria and Natal. Part 3 consists
of an account of Cunynghame's arrival at the Diamond Fields in
1875 to maintain order among the diggers. A very interesting
description of the appearance of the digging and of towns in
the neighbourhood and also of the Lovedale Institute is
included. Part 4 concerns the British annexation of the Transvaal and a description of Cunynghame's tour. Part 5 is a discussion of the Sixth Kaffir War.

182. Donkin, Sir R.S. Letterbook of Sir Rufane Shaw Donkin. ed. by
J.B. Scott. Port Elizabeth: Historical Society of Port
Elizabeth and Walmer, 1970. vii, 115pp. illus.

These letters cover the period March 1820 to June 1821 and
consist of semi-official and private letters. They cover
matters such as the arrival and establishment of the 1820
settlers, frontier affairs and matters regarding the military
forces in the colony and trade. The editor expresses the
opinion that Donkin was unfairly maligned by Lord Charles
Somerset.

183. Duly, L.C. British Land Policy at the Cape, 1795-1844: A
Study of Administrative Procedures in the Empire. Durham:
Duke University Press, 1968. xix, 226pp. maps. bibl.

Commences with the 1795 acceptance by Britain of the charter
land system established by the Dutch East India Company at the
Cape. Discusses the implementation and results of the land
system of perpetual quitrent tenure introduced by Governor
Cradock in 1813 as well as the failure of Cradock's system due
to the negligence and inefficiency of the colonial authorities
in registering land claims and issuing titles. A commission of
inquiry was appointed (1823-1826) which led to the creation of
the Cape Land Board and reformed Cradock's regulations (1828-1834). From 1840 to 1844, the British Colonial Office attempted to implement a scheme of freehold tenure and sale of
land at public auction at a minimum upset price. This system
was unpopular at the Cape and was inefficiently administered.
This inefficiency reveals that local authorities could ignore
instructions issued by London to the colonies.

184. Edwards, I. Towards Emancipation: A Study in South African Slavery. Cardiff: Gomerian Press, 1942. 249pp. bibl.

Discusses the progress of slave emancipation in South Africa from the abolition of the trade in slaves through various attempts to improve their condition and status to emancipation which took place in the first half of the nineteenth century. The beliefs and methods of English humanitarians, secretaries of state and government officials are described as well as the attitudes of Boer farmers. The situation of the slave and Hottentot 'apprentices' at the Cape is contrasted with the parallel systems in the West Indies, where the position of the slave and labourer was infinitely worse. The British authorities erred in instituting the same emancipation and apprenticeship regulations at the Cape as they had in the West Indies. The effects of slave emancipation at the Cape are evaluated and discussed.

185. Godlonton, R. A Narrative of the Irruption of the Kaffir Hordes into the Eastern Province of the Cape of Good Hope, 1834-1835; including Parts I, II and III of the Introductory Remarks. London: Richardson, 1851. Fac. repr. Cape Town: Struik, 1965. 297pp. front. map.

This detailed account of the 1834-1835 frontier war was written in great indignation against the depredations and treachery of the frontier tribes and also against the philanthropic apologies of the missionaries and government officials. There are also descriptions of trade along the frontier and of the inhabitants of Kaffraria.

186. Heese, J.A. Slagtersnek en sy Mense. Cape Town: Tafelberg, 1973. 239pp. illus. map. bibl.

A re-examination of the legend which has grown around the events of Slagtersnek. The author attempts to prove that the events did not really influence the Great Trek. After the British annexation of the Transvaal in 1877, anti-British feeling grew. Authors such as S.J. du Toit revived the legend of Slagtersnek which was increasingly used in the late nineteenth century as a means of propaganda.

187. Pama, C. Regency Cape Town: Daily Life in the Early Eighteenthirties Illustrated with the Hitherto Unpublished Johannesburg Album of Sketches by Sir Charles D'Oyly, Together with his other Cape Town Drawings and those of Frederick Knyvett. Cape Town: Tafelberg, 1975. 140pp. illus. map. bibl.

An account of the social history of Cape Town in the early 1830s, when it was visited by Sir Charles D'Oyly and his friend Frederick Knyvett. The book concludes with an alphabetical directory of Cape Town citizens and their occupations in 1833.

188. Philip, P. British Residents at the Cape, 1795-1819: Biographical Records of 4800 Pioneers. Cape Town: D. Philip, 1981. 484pp.

An alphabetically arranged list of 4800 British pioneers who lived at the Cape before 1820. Gives biographical notes on each of them. Includes useful information on Cape Town streets and squares, as well as British regiments and warships.

189. Smith, Sir Andrew. Andrew Smith's Journal of his Expedition into the Interior of South Africa, 1834-1836. ed. by W.F. Lye. Cape Town: Balkema, 1975. xii, 323pp. illus. map.

Introduction to the book supplies the historical background concerning intertribal warfare in South Africa in the early nineteenth century and also biographical details of Andrew Smith's career and expedition. The journal commences in August 1834 and concludes in March, 1836. Smith made contact with the Griquas, the Sothos under Moshweshwe, the Tlokwa of Sekonyela and the Thlaping at Kuruman (where he met Robert Moffat and the Ndebele). He met Mzilikazi and took with him to Cape Town an emissary from the chief. Illustrations in the book are reproduced from the paintings of Charles Davidson Bell, who was a member of Smith's expedition.

190. [Somerset, Sir C.] Millar, A.K. Plantagenet in South Africa: Lord Charles Somerset. Cape Town: Oxford University Press, 1965. ix, 293pp. illus. bibl.

Attempts to analyse the career of Somerset as Governor of the Cape (1814-1826) in relation to his Plantagenet ancestry, aristocratic background and upbringing. Describes the events of Somerset's rule at the Cape and discusses the positive results of Somerset's endeavours as well as the feuds and opposition which he encountered as a result of his autocratic actions. Extracts are provided from correspondence between Somerset and Commissioner J.T. Bigge which throw new light on Somerset's motives and reactions.

191. [Somerset, H.] Rivett-Carnac, D.E. Hawk's Eye. Cape Town: Timmins, 1966. xi, 178pp. illus. map. bibl.

A biography of Henry Somerset in which the achievements of the Somerset family are depicted in a favourable manner.

192. Venter, P.J. Landdros en Heemrade (1682-1827). Archives Yearbook for South African History. Vol. 3, Part 2, 1940. Cape Town: Government Printer, 1940. 242pp. bibl.

A study of the local courts of landdrost and heemraden which filled a vital administrative function between the years 1682 and 1827. Owing to poor communications, the central government of Cape Town was obliged to rely heavily on these courts in outlying districts to carry out magisterial, agricultural, municipal, military and financial duties. The central government was not always satisfied with the manner in which the local courts carried out these duties, as the incumbents were simple burghers filled with local prejudices. The local courts were abolished in 1826 on the recommendations of the Commission of Inquiry led by W.M.G. Colebrooke and J.T. Bigge.

CAPE - SETTLERS OF BRITISH ORIGIN, 1820 ONWARDS

Bibliography

193. Berning, J.M. Select Bibliography on the 1820 Settlers and Settlement; 3rd ed. Grahamstown: 1820 Settlers National Monument Foundation, 1974. 20pp.

Monographs

194. Ayliff, J. The Journal of John Ayliff, I : 1821-1830. ed. by Peter Hinchliff. Cape Town: Balkema, 1971. 130pp.

    Ayliff was an 1820 settler and pioneer Methodist missionary in the eastern Cape. The journal covers the period when Ayliff was stationed at Salem, Somerset and Butterworth. He identified himself closely with the Fingo people. Up to the present date, only volume I of Ayliff's journal has been published.

195. Ayliff, J. The Journal of 'Harry Hastings', Albany settler. ed. by L.A. Hewson and F.G. van der Riet. Grahamstown: Grocott & Sherry, 1963. 106pp.

    This journal is thought to be a partly autobiographical, semi-fictionalised account of Ayliff's own experiences as an 1820 settler. Describes the voyage of 'Harry Hastings' from London to Algoa Bay, the journey to the settlement near Bathurst and the period lasting until December 6, 1820, when many difficulties are recorded.

196. Bell, M. They Came from a Far Land. Cape Town: Maskew Miller, 1963. xv, 182pp. illus. bibl.

    A biographical account of the English settler families, the Woods and the Hooles, and their pioneering efforts in the Eastern Cape.

197. Burrows, E.H. The Moodies of Melsetter. Cape Town: Balkema, 1954. 204pp. illus. map.

A biographical account of the Moodie family tracing their early lineage from ancient times in Scotland and describing the arrival of Capt. Benjamin Moodie in the Eastern Province and finally the Moodie trek of 1892 to Eastern Rhodesia from the Orange Free State.

198. Butler, G. The 1820 Settlers: An Illustrated Commentary. Cape Town: Human & Rousseau, 1974. 366pp. illus. bibl.

A detailed history of the 1820 settlers in which the social and historical context of the period is described and the experiences and problems facing the settlers are outlined, using extracts from the settlers' own accounts. Text divided into six sections. Part 1 deals with the historical events leading to the emigration of the settlers. Part 2 is concerned with the recruitment and journey to the place of settlement. Part 3 describes the early years of the settlement and difficulties encountered. Part 4 deals with new ventures undertaken by the settlers when agricultural efforts failed. Part 5 consists of a description of public affairs and legislation, frontier affairs, the Sixth Frontier War and the arrival of the trekkers in Natal. Part 6 describes the cultural changes wrought by the arrival of the 1820 settlers, in the fields of education and religion, and the establishment of Bathurst, Grahamstown and Port Elizabeth.

199. Butler, G., ed. When Boys Were Men. Cape Town: Oxford University Press, 1969. xi, 275pp. illus. maps.

Adventures and experiences of various youthful settlers, all under the age of twenty-one, are described in the form of autobiographical extracts. The events described all took place in South Africa before 1875.

200. Caffrey, K. The British to Southern Africa. London: Gentry, 1973. ix, 118pp. (Great Emigrations Series, 3).

Discusses the importance of British emigration to South Africa from the end of the eighteenth century onwards. The social, economic, political and cultural importance of the 1820 settlers, British missionaries and traders are discussed. The discovery of gold and diamonds in the second half of the nineteenth century led to the arrival of a greater influx of emigrants, the establishment of Johannesburg and Kimberley and the Anglo-Boer War of 1899-1902.

201. Dickason, G.B. Cornish Immigrants to South Africa: The Cousin Jack's Contribution to the Development of Mining and Commerce, 1820-1920. Cape Town: Balkema, 1978. x, 122pp. illus. bibl.

Prior to the second half of the nineteenth century, few Cornish emigrants settled in South Africa. Cornish emigration increased after 1854 with the opening up of the Namaqualand copper mines, Kimberley diamond fields and gold fields of the eastern Transvaal and Witwatersrand. The Cornish influence in South Africa is evident in the mining techniques which they imported to South African mining industry, in the commercial sphere, with the establishment of various firms such as Stuttafords, in the culinary sphere and in various place names, e.g., Baragwanath Hospital.

202. Dickason, G.B. Irish Settlers to the Cape: History of the Clanwilliam 1820 Settlers from Cork Harbour. Cape Town: Balkema, 1973. 113pp. illus. maps. bibl.

Records the settlement in Clanwilliam of four parties of settlers who originated in Cork Harbour. Contains extracts from settler diaries and appendices of biographical details of settlers.

203. [Dugmore, H.H.] Van der Riet, F.G., and L.A. Hewson, eds. The Reminiscences of an Albany Settler. Grahamstown: Grocott & Sherry, 1958. 90pp. front.

Based on a lecture given by Dugmore on the occasion of the 1870 jubilee of the British settlers in Grahamstown. Dugmore recounts the early years of the settlement when he arrived with his parents at the age of nine, one of a family of six children. He also describes the Frontier War of 1835.

204. Edwards, I.E. The 1820 Settlers in South Africa: A Study in British Colonial Policy. London: Longmans, 1934. ix, 207pp. maps. bibl.

Commences in the year 1815, with an explanation of British colonial policy and of the problem of the eastern frontier of the Cape. Traces the arrival of the 1820 settlers and the reasons for their discontent with Somerset's rule. Discusses the effect of their grievances on public opinion in Britain, eventually forcing the Colonial Office to recall Somerset and pursue a more positive colonial policy at the Cape.

205. Eveleigh, W. The Settlers and Methodism, 1820-1920. Cape Town: Methodist Publishing Office, 1920. v, 198pp. illus.

An account of the Methodist Church in the eastern Cape under the leadership of the Rev. William Shaw, and his helpers, William Shepstone, John Ayliff, Thomas Jenkins and Henry Hare Dugmore. There are descriptions of missionary work done by the Wesleyans and of the Methodist church and Kingswood School in Grahamstown.

206. Ffolliott, P., and E.L.H. Croft. One Titan at a Time. Cape Town: Timmins, 1960. 222pp. illus. bibl.

Biography of John Paterson who emigrated to Port Elizabeth and became famous as a teacher, journalist, businessman and politician. Interesting facts given regarding nineteenth-century Cape Town and Port Elizabeth and also characters such as Dr. John Philip and the Kemp brothers, merchants of Cape Town and Algoa Bay.

Cape - Settlers of British Origin, 1820 Onwards

207. Findlay, J., ed. The Findlay Letters, 1806-1807. Pretoria: Van Schaik, 1954. 181pp. illus. map.

Letters are derived from two sources: the Findlay and Schreiner families. The life of Capt. John Findlay and his family reflect social and commercial life in Cape Town in the time of Lord Charles Somerset. The letters collected by Catherine Schreiner, who married a grandson of Captain Findlay, depict conditions in missionary outposts.

208. Fitzroy, V.M. Dark Bright Land. Cape Town: Maskew Miller, 1963. 327pp. map. bibl.

Semi-fictional account of the experiences of the 1820 families Pigot, Moodie, Taylor and Stuart between the years 1775 and 1881, set in the old Cape Colony, Albany district, Natal and the Boer Republics. Use has been made of letters, journals, note-books, periodicals and almanacs.

209. Godlonton, R. Memorials of the British Settlers of South Africa. Grahamstown: Godlonton, 1844. xxxvi, 126pp. Repr. Cape Town: South African Library, 1954.

A recording of the services held at Grahamstown, Port Elizabeth and Bathurst in April and May, 1844 in commemoration of the arrival of the 1820 settlers at Algoa Bay twenty-four years previously.

210. Hockly, H.E. The Story of the British Settlers of 1820 in South Africa. 2nd ed. Cape Town: Juta, 1957. 284pp. illus. maps. bibl.

Very detailed account of the events leading to the settlement of the 1820 settlers on the eastern frontier and of the hardships and struggles of the settlers up to the period immediately following the Sixth Kaffir War (1835). The cultural contribution of the settlers and the names of prominent settlers are given. There are two concluding chapters on celebrations and memorials connected with the settlers in the nineteenth and twentieth centuries.

211. Holt, B. Greatheart of the Border: A Life of John Brownlee, Pioneer Missionary in South Africa. King William's Town: South African Missionary Museum, 1976. 147pp. illus. map. bibl.

An account of Brownlee's life and achievements, mainly in the mission field. Many extracts from his correspondence are given. A briefer biography is: Rose-Innes, R.W. Rev. John Brownlee: A Veteran Missionary and the Founder of King William's Town. Lovedale: Mission Press, 1905. 26pp. Consists of a lecture in which tribute is paid to the achievements of Brownlee and in which Brownlee's career in the eastern Cape is described.

212. Jaff, F. They Came to South Africa. Cape Town: Timmins, 1963. 131pp. illus. bibl.

Short readable biographies of various personalities who have contributed to the development of South Africa; viz., Lady Anne Barnard, William J. Burchell, James Barry, Andrew Geddes Bain, Thomas Baines, David Gill, Baden-Powell, Arnold Theiler, Emily Hobhouse, Sir Herbert Baker, Anton van Wouw and Arthur Elliott.

213. Long, I., ed. The Chronicle of Jeremiah Goldswain, Albany Settler of 1820. Cape Town: Van Riebeeck Society, 1946. 2v. illus. bibl. (Van Riebeeck Society Publications, 27).

This work is greatly marred by unusual spelling errors, as Goldswain was an artisan from Buckinghamshire who wrote according to the phonetical pronunciation of his dialect. The chronicle covers forty years of his personal experiences (1819-1858) and is an interesting general record of the Albany settlers, especially as regards the frontier wars.

214. Metrowich, F.C. Frontier Flames. Cape Town: Books of Africa, 1968. 286pp. illus.

Anecdotal extracts from nineteenth-century Cape eastern frontier history. Includes descriptions of frontier wars, of various 1820 settler experiences, of daily life in the frontier towns such as Salem and Grahamstown and of prominent people of the eastern frontier.

215. Morse-Jones, E. Roll of the British Settlers in South Africa: Part I up to 1826. 2nd ed. Cape Town: Balkema, 1971. 274pp. illus. map. bibl.

Provides details of more than 2,000 heads of families and individual settlers. These are arranged in the form of lists. There are 550 more detailed biographies of prominent settlers; many of these have portraits. In addition, areas of emigration, ships' movements, location of parties, names of settlers who died in frontier wars, settlers holding legislative office and place names commemorating settlers are given.

216. [Philipps, T.] Keppel-Jones, A., and E.K. Heathcote, eds. Philipps, 1820 Settler: His Letters. Pietermaritzburg: Shuter & Shooter, 1960. 371pp. front. map.

Commences with a biographical account of Philipps' life and achievements. The letters themselves cover the period from May, 1820 to February, 1830, many being addressed to Philipps' sister, Catherine Richardson. Philipps became prominent for his efforts to promote emigration to the Cape and for his protests against government neglect of defence of the eastern frontier districts. He also favoured administrative separation of the eastern Cape from the western Cape.

Cape - Settlers of British Origin, 1820 Onwards

217. [Pigot, S.] Rainier, M., ed. The Journals of Sophia Pigot, 1819-1821. Cape Town: Balkema, 1974. xvii, 172pp. illus. map. bibl.

Provides information on the daily life of the 1820 settlers at Albany and the introductory section supplies biographical information regarding the Pigot family. The actual journal entries are very brief and cover the early years of the Pigots' arrival at the eastern Cape. An epilogue provides a summary of the events of Sophia Pigot's life after her marriage to Donald Moodie.

218. Pretorius, D.J., ed. In the Land of the Settlers. Grahamstown: Grocott & Sherry, 1956. 74pp. illus.

Booklet issued by the 1820 Settlers Commemoration Committee of Grahamstown to mark the pilgrimage on 3 September, 1956, of various groups over the original route used by the settlers to their locations.

219. Pringle, E. and others. Pringles of the Valleys. Adelaide: Eric Pringle, 1957. 242pp. illus. map.

A family history and genealogy of a well-known British settler family.

220. Pringle, T. Narrative of a Residence in South Africa. Cape Town: Struik, 1966. 352pp.

Pringle gives an interesting and informative account of the difficulties encountered by the 1820 English settlers of Albany, and of their daily life, from his own experiences at Glen-Lynden. He describes the various tribes encountered and the work of the frontier missionaries. He also relates his impressions of Cape Town, his experiences in this city and his conflict with the colonial government over the matter of freedom of the press. Covers the years 1820 to 1826.

221. [Pringle, T.] Wahl, J.R., ed. Thomas Pringle in South Africa, 1820-1826. Cape Town: Longman, 1970. xi, 208pp.

An edited version of Pringle's 'Narrative of a Residence in South Africa'. The editor has eliminated extraneous material and concentrates on Pringle's 'personal' narrative. Describes Pringle's voyage to the Cape and journey into the interior from Algoa Bay to Baviaan's River. Recounts daily life at Glen-Lynden and on the frontier as well as describing the Albany settlement in 1821 and 1825. Provides descriptions of animal and plant life of the frontier and of a journey to Cape Town across the Karroo, the author's experiences in Cape Town from 1822 to 1825 and his struggle for freedom of the press are recounted.

Cape - Settlers of British Origin, 1820 Onwards

222. Rivett-Carnac, D. Thus Came the English, 1820. Cape Town: Timmins, 1961. 147pp. illus. bibl.

    Popular readable account of the arrival, experiences, and daily life of the 1820 settlers of Albany. Intended for the non-research reader interested in the eastern province and its history.

223. Sheffield, T. The Story of the Settlement; With a Sketch of Grahamstown Together with a List of the Original Dutch and Huguenot Settlers, and of the British Settlers of 1820. Grahamstown: Grocott & Sherry, 1912. 327pp. illus.

    Attempts to outline the history of the Cape Colony up to the time of the second British occupation. Describes the life and achievement of Colonel Graham, founder of Grahamstown, the attack of the AmaXosa on Grahamstown in 1819 and the arrival of the 1820 British settlers. The misfortune and struggles of the settlers are described, particularly during the frontier wars of 1834-1835, 1846-1847 and 1851-1852. Finally describes the growth and development of Grahamstown in great detail. Concludes with a list of the 1820 settlers, the names of the heads of each 'party' into which they were divided and the names of ships in which they came.

224. Slater, F.C. Settler's Heritage. Lovedale: Lovedale Press, 1954. 261pp.

    An autobiography of a descendant of the 1820 settlers, Samuel Carey Slater, and his wife Alicia Wilmot.

225. Spilhaus, M.W. The Land They Left. Cape Town: Juta, 1969. 120pp. illus.

    A description of social, economic and political conditions in England during the period of emigration of the 1820 settlers. Author attempts to thus provide an explanation of the reaction of the settlers to South African conditions and of the influence of the settlers on the Cape Colony.

226. [Stubbs, T.] Maxwell, W.A. and R.T. McGeogh, eds. The Reminiscences of Thomas Stubbs, Including 'Men I Have Known'. Cape Town: Balkema, 1978. xvi, 302pp. illus. maps. bibl.

    Covers the period from 1819, when Stubbs embarked for the Cape as a member of the 1820 settler parties, to 1876, when Stubbs commenced his reminiscences. Valuable account of the early years of the 1820 settlement on the eastern frontier. Describes Stubbs' participation in the frontier wars of 1834-1835, 1846-1847 and 1850-1853 and his abortive attempts to earn a living as a farmer and saddler. Provides interesting descriptions of fellow settlers in his account 'Men I Have Known'.

THE GREAT TREK, 1836-1854

Bibliography

227. Grivainis, I. Material Published after 1925 on the Great Trek until 1854. Cape Town: University of Cape Town, School of Librarianship, 1967. vii, 63pp.

Monographs

228. Agar-Hamilton, J.A.I. The Native Policy of the Voortrekkers: An Essay in the History of the Interior of South Africa, 1836-1858. Cape Town: Maskew Miller, 1928. xix, 228pp. map. bibl.

    An attempt to survey the native policy of the farmers who left the Cape Colony in 1836 and organized independent states in the interior of South Africa. A preliminary sketch describes the situation in South Africa with regard to frontier conflict and Hottentot policy prior to the Trek. The expansion into Natal and the Transvaal is outlined briefly. This expansion brought conflict between the Boers and various tribes. The racial conflicts are analysed by considering the role of the missionaries. The animosities between frontiersmen and missionaries began prior to 1836 and continued as the trekkers moved into the interior and established Republics. The author attempts to analyse the justification for the missionaries' claims against the trekkers. Under the heading 'Labour and Slavery' the author discusses the 'Apprenticeship Question' by which child labourers were indentured to farmers and also discusses the 'Labour Tax' in order to examine how far these institutions were an exploitation of the Black people.

229. Bulpin, T.V. The Great Trek. Cape Town: Books of Africa, 1969. 74pp. illus.

    A readable, simple account of the events of the Great Trek up to the defeat of Dingaan at Blood River in 1840. Well-illustrated. Could be used by young readers.

230. Dreyer, A. Die Kaapse Kerk en die Groot Trek. Cape Town: de Villiers, 1929. xv, 217pp. bibl.

    Consists of archival extracts covering the years 1837 to 1852 showing the attitude of the Dutch Reformed Church to the Voortrekkers and also extracts of correspondence of various Church dignitaries who were in contact with the Voortrekkers. A later work by the same author is: 'Die Voortrekkers en hul Kerk'. Cape Town: Nasionale Pers, 1932. vi, 122pp. bibl.

231. Jansen, E.G. Die Voortrekkers in Natal: Opstelle. Cape Town: Nasionale Pers, 1938. 158pp. map.

    Eight essays concerning the Voortrekkers in Natal in which the author deals with little-known aspects concerning the trekkers which he claims to have discovered in archival sources.

232. Meintjes, J. The Voortrekkers: The Story of the Great Trek and the Making of South Africa. London: Cassell, 1973. ix, 287pp. illus. maps. bibl.

    An account of the Trek from the early nineteenth century to the establishment of the Boer Republics of the Orange Free State and South African Republic in 1854.

233. Muller, C.F.J. Die Britse Owerheid en die Groot Trek. 4th ed. Cape Town: Academica, 1977. xiv, 341pp. illus. map. bibl. First edition 1969.

    Attempts to establish the causes of the Great Trek and the reasons for British policy at the Cape which caused so much dissatisfaction to the trekkers. Isolates the following aspects influencing British colonial policy: (1) Financial factors; (2) Commercial factors; (3) Growth of imperialism and colonial rivalry with other powers and (4) Philanthropic policy towards tribal peoples. Of these factors, the financial factor; i.e., the desire to avoid undue expenditure, was the most decisive in influencing British policy.

234. Muller, C.F.J. Leiers na die Noorde: Studies oor die Groot Trek. Cape Town: Tafelberg, 1976. 165pp. illus.

    Describes the part played by certain pioneers, mostly from Uitenhage, in influencing the events of the Great Trek. Commences with an account of the adventures of Robert Scoon who visited the Transvaal in 1827 and encountered the Matabele Chief Moselikatse. His accounts influenced future Boer leaders such as Karel Landman and Piet Uys. The Voortrekker leader Karel Landman is also discussed and an account given of his career between 1796 and 1875. Piet Uys' role as a Voortrekker leader is described. Concludes with a brief description of events in Andries Pretorius' life between 1837 and 1838.

235. Muller, C.F.J. Die Oorsprong van die Groot Trek. Cape Town: Tafelberg, 1974. 464pp. illus. maps. bibl.

    Attempts to analyse conditions at the Cape which led to the Great Trek of the mid-nineteenth century. Discusses early migrations in South Africa of Black and White inhabitants and the relationship between the Black and White peoples on the eastern frontier of the Cape. Describes social, economic and political conditions at the Cape immediately prior to the Trek, the causes of the Trek, exploratory expeditions into the interior prior to the Trek and the development of the pre-Trek movement and philosophy among the Eastern Cape farmers.

Great Trek, 1836-1854 55

236. Muller, C.F.J. A Pictorial History of the Great Trek: Visual Documents Illustrating the Great Trek. Cape Town: Tafelberg, 1978. 111pp. illus. map. bibl.

Consists of close to four hundred 'visual documents', paintings, sketches, cartoons, photographs, maps, charts, official documents and reports, extracts from newspaper articles, journals, diaries and letters. These are chosen so as to form a pictorial account of events leading to the Great Trek and the Great Trek itself (1830 to 1850). There are short explanatory notes at the beginning of each section and short annotations attached to each document or group of documents. A concise chronology at the beginning of the volume provides a historical framework to the documents. The sections are entitled: 'The Land and Its People', 'The Difigane', 'Trekboers and Voortrekkers', 'Across the Orange River', 'Natal', 'The Republic of Natal', 'New Frontiers' and 'New Republics'.

237. Nathan, M. The Voortrekkers of South Africa: From the Earliest Times to the Foundation of the Republics. Johannesburg: Central News Agency, 1937. xv, 428pp. illus. maps.

This is a fairly detailed study of the Great Trek from 1835 to the creation of the Orange Free State in 1854. The work is slightly dated and more recent, better, studies of this period exist.

238. Preller, G.S., ed. Voortrekker Mense. Cape Town: Nasionale Pers, 1918-1938. 6v. illus.

Consists of extracts from diaries, letters and reminiscences of various participants in the Great Trek of 1836 onwards. These documents are taken from government archival sources, from collections of historical documents in the libraries of Pietermaritzburg and Bloemfontein and the South African Public Library in Cape Town. Also contains extracts from old Cape newspapers; e.g., 'De Zuid-Afrikaan'.

239. [Pretorius, A.] Preller, G.S. Andries Pretorius: Lewens Beskrywing van die Voortrekker Kommandant-generaal. Johannesburg: Afrikaanse Pers, 1937. xxvii, 491pp. illus. map. bibl.

A biography of Pretorius by one of the pioneer Afrikaans historians. It is very patriotic in style, but the author makes use of archival material and journals as well as secondary sources to attempt an authentic description of Pretorius' achievements.

240. [Retief, P.] Preller, G.S. Piet Retief: Lewensgeskiedenis van die Grote Voortrekker. Pretoria: Volkstem, 1912. 334pp. diagrs. bibl.

One of the earliest Afrikaans biographies of Retief in which the author attempts to make use of original documents as well as secondary sources of information.

241. Smail, J.L. Monuments and Trails of the Voortrekkers. Cape Town: Timmins, 1968. 30pp. illus. maps.

A graphic portrayal by means of annotated photographs, maps, diagrams and sketches of battle sites, monuments and statues relating to voortrekker life. There are also pictures of tools and equipment used by the voortrekkers.

242. Trichardt, L. Dagboek van Louis Trichardt (1836-1838). ed. by G.S. Preller. Cape Town: Nasionale Pers, 1938. cv, 379pp. illus. map.

Introduction discusses the origin and composition of the text of Trichardt's diary and also the existence of other versions of the diary. There are notes on the family Buys, on the tribes of the Transvaal in Trichardt's time and a biographical sketch of Trichardt's life and achievements. The Dutch text of the two diaries follows. The first diary covers the period November 1834 to December 1836. The second diary covers the period January 1837 to May 1838.

243. Trichardt, L. Die Dagboek van Louis Trigardt. ed. by T.H. Le Roux. Pretoria: Van Schaik, 1964. xxxiii, 275pp. bibl.

Editor is particularly interested in the cultural-historical and linguistic value of Trichardt's diary. In the introductory section, an historical resumé is given of Trichardt's life and career together with a discussion regarding the two diaries of Trichardt. Preller's edition of the diary is shown to have certain linguistic inaccuracies. The editor attempts to analyse the terms of Dutch language used by Trichardt and to show that it is the forerunner of Afrikaans. The diary itself is presented as close to the original form as possible. The editor indicates when he has made linguistic alterations in the text.

244. [Trichardt, L.] Fuller, C. Louis Trichardt's Trek Across the Drakensberg, 1837-1838. Cape Town: Van Riebeeck Society, 1932. (Van Riebeeck Society Publications, 13). xix, 173pp. illus. maps.

An account of Trichardt's trek based on the lectures, maps and pictures of Dr Claude Fuller. Traces Trichardt's route from Chuniespoort to Delagoa Bay.

245. Van der Merwe, P.J. Die Noordwaartse Beweging van die Boere voor die Groot Trek (1770-1842). The Hague: Van Stockum, 1937. xv, 400pp. maps. bibl.

A study of the north-westerly expansion of the colony carried out by the semi-nomadic frontier farmers in the period before the Great Trek, i.e., 1700 to 1842. These migrations were influenced by conflict with the Bushmen and Griquas, shortage of grazing land, droughts and plagues of locusts. To relieve these situations, frontiersmen crossed over the Orange River, at first occasionally, and later regularly, each season. However, these nomadic farmers, on the northern border

Great Trek, 1836-1854   57

of Graaff-Reinet, were not at first dissatisfied with British
rule at the Cape and their migrations were not originally
part of the exodus leading to the Great Trek. The Great Trek
was thus a separate movement.

246. Van der Merwe, P.J. Die Trekboer in die Geskiedenis van die
Kaapkolonie (1657-1842). Cape Town: Nasionale Pers, 1938.
xi, 334pp. bibl.

A study of the origin, history and influence of the semi-
nomadic cattle farmers of the Cape Colony who inhabited the
frontier regions of the Colony and preceded the Voortrekkers.
Describes the origin of cattle farming at the Cape in the
seventeenth century and the encouragement given to this farming by W.A. van der Stel. Cattle farmers became semi-nomadic
and as grazing land became scarcer, the need arose for barter
with Hottentots and hunting expeditions became profitable.
Successive governments attempted unsuccessfully to curb the
nomadic habits of the cattle farmers. Discusses the origin
of the system of grazing licences issued by the government
which led to the system of loan farms for cattle farmers.
During the eighteenth century the Cape Colony expanded
rapidly eastwards and northwards. The frontier farmers
developed a tradition of independence but were inclined to
despise manual labour due to the prevalences of slave and
Hottentot labour. A description is given of economic and
social life on the frontier. Many amenities of 'civilized
life' were absent. Religion played a major role in daily life.
The first conflict with the Xhosa occurred towards the end of
the eighteenth century.

247. Van der Merwe, P.J. Trek: Studies oor die Mobiliteit van die
Pioniers Bevolking aan die Kaap. Cape Town: Nasionale Pers,
1945. x, 312pp. bibl.

A study of the nomadic tendencies of the cattle farmers at
the Cape. This phenomenon is studied independently of the
Great Trek and continued after the Trek, even into modern
times, in areas such as Namaqualand, Bushman land, Gordonia
and South West Africa. Describes the origin and development
of extensive cattle farming at the Cape from the seventeenth
to the nineteenth century. Analyses the importance of barter-
ing and hunting in the life of the nomadic farmer. Describes
the tendency of the nomadic farmers to favour a life of freedom, unfettered by ties to a particular area and migrating
seasonally to various grazing areas. This form of seasonal
migration was also influenced by factors such as drought or
locusts. Migrations became a less noticeable phenomenon at
the beginning of the twentieth century, because cattle farmers
could no longer find unoccupied land to which they could trek.
Crown land decreased in area and farmers had to pay grazing
licences for land which was available. Agricultural methods
improved and water conservation was introduced, so that
seasonal droughts were less common.

248. Van Jaarsveld, F.A. Die Eenheidstrewe van die Republikeinse Afrikaners. Deel 1: Pioniers Hartstogte (1856-1864). Johannesburg: Impala, 1951. 336pp. map.

    A study of the attempts of the Orange Free State and South African Republic to achieve unity in the second half of the nineteenth century.

249. Van Rooyen, G.H. Kultuurskatte uit die Voortrekker-tydperk: 'n Kultuur-historiese Studie. Bloemfontein: Nasionale Pers, 1938-1941. 2v. illus. bibl.

    Attempts to delineate the daily life of the Voortrekkers, by describing equipment, the structure of the ox wagon, furniture, bibles, tools and implements used by these pioneers. Also discusses, education, medicine, clothes, toys and houses of the pioneer era. Useful book for young people.

250. Walker, E.A. The Great Trek. 5th ed. London: Black, 1934. viii, 388pp. illus. maps.

    The events of the Trek are recounted from the years 1836 to 1848, in a readable and interesting manner. There are descriptions of the daily life and appearance of the trekkers and of the causes of the Great Trek. The conflict with the Matabele under Mzilikazi, the settlement in Natal after the death of Piet Retief, and the establishment of a Boer Republic in the Transvaal, after the second British occupation of Natal, are all described.

CAPE - 1836-1899

Bibliographies

251. Barker, M. Sir Benjamin D'Urban's Administration of the Eastern Frontier of the Cape of Good Hope during the Period 1834-1838: A Bibliography. Cape Town: University of Cape Town, School of Librarianship, 1964. v, 33pp.

252. Jennings, B. The Seventh Kaffir War or the War of the Axe: A Bibliography. Cape Town: University of Cape Town School of Librarianship, 1957. iii, 25pp.

253. Moodie, A.D. The Eighth Kaffir War, 1850-1853: A Bibliography. Cape Town: University of Cape Town School of Librarianship, 1955. iv, 24pp. Unpublished.

254. Southey, N.M. Kimberley and the Diamond Fields of Griqualand West, 1869-1900. Cape Town: University of Cape Town School of Librarianship, 1952. v, 28pp.

Cape - 1836-1899

Monographs

255. Adams, W.J. The Narrative of Private Buck Adams, 7th (Princess Royal's) Dragoon Guards on the Eastern Frontier of the Cape of Good Hope, 1834-1848. ed. by A. Gordon-Brown. Cape Town: Van Riebeeck Society, 1941. xx, 316pp. illus. map, bibl. (Van Riebeeck Society Publications, 22).

    Depicts military events on the eastern frontier and living conditions from the point of view of the ordinary soldier. Adams' account is said to be generally truthful and accurate. Adams took part in the action at Zwart Koppies against the Boer farmers beyond the Orange River in 1845, and in the frontier War of the Axe in 1846-1847. He returned to England with his regiment early in 1848.

256. Angove, J. In the Early Days: The Reminiscences of Pioneer Life on the South African Diamond Fields. Kimberley: Handel House, 1910. 212pp. illus.

    This history of the diamond fields is recounted by a pioneer of the 1870s and 1880s when the first diggings began at the junction of the Orange and Vaal Rivers and the city of Kimberley was founded. An index to this volume was compiled in 1958 by Eric Rosenthal and Ena Cloete (Johannesburg: Public Library).

257. Appleyard, J.W. The War of the Axe and the Xosa Bible: The Journal of the Rev. J.W. Appleyard. ed. by S. Frye. Cape Town: Struik, 1971. xii, 157pp. illus. maps. bibl.

    An accurate eye-witness account of the eastern frontier 'War of the Axe' which occurred between 1846 and 1847. Appleyard, as a member of the Wesleyan Missionary Society, was active on the eastern Cape frontier during the war and devoted four chapters of his journal to descriptions of skirmishes and fatalities. Chapter 5 is devoted to a description of Appleyard's translation of the Bible in Xosa.

258. [Barkly, H.] Macmillan, M. Sir Henry Barkly: Mediator and Moderator, 1815-1898. Cape Town: Balkema: 1970. viii, 302pp. illus. bibl.

    Discusses Barkly's career as governor of British Guiana, Jamaica, Australia, Mauritius and the Cape. Maintains that Barkly successfully introduced responsible government at the Cape and that he was unjustly accused of being responsible for the failure of the federation movement in South Africa. Barkly is described as an upholder of liberal democracy who refused to accept any form of confederation in which the Black peoples would be unjustly treated.

259. Bevan, D. Drums of the Birkenhead. Cape Town: Purnell, 1972. xvi, 190pp. illus.

    A detailed account of the wreck of the 'Birkenhead' off Danger Point on 26 February, 1852.

260. Boyle, F. To the Cape for Diamonds. A Story of Digging Experiences in South Africa: With Comments and Criticisms, Political, Social and Miscellaneous, upon the Present State and Future Prospects of the Diamond Fields. London: Chapman & Hall, 1873. 415pp.

Describes the discovery of diamonds and a visit paid by the author to the diamond fields at Pniel, Dutoitspan, Bultfontein, Alexandersfontein, Klipdrift, Hopetown and other areas where diggings had been opened up. Many interesting descriptions of the operation of the diamond fields and methods used by the diggers and also of daily life on the diamond fields in the 1870s. The following five books (entries 261-266) also deal with the discovery of diamonds.

261. Chilvers, H.A. The Story of De Beers: With Some Notes on the Company's Financial, Farming, Railway and Industrial Activities in Africa, and Some Introductory Chapters on the River Diggings and Early Kimberley. London: Cassell, 1939. xvii, 344pp. illus.

Covers the years 1888 to 1938. Commences with a survey of the history of diamond mining in ancient and modern times. Describes the early digger camps on the Vaal River and discovery of the 'dry' mines a few miles distant in 1869-1871, leading to the foundation of Kimberley. The formation of 'De Beers' under the guidance of Cecil Rhodes and the growth of the company up to and including the period of Sir Ernest Oppenheimer is comprehensively surveyed. Appendices provide extracts from the company's records from 1888-1938, alphabetical list of past and present members of the board of De Beers, lists of life governors, chairmen and deputy chairmen, notes on Voorspoed Diamond Mines and De Beers dividend payments between 1889 and 1901.

262. Chilvers, H.A. The Seven Lost Trails of Africa: Being a Record of Sundry Expeditions, New and Old, in Search of Buried Treasure. London: Cassell, 1930. xiii, 241pp.

An attempt to describe some of the exploits of African treasure-hunters. Most of these searches were carried out for mythological or legendary treasures said to be hidden in various parts of Southern Africa. These legendary treasures include the 'Grosvenor' treasure, the great diamond craters, Lobengula's buried treasure and the Kruger millions. There are also descriptions of the history of Southern African towns such as Cape Town, Johannesburg, Pretoria, Durban, Maritzburg, East London, Bloemfontein, Port Elizabeth, Kimberley and Lourenco Marques (Maputo).

263. Doughty, O. Early Diamond Days: The Opening of the Diamond Fields of South Africa. London: Longmans, 1963. v, 237pp. illus. map. bibl.

A description of the early diamond diggings along the Vaal River and also of the dry diggings at Dutoitspan and Kimberley. The everyday life of the diggers, the appearance of the mining

Cape - 1836-1899

camps and the events and social conditions of the diggings are comprehensively described. Much information was obtained from pioneer reminiscences on the South African diamond fields discovered by the author in the library of Rhodes House, Oxford.

264. Reunert, T. Diamonds and Gold in South Africa. Cape Town: Juta, 1893. xvi, 242pp. illus. maps.

A detailed history of the foundation and operation of the South African diamond and gold mining industry during the nineteenth century. The appendices contain articles by experts who are now regarded as pioneers e.g., H.W. Struben, W.E. Fairbridge, J.S. Macarthur and J. Hamilton Smith.

265. Roberts, B. Kimberley: Turbulent City. Cape Town: Philip, 1976. 413pp. illus. bibl.

A detailed history of Kimberley covering the period 1859 to 1947. There are interesting descriptions of the discovery of diamonds, the first shanty town and the gradual progress of the town after the creation of a railway in 1886. The diamond magnates who played an important part in the development of Kimberley also feature prominently in the book and include names such as Rhodes, Barnato and Robinson.

266. Rosenthal, E. River of Diamonds. Cape Town: Timmins, n.d. 161pp. illus. map.

Consists of various anecdotes connected with the diamond diggings at the Vaal River during the second half of the nineteenth century. Little-known facts about pioneer prospectors are recounted as well as events forming the daily life of the diggers.

267. Bradlow, E., and F. Bradlow. Here Comes the 'Alabama': The Career of a Confederate Raider. Cape Town: Balkema, 1958. 128pp. illus.

An account of the origin of the song sung by the Coloured community at the Cape. The adventures of the 'Alabama', a Confederate raiding ship, are traced in the year 1863, when the ship visited the Cape before being sunk in the English Channel the following year.

268. Brinton, W. History of the British Regiments in South Africa, 1795-1895. Cape Town: University of Cape Town, Department of Extra-Mural Studies, 1977. 308pp.

Describes the role of the British regiments in the frontier wars of the nineteenth century, including the Zulu War of 1879. Detailed descriptions are given of skirmishes and battles fought during the frontier wars. The First Boer War of 1880-1881 is discussed in an objective manner, the author confining himself mainly to describing briefly events leading to the war, details of the military engagement and analysis of military tactics used during the war.

269. Brownlee, F. The Transkeian Native Territories; Historical Records. Lovedale: Lovedale Press, 1923. xii, 135pp. map.

These historical records concern the history and government of the Transkeian territories, including Tembuland, Griqualand East and Mount Ayliff, Pondoland and Port St. Johns, up to the year 1885. The records consist of the Cape Government Blue Book on Native Affairs, 1885; Report of Commission on Native Laws and Customs, 1883; the Maitland Treaty with Faku, chief of the Amapondo (1884); Report of Meeting with Umqikela's Pondos; History of the Amaxesibe as narrated by the Pondos (1880); History of the Amaxesibe as narrated by their chief Jojo (1874); Conditions under which the Amabaca chief Makaula and his people became British subjects (1883); Brief history of the Pondomise tribe by Mabasa; Report of a Commission to enquire into the causes of the outbreak in Griqualand East, 1879; and Mr Orpen's report regarding certain tribes (1873).

270. Burton, A.W. Sparks From the Border Anvil; A Record of Remarkable and Inspiring Events. King William's Town: Provincial Publications Co., 1950. xviii, 298pp. illus. map.

There are two sections to this book. Book 1 describes the prophecy of Nonquase and its effect on the Xhosa (1856/1857). Book 2 is devoted to the incidents of the Tshangane or Sligo mystery (1875-1876), a bank robbery in 1876, floods of the Buffalo River and various other incidents occurring on the border in the second half of the nineteenth century.

271. Campbell, W.B. The South African Frontier, 1865-1885: A Study in Expansion. (Ph.D. Thesis. University of California). Archives Yearbook for South African history. Vol. 22, Part 1, 1959. Pretoria: Government Printer, 1960. 247pp. bibl.

A study of British and colonial expansion between 1865 and 1885 which resulted in embittered Boer-British and White-Black relations as well as largely determining the present political and tribal divisions of South Africa. The frontiersmen, consisting of missionaries, settlers and traders and local administrators, advanced the political frontiers despite the reluctance of the Cape legislature and the British government's preference for relying on influence rather than control over the tribes and republics beyond the colonial borders. By 1885, the Cape Colony had annexed all native territories as far as Natal except for the protectorate of Pondoland. The diamond fields and Basutoland had been wrested from the Boer Republics. The Boers had been barred from access to key parts and from the missionaries route to the interior. Much use is made in this study of archival material; e.g., Richard Southey's semi-official papers, correspondence of missionaries and officials, British and Cape parliamentary papers and debates and frontier newspapers.

Cape - 1836-1899   63

272. Cathcart, Sir G. Correspondence of Lieut.-General the Hon.
      Sir George Cathcart, K.C.B., relative to his military
      operations in Kaffraria. 2nd ed. London: John Murray,
      1857. 401pp.
      Contains Cathcart's despatches and letters relative to the
      Frontier War of 1852 to 1853.

273. Davenport, T.R.H. The Afrikaner Bond: The History of a South
      African Political Party, 1880-1911. Cape Town: Oxford University Press, 1966. xiii, 431pp. illus. maps.
      Discusses the origins and growth of the Afrikaner Bond in
      the Cape Province. Describes how its members later joined up
      with 'Het Volk' (Transvaal), the 'Orangia Unie' (Orange Free
      State) and the 'Volks Vereniging' (Natal) to form, after unification, The South African Party under Botha's leadership.
      The Afrikaner Bond was the ancestor of both the government
      party and opposition party of mid-twentieth-century South
      Africa.

274. Davies, J.H. Palgrave and Damaraland. (M.A. Thesis. University of South Africa, 1939). Archives Yearbook for South
      African History. Vol. 5, Part 2, 1942. Pretoria: Government Printer, 1943. pp.93-203.
      Covers the years 1875 to 1885 when Palgrave made an abortive
      attempt to annex Namaqua-Damaraland on behalf of the Cape
      Colony. The territory was finally annexed by Germany in 1884
      but the Cape Colony government was largely to blame for the
      loss of this territory, as the Cape authorities had not acted
      promptly and decisively, when they had the opportunity to
      interfere in the Namaqua-Damara War of 1880.

275. De Kock, W.J. Ekstraterritoriale Vraagstukke van die Kaapse
      Regering (1872-1885): Met Besondere Verwysing na die Transgeriep en Betsjoeanaland. Archives Yearbook for South
      African History. Vol. 11, Part I, 1948. Cape Town: Government Printer, 1948. 306pp. illus. map. bibl.
      A study of the attempted expansion of Cape provincial boundaries between the Orange and Kunene ribers and in the Bechuanaland area, between the years 1872 to 1885.
      The Cape received responsible government in 1872 and successive governments under Molteno, Sprigg, Scanlen and Upington
      seemed anxious to further Cape territorial interests. They
      were assisted by the patriotism of the Afrikaner Bond under
      Hofmeyr. However, by 1885, it was clear that Cape interests
      had been defeated by a combination of factors. Molteno and his
      successors were half-hearted and dilatory in pursuing expansionist policies. Palgrave's mission as Cape representative in
      Damaraland was fruitless and involved Palgrave in inter-tribal
      wars. The Cape Colony was plagued by frontier wars and Britain
      discouraged territorial expansion in order to avoid expenditure.
      Germany finally arrested Cape expansion in the south-west area
      by claiming the territory for herself. The area of Bechuanaland was also subject to fierce inter-tribal warfare and the

land claims of White settlers. The Cape was in the grip of
economic depression and was unable to deal with these problems.
In 1885 Britain annexed southern Bechuanaland as a Crown
Colony.

276. Dracopoli, J.L. Sir Andries Stockenstrom, 1792-1864: The
Origins of the Racial Conflict in South Africa. Cape Town:
Balkema, 1969. xii, 211pp. illus. maps. bibl.

Attempts to give an account of the problems facing Stockenstrom on the eastern frontier of the Cape in the first half of
the nineteenth century. Maintains that the policy of
'apartheid' had its origins during the period under discussion.
The second lesson to be learned from Stockenstrom's rule is
the advisability of negotiating with the leaders of the Black
people to achieve a lasting peace. The third point emerging
from the study is the effect of external pressure groups; e.g.,
the evangelical group, on South Africa's internal policy. The
final point made is the degree of British responsibility for
the creation of the racial problem, due to the mutual antagonism constantly existing between Boer and Briton.

277. Duff-Gordon, Lady Lucie. Letters from the Cape. Annotated by
Dorothea Fairbridge. London: Oxford University Press, 1927.
xii, 163pp. illus.

The letters cover the period from July, 1861 to May, 1862
and contain descriptions of Cape Town, Caledon and Genadendal.
The letters are preceded in each case by the editor's introductory paragraphs explaining the background to the period of
Lady Duff Gordon's family history.

278. Du Toit, A.E. The Cape Frontier: A Study of Native Policy with
Special Reference to the Years 1847-1866. (D.Phil. Thesis.
University of Pretoria). Archives Yearbook for South African
history. Vol. 17, Part 1, 1954. Pretoria: Government
Printer, 1955. 309pp.

A detailed discussion of the military and frontier problems
existing in the eastern Cape during the first half of the
nineteenth century. Describes the efforts of successive
governors to solve the frontier problem. The Treaty System, as
advocated by Dr. Philip, was used in the 1830s in an attempt to
conciliate the tribal chiefs. Earl Grey, Secretary of State
for the Colonies, advocated in 1846 the annexation of Kaffraria,
and this policy was carried out by Sir Harry Smith, who also
annexed to the Cape the area between the Orange and Vaal River.
By 1853, a further frontier war had brought a reversal of
Smith's policy. The Orange River Sovereignty was abandoned.
Discusses Sir George Grey's administrative reforms in British
Kaffraria and his attempt to settle White farmers in the area.
Grey also favoured a federation scheme to extend British
responsibility throughout South Africa. Wodehouse, the next
governor at the Cape, forced the Cape parliament to pass the
Kaffrarian Annexation Act of 1865. Xhosas within this area

Cape - 1836-1899

were administered by government officials who had experience of tribal law and customs. Missionaries reduced the vernacular to writing and used it in instruction.

279. [Frere, B.] Martineau, J. The Life and Correspondence of Sir Bartle Frere. London: John Murray, 1895. 2v. illus. maps. bibl.

Volume 2 contains a description of Frere's appointment as High Commissioner of South Africa (1877). Outlines the part played by Frere in affairs of the Cape frontier, the Zulu War (1879) and in the affairs of the Transvaal Republic. Maintains that Frere was unjustly criticised for events of the Zulu War and his recall was due to party politics and public ignorance in Britain.

280. [Frere, B.] Worsfold, B. Sir Bartle Frere: A Footnote to the History of the British Empire. London: Butterworth, 1923. 352pp. front.

Attempts to provide more information regarding Frere's period of office as High Commissioner of South Africa (1877-1880). Examines and discusses the private correspondence of Sir Michael Hicks Beach, the Colonial Secretary, and also the correspondence of Lord Carnarvon and Lord Beaconsfield in order to determine the exact instructions issued to Frere by his superiors in Britain. Concludes that Frere was unjustly treated and made to suffer for the errors of judgment of the Beaconsfield cabinet.

281. Fryer, A.K. The Government of the Cape of Good Hope, 1825-1854: The Age of Imperial Reform. (D.Phil. Thesis. Rhodes University). Archives Yearbook for South African history. Vol. 27, Part 1, 1964. Pretoria: Government Printer, 1964. 156pp. bibl.

An attempt to examine in detail the structure of the Cape Colonial government before 1854 in order to make possible a greater understanding of the parliamentary period that followed. Discusses local political events at the Cape between 1825 and 1853, the most notable being the appointment of a lieutenant-governor for the eastern province in 1827 and the growing demand for representative government which was reflected in the anti-convict agitation of 1849. Analyses the development of the executive council of the Cape Colony (1825-1854), the powers of the Colonial Secretary and lesser executive counsellors at the Cape, the political crisis over the Constitution Ordinance (1851) and the incidence of patronage in the civil service. Concludes with a discussion of the post of High Commissioner created in 1847 and conferred on the governors of the Cape until 1901.

282. Godlonton, R., and E. Irving. A Narrative of the Kaffir War
of 1850-51-52. Cape Town: Struik, 1962, 351, 160pp. illus.
maps. Includes facs. repr. of v.1. of the Grahamstown ed.
of 1851, published by Godlonton and White.

Deals with the Eighth Kaffir War from the point of view of
the White frontier farmers. Outlines events which preceded
the war, dealing with unrest as far back as 1817. Details
given of military posts along the frontier and of treaties
with the Xhosa up to the commencement of the war. The war
itself and the treasonable actions of Hottentots and Xhosa are
described in detail and documented. Godlonton, as editor of
the 'Grahamstown Journal' and member of the Cape Legislative
Assembly, had access to much information, but he has been
accused of prejudice towards Xhosa tribes.

283. [Gray, Lucy.] Hattersley, A.F. A Victorian Lady at the Cape,
1849-1851. Cape Town: Maskew Miller, 1951. vii, 111pp.
illus.

This account of life at Cape Town and on the eastern frontier, is based on the journal and letters of Lucy Gray, sister
of Samuel Gray, who served as Vicar of Cradock from 1848 to
1855.

284. [Grey, Sir G.] Rutherford, J. Sir George Grey, K.C.B., 1812-
1898: A Study in Colonial Government. London: Cassell, 1961.
viii, 709pp. illus. maps. bibl.

Biography concerned mainly with Grey's official career as
governor of Australia, New Zealand, South Africa and New Zealand again between the years 1841 to 1898. Source material
for the biography was drawn from archives. Part III covers
Grey's term of office in South Africa (1854-1861). Discusses
his achievements in frontier policy and his policy towards the
Xhosa after the cattle-killing delusion (1856-1857). He
became involved in various disagreements with the War Office
and Colonial Office in London over lack of financial and
military support for frontier development. His final recall
was due to his support of a political and economic federation
scheme for South Africa at a time when Britain desired to
limit her responsibilities in the region.

285. Hattersley, A.F. The Convict Crisis and the Growth of Unity:
Resistance to Transportation in South Africa and Australia,
1848-1853. Pietermaritzburg: Shooter & Shuter, 1965. 142pp.
illus. bibl.

Attempts to show that the anti-convict agitation of 1849
against the landing of the convict ship 'Neptune' was one of
the first occasions on which White South Africans united in a
common goal. One effect of this anti-convict agitation was the
growth of the movement towards responsible government.

286. Hyatt, S.P. The Northward Trek. London: Andrew Melrose, 1909. xxi, 309pp. illus. maps.

The author summarizes the period of expansion of the White man's control over Southern Africa up to the year 1880. The main body of the work deals with the efforts of John Mackenzie and Cecil Rhodes to increase the area of British rule in Southern Africa. The author is pro-British in outlook and also sympathetic to the claims and rights of Lobengula, the Matabele king. The book concludes with the ratification of the Anglo-Portuguese treaty of June, 1891.

287. Innes, Sir James Rose. Sir James Rose Innes: Selected Correspondence (1884-1902). ed. by H.M. Wright. Cape Town: Van Riebeeck Society, 1972. 366pp. front. map. bibl. (Van Riebeeck Society Publications, 2nd Series, No. 3).

Between 1884 to 1902, Innes was a member of the Cape House of Assembly. From 1890 to 1893 he served as Attorney-General in Cecil Rhodes' ministry. From 1896 to 1897 he acted as leader of the parliamentary opposition. His final period of office at the Cape was as Attorney-General in the Sprigg ministry from 1900 to 1902. The correspondence selected for this volume covers the period of Innes' political career and is drawn from papers and letterbooks in the South African Library and from the family papers in Vermont, which were written to Innes' wife.

288. Le Cordeur, B., and C. Saunders. The War of the Axe, 1847. Sandton: Brenthurst Press, 1981. 288pp. illus. maps.

A detailed account, with contemporary illustrations and based on unpublished manuscript material of the Seventh Frontier War in the Ciskei and eastern Cape. This war was of crucial political, military and social significance.

289. Le Cordeur, B. The Politics of Eastern Cape Separatism. Cape Town: Oxford University Press, 1981. 314pp. illus. maps. bibl.

A study of the eastern Cape Separatist Movement from the time of the arrival of the 1820 English settlers to the granting of representative government to the Cape Colony (1854). The demands for separation of western and eastern administration of the Cape Colony originated in certain frontier areas, particularly Grahamstown. Later the movement spread to Port Elizabeth, Graaff-Reinet and Uitenhage. Leaders of the agitation consisted of prominent English farmers and businessmen who desired political influence in order to further their frontier trade and expansion and curb unrest among frontier tribes. The most notable of these leaders were Robert Godlonton and J.C. Chase.

290. McCracken, J.L. The Cape Parliament, 1854-1910. Oxford: Clarendon Press, 1967. ix, 156pp. illus. maps. tabs. bibl.

Discusses the origin and development of the Cape parliament during the second half of the nineteenth century. Examines some of the problems faced by the Cape parliament; e.g., the difficulties of holding elections in rural areas and the extension of the franchise to Coloured and Black peoples. Discusses the growth of political parties in the 1880s, the question of federation, which was discussed in parliament from the 1850s onwards, the nature of the membership and method of conducting business in parliamentary houses.

291. McKay, J. Reminiscences of the Last Kafir War. Cape Town: Struik, 1970. 318pp. illus.

Account by a former sergeant of the 74th Highlanders of the Frontier War of 1851 to 1853. Presents a description of the life of the common soldier on the eastern frontier and also of the battles fought against the tribes.

292. [Merriman, J.X.] Laurence, P. The Life of John Xavier Merriman. London: Constable, 1930. viii, 428pp. illus.

A biography of Merriman written soon after his death. The biographer, although having access to Merriman's correspondence, was unable to quote freely from these papers for fear of offending personages alive at the time. The style of the biography is thus somewhat reticent in manner.

293. [Merriman, J.X.] Lewsen, P. John X. Merriman: Paradoxical South African Statesman. Johannesburg: Donker, 1982. xii, 431pp. illus. maps. bibl.

A shortened version of a much fuller, unpublished work, copies of which are in the British Library, South African Library and the University of the Witwatersrand Library. Concentrates in great detail on Merriman's parliamentary career, his participation in the Molteno, Scanlen, Rhodes and Schreiner ministries and his role as the last Cape prime minister in 1908. Merriman's liberal views were unique at that period. He was equally opposed to the extremes of British imperialism and Afrikaner nationalism and after 1910 attempted in vain to retain civil liberties on behalf of Indians, Blacks and Coloureds.

294. Merriman, J.X. Selections from the Correspondence of J.X. Merriman, 1870-1890. ed. by P. Lewsen. Cape Town: Van Riebeeck Society, 1960-1966. 3v. illus. maps. bibl. Van Riebeeck Society Publications, 41, 44, 47).

An introduction outlines Merriman's career and importance as a Cape politician and finally as Prime Minister of the Cape prior to Union (1869-1910). The papers consist of c.14,500 items, comprising Merriman's personal and political correspondence, diaries, letter-books and note books, copies of memoranda and political papers and his wife's correspondence. These have been arranged in chronological order and edited. Volume 1 (1870-1890) covers the period from Merriman's second year in the Cape parliament to the beginning of his third term of Cabinet office. Includes experiences as a land surveyor and on mining camps of Griqualand West, Barberton and Johannesburg. Volume 2 begins in June, 1890, when Merriman became Treasurer in the first Rhodes Ministry and ends on New Year's Day 1899, with his letter to President Steyn defining the Schreiner Ministry's peace policy. Consists mainly of letters and shorter extracts. Gives information on the ascendancy of Rhodes, imperial policy and social and economic problems such as poor White question, race relations, education, agriculture and finances. Volume 3 centres around the Anglo-Boer War, which Merriman strongly opposed as a threat to personal rights and parliamentary privileges. Contains correspondence with Republican leaders, Cape politicians and English liberals as well as diary entries.

295. Merriman, N.J. The Cape Journals of Archdeacon N.J. Merriman, 1848-1855. ed. by D.H. Varley and H.M. Matthew. Cape Town: Van Riebeeck Society, 1957, xv, 243pp. illus. map. bibl. (Van Riebeeck Society Publications, 37).

These journals cover the period November, 1848 to August, 1855. Are of interest in that they record Merriman's impressions of the eastern Cape, through which Merriman took long excursions on foot. Describes Dutch and British frontier life and hospitality, the devastation caused by the frontier wars and various individuals such as Umhala and Kreli, who were Xhosa chiefs.

296. Metrowich, F.C. Assegai over the Hills. Cape Town: Timmins, 1953. 215pp. illus.

Anecdotes of pioneer days of the eastern Cape and the eastern Cape towns such as Grahamstown, Salem and Bathurst. Interesting personages are described, such as: Makana, Dr. G. Atherstone, Jeremiah Goldswain, Jeremiah Long, Richard Gush, Andrew Geddes, Bain and Joshua Norton.

297. Metrowich, F.C. The Valiant but Once. Cape Town: Timmins, 1956. 230pp. illus. map.

Each chapter an anecdote concerning various heroes of the eastern Cape in the nineteenth century. These heroes include Colonel Graham, Henry Austen, Jacob Glen Cuyler, Bishop Burnett, Thomas Pringle, John Jarvis Bisset, George Jordan, Sir Harry Smith, Rev. George Brown and Rev. Robert Niven. The author shows a definite bias in favour of the White settlers of the frontier.

298. [Milner, A.] Crankshaw, E. The Forsaken Idea: A Study of
Viscount Milner. London: Longmans Green, 1952. 178pp.

A sympathetic study of Lord Milner's ideas as reflected in
his writings, speeches and actions. Discusses Milner's career
from his early years to 1906 and attempts to show that Milner
was a true patriot whose imperialism was devoted to the survival and prosperity of Britain. While critical of certain
aspects of British policy; e.g., the British party system
which led to a vacillating Colonial system, Milner devoted his
life to the welfare of Britain. The author considers that
Milner was betrayed by the Liberal Party. The author admits
that he shows bias in favour of Milner's brand of imperialism,
as he feels that neglect of Milner's ideas led to Britain's
weakness and involvement in two World Wars.

299. [Milner, A.] Halperin V. Lord Milner and the Empire: The
Evolution of British Imperialism. London: Odhams, 1952.
256pp. front. bibl.

Aims at presenting a study of late nineteenth-century
British imperialism as personified by Milner. Milner is described as the embodiment of both militant and 'pacific
imperialism' and exemplified this quality in his administrative reforms.

300. [Milner, A.] Headlam, C., ed. The Milner Papers: vol. 1:
South Africa, 1897-1899. London: Cassell, 1931. 591pp.
illus.

A brief biographical introduction outlines Milner's career
before arrival in South Africa. The documents concerned with
his term of office in South Africa are arranged so as to
illustrate the actions and events of the period. The editor
accompanies each set of documents with an explanatory commentary. The Milner papers consist mainly of letters, telegrams
and despatches. Subsequent volumes did not deal with South
Africa.

301. [Milner, A.] Marlowe, J. Milner: Apostle of Empire. London:
Hamish Hamilton, 1976. 394pp. illus. bibl.

Interesting and readable biography of Milner based largely
upon the Milner papers in the Bodleian Library, New College,
Oxford, and upon those edited by Cecil Headlam. Approximately
one-third of the volume is devoted to Milner's career in South
Africa.

302. [Milner, A.] O'Brien, T.H. Milner: Viscount Milner of St.
James's and Cape Town, 1854-1925. London: Constable, 1979.
447pp. illus. bibl.

Attempts to present a balanced description of Milner's
talents, aims and achievements, as the author believes that
Milner's achievements have hitherto been undervalued. The
work is very extensively documented and full use has been made
of the Milner papers to depict his career from infancy to the

post-World War I period. Part 2 of the work deals with
Milner's term of office as High Commissioner in South Africa.
This section is very short and is only a summary (fifty-eight
pages). The greater part of the work is devoted to Milner's
career between 1905-1921, which the author feels has never
been properly documented.

303. [Milner, A.] Walker, E.A. Lord Milner and South Africa.
London: Humphrey Milford, 1942. 26pp. (Raleigh Lectures
in History). Reprinted from Proceedings of the British
Academy. Vol. 27.

An analysis of Milner's achievements between the years 1897
and 1905. Outlines the difficulties Milner encountered on his
arrival in South Africa, particularly with regard to the South
African Republic under Kruger. Defines Milner's aims as the
reaffirmation of British paramountcy in South Africa and the
desire to improve relations between British and Afrikaners.
Up to the year 1898, Milner hoped for voluntary reform within
the South African Republic and the election of a more liberal
government. When this failed to happen, Milner supported the
Uitlanders' demands for a five-year franchise in order to
anglicize the Transvaal. Discusses Milner's achievements in
post-war reconstruction from 1901 onwards, in which his aim
remained to build up industry in the Transvaal so as to
attract more British emigrants to the towns and anglicize the
Transvaal. He desired a confederation of South African states
under British control and opposed Responsible Government for
the British colonies. Discusses the success and weaknesses of
Milner's legal, fiscal, economic and social reforms. His
greatest error lay in neglect of native policy. Milner's
Anglicization policy failed, but his reconstruction policy
paved the way for union on a sound economic footing.

304. [Milner, A.] Worsfold, W.B. Lord Milner's Work in South
Africa from its Commencement in 1897 to the Peace of
Vereeniging in 1902. London: John Murray, 1906. viii,
620pp. illus. map.

Author attempts to portray Lord Milner's regime in South
Africa in a sympathetic light. Is very scathing in descriptions of the Afrikaner Bond, of Cape politicians such as
Merriman and Schreiner, of the British government's vacillating policy in South Africa and of the intransigence of the
Boer republics. The British Liberal Party is blamed for providing encouragement to the rebellious Boer republics. The
positive aspects of Lord Milner's patience, diplomacy and
administrative skill are stressed.

305. [Milner, A.] Wrench, J.E.L. Alfred Lord Milner: The Man of
no Illusions, 1854-1925. London: Eyre & Spottiswoode, 1958.
398pp. front.

A biography of Milner in which the author shows a definite
bias towards Milner's imperial ideals.

306. Molteno, Sir James T. The Dominion of Afrikanerdom: Recollections pleasant and otherwise. London: Methuen, 1923. xii, 257pp. illus.

Describes Molteno's experiences and views during the period 1885 to 1902, covering the period of the Rhodes ministry, Jameson Raid and Anglo-Boer War.

307. Molteno, Sir James T. Further South African Recollections. London: Methuen, 1926. 236pp. illus.

Deals with Molteno's political life from 1902 to 1910; i.e., the aftermath of the Anglo-Boer War, the National Convention and the birth of the Union of South Africa.

308. [Molteno, Sir John C.] Molteno, P.A. The Life and Times of Sir John Charles Molteno, K.C.M.G., First Premier of Cape Colony, Comprising a History of Representative Institutions and Responsible Government at the Cape and of Lord Carnarvon's Confederation Policy and of Sir Bartle Frere's High Commissionership of South Africa. London: Smith, Elder, 1900. 2v. illus. maps.

A very detailed account of constitutional development of the Cape during the second half of the nineteenth century. Author shows definite bias in favour of Molteno and against the confederation policy of Lord Carnarvon and also against Sir Bartle Frere's 'dictatorial' rule.

309. [Molteno, P.A.] Solomon, V., ed. Selections from the Correspondence of Percy Alport Molteno, 1892-1914. Cape Town: Van Riebeeck Society, 1981. (Van Riebeeck Society Publications, 2nd Series, No. 12). 367pp. illus. bibl.

A selection of the correspondence of Percy Alport Molteno housed in the South African library, Cape Town. Molteno was the son of Sir John Molteno, Prime Minister of the Cape from 1872 to 1878. Percy Molteno became a partner in the Union Castle shipping line, London, but remained patriotic towards South Africa. He opposed British imperialism as embodied in Rhodes, Chamberlain and Milner and favoured self-government for South Africa and closer union between English and Afrikaner. His views are evident in his correspondence to J.H. Hofmeyr, J.W. Sauer and J.X. Merriman. Molteno was able to use his influence in support of the Boer cause during the Anglo-Boer War of 1899-1902 and in post-war reconstruction. He was disillusioned by the colour bar restrictions contained in the Act of Union (1909) and by the rise of exclusive Afrikaner nationalism.

310. Noble, J. South Africa, Past and Present: A Short History of European Settlement at the Cape. London: Longmans, 1877; Cape Town: Juta, 1877. xiv, 345pp.

Aims at giving an account of European colonization from the end of the eighteenth century to 1877. Emphasizes important

Cape - 1836-1899

events in the political history of the colonies and states of
South Africa in the hope that these might soon be included in
a confederation.

311. Pama, C. Bowler's Cape Town: Life at the Cape in Early Victorian times, 1834-1868. Cape Town: Tafelberg, 1977. 132pp. illus. map. bibl.

A description of the social, economic and religious life of
Cape Town during the time of the artist, Thomas Bowler, who
illustrated many scenes of Cape Town life.

312. Picard, H.W.J. Lords of Stalplein: Biographical Miniatures of the British Governors of the Cape of Good Hope. Cape Town: H.A.U.M., 1974. 176pp. illus. bibl.

Contains short biographical descriptions of British governors of the Cape from 1795 to 1910. Popular book containing only a few facts concerning each governor's regime.

313. [Rhodes, C.J.] Baker, Sir H. Cecil Rhodes, by His Architect. London: Oxford University Press, 1934. xv, 182pp. illus.

Biography in which Rhodes is depicted as a nature lover and patron of the arts. Contains descriptions of architecture and memorials erected in Rhodes' era and after his death in his honour.

314. [Rhodes, C.J.] Burke, E.E. A Bibliography of Cecil John Rhodes, 1853-1902. Repr. from 'The Story of Cecil Rhodes, 1953'. Salisbury: Central African Archives, 1953. pp.117-192.

315. [Rhodes, C.J.] Flint, J. Cecil Rhodes. Boston: Little Brown, 1974. xx, 268pp. illus. maps. bibl.

Biography of Rhodes in which the author attempts to reassess the traditional view of Rhodes as the 'archetype of imperialism'. Claims that Rhodes was antagonistic to imperial interference and manipulated the concept of imperialism to achieve his aims of colonial expansion. Discusses the influence of Rhodes' aims in the South African economic sphere, in the development of Marxism and German Nazism and in the political development of Rhodesia in the twentieth century.

316. [Rhodes, C.J.] Gross, F. Rhodes of Africa. London: Cassell, 1956. 433pp. illus.

Popular biography of Rhodes.

317. [Rhodes, C.J.] Hensman, H. Cecil Rhodes: A Study of a Career. Edinburgh: Blackwood, 1901. xii, 381pp. illus. map.

Early biography of Rhodes in which the author attempts to present an impartial, unbiased description of Rhodes' life and achievements. Contains strong prejudices which are especially evident in the author's assessment of Kruger's ambitions and in his antipathy towards the Afrikaner Bond in the Cape Colony.

318. [Rhodes, C.J.] Lockhart, J.G., and C.M. Woodhouse. Rhodes. London: Hodder & Stoughton, 1963. 511pp. illus. bibl.

Attempts to make full use of the Rhodes Papers at Rhodes House, Oxford, in order to present an unbiased and accurate account of Rhodes' ambitions and career. Endeavours to describe all facets of Rhodes' personality, strengths and weaknesses.

319. [Rhodes, C.J.] McDonald, J.G. Rhodes: A Life. London: Philip Allan, 1927. xi, 403pp. illus. maps.

Popular biography of Rhodes based on secondary sources and on personal acquaintance with Rhodes.

320. [Rhodes, C.J.] Millin, S.G. Rhodes. London: Chatto & Windus, 1933. 389pp. front. maps. bibl.

Popular biography of Rhodes written in an interesting and vivid style.

321. [Rhodes, C.J.] Mitchell, L. The Life of the Rt. Hon. Cecil John Rhodes, 1853-1902. London: Edward Arnold, 1910. 2v. illus.

Early biography of Rhodes which is biased in its approach as it was written by a colleague and supporter of Rhodes' policies.

322. [Rhodes, C.J.] Vindex, pseud. Cecil Rhodes: His Political Life and Speeches, 1881-1900. London: Chapman and Hall, 1900. xliii, 859pp. front. map.

Consists of a selection of Rhodes' speeches as they appeared in journals including the Cape Argus, Cape Times, Bulawayo Chronicle and Diamond Fields Advertiser. Also includes speeches appearing in the reports of the Chartered Company and De Beers'. These speeches are preceded by a historical introduction and commentary which is extremely biased in favour of Rhodes and British imperial sentiment. Cover such topics as northern expansion in Bechuanaland and Matabeleland, the native question, progressive government, the revolutionary movement at Johannesburg, the political situation at the Cape, 1896-1899, the crisis in South Africa, 1899, and financial speeches.

323. [Rhodes, C.J.] Williams, B. Cecil Rhodes. London: Constable, 1921. vii, 353pp. illus. map. bibl. (Makers of the Nineteenth Century Series).

Interesting biography of Rhodes in which the author attempts to maintain an impartial attitude, but nevertheless tends to stress the positive contributions which Rhodes made to South African history. The author has provided an extensive bibliography, including the personal recollections of Rhodes' colleagues and contemporaries, archival material, published books on Rhodes, books relating to the period and government publications.

Cape - 1836-1899

324. Rutherfoord, E. In Mid-Victorian Cape Town: Letters from Miss Rutherfoord (1852-1856). ed. by J. Murray. Cape Town: Balkema, 1953. 157pp.

These letters were written by Emma Rutherfoord and addressed mainly to her married sister, Mary Murray in Bloemfontein. The letters are valuable in that they give a description of middle-class family life in Cape Town during the 1850s.

325. [Schreiner, W.P.] Walker, E. W.P. Schreiner: A South African. London: Oxford University Press, 1937. xii, 386pp. illus.

Biography of Schreiner based on the Schreiner papers in the South African Library, Cape Town. This biography is valuable in throwing fresh light on the policy of the self-governing Cape Colony between the years 1898 to 1900. During the Anglo-Boer War, Schreiner prevented the colonial Afrikaners from rising in support of the Boer republics. His ministry was defeated by his insistence that colonial rebels should be punished. He was anxious to uphold the rights of the Black peoples and favoured a loose federation of the South African states instead of union, as he feared that the traditionally liberal policies of the Cape towards non-White peoples would be over-borne by the racial frontier policies of Transvaal, Orange Free State and Natal. He attempted to defend the Zulu chief Dinuzulu and unsuccessfully opposed the draft South Africa Act. In 1914 he became Union High Commissioner in London and died in 1919.

326. Smith, H. The Autobiography of Lieutenant-General Sir Harry Smith. ed. by G.C. Moore. London: John Murray, 1902. 2v. illus. map. bibl.

The autobiography of Sir Harry Smith covers the period 1787 to 1846. Supplementary chapters, contributed by the editor, have been added for the period 1846 to 1860. Volume 2 contains an account of Smith's period of military service at the Cape from 1829 to 1840 and finally his appointment as governor of the Cape from 1847 to 1852.

327. [Smith, Sir H.] Harington, A.L. Sir Harry Smith - Bungling Hero. Cape Town: Tafelberg, 1980. 299pp. illus. map. bibl.

Analyses the achievements and failures of Sir Harry Smith during a fifteen-year period at the Cape (1829-1840; 1847-1852). Discusses Smith's behaviour as military commander of the British troops from 1821 to 1840, particularly as regards the death of Hintsa, the Gcaleka chief in May, 1835. From 1847 to 1852 Smith served as Governor of the Cape and High Commissioner. The weaknesses of his policy with regard to the Orange River Sovereignty, his dealings with the Voortrekker leader, Andries Pretorius, and the failure of his settlement on the eastern frontier, culminating in the Frontier War of 1850, are discussed as factors leading to Smith's recall.

328. [Smith, Sir H.] Lehmann, J.H. Remember You Are an Englishman: A Biography of Sir Harry Smith. London: Jonathan Cape, 1977. 384pp. illus. bibl.

Biography based on private papers of Sir Harry Smith. Concentrates on the military career of Smith in the Americas, South Africa, India and during the Napoleonic Wars. Approximately one-third of the book is devoted to Smith's period of frontier office in South Africa during the Sixth Frontier War (1834-1835) and his term of office as Governor of the Cape, 1846-1852.

329. [Southey, Sir R.] Wilmot, A. The Life and Times of Sir Richard Southey. London: Sampson Low, Marston, 1904. xiv, 439pp. illus.

Account of the life of Southey from the time of his arrival with the 1820 settlers to his death in 1901. Presents a very sympathetic attitude towards the position of the eastern frontier colonists in their struggles against the Xhosa tribes. Describes the part played by the Southeys in the 1834 Frontier War, Richard Southey's appointment as Civil Commissioner of Swellendam (1849), Acting Colonial Secretary (1853) and finally Colonial Secretary (1861). Discusses Southey's role in the dispute over the ownership of the Griqualand West Diamond Fields and his appointment as Lieutenant-Governor of Griqualand West. Important correspondence and extracts from official documents are included. The biography covers a great deal of the history of the Cape in the late nineteenth century but shows bias towards the colonists.

330. Staples, I. A Narrative of the Eighth Frontier War of 1851-1853. Pretoria: State Library, 1974. 59pp. illus. map. bibl.

Published in commemoration of the opening of the 1820 Settlers National Monument in Grahamstown. Consists of the reminiscences of Isaiah Staples, who had participated in the Frontier War of 1851-1853. Staples was the son of John Beth Staples, an 1820 settler. Isaiah Staples lived near the Kat River when war began. Isaiah describes the war from memory, as he wrote this account in old age. The savagery of the war was due to the fact that many Hottentot soldiers enrolled in the colonial forces, rebelled and joined the Xhosas.

331. Strydom, C.J. Scheepers, and others. Afrikaners in die Vreemde. Cape Town: Tafelberg, 1976. 262pp. illus. bibl. (Die Afrikaner en sy kultuur, deel 5).

Describes the experiences of Afrikaners who left their homeland to explore the unknown interior of Africa, or who journeyed through other continents during the second half of the nineteenth century. These areas of exploration include South West Africa and Angola, Rhodesia, Gazaland, and as far north as Zambia and Zaire. In the late nineteenth and early twentieth centuries Afrikaners emigrated to Argentina and North America. Includes personal family histories.

CHAPTER V
NATAL - HISTORY AND DESCRIPTION

Bibliographies

332. Duminy, A.H. A Guide to Unofficial Sources Relating to the History of Natal. Durban: University of Natal, Department of History and Political Science, 1977. 103pp.

333. O'Byrne, S.P.M. The Colony of Natal to the Zulu War, 1843-1878: A Bibliography. Cape Town: University of Cape Town, School of Librarianship, 1965. v, 22pp.

334. Simmonds, H.A. European Immigration into Natal, 1824-1910: A Bibliography. Cape Town: University of Cape Town, School of Librarianship, 1964. iv, 38pp.

335. Sumner, J.A. Natal, 1881-1911: A Bibliography. Cape Town: University of Cape Town, School of Librarianship, 1965. iv, 30pp.

336. Webb, C. de B. A Guide to the Official Records of the Colony of Natal. Pietermaritzburg: University of Natal Press, 1965. 318pp.

Monographs

337. Bird, J. The Annals of Natal: 1495 to 1845. Facs. repr. Cape Town: Struik, 1965. 2v.

An introduction to the work provides an outline of events in Natal from 1495 to 1845. This is followed by a chronologically arranged series of documents consisting of historical extracts, narratives, official documents, letters and other primary sources of historical information drawn from the Natal and Cape Government Archives and the archives at Pretoria, the Public Record Office in London, the Public Library in Cape Town and the library of C.A. Fairbridge.

338. Bleek, W.H.I. The Natal Diaries of Dr. W.H.I. Bleek, 1855-1856. tr. by O.H. Spohr. Cape Town: Balkema, 1965. ix, 117pp. illus. map. bibl.

A biographical introduction precedes the published diaries and manuscripts diaries. An epilogue outlines Bleek's subsequent career.

Natal - History and Description

339. Bosch, D.W. The Wilgefontein Settlement, 1880. Archives Yearbook for South African History. Vol. 27, Part 1, 1964. Pretoria: Government Printer, 1965. pp.239-288. maps. bibl. (M.A. Thesis. University of Natal, 1949).

Describes the attempt of the Land and Immigration Board of Natal to stimulate agriculture and promote immigration in Natal by means of the establishment of special settlements, of which the Wilgefontein scheme was the first (1880). The scheme, which was experimental, had negligible results.

340. Brookes, E.H., and C. de B. Webb. A History of Natal. Pietermaritzburg: University of Natal Press, 1965. 371pp. illus. maps. bibl.

Covers the history of Natal and Zululand from the year 1300 to 1961. Attempts to give an impartial history of Africans and Indians as well as the White settlers. Also attempts to give impartial views of various prominent personalities such as Lieutenant-Governor Martin West, Theophilus Shepstone, Benjamin Pine, Bishop Colenso and the various Zulu chiefs. The book is well-documented.

341. Bryant, A.T. Olden Times in Zululand and Natal, Containing Earlier Political History of the Eastern-Nguni Clans. London: Longmans, 1929. xxi, 710pp. illus. maps. Repr. Cape Town: Struik, 1965.

Deals with the tribal history of the Eastern-Nguni during the period 1497-1828, which covers the period of first contact with the White man to the death of Shaka. Detailed genealogical information and tables of clans are given.

342. Bulpin, T.V. Natal and the Zulu country. Cape Town: Books of Africa, 1966. 456pp. illus. bibl.

This work includes information contained in 'Shaka's Country' and 'To the Shores of Natal'. Covers the history of Natal from 1497 onwards. Written in a popular, readable style. Interesting anecdotes about personalities and places within Natal and Zululand.

343. Bulpin, T.V. To the Shores of Natal. Cape Town: Nelson, 1953. 340pp. illus. maps.

The history of Natal recounted in readable style. Interesting descriptions of pioneers, tribes and of origin of towns and place names within Natal.

344. Campbell, E.D. The Birth and Development of the Natal Railway. Pietermaritzburg: Shuter & Shooter, 1951. 170pp. illus.

Detailed history of Natal railways from the period 1859 onwards.

Natal - History and Description   79

345. Chase, J.C. The Natal Papers, 1498-1843... Grahamstown:
      Godlonton, 1843. 2v. Facs. repr. in 1v. Cape Town:
      Struik, 1955. iv, 135, 310pp.

      In chronological order, the author mentions the most impor-
      tant documents and descriptions connected with Natal. The
      author in each case briefly describes each document and the
      circumstances under which it was written and gives extracts
      from the document concerned. In addition the author expresses
      rather subjective opinions about these documents, particularly
      extracts from government proclamations and notices.

346. Churchill, J., and M. Churchill. A Merchant Family in Early
      Natal: Diaries and Letters of Joseph and Marianne Churchill,
      1850 to 1880, with a Narrative of Pioneering Travels to
      Potchefstroom and the Soutpansberg. ed. by D. Child. Cape
      Town: Balkema, 1979. x, 198pp. illus.

      Consists of the journal of Joseph Fleetwood Churchill and the
      letters of his sister Marianne who emigrated to Natal in 1850
      and 1854 respectively. Provides a well-written account of the
      social life in Durban, the difficulties of travel by ox wagon,
      and the economic problems faced by the firm of Evans and
      Churchill due to inefficient communications and faulty market-
      ing information. Recounts the marriages of Joseph to Emma
      Gillespie and of Marianne to Hugh Gillespie. Provides an
      account of the family life of the Churchills until Joseph's
      death in 1880.

347. Colenso, F. Colenso Letters from Natal. ed. by W. Rees.
      Pietermaritzburg: Shuter & Shooter, 1958. 440pp. illus.
      bibl.

      A selection of some three hundred letters written between
      1865 and 1893 by Frances Colenso, wife of Bishop John Colenso
      to Lady Mary Lyell and Mrs. Catherine Lyell. Each section has
      an introductory historical explanation.

348. Dobie, J.S. John Sheddon Dobie: South African Journal, 1862-
      1866. ed. by A.F. Hattersley. Cape Town: Van Riebeeck
      Society, 1945. xxxvi, 207pp. map. (Van Riebeeck Society
      Publications, 26).

      Introduction describes Dobie's life and career. The journal
      supplies a detailed description of life in the farming dis-
      tricts to the north and west of Pietermaritzburg in the mid-
      nineteenth century and also of Dobie's three journeys through
      Namansland to the Cape Colony for the purchase of sheep. Gives
      an account of the losses suffered by sheep farmers of Natal
      through illness among their stock and through the economic
      slump which began in 1865. In June, 1866, Dobie left Natal.

349. Fynn, H.F. The Diary of Henry Francis Fynn. ed. by J. Stuart and D.M. Malcolm. Pietermaritzburg: Shuter & Shooter, 1969. xvi, 341pp. illus. map. bibl.

Covers the period 1824-1836. Fynn, a pioneer trader of Natal, kept a diary on which the present work is based. Commences with a historical introduction by Fynn giving a brief account of Zulu history prior to Fynn's arrival in Natal. The diary itself was originally written in fragmentary form and transcribed more fully in later years (1859-1861). The work concludes with an epilogue summarising events in Natal up to the arrival of the Voortrekkers, together with additional notes on the customs and social life of the Zulus as observed by Fynn.

350. [Gardiner, A.F.] Marsh, J.W. A Memoir of Allen F. Gardiner, Commander, R.N. London: James Nisbet, 1857. iv, 399pp. front.

A biography of Gardiner emphasizing his role of missionary. The period which he spent in Natal, between the years 1834 to 1838, is described on pp.55-119.

351. Hattersley, A.F. The British Settlement of Natal: A Study in Imperial Migration. Cambridge: University Press, 1950. viii, 351pp. map.

Written to commemorate the centenary of the first organized emigration from Great Britain to Natal. Describes the causes, progress and results of the emigration between 1848-1851. Discusses British emigration companies, areas of Britain from which emigrants came, activities in which British settlers to Natal engaged, and the economic, agricultural, political, social and cultural achievements of the settlers.

352. Hattersley, A.F. A Camera on old Natal. Pietermaritzburg: Shuter & Shooter, 1960. 81pp. illus.

Annotated photographs of historic buildings in Durban, Pietermaritzburg, and outlying areas have been preserved in this book, because the author feels that many older buildings of Natal are fast being demolished.

353. Hattersley, A.F. More Annals of Natal: With Historical Introductions and Notes. Pietermaritzburg: Shuter & Shooter, 1936. 256pp. illus.

Accounts by settlers in Natal prior to 1852 of the early years of the Colony. These accounts are based on material collected by C. Bird in 1896. The scope of the volume covers the years 1845-1875 and the author has added introductory sections to each narrative account to explain the background of political events in Natal.

Natal - History and Description

354. Hattersley, A.F. Later Annals of Natal. London: Longman, 1938. xiii, 286pp. illus.

    A continuation of Hattersley's book, 'More Annals of Natal'. Covers the years 1860 to 1900. Extracts are taken from the writings of various people connected with the history of Natal at this time, of visitors to Natal; e.g., Thomas Baines, J.J. Aubertin, Shepstone and Harry Escombe. These extracts are linked by the author's explanatory introductions.

355. Hattersley, A.F. The Natalians: Further Annals of Natal. Pietermaritzburg: Shuter & Shooter, 1940. 200pp. illus.

    The author has made use of extracts from diaries, memoirs, letters and official papers to depict the daily life and problems of settlers in Natal from 1849 to 1870. Economic and social conditions of the Colony are described. An account is given of the Byrne emigration scheme.

356. Hattersley, A.F. Portrait of a Colony: The Story of Natal. Cambridge: University Press, 1940. x, 233pp. illus.

    Describes the British settlement in Natal, particularly the social and political life of the colonists in the nineteenth century. The final chapter describes the customs of the Zulus and the attitudes and policy of the White settlers towards them.

357. Holden, W.C. History of the Colony of Natal. London, 1855. Facs. repr. Cape Town: Struik, 1963. viii, 463pp. illus. maps.

    The author commences with a description of the Bay of Natal and adjacent country which is historically interesting. The history of Natal is summarized to the time of the British annexation of Natal. The laws and regulations of the British government in Natal are described. The author is critical of British policy towards the Zulus, because the Zulus were allowed to retain their laws and customs. Interesting descriptions of mid-nineteenth century Durban, Pietermaritzburg and smaller settlements. Author tries to encourage emigration to Natal and discusses agricultural prospects such as cultivation of sugar and coffee. In the appendix, the history of the Orange River sovereignty is discussed.

358. Hurwitz, N. Agriculture in Natal, 1860-1950. Cape Town: Oxford University Press, 1957. 123pp. illus. maps. (Natal Regional Survey, v.12).

    A study based on material submitted to the University of Stellenbosch for the D.Com. degree. Discusses the manner in which successive groups of immigrants into Natal during the nineteenth century influenced agricultural growth and developed it into an organised and commercialised industry. These groups included Voortrekkers, pastoral Black tribes, English settlers, German and Norwegian settlers and Indians. Discusses agriculture in relation to the general economic development of Natal.

Demonstrates how land, labour and credit policies affected agricultural growth. Describes the development of the sugar and wattle industries, the efforts made to introduce various field crops, the development of horticulture and market-gardening and livestock and dairy industries.

359. Ingram, J.F. Natalia: A Condensed History of the Exploration and Colonisation of Natal and Zululand. London: Harvey, Greenacre, (1897). xvi, 197pp. illus. map.

   An account of the history of Natal from the year 600 B.C., when the Phoenicians sailed past the shores of Natal, to the end of the nineteenth century. Photographs of great interest show scenes of the landscape, buildings of Durban and Pietermaritzburg and tribal scenes from Zululand.

360. [Isaacs, N.] Herrman, L., ed. Travels and Adventures in Eastern Africa. Cape Town: Van Riebeeck Society, 1936. 2v. illus. map. (Van Riebeeck Society Publications, 16, 17).

   These volumes were first published in 1836 and contain valuable descriptions of the Zulus. Cover the period of Isaacs' life from 1825 when Isaacs first arrived at Port Natal to 1832, when he left Natal. Isaacs is regarded as one of the founders of Natal. He explored Natal and Zululand during his trading expeditions and came into contact with Chaka and Dingaan. Was anxious for Britain to colonise Natal but left Natal before the British annexation.

361. [Langalibalele.] Guest, W.R. Langalibalele: The Crisis in Natal, 1873-1875. Durban: Department of History and Political Science, University of Natal, 1976. (Research Monographs, 2). v, 145pp. map. bibl.

   This study was based upon research towards a Master's degree (1967) at the University of Natal in Durban. Describes the political and economic progress of Natal as a British colony from 1846 to 1875. Discusses Shepstone's policy as native administrator of Natal and the growth of tension between the Amahlubi under Langalibalele and the Natal authorities. Describes the events of 1873 to 1875 which led to Langelibalele's arrest and trial on charges of treason and also led to condemnation of Governor Pine's action in regard to the trial. Analyses the effects of the trial on the subsequent careers of Archbishop Colenso and Shepstone and on the future course of 'native policy' in Natal.

362. [Langalibalele.] Herd, N. The Bent Pine: The Trial of Chief Langalibalele. Johannesburg: Ravan Press, 1976. 166pp. illus. maps.

   Describes the circumstances leading to the trial of Langalibalele in 1874, chief of the Amahlubi tribe of the Drakensberg foothills. Discusses the political implications of the trial which caused a serious rift between Archbishop Colenso and Governor Pine, who was supported in his action against Langalibalele by Theophilus Shepstone.

Natal - History and Description 83

363. Leverton, B.J. Government Finance and Political Development in Natal, 1843 to 1893. (Ph.D. Thesis. University of South Africa). Archives Yearbook for South African History. Vol. 33, Part 1, 1970. Pretoria: Government Printer, 1971. 317pp.

Investigates the extent to which (1) the commerce, economy and governmental finance of Great Britain affected the political development of Natal, (2) the humanitarian principles of Britain were affected by the commerce, economics and governmental finance of Natal and the British government, and (3) how the commerce, economy and governmental finance of Natal affected the political advancement of Natal to responsible government. During the greater part of the period under review in this thesis, Natal had representative government (1856 to 1892). The Legislative Council was in constant conflict with the British government for control of local financial affairs and native policy in order to ensure an adequate labour force. The traditional chronological divisions of Natal's history are substituted, in this study by 'business cycle' divisions of economic boom, recession, depression and recovery as they affected both Natal and South Africa. The study concludes by analysing the success of Natal's native policy, defence policy, financial, commercial and economic situation when responsible government was granted in 1893. Discusses imperial strategy pursued by Britain in Natal and weaknesses in Natal's constitution at that period.

364. Lugg, H.C. Historic Natal and Zululand. Pietermaritzburg: Shuter and Shooter, 1949. 176pp. illus. maps.

The author has divided the magisterial districts of Natal into separate units, and discusses the origin, history and description of each district and various places of interest within the districts. These entries are interspersed with biographical entries of famous persons who resided within the various districts under discussion.

365. Mackeurtan, G. The Cradle Days of Natal. London: Longmans, 1931. xii, 348pp. illus. bibl.

Covers the history of Natal from 1497 to the middle of the nineteenth century. Interesting descriptions given of travellers and ships which called at Natal during the sixteenth, seventeenth and eighteenth centuries. Detailed description of English settlement at Port Natal and of missionaries at kraals of Shaka and Dingaan. The section dealing with the Voortrekkers in Natal is much briefer and not as authoritative. The annexation of Natal and the social life of Durban and Pietermaritzburg at this period is amusingly described. Concludes with a description of the work of the American missionaries.

Natal - History and Description

366. MacLeod, E. Dear Louisa: History of a Pioneer Family in Natal, 1850-1888; Ellen McLeod's Letters to Her Sister in England from the Byrne Valley. ed. by R.E. Gordon. Cape Town: Balkema, 1970. xii, 280pp. illus. maps. tabs.

    Letters revealing the hardships and triumphs of the MacLeods, the first British family to settle in the Byrne Valley in Natal have been arranged so as to form a continuous narrative of pioneer life in Natal in the nineteenth century. Each chapter has an introduction by the editor.

367. [Moreland, J.] Clark, J. Natal Settler-agent: The Career of John Moreland, Agent for the Byrne Emigration-scheme of 1849-1851. Cape Town: Balkema, 1972. xvi, 312pp. illus. maps. bibl.

    Biography based on original documents of the Moreland family and papers in the Natal Archives. John Moreland acted as agent in Natal for Joseph Charles Byrne, who sent 2,200 British settlers to Natal between 1849 and 1851. The scheme collapsed in 1859 and the reasons for its failure are analysed in a survey of the letters exchanged between Byrne and Moreland.

368. Peace, W. Our Colony of Natal. London: Edward Stanford, 1883. iv, 183pp. map.

    A description of the colony of Natal, supplemented by statistical tables, for the benefit of would-be emigrants from Britain. Information is given regarding the political, social and economic conditions of the colony.

369. Phipson, T. Letters and Other Writings of a Natal Sheriff. Thomas Phipson, 1815-1876. ed. by R.N. Currey. Cape Town: Oxford University Press, 1968. xxx, 248pp. illus. bibl.

    There is a biographical introduction and account of Phipson's career prior to his arrival at Natal in 1849. Most of the letters quoted appeared in the 'Natal Witness', 'Natal Mercury', 'Times of Natal' and 'Natal Colonist'. These letters reveal Phipson's views on politics, the law, matters of public interest and agricultural problems.

370. [Pretorius, A.] Liebenberg, B.J. Andries Pretorius in Natal. Pretoria: Academica, 1977. 396pp. maps. bibl. Afrikaans text.

    Scholarly description of the period in Pretorius's life covering the decade 1838 to 1848, when Pretorius initially emerged as a national leader, first, in directing operations against the Zulus and other Black tribes of the Natal region, and second, as an opponent of British annexation of Natal.

371. Rowell, T. Natal and the Boers: The Birth of a Colony. rev. ed. London: Dent, 1902. viii, 231pp.

    A history of Natal from 1497 to 1902 written for the benefit of the English reading public. The author attempts to recount historical events and also to enlighten his readers as to the 'Boer character' in the light of events past and present. The author makes much use of John Bird's 'Annals of Natal'.

372. [Shepstone, T.] Geyser, O. Die Bantoebeleid van Theophilus Shepstone, 1845-1875. (Ph.D. Thesis. University of Pretoria). Archives Yearbook for South African History. Vol. 31, Part 1, 1968. Pretoria: Government Printer, 1969. 166pp. bibl.

A detailed examination of the administrative system established by Shepstone in regard to Natal's Black inhabitants. Shepstone's policy was based on retention of the Black people as a separate nation with their own identity and culture. He favoured territorial segregation and the location system. Also advocated that Zulu peoples retain their traditional social customs; e.g., lobolo and polygamy. Shepstone's policy was criticised by the colonists of Natal who wished for the economic integration of the Zulu in order to ensure adequate labour. He was also criticised in that he was accused of retaining the Black peoples of Natal in a state of barbarism.

373. [Shepstone, T.] Sullivan, J.R. The Native Policy of Sir Theophilus Shepstone. Johannesburg: Walker and Snashall, 1928. 143pp. bibl.

Detailed examination of the native policy of Shepstone's of which the author whole-heartedly approves. The keystone of the policy is defined as the development and preservation of tribal life and customs. Analyses Shepstone's land policy, by means of which tribes were guaranteed certain areas of land in perpetuity under the supervision of trustees. Discusses the methods used by Shepstone to put his land scheme into operation in Natal from 1852 onwards and analyses his administrative system within the native reserves. Maintains that General Hertzog, in formulating a native policy for the Union in 1925, was greatly influenced by Shepstone's policy.

374. [Shepstone, T.] Uys, C.J. In the Era of Shepstone: Being a Study of British Expansion in South Africa (1842-1877). Lovedale: Lovedale Press, 1933. xix, 469pp. illus. map. bibl.

Attempts to analyse the motivation behind British colonial policy during Shepstone's era. He was concerned mainly with commercial motives and fear of rival 'foreign' expansion in South Africa. Both Shepstone as diplomatic agent in Natal, and Sir George Grey, governor of the Cape, opposed the granting of independence to the Orange Free State and South African Republic by the terms of the Sand River and Bloemfontein Conventions (1852, 1854). Grey initiated the federation policy for South African states. Shepstone was anxious to prevent Transvaal expansion towards the coast and in 1873 opposed the acquisition by the South African Republic of St. Lucia Bay. Shepstone was concerned that the Transvaal might construct a railway to Delagoa Bay. President Burgers of the South African Republic became increasingly unpopular due to the war against

Sekukuni, ineffective government and financial bankruptcy. Shepstone took advantage of this situation to interfere in the Republic's affairs and carry out the annexation of the Transvaal in 1877. This annexation united the Boers of South Africa against Britain.

375. [Shepstone Family.] Gordon, R.E. Shepstone: The Role of the Family in the History of South Africa, 1820-1900. Cape Town: Balkema, 1968. 421pp. illus. map. bibl.

A biographical account of the Shepstone family from the time of arrival with the 1820 settlers to the death of John Wesley Shepstone in 1916. Part 1 deals mainly with John William Shepstone, missionary on the eastern Cape frontier. Part 2 is concerned mainly with Theophilus Shepstone, son of John William Shepstone, who was responsible for the organisation of Zulu locations in Natal and for the annexation of the Transvaal. There is finally a brief biography of John Wesley Shepstone.

376. Shuter, C.F. Englishman's Inn, 'Engelschelogie': An Account of the Experiences of the British Settlers and Colonists of Natal, 1824-1885. Cape Town: Timmins, 1963. 116pp. illus. maps. bibl.

Commences with the founding of the British settlement in Natal in 1824 and the first civic settlement in Durban in 1835. Deals briefly with the arrival of the trekkers in Natal in 1837 and annexation of Natal by Britain in 1842. The heart of the book is devoted to the British settlers of 1849-1851 and describes their difficulties and achievements.

377. Smail, J.L. With Shield and Assegai. Cape Town: Timmins, 1969. 172pp. illus. maps.

A historical guide to Natal and Zululand, presenting in the form of notes and photographs, relics of Natal's past from 1497 to 1879. The text covers the history of the Zulu nation as well as the history of the earliest discovery of Natal by the Portuguese and the subsequent history of the White settlers.

378. [Smith, A.] Kirby, P.R., ed. Andrew Smith and Natal: Documents Relating to the Early History of that Province, 1832-1841. Cape Town: Van Riebeeck Society, 1955. v, 253pp. illus. map. (Van Riebeeck Society Publications, 36).

Andrew Smith's expedition to Natal was made on the secret instructions of Sir Lowry Cole. Smith left no official record regarding this expedition. Information was obtained from notes present in one of the 'unpublished volumes of Smith manuscripts in the South African Museum', from the manuscript diary of Carl Friedrich Drège, who accompanied Smith, and from information supplied by H.F. Fynn and F.G. Farewell to Smith. Smith's field notes are of interest because of his scientific descriptions of tribal people and customs. The book concludes with a memorial from the Cape Town merchants requesting a settlement at Port Natal and also from the South African Land

Natal - History and Description 87

and Emigration Association formed in London to promote colonization of Natal. This memorial was forwarded to London by Sir Benjamin D'Urban but was unsuccessful.

379. Spencer, S. O'Byrne. British Settlers in Natal, 1824-1857: A Biographical Register. Volume I: Abbot-Ayres. Pietermaritzburg: University of Natal Press, 1981. 128pp. bibl.

An attempt to record details of British men and women who settled in Natal between 1824 and 1857. Entries are alphabetically arranged under the names of heads of families or single men and women who arrived without parents. Information is supplied under three headings: a biography, a list of children and a source list. Only the first volume comprising ninety-three entries has appeared. The complete work will consist of approximately 2,600 entries.

380. Tabler, E.C. Pioneers of Natal and Southeastern Africa: 1552-1878. Cape Town, Balkema, 1977. vii, 118pp. bibl.

A biographical dictionary, alphabetically arranged, giving a summary of the achievements of adult male foreigners who explored Natal and south east Africa from 1552 until the end of 1878.

381. Theal, G. McCall. Republic of Natal: The Origin of the Present Pondo Tribe. Original ed. Cape Town: Saul Solomon, 1886. 69pp. (William Hiddingh. Repr. Series, no. 16, University of Cape Town Library and South African Library, 1961).

Brief outline of events in Natal between 1840 and 1845, covering imperial treaties with the Pondo and establishment of the colony of Natal.

382. Welsh, D. The Roots of Segregation: Native policy in Colonial Natal, 1845-1910. Cape Town: Oxford University Press, 1971. viii, 381pp. tabs. bibl.

Discusses and assesses the administrative system created by Sir Theophilus Shepstone in Natal for the Zulu people. Shepstone's policy was the precursor of 'segregation' and 'apartheid'. Natal's policies influenced settlers and administrators moving into Malawi, Zambia and Rhodesia. The beginnings of African nationalism are apparent in Zulu reactions to land and franchise policies and in the pressure to provide labour for farms and public services; e.g., road making. The Natal legislature also attempted to reform traditional Zulu marriage concepts of lobolo and polygamy but met Shepstone's opposition in this matter. The Natal government failed to promote the economic development of the African reserves and the number of migrant workers rose as poverty increased. After Shepstone's retirement (1875), Natal colonists accepted his policy of retention of the Zulu traditional system and opposed the efforts of missionaries to educate and convert Africans. The power of the chiefs was steadily eroded by the government. This resulted in the Zulu revolt of 1906.

383. [Wolseley, Sir G.] Lehmann, J.H. All Sir Garnet: A Life of Field-Marshal Lord Wolseley. London: Jonathan Cape, 1964. 415pp. front. maps. bibl.

Biography based largely on correspondence and papers of the Wolseley family and on official papers at the War Office Library. Four chapters are devoted to Wolseley's period of office as governor of Natal (1874-1876), his participation in the Zulu War (1879) and annexation of the Transvaal (1879-1880). At the end of Wolseley's career, he was involved, as commander-in-chief of the British army, in preparations for the conduct of the Anglo-Boer War (1899-1902). Well-written and interesting account.

384. [Wolseley, Sir G.] Maurice, F.B., and G. Arthur. The Life of Lord Wolseley. New York: Doubleday, Page, 1924. xxiii, 375pp. illus. map. bibl.

Wolseley's career in Natal (1875) and South Africa (1879-1880) is described in Chapters 5 and 6 respectively (pp. 76-132). The part which he played in preparations for the Anglo-Boer War from 1896 onwards, is described in Chapter 12, pp. 310-32.

385. [Wolseley, Sir G.] Preston, A., ed. The South African Diaries of Sir Garnet Wolseley, 1875. Cape Town: Balkema, 1971. 293pp. illus. bibl. (South African Biographical and Historical Studies, 11).

Part 1 consists of an introduction analysing the significance of Wolseley's role in South Africa, particularly in Natal during the second half of the nineteenth century. The four collections of Wolseley's manuscripts and diaries are described. A biographical outline is given, describing Wolseley's career up to 1875 and details regarding his Natal mission and annexation of Zululand. Part 2 consists of the Natal diaries covering the period 20 March to 10 September, 1875.

386. Wood, A.A. Natal Past and Present. Ilfracombe: Arthur H. Stockwell, 1962. 176pp.

The history of the Natal Mounted Police and Natal Police from 1874 onwards.

CHAPTER VI
ZULULAND

Bibliographies

387. Cope, A.T. A Select Bibliography Relating to the Zulu People of Natal and Zululand. Durban: University of Natal, Department of Bantu Languages, 1974. 72pp.

388. Galloway, M.H. Zululand and the Zulus: A Bibliography. Cape Town: University of Cape Town, School of Librarianship, 1963. 16pp.

ZULULAND - TO 1879

Monographs

389. Bryant, A.T. The Zulu People as They Were Before the White Man Came. 2nd ed. Pietermaritzburg: Shuter & Shooter, 1967. xiv, 769pp. bibl. First published 1949.

    Gives the history of the Zulus from the sixteenth to the seventeenth century. Describes in great detail everyday life and customs of the Zulu before they encountered the White man.

390. Bulpin, T.V. Shaka's Country: A Book of Zululand. Cape Town: Nelson, 1952. x, 306pp. illus. bibl.

    A history of the Zulu from the seventeenth century to the end of the Bambata Revolt (1907).

391. [Champion, G.] Booth, A.R., ed. The Journal of the Reverend George Champion, American Missionary in Zululand, 1835-1839. Repr. Cape Town: Struik, 1967; London: Cass, 1969. xvi, 149pp. Originally published Boston: 1888, 1896.

    A description of life in Natal from 1835 to 1838. Champion worked as a missionary of the American Board of Missions during the reign of Dingane.

392. [Dingane.] Becker, P. Rule of Fear: The Life and Times of Dingane, King of the Zulu. London: Panther, 1972. 284pp. bibl. First published London: Longmans Green, 1964.

    Authoritative biography of Dingane.

393. Farrer, J.A. Zululand and the Zulus. London: Kerby & Endean, 1879. 151pp.

Recounts the history of the Zulus from the time of the English settlement at Natal and first interview with Shaka to 1878. There is also some account of Zulu customs and beliefs and government and the difficulties encountered by missionaries. Interesting facts on the methods of government of chiefs Shaka, Dingane, Panda and Cetewayo.

394. Fuze, M.M. The Black People and Whence They Came: A Zulu View. Tr. by H.C. Lugg; ed. by A.T. Cope. Pietermaritzburg: University of Natal, 1979. 206pp. illus.

This work, originally published in Zulu in 1922 as 'Abantu Abamnyama', was the first major historical work written in the vernacular by a native speaker of the language. It was written at the turn of the century by a Christian convert and friend of Bishop Colenso. Fuze remained loyal to Zulu traditions and makes use of this knowledge when discussing Zulu customs and Zulu history. His account covers the origin of the Black peoples and the reigns of the Zulu kings from Shaka to Dinuzulu.

395. Gibson, J.Y. The Story of the Zulus. London: Longmans, 1911. vii, 338pp. illus.

An attempt by the author to present an impartial account of Zulu history from the seventeenth to the end of the nineteenth century. By virtue of his position as magistrate in Zululand, Gibson attempts to verify accounts of Zulu conflicts with White settlers by questioning Zulu survivors of the various wars. The author believes that the expansion of European occupation and the creation of the Union of South Africa was greatly influenced by the actions of the Zulu nation under their kings.

396. Grout, L. Zululand; or, Life among the Zulu-kafirs of Natal and Zululand, South Africa. Philadelphia: Presbyterian Publication Committee, 1864. 351pp. illus. map.

Account of the history, social customs, government, religion, daily life, language and literature of the Zulus by a missionary who spent fifteen years in South Africa as representative of the American Board of Commissioners for Foreign Missions. Also describes the history of the American and European missions in Zululand in the first half of the nineteenth century, the geological, botanical and zoological features of Natal, European enterprise in Natal and affairs in Zululand.

397. Holden, W.C. British Rule in South Africa: Illustrated in the Story of Kama and His Tribe and the War in Zululand. London: Wesleyan Conference Office, 1879. 218pp. illus. maps.

The biography of the Christian Chief Kama is sympathetically recounted by Holden, who was a missionary with Kama's people.

Zululand - To 1879

The account of the war in Zululand is an attempt to justify Britain's participation in the war. Holden contrasts the noble behaviour of the Christian Chief Kama with the barbarism of the savage 'Kechwayo'.

398. Lloyd, A. The Zulu War, 1879. London: Hart-Davis, MacGibbon, 1973. 173pp. illus. maps. bibl.

Popular account of the Zulu War based on secondary sources. Written in a very readable style. Suitable for non-specialist readers.

399. Morris, D.R. The Washing of the Spears: A History of the Rise of the Zulu Nation Under Shaka and its Fall in the Zulu War of 1879. New York: Simon and Schuster, 1965. 655pp. illus. bibl.

Detailed account of the history of the Zulu nation from the time of Dingiswayo to recent times.

400. Mutwa, V.C. Indaba, My Children. Johannesburg: Blue Crane Books, 1965. xix, 562pp. illus.

The history of the Zulu nation is reconstructed from a Zulu historian's point of view. The early history of the tribe is told in the form of folk tales and epic poems. The religion, beliefs and laws of the Zulu and also the reason for the murder of Piet Retief are revealed.

401. Owen, F. The Diary of the Rev. Francis Owen ... Missionary with Dingaan in 1837-1838; Together with Extracts from the Writings of Messrs. Hulley and Kirkman. ed. by G. Cory. Cape Town: Van Riebeeck Society, 1926. 189pp. (Van Riebeeck Society Publications, 7).

Commences with the arrival of Owen at Cape Town in March 1837. From Grahamstown, he journeyed overland to Port Natal, and in August 1837, arrived at Dingaan's kraal. The greater part of the diary contains a description of his stay among the Zulus, the death of Retief's party at the hand of Dingane and Owen's departure from Zululand at the beginning of 1838. A summary is given of the rest of Owen's stay in South Africa and his attempt to establish a mission in Moselikatze's country. He left South Africa in 1841. The short accounts of Joseph Kirkman, interpreter to the Rev. Mr. Champion, and R.B. Hulley interpreter to Owen, give further information regarding Retief's death and Owen's stay in Zululand.

402. Peires, J.B., ed. Before and after Shaka: Papers in Nguni History. Grahamstown: Institute of Social and Economic Research, Rhodes University, 1981. 267pp. map. bibl.

A collection of papers presented at a Nguni workshop held at Rhodes University in 1979. The topics covered include a discussion of the political structure of the Zulu kingdom in the nineteenth century, Nguni society, migrant labour and Zulu trade with Delagoa Bay. There are also descriptions of the various Nguni peoples.

403. Roberts, B. The Zulu Kings. London: Hamish Hamilton, 1974. xii, 388pp. illus. map. bibl.

Provides detailed biographical accounts of the lives of Shaka and Dingane. Events in the reigns of Cetshwayo and Dinuzulu are dealt with very briefly. Many descriptions are given of White travellers who visited the kraals of Zulu kings and of the effect of the intrigues of White adventurers on the fate of the Zulu kings; e.g., Isaacs, Fynn and Farewell.

404. [Shaka.] Bond, G. Chaka the Terrible. London: Arco, 1961. 176pp.

Semi-fictional account of Shaka's life and career. Suitable for young readers.

405. [Shaka.] Mofolo, T. Chaka: An Historical Romance. Tr. from the original Sesuto by F.H. Dutton. London: Oxford University Press for International Institute of African languages and cultures, 1931. xv, 198pp.

Fictionalised account of Shaka's life and career by a Sotho author.

406. [Shaka.] Ritter, E.A. Shaka Zulu: The Rise of the Zulu Empire. London: Longmans Green, 1955. xvi, 383pp. illus. bibl.

Popular biography of Shaka.

407. Shooter, J. The Kafirs of Natal and the Zulu Country. London: Stanford, 1857. x, 402pp. illus.

The author lived for about four years in Natal and during this period conducted researches into the social customs, political system, beliefs, and history of the Zulu people.

408. Smail, J.L. From the Land of the Zulu Kings. Durban: Pope, 1979. viii, 185pp. illus. maps. bibl.

A richly illustrated summary of Natal and Zulu history from the fifteenth to the nineteenth centuries. Contains many reproductions of historical paintings depicting events and photographs of historical monuments, buildings and objects from museums. There are various useful lists and tables; e.g., forts, fortifications and laagers in Natal and Zululand (1842-1906), wars, rebellions and expeditions in Southern Africa from 1510-1953.

ZULULAND - WAR OF 1879

Bibliography

409. Jaffe, E.L. The Zulu War of 1879: A Bibliography. Cape Town: University of Cape Town, School of Librarianship, 1956. vii, 78pp.

Monographs

410. Ashe, W., and E.V.W. Edgell. The Story of the Zulu campaign. London: Sampson Low, 1880. xv, 408pp. map.

    An account of the Zulu campaign written from details supplied by Captain E.V. Wyatt Edgell, who was killed at Ulundi. The author attempts to vindicate the action of the British military command and soldiers whom he feels were unjustly criticised by the British press and public. Also attempts to arouse sympathy for the death of Prince Louis Napoleon. Descriptions of military campaigns given in great detail.

411. Barthorpe, M. The Zulu War: A Pictorial History. Poole: Blandford Press, 1980. ix, 181pp. illus. maps. bibl.

    The author attempts to present a concise account of the events of the Zulu War, including conditions in Zululand leading up to the war (1816-1879), the first and second British invasions of Zululand (1879) and aftermath (1879-1897). The emphasis throughout the book is on old photographs of scenes of battle and of the protagonists and also on contemporary paintings, drawings and engravings.

412. [Cetshwayo.] Binns, C.T. The Last Zulu King: The Life and Death of Cetshwayo. London: Longmans, 1963. xv, 240pp. illus.

    Readable biography, sympathetic towards Cetshwayo, and based on eye-witness accounts and research into original documents.

413. [Cetshwayo.] Vijn, C. Cetshwayo's Dutchman: Being the Private Journal of a White Trader in Zululand During the British Invasion. Tr. by J.W. Colenso. London: Longmans Green, 1880. xvii, 196pp. front. Repr. New York: Negro Universities Press, 1969.

    Covers the period 1878 to 1879 and contains a description of the Zulu War of 1879 by the trader Vijn, who had been four and a half years in Natal. Describes the reluctance of Cetshwayo to make war on the White people. Lays considerable blame for the unrest in Zululand on John Dunn, an untrustworthy colonist of Natal. Colenso adds notes to Vijn's account further attempting to prove Cetshwayo's reluctance to make war on Natal. Colenso believes that Sir Bartle Frere deliberately attempted to slander Cetshwayo in order to justify Britain's actions in the war of 1879.

414. [Cetshwayo.] Webb, C. de B., and J.B. Wright, eds. A Zulu King Speaks: Statements Made by Cetshwayo KaMpanda on the History and Customs of His People. Pietermaritzburg: University of Natal Press, 1978. 126pp. illus. maps.

Three documents are reprinted containing statements made by Cetshwayo between 1880 and 1881 while he was in detention at the Cape. These documents provide a comprehensive description of the history, functioning and downfall of the Zulu empire in the nineteenth century. An introduction provides a biographical sketch of Cetshwayo and description of the Zulu War (1879). The first document was originally published under the title 'Cetywayo's story of the Zulu Nation and the War' in 'Macmillan's Magazine' of February 1880. The second consists of a letter written by Cetshwayo to the Governor of the Cape, Sir Hercules Robinson, requesting his release and setting out his view of events leading to the war of 1879. The third document consists of minutes of evidence supplied by Cetshwayo in 1881 to the Cape Government Commission on Native Laws and Customs and published in 1883 in the Commission's official report.

415. Clammer, D.G. The Zulu War. Newton Abbot: David and Charles, 1973. 239pp. illus. maps. bibl. Repr.: Pan, 1975.

Survey of the causes and events of the Zulu War of 1879. Suitable for non-specialist readers. Concentrates mainly on descriptions of the military campaigns. Contains very little information on the effects of the war or of events subsequent to the Battle of Ulundi (June, 1879).

416. Clarke, S., ed. Invasion of Zululand, 1879: Anglo-Zulu War Experiences of Arthur Harness; John Jervis, 4th Viscount St. Vincent; and Sir Henry Bulwer. Johannesburg: Brenthurst Press, 1979. 296pp. illus. maps. bibl.

Part 1 consists of editorial commentary and historical background to tne Zulu War. Also contains the unpublished letters of Arthur Harness (January, 1878 to October, 1879). Part 2 consists of the diary of John Jervis, later Lord St. Vincent, and covering the Zulu War period. Part 3 contains the letters of Henry Bulwer, dated December, 1878 to September, 1882. There are in addition, biographical sketches of some British officers connected with the Zulu War and a letter by Arthur Harness on Chelmsford's conduct of the war, taken from 'Fraser's Magazine' April, 1880, pp. 477-88.

Zululand - War of 1879

417. Clements, W.H. The Glamour and Tragedy of the Zulu War.
London: John Lane, 1936. xxi, 348pp. illus.

Detailed history of the Zulu War of 1879 by a contemporary
settler of Natal, who was a member of the Natal Mounted Police
and later a journalist. The origin and history of the Zulu
nation and events leading up to the war are described. The
campaigns and events of the war are described in great detail.

418. Colenso, F.E., and E. Durnford. History of the Zulu War and
its Origin. 2nd ed. London: Chapman & Hall, 1881. 445pp.

A history of the causes and events of the Zulu War of 1879,
in which the authors display great sympathy towards the Zulu
nation and indignation against the action of the British.

419. Colenso, F.E. The Ruin of Zululand: An Account of British
Doings in Zululand Since the Invasion of 1879. London:
William Ridgway, 1884-1885. 2v.

This is a sequel to 'The History of the Zulu War'. The
author contends that Cetshwayo was very unjustly treated by
the Natal officials, particularly Bulwer. The partition of
Zululand is also condemned.

420. [Colenso, J.W.] Cox, G.W. The Life of John William Colenso,
D.D.: Bishop of Natal. London: Ridgway, 1888. 2v. front.

An attempt to vindicate the acts, beliefs and writings of
Colenso. A great part of the two volumes is devoted to a
vindication of Colenso's theological beliefs. Volume 2 contains a description of Colenso's actions during the Zulu War
of 1879.

421. [Colenso, J.W.] Bringing Forth Light: Five Tracts on Bishop
Colenso's Zulu Mission; edited by R. Edgecombe. Pietermaritzburg: University of Natal Press, 1983. 298pp. illus.
(Killie Campbell Africana Library Reprint Series, 4).

A recent reprint relating to J.W. Colenso's work in Zululand.
The volume includes Colenso's 'First Steps of the Zulu Mission'
and 'Three Native Accounts of the Visit of the Bishop of Natal
in September and October 1859 to Umpande, King of the Zulus'.
The latter work was written by three Zulu converts. There are
also lesser known publications of Colenso included in this
work.

422. Cope, R.L., and J.J. Guy. The Anglo-Zulu War of 1879: Two
Centenary Lectures. Johannesburg: Friends of the Library,
University of the Witwatersrand, 1979. 29pp.

Consists of two lectures, 'The Zulu Kingdom and its White
Neighbours, 1824-1879' and 'The Centenary of the British
Invasion of Zululand'. In these lectures, an attempt is made
to reassess events leading up to the war and evaluate the
consequences of the war for the people of South Africa.

423. Coupland, R. Zulu Battle Piece: Isandhlwana. London: Collins, 1948. 148pp. illus. maps. bibl.

A detailed description of the battle of Isandhlwana and analysis of the results of the battle. The author asserts that the British defeat led to the recall of Frere and thus delayed the process of federation of the South African states.

424. Duminy, A.H., and C. Ballard. The Anglo-Zulu War: New Perspectives. Pietermaritzburg: University of Natal Press, 1981. 198pp. maps.

Includes a variety of historical interpretations contributed by scholars at a centenary conference held in Durban in February, 1979. Contents include: 'The Origins of the War' (C. de B. Webb), 'Anglo-Zulu Relations, 1856-1878' (N.A. Etherington), 'The War, Natal and Confederation' (W.R. Guest), 'The Zulu Political Economy on the Eve of the War' (P.J. Colenbrander), 'Confronting Imperialism' (E. Unterhalter), Sir Garnet Wolseley and John Dunn : the Architects and Agents of the Ulundi Settlement' (C. Ballard) and 'The Role of Colonial Officials in the Destruction of the Zulu Kingdom' (J.J. Guy).

425. Emery, F. The Red Soldier: Letters from the Zulu War, 1879. London: Hodder & Stoughton, 1977. 288pp. illus. maps. bibl.

An account of the Zulu campaign of 1879 drawn from the correspondence of officers and private soldiers who participated in the campaign. This correspondence is divided into five sections; massacre at Isandhlwana, Rorke's drift, Evelyn Wood's column, Pearson's column and Cetshwayo's defeat.

426. French, G. Lord Chelmsford and the Zulu War. London: John Lane, 1939. ix, 436pp. illus. maps.

Based on the private and official correspondence of Lord Chelmsford, commander of the British army during the Zulu War of 1879. Attempts to vindicate Chelmsford, who was severely criticised for his conduct of the war.

427. Furneaux, R. The Zulu War: Isandhlwana and Rorke's Drift. London: Weidenfeld & Nicolson, 1963. 210pp. illus. maps.

An analysis of the Zulu War, in which the author maintains that the blind prejudice of Sir Bartle Frere was the main reason for the war. Describes the conduct of the war and the failure of the British government to establish an efficient and just policy toward Zululand in the post-war years.

428. Glover, M. Rorke's Drift: A Victorian Epic. Cape Town: Purnell; London: Leo Cooper, 1975. xi, 146pp. illus. map. bibl.

Attempts to show that the defence of Rorke's Drift became a Victorian legend because it was exploited by Lord Beaconsfield as a means of offsetting the British defeat by the Zulus at Isandhlwana. The British public were thus encouraged to

Zululand - War of 1879

maintain their faith in the bravery of the British soldier and in the effectiveness of British military weapons.

429. Gon, P. The Road to Isandlwana: The Years of an Imperial Battalion. Johannesburg: Ad Donker, 1979. 288pp. illus.

   Traces the history of the 1st battalion of the 24th Regiment between December, 1875 and January, 1879. Describes their participation in quelling the 'Black Flag' rebellion in Kimberley and a Griqua uprising, and also in subduing the chief Sekhukhune. Discusses the Ninth Frontier War (1877-1878) in which the Xhosa were defeated and the manner in which British military tactics applied in this campaign were misapplied at the Battle of Isandlwana, where the first 24th battalion was decimated.

430. Harford, H. The Zulu War Journal of Colonel Henry Harford, C.B. ed. by D. Child. Pietermaritzburg: Shuter & Shooter, 1978. 88pp. illus.

   Describes the experiences of a member of Lord Chelmsford's column at the battle of Isandhlwana and defence of Rorke's Drift. Harford was responsible for recovering the regimental colours at Fugitives Drift. He participated in the capture of Cetshwayo, whom he later came to know well when stationed at Cape Town in 1881.

431. Lloyd, A. The Zulu War. London: Hart-Davis, MacGibbon, 1973. 173pp. illus. maps. bibl. (Colonial Wars Series).

   Popular account of events of the Zulu War (1879) written in a readable style. Based on secondary sources.

432. Lucas, T.S. The Zulus and the British Frontiers. London: Chapman & Hall, 1879. xvi, 371pp.

   An account by a former captain of the Cape Mounted Rifles, who maintains that defence against the Zulus should be brought about by forts and frontier garrisons, as was the case at the Cape. Describes the physical features of eastern South Africa, the customs and conflicts of the Xhosa, the rise of the Zulu and Natal government policy towards the Zulu up to the year 1879, and the events leading to the annexation of the Transvaal. The account concludes with a description of the Battle of Isandhlwana.

433. Natal Provincial Museum Advisory Board. The Zulu War and the Colony of Natal; ed. by G.A. Chadwick and E.G. Hobson. Mandini: Qualitas Publishers, 1979. 188pp. illus.

   Consists of articles describing the impact of the war on Black and White inhabitants of Natal. Deals with political and economic aspects of the war, the social life of the colony, the volunteer units, the death of the Prince Imperial of France, the influence of the war on specific towns and areas, the role played by the Natal Native Corps, some colonial personalities and contemporary reminiscences.

434. Norris-Newman, C.L. In Zululand with the British Throughout the War of 1879. London: W.H. Allen, 1880. xv, 343pp. illus. maps.

A detailed account of the Zulu War by an officially appointed special war correspondent who had a knowledge of the country and of Zulu language and customs. The author gives a summary of the causes of the war, and an unbiased and factual eye witness account of the war.

435. Wilmot, A. A History of the Zulu War. London: Richardson & Best, 1880. viii, 249pp. map.

An account of the Zulu War in which the author shows great prejudice against the Zulu people and upholds the policy of Sir Bartle Frere in initiating the war. Contains a long description of the death of Prince Louis Napoleon and of the military campaigns conducted during the war. Concludes by condemning the peace settlement in Zululand which left the chiefs in power and did not attempt to convert the Zulus from their heathenism and polygamy.

436. Wolseley, Sir G. The South African Journal of Sir Garnet Wolseley, 1879-1880. ed. by A. Preston. Cape Town: Balkema, 1973. viii, 359pp. bibl.

Introduction provides historical background of British colonial policy and of Wolseley's career and ambitions between 1875 and 1879. The diary entries cover the period from Wolseley's arrival in South Africa in June, 1879 until his return to England in May, 1880. He was charged with the pacification of Zululand and the Transvaal, but became involved in a war in Zululand and increasing Boer discontent owing to the British annexation of the Transvaal. This period is described as the least known and most neglected of Wolseley's career.

ZULULAND - AFTER 1879

437. Brookes, E.H., and N. Hurwitz. The Native Reserves of Natal. Cape Town: Oxford University Press, 1957. ix, 195pp. illus. maps. (Natal Regional Survey, v.7).

Published as part of a study, entitled 'Natal Regional Survey', undertaken by the University of Natal. Discusses the history of the reserves from 1841 to 1951. Describes the administration, natural environment, road and rail transport, population, agriculture, industrial and commercial development, health, education, rehabilitation schemes and social welfare of the Reserves in the 1950s. In conclusion makes certain recommendations as to improvements which could be carried out in all the above-mentioned areas.

Zululand - After 1879   99

438. [Dinuzulu.] Binns, C.T. Dinuzulu: The Death of the House of
     Shaka. London: Longmans, 1968. xi, 306pp. illus. maps.
     bibl.

     A sympathetic biography of Dinuzulu which gives an account
     of the trials and tribulations of the Zulu nation between the
     years 1868 and 1913.

439. Guy, J.J. The Destruction of the Zulu Kingdom: The Civil War
     in Zululand, 1879-1884. London: Longman, 1979. x, 273pp.
     illus. maps. bibl.

     An unbiased account which attempts also to present the Zulu
     viewpoint as expressed by the Bishop of Natal (John William
     Colenso) and his family. Includes information collected by
     James Stewart from Zulu informants at the end of the nine-
     teenth century as well as an account given by a Zulu war
     participant, Mapheluka Mkhosana.

440. Marks, S. Reluctant Rebellion: The 1906-1908 Disturbance in
     Natal. Oxford: Clarendon Press, 1970. xxv, 404pp. maps.
     bibl.

     A study of the causes and events of the Zulu Rebellion of
     1906 to 1908 which, although crushed, contributed to the grow-
     ing movement for a political organization which would embrace
     Black people all over South Africa. This led to the formation
     of the South African Native National Congress in 1912.

441. Selby, J. Shaka's Heirs. London: Allen & Unwin, 1971. 232pp.
     illus. bibl.

     An account of the military achievements of the Zulus and
     Matabele who employed Shaka's military system, from the Battle
     of Isandhlwana (1879) to the downfall of Lobengula (1893).

442. Stuart, J. A History of the Zulu Rebellion (1906) and Dinu-
     zulu's Arrest, Trial and Expatriation. London: Macmillan,
     1913. xvi, 581pp. illus. maps.

     This work was begun in an official capacity, when the author
     was Assistant Secretary for Native Affairs, and much use has
     been made of official records to ensure accuracy. A de-
     scription is given of native administration in Natal prior to
     the rebellion, military organization in Natal and Zulu military
     system. The events leading up to and during the rebellion are
     described in great detail. In conclusion the causes of the
     rebellion and aims of the rebels are analysed.

CHAPTER VII
ORANGE FREE STATE
1854-1899

Bibliographies

443. Eales, M. Annotated Guide to the Pre-Union Government Publications of the Orange Free State, 1854-1910. Boston: Hall, 1976. 523pp.

444. Muller, D.J. The Orange River: A Bibliography. Cape Town: University of Cape Town, School of Librarianship, 1953. v, 21pp.

445. Van Schoor, M.C.E., and S.I. Malan. 'n Bibliografie van Werke oor die Oranje-Vrystaat vanaf die Vroegste Tye tot 1910. Bloemfontein: The Compilers, 1954. vii, 113pp.

Monographs

446. Attree, E.M. The Closer Union Movements Between the Orange Free State, South African Republic and Cape Colony (1838-1863). (M.A. Thesis. University College of the Orange Free State, 1946). Archives Yearbook for South African History. Vol. 12, Part 1, 1949. Pretoria: Government Printer, 1950. pp.303-77.

Maintains that the factors militating against the union of South African states in the mid-nineteenth century were the individualism and jealousies among the various parties of the Boer republics and Britain's reluctance to assume responsibility for control beyond the Orange River. Discusses the effects of the Sand River and Bloemfontein Conventions (1852-1854), which recognised independence of the Orange Free State and South African Republics but left the Orange Free State in a weak position regarding Basuto incursion. Certain Boers of the Orange Free State favoured union with the Transvaal under M.W. Pretorius. Another party in the Orange Free State looked to the Cape government and Britain for assistance. Sir George Grey, governor of the Cape, favoured federation, but his scheme was rejected. In 1859, the movement favouring union with the Transvaal seemed to be progressing in the Orange Free State, following the election of M.W. Pretorius as President of the Orange Free State. However, Grey opposed

Orange Free State - 1854-1899

this Union. President Brand finally rallied forces of the
Orange Free State and defeated the Basuto (1866). Britain
annexed Basutoland to the disappointment of the Orange Free
State. This caused much anti-British sentiment.

447. [Brand, J.H.] Barlow, T.B. President Brand and His Times.
Cape Town: Juta, 1972. ix, 267pp. illus. maps. bibl.

Covers the whole period of Brand's career to his death in
1888. Well-documented account written in a simple narrative
style. The author, whose grandfather was a personal friend
of President Brand, presents a very sympathetic portrait of
the statesman and demonstrates his sagacity in administration,
in dealing with the Basuto problem, the question of the Griqualand West diamond fields and in his intervention in the first
Anglo-Boer War.

448. [Brand, J.H.] Scholtz, G.D. President Johannes Henricus
Brand. Johannesburg: Voortrekkerpers, 1957. 304pp. front.
bibl.

Well-documented biography of Brand, written in Afrikaans, by
a former citizen of the Orange Free State. Much use has been
made of archival sources, such as the official records of the
Volksraad of the Orange Free State, official correspondence and
extracts from newspapers prominent in the Free State during
Brand's term of office.

449. Collins, J.A. The Struggles of an Infant State; Being Some
Glimpses into the History of the Late Orange Free State
Republic. Cape Town: Juta, 1925. 102pp. illus. Facs.
repr. Cape Town: Struik, 1965.

Provides a brief history of the Orange Free State from 1845
to 1899. Lacks documentation.

450. Collins, W.W. 'Free Statia'; or, Reminiscences of a Lifetime
in the Orange Free State., South Africa, from 1852 to end
of 1875: 23 years. Bloemfontein: Friend Printing and Publishing Co., 1907. 391pp. Repr. Cape Town: Struik, 1965.
344pp. illus.

Written by an English pioneer settler in the Orange Free
State. Describes political events and the struggle of the
Orange Free State for independence; early Bloemfontein and
the social and religious life of its inhabitants; the problems
of the farmers and economic affairs of the settlement. The
Basuto wars, discovery of diamonds, the appearance of a comet
(1874) and the earthquake at Bloemfontein (1875) are among
other interesting events described.

451. Hamelberg, H.A.L. Die Dagboek van H.A.L. Hamelberg, 1855-1871 ... met 'n Verkorte Weergawe in Engels Vertaal deur N.G. Sabbagha. ed. by F.J. du Toit Spies. Cape Town: Van Riebeeck Society, 1952. xx, 275pp. illus. map. bibl. (Van Riebeeck Society Publications, 33).

    Diary of a Dutch advocate who became prominent in the Orange Free State between 1856 and 1871. The diary covers Hamelberg's voyage from the Netherlands to the Cape in 1855, his impressions of a six-month visit to Cape Town, his journey to Bloemfontein and his impressions of Bloemfontein and of political events there in which he participated.

452. [Hamelberg, H.A.L.] Muller, H.P.N. Oude Tyden in den Oranje-Vrystaat: naar Mr. H.A.L. Hamelberg's Nagelaten Papieren Beschreven. Leiden: Brill, 1907. 374pp. illus.

    Account of the history of the Orange Free State between the years 1846 to 1896, based largely on material found in the Orange Free State Archives and connected with the career of H.A.L. Hamelberg, who acted as consul-general for the Orange Free State from 1872-1896.

453. Kieser, A. President Steyn en die Krisisjare, 1896-1899. Cape Town: Nasionale Boekhandel, 1939. ix, 213pp. illus. bibl.

    Steyn is depicted as the greatest statesman of the Orange Free State, with ambition to improve agriculture and education and to encourage the growth of Afrikaner nationalism by combating the growing Anglicisation of the Orange Free State and by close ties with the South African Republic. He aimed at eventual federation of all the South African colonies, in a system where Afrikaner aspirations would unite, but was defeated by Milner's imperialism.

454. Lamb, D. The Republican Presidents. Johannesburg: Perskor, 1974-1976. 2v. illus. bibl.

    Consists of the biographies of Boer statesmen of the nineteenth century. Volume 1 deals with J.P. Hoffman, J.N. Boshof, M.W. Pretorius and J.H. Brand. Volume 2 includes biographies of F.W. Reitz, M.T. Steyn, T.F. Burgers and S.J.P. Kruger.

455. Lindley, A.F. Adamantia: The Truth about the South African Diamond Fields. London: Collingridge, 1873. xiii, 423pp. illus. maps.

    The author attempts to show that the British colonial government acted illegally in annexing the diamond fields to the Cape. He examines the case for the Griquas and finds that their claim to the fields is weak and that Sir Henry Barkly gravely wronged the Orange Free State.

Orange Free State - 1854-1899

456. Malan, J.H. Die Opkoms van 'n Republiek; of, Die Geskiedenis van die Oranje Vrystaat tot die Jaar 1863. Bloemfontein: Nasionale Pers, 1929. 532pp.

A detailed history of the Orange Free State from 1819 to 1863, in which some bias is shown in favour of the White settlers of the Orange Free State.

457. Malan, S.F. Politieke Strominge onder die Afrikaners van die Vrystaatse Republiek. Durban: Butterworth, 1982. 413pp. illus. bibl.

A study of the development of national awareness among the Afrikaners of the Orange Free State, with particular reference to the years 1868 to 1899. This national awareness was evident in political, economic and cultural spheres and began during the period of office of President J.H. Brand. Factors which stimulated the growth of nationalism were British imperialistic actions, such as the annexations of the Kimberley diamond fields and of the Transvaal in 1879. The success of the Boer forces against Britain in the Transvaal War of Independence (1880-1881) inspired the Republicans of the Orange Free State to form the Afrikaner Bond in 1880. This organization was very influential in the 1880s and was supported by co-operative farming organizations and youth movements. The people of the Orange Free State were also bound by church and family ties and by loyalty to a very democratic constitution. The greatest limitation to their freedom resulted from their economic dependence on British dominated coastal regions for trade and imports. The final breakdown in relations with Britain came with the events of the Jameson Raid (1895) and President Steyn's unsuccessful efforts to mediate between Kruger and Milner at the Bloemfontein Conference (1899).

458. Midgley, J.F. The Orange River Sovereignty, 1848-1854. (D.Phil. Thesis. University of Cape Town). Archives Yearbook for South African History. Vol. 12, part 2, 1949. Cape Town: Government Printer, 1950. xxiv, 597pp. maps. bibl.

Attempts to present a detailed authoritative and unbiased narrative of the history of the Orange River Sovereignty between 1848 and 1854. Describes events in Transorangia prior to the proclamation of the sovereignty with particular emphasis on relationships between the Boers and various tribes. The British Secretary of State for the Colonies was extremely reluctant to extend British control over Transorangia. This step was undertaken by Sir Harry Smith in 1848 to provide a more adequate system of government for that region and to resolve land disputes between farmers and tribes. The annexation failed due to lack of adequate revenue for administration and because of inefficiency of administrative personnel. Warden, the British Resident, erred in attempting to control and interfere in the quarrels of the various tribes in the sovereignty. This problem reached its zenith at the Battle of Viervoet where British forces were rebuffed.

459. Orpen, J.M. Reminiscences of Life in South Africa from 1846 to the Present Day. Cape Town: Struik, 1964. xix, 344pp. illus.

Originally consisted of two volumes, of which volume 2 appeared only as newspaper articles in the 'Natal Advertiser'. Volume 1 originally published in 1908. Contains interesting accounts of the Orange River Sovereignty (1851), where Orpen acted as surveyor, and of the early days of the Orange Free State, where Orpen represented Harrismith in the Volksraad and also acted as landdrost of Winburg and Harrismith. Concludes with the intervention of Sir George Grey in the Basuto War (1855).

460. Spies, F.J. du Toit, ed. 'n Nederlander in Diens van die Oranje Vrystaat: Uit die Nagelate Papiere van dr. Hendrik P.N. Muller, oud-Konsul-generaal van die O.V.S. Amsterdam: Swets & Zeitlinger, 1946. 311pp. illus.

A biography of a Dutch merchant who visited South Africa in 1883 and was appointed Dutch consul-general for the Orange Free State from 1896 to 1898. During the Anglo-Boer War, Muller attempted to awaken pro-Boer sympathy in Europe and America and organised charitable relief for victims of the war.

CHAPTER VIII
TRANSVAAL
1852-1899

Bibliographies

461. Hughes, E.B. Personal Reminiscences of Early Johannesburg in Printed Books, 1884-1895: An Annotated Bibliography. Johannesburg: University of the Witwatersrand, Department of Bibliography, Librarianship and Typography, 1966. vii, 76pp.

462. Shaw, T.R. The Growth of Johannesburg, 1886-1939. Johannesburg: University of the Witwatersrand, Department of Bibliography, Librarianship and Typography, 1963. 39pp.

463. Winter, J.S. First-Hand Accounts of Johannesburg in English Language Periodicals, 1886-1895. Johannesburg: University of the Witwatersrand, Department of Bibliography, Librarianship and Typography, 1967. 42pp.

Monographs

464. Agar-Hamilton, J.A.I. The Road to the North: South Africa, 1852-1886. London: Longmans Green, 1937. xiv, 458pp. maps. bibl.

An account of the efforts of the Cape Colony, Boer Republics and Great Britain to obtain control over the road which led through Bechuanaland to Central Africa in the second half of the nineteenth century. In 1852, Britain recognised the independence of the Transvaal Boers who commenced raids against various tribes of Bechuanaland. After the discovery of diamonds (1867) Presidents Pretorius and Burgers attempted to control all land as far as the Kalahari. This move was thwarted by Cape annexation of the diamond fields (1871) and British annexation of the Transvaal (1877). In 1881 the Transvaal successfully revolted and attempted to establish republics in Stellaland and Goshen (1881-1886). Rhodes persuaded Britain to annex Bechuanaland and by 1886 the Road to the North was in British hands.

465. Allen, V. Kruger's Pretoria: Buildings and Personalities of the City in the Nineteenth Century. Cape Town: Balkema, 1971. xi, 259pp. illus.

Attempts to recreate the Pretoria of Kruger's period by means of descriptions and illustrations of famous contemporary buildings and personalities.

466. Aylward, A. The Transvaal of Today: War, Witchcraft, Sport and Spoils in South Africa. Edinburgh: Blackwood, 1878. xii, 428pp. map.

The author, drawing on ten years experience of South Africa, describes the Boers of the Transvaal, the conflicts with the Bapedi tribe, the Lydenburg Volunteer Corps and discusses the weaknesses of the British annexation of the Transvaal.

467. Botha, P.R. Die Staatkundige Ontwikkeling van die Suid Afrikaanse Republiek onder Krüger en Leyds: Transvaal, 1844-1899. Amsterdam: Swets & Zeitlinger, 1926. 848pp. illus. bibl.

Detailed account of the political development of the South African Republic between the years 1844 to 1899, based on archival material supplied mainly by W.J. Leyds and partly by the Pretoria Archives. The work reveals a strong antipathy towards Britain and great admiration for the role played by Leyds in the administration of the South African Republic.

468. Bulpin, T.V. Lost Trails of the Transvaal. Rev. ed. Cape Town: Books of Africa, 1965. 461pp. First published 1956. illus. bibl.

Covers the period of Transvaal history from 1837 to 1899. This revised edition represents the combined material from his earlier works, 'Lost Trails of the Low Veld', 'The Golden Republic', 'Storm over the Transvaal', and 'Lost Trails of the Transvaal' (1956 edition).

469. Bulpin, T.V. The Golden Republic: The Story of the South African Republic, from its Foundation until 1883. Cape Town: Books of Africa, 1953. 236pp. illus. maps. bibl.

Interesting and readable account of the early history of the South African Republic, with good descriptions and anecdotes of chiefs such as Mzilikaze, trekkers such as Hendrik Potgieter, and also of various unusual characters such as Gunn and his Highlanders.

470. Bulpin, T.V. Low Veld Trails. Cape Town: Books of Africa, 1968. 76pp. illus.

Recounts interesting anecdotes concerning places of interest in the low veld and supplies the historical background to these places.

471. Bulpin, T.V. Storm over the Transvaal. Cape Town: Books of Africa, 1955. 319pp. illus. maps. bibl.

The history of the Transvaal from 1884 to 1900 described in a readable anecdotal style. Interesting details of eccentrics and notable personages of early Johannesburg.

472. [Burgers, T.F.] Appelgryn, M.S. Thomas Francois Burgers; Staatspresident, 1872-1877. Pretoria: H.A.U.M., 1979. 283pp. illus. bibl.

Attempts to present a more sympathetic and unprejudiced description of Burgers' achievements and frustration than exists in previous historical works. Commences with Burgers' election as President of the South African Republic in 1872. Discusses the financial, economic, administrative, political and educational reforms introduced by Burgers, his policy towards the tribes of the Transvaal, and the campaign against Sekukuni. Analyses the desperate attempts made by Burgers to prevent British annexation by introducing administrative reforms into the South African Republic and the frustration of his efforts by the Volksraad. Maintains that Shepstone deliberately misled the British authorities into believing that Burgers favoured annexation. Describes Burgers' final resignation and humiliation.

473. [Burgers, T.F.] Engelbrecht, S.P. Thomas Francois Burgers: A Biography. Pretoria: J.H. de H. Bussy: Cape Town: Dusseau, 1946. 342pp.

A translation of an Afrikaans work which appeared in 1934. Based on research in the Transvaal Archives. Attempts to vindicate the policy pursued by Burgers while President of the South African Republic (1872-1880).

474. Carter, T.F. A Narrative of the Boer War; its Causes and Results. London: Remington, 1883; Cape Town: Juta, 1899. viii, 574pp.

Author attempts to discuss, impartially, the causes of the Anglo-Boer War of 1880-1881, and to describe in great detail the battles and conduct of the war. The author also evaluates the results of the war and of the Convention by which the British restored self-government to the Transvaal.

475. Cartwright, A.P., and N. Cowan. The Old Transvaal: 1834-1899. Cape Town: Purnell, 1978. 154pp. illus.

A well-illustrated brief history of the Transvaal. Contains reproductions of many early photographs of the Transvaal, dating from the second half of the nineteenth century, taken by itinerant photographers from the Cape. These include scenes from the campaign against Sekukuni, the siege of Pretoria (1880), the Battle of Majuba, early gold-mining camps and everyday life of the people. The text is written in an interesting and readable style, providing an historical background to the photographs.

476. Chilvers, H.A. Out of the Crucible: Being the Romantic Story of the Witwatersrand Goldfields; and of the Great City which arose in their Midst; and an Epilogue 1929-1948: the Incredible City by Alexander Campbell. London: Cassell, 1948. xi, 298pp. illus.

History of Johannesburg and the Witwatersrand from the 1860s to 1948, written in a simple and anecdotal style. Interesting descriptions of pioneers of Johannesburg and of daily life and events of these years.

477. Coetzee, D.J. Spoorwegontwikkeling in die Suid-Afrikaanse Republiek, 1872-1899. Cape Town: Nasionale Pers, 1940. 233pp. map. bibl.

A detailed examination of the attempts made by the South African Republic in the late nineteenth century to construct a railway network within the Transvaal, through to Delagoa Bay, in order to obtain independent access to the outside world and thus preserve independence from British control.

478. Collier, J. The Purple and the Gold: The Story of Pretoria and Johannesburg. Cape Town: Longmans, 1965. 186pp. illus. bibl.

Relates the history of Pretoria and Johannesburg from the time these two towns were founded. Written in a popular style. Interesting anecdotes given of prominent citizens who influenced the growth of the towns and also of daily life and architecture of the era.

479. Crisp, R. The Outlanders: The Men Who Made Johannesburg. London: Davies, 1964. xii, 435pp.

The story of the 'Uitlanders' is told from the discovery of gold in 1886 to the surrender of Johannesburg to Lord Roberts in 1900. The style of the book is semi-fictional and the author admits in the preface that his interpretation does not always coincide exactly with the accepted version.

480. Fitzpatrick, J.P. The Transvaal from Within: A Private Record of Public Affairs. London: Heinemann, 1900. xxvi, 364pp. map.

An attempt to present the case for the Uitlander cause in the Transvaal, as the author had served as Secretary for the Reform Committee prior to the Jameson Raid. The history of the Transvaal Republic both prior and subsequent to the first British annexation and war of 1880-1882 is discussed. The grievances of the Uitlanders, formation of the Reform Committee and failure of the Jameson Raid are described. The arrested members of the Reform Committee are shown to have been unjustly treated during their trial at Pretoria and were subject to miserable conditions in gaol. This injustice weakened Kruger's position in world opinion.

Transvaal - 1852-1899

481. [Fitzpatrick, J.P.] Cartwright, A.P. The First South African: The Life and Times of Sir Percy Fitzpatrick. Cape Town: Purnell, 1971. 256pp. illus.

   Popular biography of a prominent author, Johannesburg mining magnate, member of the Reform Committee during the Jameson Raid and member of parliament for Pretoria-East from 1910 to 1924.

482. [Fitzpatrick, J.P.] Wallis, J.P.R. Fitz: The Story of Sir Percy Fitzpatrick. London: Macmillan, 1955. xi, 278pp. illus. bibl.

   Popular biography of Fitzpatrick, in which the author pays tribute to Fitzpatrick's patriotism as one of the prime architects of the Union of South Africa, a supporter of liberal causes, and a founder of the Sundays River Settlement. Fitzpatrick worked continuously for national unity and was responsible for the erection of the Delville Wood Memorial. Fitzpatrick was also a gifted author and speaker.

483. [Fitzpatrick, J.P.] Wilson, G.M., ed. South African Memories. London: Cassell, 1932. 319pp. illus.

   Reminiscences of Fitzpatrick relating to the history of the Transvaal prior to the South African War (1899-1902). Cover subjects such as author's impressions of Rhodes, Beit, early days of diamond and gold mines, Balfour, the Battle of Colenso (1899), General J.H. de la Rey, the Jameson Raid, and Lord Cromer. Popular biography written in narrative style.

484. Garson, N.G. The Swaziland Question and the Road to the Sea 1887-1895. Archives Yearbook for South African History, Vol. 20, Part 2, 1957. Pretoria: Government Printer, 1958. pp.263-434. bibl.

   A detailed, scholarly study of negotiations between Britain and the Transvaal Republic for control of Swaziland and the area to the east between Portuguese East Africa and Zululand, as far as the sea. This area was in 1887, the Transvaal Republic's only method of expansion towards the coastline. Britain attempted to extract certain conditions from President Kruger in return for British recognition of the Transvaal's right to the disputed area. President Kruger, however, refused to join a South African commercial union as a prelude to a British sponsored closer political union. Finally, in 1894, Swaziland was ceded to the Transvaal Republic but Britain blocked any further eastward expansion by annexing the territories east of Swaziland, including Tongaland. In all these negotiations the wishes of the tribal inhabitants were disregarded.

485. Glynn, M.T. Game and Gold: Memories of over 50 years in the Lydenburg District, Transvaal. London: Dolman, 1938. 221pp. illus.

Reminiscences of a pioneer who hunted and prospected for gold at Lydenburg, Pilgrim's Rest and Sabie (1873-1925).

486. Gordon, C.T. The Growth of Boer Opposition to Kruger, 1890-1895. Cape Town: Oxford University Press, 1970. xxii, 290pp. bibl.

Traces the growth of a burgher opposition party to Kruger's rule during the years 1890 to 1895. This party was led by Commandant-General P.J. Joubert and known as the Progressive Party. The Progressive Party claimed that Kruger had illegally won the elections of 1893 and the author investigates the truth of this allegation. Discusses the issues around which opposition to Kruger coalesced; e.g., the Republic's weak financial situation, Kruger's promotion of concessions and monopolies, railway policy, administrative inefficiency, education policy, favouritism shown towards Hollanders as officials and the franchise question. The author analyses the nature of Joubert's leadership of the Progressive Party and the extent to which Joubert could be termed 'Progressive' in the modern sense of the word. Source material includes the Dutch-language papers of the Republic; e.g., 'Volksstem' and 'Land en Volk', English editions of the 'Press' and 'Weekly Press' and also the proceedings of the first and second Volksraads.

487. Grey, P.C. Eilande in die Vaal Rivier: Die Oplossing van 'n Grenskwessie tussen die Suid-Afrikaanse Republiek en die Oranje-Vrystaat, 1884-1895. Summary in English. Pretoria: University of South Africa, 1965. 62pp. maps. tabs. bibl.

Discusses the dispute between the Orange Free State and South African Republic in the late nineteenth century regarding the ownership of certain islands in the Vaal River. Describes the appointment of Island Commissions to settle the dispute (1887) and the signing of the Vaal River Island Treaty (1895) which finally determined the boundary.

488. [Jacobsz, W.H.] Duvenhage, G.D.J. Willem Hendrik Jacobsz se Rol in die Onafhanklikheid en Eenheidstrewe van die Voortrekkers op die Hoëveld, (1847-1852). Archives Yearbook for South African History, Vol. 19, Part 1, 1956. Pretoria: Government Printer, 1956. pp.159-264. maps. bibl.

Discusses the role of Jacobsz, a Voortrekker leader, in the establishment of the South African Republic. Analyses his deep mistrust of British rule during his period of office as Landdrost of Winburg and his unfavourable reaction to the British annexation of Transorangia in 1848. Describes his opposition to the armed revolt led by M.W. Pretorius at Boomplaats, which resulted in a rivalry between the two leaders. This rivalry persisted during the period 1849 to 1852, when both leaders were active in the Transvaal, and seriously

hampered the formation of a stable government within the new
Republic. However, in 1852, Britain recognised the independance of the South African Republic.

489. Jeppe, C. The Kaleidoscopic Transvaal. Cape Town: Juta, 1906.
x, 266pp.

Describes events in the Transvaal from 1870 to 1902, and is
based on the personal reminiscences of the author, who was
Consul-General of the Transvaal Republic in Cape Town.

490. Kistner, W. The Anti-slavery Agitation Against the Transvaal
Republic, 1852-1868. Archives Yearbook for South African
History, Vol. 15, Part 2, 1952. Pretoria: Government
Printer, 1952. pp.197-278. bibl.

Investigates the accusations of slavery against the Transvaal and the part they played in the relations between Great
Britain and the northern Boer Republic from 1852 to 1868.
Discusses the origin and development of British philanthropy
in the nineteenth century and the origin and development of
the Boer attitude towards the various tribes. Describes the
attitude of mutual mistrust experienced by the Boers on the
one hand and the missionaries and traders on the other.
Analyses the apprenticeship system and anti-slavery laws of
the Transvaal and the degree to which the Transvaal government
succeeded or failed to enforce obedience to its legislation.
Describes the course of the anti-slavery agitation against the
Transvaal from 1852 to 1868 and finally, the attitude of the
imperial government towards this agitation.

491. Kruger, D.W. Die Weg na die See of die Ooskus in die Boere-
Beleid voor 1877 met Besondere Verwysing na die Verhouding
tot die Portugese. Archives Yearbook for South African History, Vol. 1, Part 1, 1938. Pretoria: Government Printer,
1938. pp.33-232. bibl.

A study of the efforts of the Boer Republics to obtain in
the second half of the nineteenth century, an outlet to the
sea, which would be independent of British control. This
study covers the period 1837 to 1877. By 1838 the Portuguese
were established along the east coast of Africa. Louis
Trichardt was the first voortrekker to attempt contact with
the Portuguese at Delagoa Bay in 1837. After the British
annexation of Natal (1843), the Voortrekkers lost the opportunity to gain possession of Port Natal or Lucia Bay. The
Boers formed a Republic in north and north-eastern Transvaal.
A.H. Potgieter attempted in 1844 to establish contact with
the Portuguese at Delagoa Bay. These efforts were continued
by President M.W. Pretorius and President Burgers. These
efforts ended temporarily with Shepstone's annexation of the
Transvaal in 1877.

492. Kruger, S.J.P. The Memoirs of Paul Kruger: Four Times President of the South African Republic. New York: Century Co., 1902. xiii, 444pp. front.

Based upon the memoirs dictated by Kruger to his private secretary, H.C. Bredell and to Piet Grobler, former Under Secretary of State of the South African Republic.

493. [Kruger, S.J.P.] Changuion, L., ed. Foto Biografie: Paul Kruger, 1852-1904. Johannesburg: Perskor, 1973. 229pp. illus.

A photographic and pictorial record of the life of Paul Kruger, from the years 1825 to his death in 1904. Each illustration is annotated, but there is no accompanying text.

494. [Kruger, S.J.P.] Du Plessis, J.S., comp. President Kruger aan die Woord: Verkiesings Manifeste, Intreeredes en Toespraake van President S.J.P. Kruger. Bloemfontein: Sacum, 1952. 157pp. illus.

A selection of Kruger's public speeches which contain the essence of his political beliefs. These are divided into election manifestos, inaugural speeches, parliamentary debates, and public addresses. They cover the years 1881 to 1898.

495. [Kruger, S.J.P.] Engelbrecht, S.P., ed. Paul Kruger's Amptelike Briewe, 1851-1877. Pretoria: Volkstem, 1925. 226pp.

Consists of the correspondence of Paul Kruger between the years 1851 to 1877. The letters are preceded by an introduction providing an historical background to the correspondence. The correspondence consists of official letters which Kruger wrote in his capacity as Commandant-General of the South African Republic.

496. [Kruger, S.J.P.] Fisher, J. Paul Kruger: His Life and Times. London: Secker & Warburg, 1974. 278pp. illus. bibl.

Interesting, popular biography of Kruger which is well-documented and provides a clear description of personalities and events of the second half of the nineteenth century.

497. [Kruger, S.J.P.] Juta, M. The Pace of the Ox: The Life of Paul Kruger. London: Constable, 1937. xiii, 338pp. illus. maps. bibl.

Popular biography of Kruger written in a narrative style. Contains many anecdotes regarding Kruger's early life and period of office as President of the South African Republic.

498. [Kruger, S.J.P.] Meintjes, J. President Paul Kruger: A Biography. London: Cassell, 1974. 295pp. illus. bibl.

Popular biography of Kruger in which the author attempts to present an unbiased description of the main character whom he contends has hitherto been the subject of both vilification and idolatry.

499. [Kruger, S.J.P.] Nathan, M. Paul Kruger: His Life and Times.
Durban: Knox, 1941. 510pp. illus. bibl.
Popular readable biography.

500. [Kruger, S.J.P.] Smit, F.P. Die Staatsopvattinge van Paul
Kruger. Pretoria: Van Schaik, 1951. xi, 210pp. illus.
bibl.

A survey of Kruger's political philosophy, mainly deduced
from his speeches, covering a period of twenty-five years.
The following aspects are covered: Kruger's religious principles, his concepts of republicanism, the rights of the
individual, racial policy, the vote, political unity, the
duties of parliament, the executive council, the duty of the
president and the judiciary.

501. [Kruger, S.J.P.] Steenkamp, A.J. Die Lewe van President
S.J.P. Kruger: 'n Bibliografie. Stellenbosch: University
of Stellenbosch, 1969. 15pp.

502. [Kruger, S.J.P.] Uys, C.J. Paul Kruger: Van die Wieg tot die
Graf, 'n Studie om Vas te Stel waar die President Gebore is,
Met 'n Hoofstuk oor Wanopvattings omtrent sy Lewe en Werk.
Cape Town: Balkema, 1955. 75pp. illus. map. bibl.

Author attempts to establish the correct birthplace of Paul
Kruger and refutes the belief that Kruger was born at Bulhoek,
near Steynsburg. Also attempts to refute certain myths and
misconceptions regarding Kruger's life and career; e.g.,
Kruger is falsely credited with having participated in the
Battle of Vegkop in 1836, at the age of eleven. Also maintains
that President Kruger's final message to the Afrikaans nation
was drawn up by Dr. W.J. Leyds. Kruger was unjustly accused
of having deserted the Transvaal commandos against Sekukuni in
1876, because of a personal vendetta against President Burgers.
A further misconception regarding Kruger is that he deliberately provoked Britain into declaring war in 1899 on the South
African Republic. He was misled by his advisers, particularly
F.W. Reitz.

503. Leonard, C. Papers on the Political Situation in South Africa,
1885-1895 with Papers by Advocate Wessels and Advocate Auret.
London: Arthur Humphreys, 1903. 469pp.

Consists of various pamphlets and other papers compiled by
the English political association known as the Empire League,
by Charles Leonard himself and extracts from various newspapers, public addresses and petitions, all relating to
grievances of the Uitlanders in the Transvaal between 1885-
1895. Leonard prepared a statement on the position of the Uitlanders in the Transvaal for the Committee of the House of
Commons, gave evidence before a select Committee on British
South Africa, 1897 and issued a Manifesto in May, 1897, on
behalf of the Uitlanders. The volume concludes with the report
of the Select Committee on the Jameson Raid (July, 1897).

504. Leyds, G.A. A History of Johannesburg: The Early Years. Cape Town: Nasionale Pers, 1964. 318pp. illus. bibl.

   Account of early Johannesburg based on the reminiscences of a pioneer of 1892, nephew of Dr. W.J. Leyds, Kruger's adviser. Provides descriptions of events such as the discovery of gold and the Jameson Raid, of notable personalities of the period and of famous landmarks within the city. Also describes local administration of the city, including the period of Milner's 'kindergarten'.

505. Leyds, W.J. The First Annexation of the Transvaal. London: Fisher Unwin, 1906. xxiii, 378pp. map.

   Deals firstly with the early relations of the Boers and British government; i.e., the first and second British annexations of the Cape. Attempts to show that the Boer resentment of Britain was built up through centuries of British injustice, factors which led to the Great Trek and establishment of the Orange Free State and South African Republic. Part 2 deals with the British annexation of the South African Republic. Here again the case is presented in favour of the Boers and against Britain. The author attempts to strengthen his case against Britain by quoting from British authorities, Blue Books, and reports and despatches to demonstrate the authenticity of claims of British injustice.

506. Leyds, W.J. The Transvaal Surrounded: A Continuation of 'The First Annexation of the Transvaal'. London: Fisher Unwin, 1919. xiii, 603pp. maps.

   Attempts to prove that the British government had no intensions of adhering to the London Convention of 1884 and made every effort to interfere with the independence of the South African Republic by encircling it with a barrier of British territory. Zululand, Bechuanaland, Swaziland, Amatongaland, Matabeleland and Mashonaland all came under British domination.

507. Livingstone, D. David Livingstone: South African Papers, 1849-1853. ed. by I. Schapera. Cape Town: Van Riebeeck Society, 1974. 187pp. illus. map. bibl. (Van Riebeeck Society Publications, 2nd Series, No. 5).

   Contains a selection of Livingstone's writings on South African racial and missionary affairs with supplementary material. The first two articles, published in the 'Banner' in 1849, were entitled 'The Peacemakers of the Interior of South Africa'. In these, Livingstone denounces the policy of the Transvaal Boers towards the tribes of the Transvaal. 'The Story of the Black Pot' concerns a further dispute between Livingstone and the Transvaal Boers. Livingstone further denounces the Boers in his correspondence to the Lt.-Governor and the Secretary of State for the Colonies regarding the sack of Kolobeng. 'The South African Boers and Slavery', 'Missions in South Africa' and 'Missionaries and Trade' are the three remaining topics discussed by Livingstone. Each of the articles appearing in the volume is fully annotated by the editor, who also provides the historical background to the events described in the articles and discusses the validity of Livingstone's assertions.

508. MacDonald, T. Transvaal Story. Cape Town: Timmins, 1961. 252pp. illus.

    Personal reminiscences of a newspaper reporter who writes in anecdotal style of various towns in the Transvaal such as Potchefstroom, Pietersburg and Pilgrim's Rest. In each case, the history of these places is discussed.

509. [Nellmapius, A.H.] Kaye, H. The Tycoon and the President: The Life and Times of Alois Hugo Nellmapius, 1847-1893. Johannesburg: Macmillan, 1978. 120pp. illus. bibl.

    An account of the life of the adventurer, Nellmapius, who made his first fortune at Pilgrim's Rest and Mac Mac and pioneered the wagon road from the Portuguese border to Pilgrim's Rest. He became one of the first industrialists in the South African Republic and a friend of President Kruger who granted him various concessions. He died bankrupt.

510. Nixon, J. The Complete Story of the Transvaal from the Great Trek to the Convention of London. London: Sampson Low, 1885. xx, 372pp. map.

    This account is written by a British subject resident in the Transvaal during the years 1877 to 1884. In describing the war of 1880 to 1882, the writer is able to supply a first-hand account of events. However, his account is biased because he is filled with indignation towards the actions of Gladstone's government and the manner in which the military engagements were carried out.

511. Preller, G.S. Die Grobler-Moord; Historiese Rekonstruksie van die Opkoms en Ondergang van die Matabele Dinastie. Pretoria: Noordelike Drukpers, 1930. 2v. illus. bibl.

    Discusses the rise to power of the Matabele under their chiefs Mzilikaze and Lobengula in the area north of the Limpopo. Describes the circumstances leading to the death of Transvaal Consul Piet Grobler in British Bechuanaland in 1888 and denounces the attempt of the administrator of British Bechuanaland, Sir Sidney Shippard, to absolve the Bamangwatos of guilt in treacherously attacking Grobler. Lord Knutsford, British Colonial Secretary, set aside Shippard's biased decision and ordered Khama to pay an annual pension to Grobler's widow as compensation. President Kruger suspected British complicity in the murder of Grobler in order to prevent South African Republic gaining a concession from Lobengula before the Rhodes concession could be finalised. Descriptions are given of Britain's aggressive policy with regard to Swaziland, Rhodes' ambitions in Bechuanaland and Matabeleland and the establishment of a Chartered Company in Rhodesia. Concludes by discussing the Matabele rebellion of 1896.

512. Schreuder, D.M. Gladstone and Kruger: Liberal Government and Colonial 'Home Rule', 1880-1885. London: Routledge & Kegan Paul, 1969. 558pp. illus. bibl.

A study of the attempts of the British Liberal party to preserve the imperial connection in South Africa in the face of growing Afrikaner nationalism during the first Anglo-Boer War (1880-1881), particularly following the Battle of Majuba. Gladstone decided to pursue a conciliatory policy in South Africa and in Ireland and introduce qualified self-government; i.e., 'Home Rule'. The Pretoria Convention of 1881 was an attempt to retain suzerainty over the Transvaal and at the same time to grant limited self-government to the Boers. The London Convention (1884) was deliberately vague on the question of British suzerainty and thus sowed the seeds of future confusion and discord in South African politics. Other threats to British supremacy in South Africa were the ambitions of Germany in South West Africa and the rise of the Afrikaner Bond under Hofmeyr at the Cape.

513. South Africa. State Archives. South African Archival Records, Transvaal, nos. 1-7: Notule van die Volksraad van die Suid-Afrikaanse Republiek ... 1844-1868. ed. by J.H. Breytenbach, H.S. Pretorius and D.C. Joubert. Cape Town: Government Printer, 1949-1966. 7v.

Minutes of the Volksraad of the South African Republic, with annexures.

514. Stals, E.L.P., ed. Afrikaners in die Goudstad. Cape Town: H.A.U.M., 1978. 207pp. illus. bibl.

Part 1 has been completed and covers the period 1886-1924. The author is J.J. Fourie. The aim of the series is to present a comprehensive account of the history of the Afrikaans community of the Witwatersrand. The pastoral activities of the Afrikaner prior to 1886 are discussed, as is the role of the Afrikaner in the discovery of gold and in the establishment of the mining industry and the political, educational, religious, social and cultural contributions of the Afrikaner to the growth of the Johannesburg community.

515. Struben, C. Vein of Gold. Cape Town: Balkema, 1957. 190pp. illus.

Memoirs of Charles Struben, son of Henry Struben. Interesting descriptions of life in Pretoria from 1877 to 1887 and of political events in South Africa in the first half of the twentieth century. A popular biography.

516. Struben, H.W. Recollections of Adventures: Pioneering and Development in South Africa, 1850-1911. Cape Town: Maskew Miller, 1920. 208pp.

Reminiscences of one of the first English pioneers in the Transvaal, written in old age and edited by his daughter, Edith Struben. Informal, narrative style.

517. Tingay, P., and J. Johnson. Transvaal Epic. Howick: Khenty Press, 1978. 195pp. illus. bibl.

A brief and well-illustrated survey of Transvaal history from the beginning of the nineteenth century to 1910.

517a. Van Onselen, C. Studies in the Social and Economic History of the Witwatersrand 1886-1914. Johannesburg: Ravan Press, 1982. 2v. illus. maps. bibl. Volume 1 sub-titled 'New Babylon'. Volume 2 sub-titled 'New Nineveh'.

A study of the poorer classes of the Witwatersrand during the period 1886-1914. Volume 1 describes the social conditions of the miners, liquor sellers, prostitutes and cab drivers. Volume 2 is concerned with the daily existence of the domestic servants, Afrikaner working classes and Black proletariat. The ruling capitalist class gradually asserted control over all sections of the population and influenced every aspect of their existence.

518. Van Rooyen, T.S. Die Verhoudinge tussen die Boere, Engelse en Naturelle in die Geskiedenis van die Oos-Transvaal tot 1882. (Doctoral Thesis. University of Pretoria). Archives Yearbook for South African History. Vol. 14, Part 1, 1951. Pretoria: Government Printer, 1951. xi, 391pp. bibl.

Attempts to demonstrate that the history of the eastern Transvaal between 1845 and 1876, was largely the history of the relationships between the Boer farmers on the one hand, and the Pedi and Zulu nations on the other. This confrontation led to frequent conflicts. Maintains that Britain annexed the Transvaal at a critical stage in this conflict (1880), and inherited the problems of dealing with Zulu and Pedi nationalism. Discusses the weak political position of the Boer farmers at this period and maintains that their lack of unity was due to differences among the various leaders, which only disappeared after the annexation of the Transvaal by Britain. Also discusses the role of the Berlin Missionary Society in the eastern Transvaal prior to 1882.

519. Van Zyl, M.C. Die Protesbeweging van die Transvaalse Afrikaners (1877-1880). Pretoria: Academica, 1979. 212pp. illus. bibl.

Traces the origins and growth of the Afrikaner protest movement in the Transvaal which resulted from the annexation of South African Republic in April 1877 and culminated in the War of Independence of 1880 to 1881. Describes the difficulties faced by Shepstone in the administration of the Transvaal; the departure of the first and second deputations of Boer Leaders to London (April 1877 and May 1878 respectively) to protest against the annexation and the role played by Sir Bartle Frere, Garnet Wolseley and Lanyon in the further disillusionment of the Afrikaners towards British rule. Concludes with the outbreak of hostilities and re-establishment of the republican government in December, 1880.

520. Younghusband, F. South Africa of To-day. London: Macmillan, 1898. xii, 177pp. illus.

Account of a visit to South Africa from December, 1895 to December, 1896 by a correspondent of 'The Times'. Describes a visit to the Transvaal, the Jameson Raid and the economic, social and political conditions generally prevailing in the South African Republic. The author also visited Rhodesia just after the conclusion of the Matabele war and he discusses the war and conditions in Rhodesia. Describes the problems caused by Indian immigration to Natal. Concludes by analysing the various tensions building up between English and Afrikaans sections of the population in South Africa. Considers that Britain should abstain from interfering in affairs of the Transvaal, and should seek only to protect the rights of British citizens in the Transvaal. Britain should also attempt to conciliate Afrikaners in the Cape, Natal and the Free State.

TRANSVAAL WAR OF INDEPENDENCE, 1880-1881

Bibliography

521. Jordan, R.A. The Transvaal War 1880-1881. Johannesburg: University of the Witwatersrand, Department of Bibliography, Librarianship and Typography, 1969. 73pp.

Monographs

522. Bellairs, B. St. J., ed. The Transvaal War, 1880-1881. Edinburgh: Blackwood, 1885. xxiv, 491pp. illus. map. facs. repr. Cape Town: Struik, 1972.

An account of the causes of the Anglo-Boer War of 1880-1881, and of the main events of the war. The author is very sympathetic to the Boer cause and ascribes the war to a 'too great eagerness to carry out a federation scheme'. The causes of the war are discussed at great length. The work also describes various battles and military engagements and events following the armistice and peace settlement. Lady Bellairs, although the wife of a British soldier (Brigadier-General Bellairs), is critical of British imperialism in South Africa and concludes that South Africans should be allowed complete control over their internal affairs.

Transvaal War - 1880-1881

523. Breytenbach, J.H. Majuba Gedenkboek: Uitgegee ter Herdenking van die Boere se Stryd ter Verkryging van hul Onafhanklikheid 'n Eeu Gelede. Roodepoort: Cum Books, 1980. 226pp. illus. maps.

    A richly illustrated volume issued to commemorate the centenary of the Battle of Majuba. Designed for popular reading.

524. Clark, G.B. British Policy Towards the Boers. London: William Ridgway, 1881. 56pp.

    Compiled by the secretary of the Transvaal Independence Committee. An attempt to present the grievances of the Boers of the Transvaal engaged in the first War of Independence against Britain. Refutes the statement of Sir Bartle Frere that Kruger and Jorissen agreed to the British annexation of the Transvaal. Summarizes events leading to the annexation up to the outbreak of war in 1880.

525. Davey, A.M. The Siege of Pretoria, 1880-1881. (M.A. Thesis. University of South Africa). Archives Yearbook for South African History. Vol. 19, Part I, 1956. Pretoria: Government Printer, 1957. pp.269-316. bibl.

    Describes the Boer siege of Pretoria during the first Anglo-Boer War. The British garrison within the town was assisted by English speaking volunteers. Maintains that the strategy of this siege was repeated by the Boer leaders Erasmus, Schoeman, Cronjé and Joubert during the second Anglo-Boer War (1899-1902) during the sieges of Ladysmith, Mafeking and Pretoria. However, these tactics were by now out-dated and did not result in the same degree of success.

526. Duxbury, G.R. David and Goliath: The First War of Independence, 1880-1881. Johannesburg: South African National Museum of Military History, 1981. 90pp. illus. maps. bibl.

    A commemorative volume of the centenary of the Transvaal War of Independence, 1880-1881. The emphasis is placed on descriptions of battles and sieges which took place during the war.

527. Lehmann, J.H. The First Boer War. London: Jonathan Cape, 1972. 330pp. illus. bibl.

    A detailed description of the first Boer War (1880-1881), commencing with the annexation of the Transvaal by Britain (1877). The effects of the war are discussed, particularly as regards the influence of the first Boer War on events leading up to the second Anglo-Boer War and also on military strategy pursued by the Boers during the second Anglo-Boer War (1899-1902).

528. Norris-Newman, C.L. With the Boers in the Transvaal and Orange Free State in 1880-1881. London: Allen, 1882. xxi, 359pp.

Traces briefly the early development of the Cape Colony, the events of the Great Trek, the establishment of Boer Republics, Orange Free State and Transvaal and the British annexation of the Transvaal (1877). Describes events leading to the Transvaal War of 1880-1881. The author recounts his experiences as special war correspondent, attached to the Boer army. Describes the Battle of Amajuba and various battles within the Transvaal. The book concludes immediately prior to the ratification of the Peace Convention by the Volksraad.

529. Ransford, O. The Battle of Majuba Hill; the first Boer War. London: John Murray, 1967. ix, 154pp. illus. maps. bibl.

A very detailed account of events leading up to the Battle of Majuba Hill (February 1881) and of the battle itself. The participants in the battle and the consequences of the British defeat are carefully analysed.

530. Van Jaarsveld, F.A., A.P.J. van Rensburg and W.A. Stals, eds. Die Eerste Vryheidsoorlog: Van Verset en Geweld tot Skikking deur Onderhandeling 1877-1884. Pretoria: H.A.U.M., 1980. 282pp. illus. bibl.

Essays compiled to commemorate the centenary of the Battle of Majuba. The contributors consist mainly of post-graduate students and members of the history department of the University of Pretoria. Essays deal chronologically with the origins of the Transvaal War of Independence, the conduct of the war, the peace settlement and the rise of Afrikaner nationalism.

531. [Wood, H.E.] Williams, C. The Life of Lieutenant-General Sir Henry Evelyn Wood. London: Sampson Low, Marston, 1892. vi, 309pp. front.

Wood's period of service in the British army in Zululand (1879) and during the first Anglo-Boer War (1881) is described in Chapters 5 and 6. During the first Anglo-Boer War, after Colley's death, Wood became Major-General of the British army and High Commissioner. Attempts to vindicate Wood of all charges of cowardice and neglect during the course of the war, maintaining that Wood was overridden by the policy of Gladstone, who desired peace at all costs with the Boers.

DISCOVERY OF GOLD IN THE TRANSVAAL, 1886-1899

Bibliographies

532. Bischoff, L.R. The Search for Gold in South Africa from 1842-1872. Johannesburg: University of the Witwatersrand, Department of Bibliography, Librarianship and Typography, 1970. 22pp.

533. Watts, B.H. Gold-mining in the Eastern Transvaal; A Bibliography. Cape Town: University of Cape Town School of Librarianship, 1955. vi, 26pp.

Monographs

534. Cartwright, A.P. The Corner House: The Early History of Johannesburg. Cape Town: Purnell, 1965. xvii, 293pp. illus.

Deals with the period 1866-1910 in the formation of the gold mining industry and particularly the part played by the Rand Mines and Central Mining and Investment Corporation.

535. Cartwright, A.P. The Gold Miners. Cape Town: Purnell, 1962. 339pp. illus.

Account of the history of gold mining in South Africa from 1886 to 1959. Interesting descriptions of various personalities involved in the gold mining industry.

536. Cartwright, A.P. Gold Paved the Way: The Story of the Gold Fields Group of Companies. London: Macmillan, 1967. x, 326pp. illus. map.

The history of the Gold Fields Company commenced with the arrival of Rudd and Rhodes on the Witwatersrand in July 1886. The Company was registered in February, 1887, and prospered until the events of the Jameson Raid and Anglo-Boer War. The fortunes of the Company declined until the 1930s when South Africa went off the gold standard, and West Witwatersrand Area Limited was launched as a new mine. After the second World War, the Company became a world-wide organization.

537. Cartwright, A.P. Golden Age: The Story of the Industrialization of South Africa and the Part Played in it by the Corner House Group of Companies, 1910-1967. Cape Town: Purnell, 1968. xviii, 363pp. illus.

A sequel to 'The Corner House', (entry 534). A continuation of the history of the Central Mining and Rand Mines Companies to the year 1967.

538. Cartwright, A.P. Valley of Gold. Cape Town: Timmins, 1961. 194pp. illus.

Account of the discovery of gold at Pilgrim's Rest in the 1870s. Written in a popular, readable style.

539. Consolidated Gold Fields of South Africa Ltd. The Gold Fields 1887-1937. London: Consolidated Gold Fields, 1937. 185pp. illus.

A history of the company from the time of its foundation in 1887. The biography of Cecil Rhodes is given and also the circumstances which led to the company's formation. The company's achievements up to the year 1937 are discussed. There are also notes on subsidiary companies: 'Robinson Deep', 'Simmer and Jack Mines', 'Knights Deep', 'Sub Nigel', 'Gold Fields Deep', 'Luipaards Vlei Estate and Gold Mining Company' and 'Rietfontein Consolidated'.

540. Emden, P.H. Randlords. London: Hodder & Stoughton, 1935. 368pp. illus. bibl.

A description of the period from the end of the 1860s to the late 1890s, when the mining magnates became prominent due to the discovery of diamonds and gold in South Africa. The formation of De Beers Amalgamated Mines is discussed. The careers of Rhodes, Robinson, Beit, Lionel Phillips, members of the Corner House group and other prominent Rand mine owners and speculators are described. The speculative boom of 1895 and the subsequent crisis on the stock exchange are analysed. There are useful supplementary notes at the end of the text.

541. Gray, J. Payable Gold; an Intimate Record of the History of the Discovery of the Payable Witwatersrand Goldfields and of Johannesburg in 1886 and 1887. Johannesburg: Central News Agency, 1937. 286pp. illus. maps.

Based on research in the State Archives, Pretoria, where extracts were made from approximately two thousand documents concerning the discovery of the auriferous conglomerates of the Witwatersrand. Sources of information consist of correspondence of the State Secretary, resolution of the Executive Council and official notices and proclamations published in the 'Government Gazette', correspondence of Landdrosts of Pretoria, Heidelberg and Potchefstroom, records of the Mining Commissioner of the Witwatersrand goldfields and early newspapers. The period of discovery of gold discussed in the book covers the years 1850 to 1887. Forms a valuable source of information for the period and contains many quotations from original documents.

542. Gray, J., and E. Gray. A History of the Discovery of the Witwatersrand Goldfields. Johannesburg: Privately published, 1940. 198pp. illus.

A sequel to the author's volume 'Payable Gold'. Based on the examination of photographed records in the Transvaal

Discovery of Gold - 1886-1899

Archives, Pretoria and archival records of the Mining Commissioner of Johannesburg, the Supreme Court, Pretoria, and the Registrar of Mining Titles, Johannesburg. The various pioneers of gold discovery are discussed including the Strubens, George Harrison and George Walker. Extracts are reproduced from various official documents regarding these early discoveries and claims.

543. Jacobson, D. Fifty Golden Years of the Rand, 1886-1936. London: Faber, 1936. 206pp. illus. map.

Describes the history of the Rand, the technical aspects of mining, geology of the reefs and methods of modern mining. There are chapters on the administration of the mines and the rise and growth of Johannesburg.

544. Jeppe, C.B. Gold Mining on the Witwatersrand. Johannesburg: Transvaal Chamber of Mines, 1946. 2v. illus. maps. bibl.

Chapter 1 contains a survey of the history of gold mining on the Witwatersrand. The remainder of the two volumes is devoted to methods used in the mining of gold.

545. Kubicek, R. Economic Imperialism in Theory and Practice: The Case of South African Gold Mining Finance, 1886-1914. Durham: Duke University Press, 1979. 239pp. maps. charts. tabs. bibl.

A study of late nineteenth century economic imperialism. The author examines the capital flow from Europe into the gold industry, the strategies adopted by the mining promoters to encourage investment in South African mines and the administrative structure of each mining house. The larger mining houses such as the Corner House organization were development orientated. Others such as the smaller less reputable firms combined a development function with intensive speculative operations. The fringe operators such as Abe Bailey were simply speculators with very little actual gold production. The London stock market, the Paris private banks and the German corporate banks all actively provided capital or speculated in gold shares.

546. Letcher, O. The Gold Mines of Southern Africa: The History, Technology and Statistics of the Gold Industry. Johannesburg: The Author, 1936. 580pp. illus. maps. bibl.

Published on the fiftieth anniversary of the city of Johannesburg and of the proclamation of the Witwatersrand. Traces the presence of gold in Africa to ancient times and describes the development of mines in South Africa to the end of 1935. In the second section, gold fields other than those of the Transvaal are described, from the Cape Province to the Equator. The third section is devoted to a description of Johannesburg and Reef townships. The fourth section covers the gold mining industry and its administration. Appendices contain statistical tables and various miscellaneous items of information; e.g., the Tati goldfields; the Sterkfontein Junction Syndicate.

547. Preller, G.S., ed. Argonauts of the Rand: Story of the Discovery of the Main Reef, with the Marais Diary. Pretoria: Wallachs, 1935. 200pp. illus.

Attempts to trace historically the earliest gold discoveries in the Transvaal, particularly as regards the Witwatersrand Main Reef. Also supplies information regarding the discoveries of an early prospector, Pieter Jacob Marais, accompanied by extracts from Marais' diary.

548. Reunert, T. Diamonds and Gold in South Africa. Cape Town: Juta, 1893. xvi, 242pp. illus. maps.

For description see entry 264.

549. Rosenthal, E. Gold Bricks and Mortar: 60 Years of Johannesburg History. Johannesburg: Printing House, 1946. 186pp. illus.

The events that led to the discovery of gold on the Witwatersrand, descriptions of pioneers of the Rand and anecdotes of early Johannesburg are told in a simple style for the general reader.

550. Rosenthal, E. Gold! Gold! Gold! The Johannesburg Gold Rush. London: Macmillan, 1970. 372pp. illus. Repr. Johannesburg: Donker, 1979.

A readable account of the discovery of gold on the Witwatersrand from 1850 to 1902. Describes the arrival of the gold prospectors, the growth of Johannesburg and the effects of the growth of gold companies and 'Uitlander' demands for the franchise, on the politics of the South African Republic. Concludes with the Anglo-Boer War of 1899-1902.

JAMESON RAID, 1896

Bibliography

551. Moggridge, C.A. The Jameson Raid, An Annotated Bibliography. Cape Town: University of Cape Town, School of Librarianship, 1962. v, 38pp.

Monographs

552. Butler, J. The Liberal Party and the Jameson Raid. Oxford: Clarendon Press, 1968. xii, 336pp. map. bibl.

Attempts to explain in detail and describe the reactions of Liberal statesmen to the situation following the Jameson Raid.

Based on a study of private collections left behind by various statesmen. The leader of the Liberal Party, Sir William Harcourt strongly condemned the Jameson Raid and insisted on an inquiry into its origin. The South African Committee of 1897 failed to investigate properly the part played by officials and by Joseph Chamberlain. However, the Liberal opposition did not attempt to pursue the matter further. The author discusses the motives and reasons for the restraint exercised by the Liberals and also discusses the central problem of the distinction between public and private knowledge which influenced Chamberlain's actions in regard to the Raid and which was a distinction equally understood by the Liberal opposition.

553. Danziger, C. The Jameson Raid. Cape Town: Macdonald, 1978. 24pp. illus. maps. (Looking at South African History).

    A concise account of the Jameson Raid which would be suitable for high school students. Has no bibliography.

554. Garrett, E., and E.J. Edwards. The Story of an African Crisis. Westminster: Constable, 1897. xxxi, 308pp. illus.

    An attempt to present the truth about the Jameson Raid and to determine how far Chamberlain and Rhodes were involved in the planning of the Raid. The events leading up to the Raid, the Raid itself and the results of the Raid are described in great detail.

555. Hole, H.M. The Jameson Raid. London: P. Allan, 1930. xiii, 306pp. illus.

    An account of the Raid written by a former private secretary to Jameson (1891-1893) who became a Civil Commissioner of Bulawayo. A detailed analysis of the events of the Raid, the motives of its leaders particularly Jameson and the consequences of the Raid for Jameson and Rhodes.

556. [Jameson, L.S.] Colvin, I. The Life of Jameson. London: Edward Arnold, 1923. 2v. illus. map.

    Interesting, detailed biography. Lacks a bibliography.

557. Longford, E. Jameson's Raid: The Prelude to the Boer War. Johannesburg: Jonathan Ball, 1960. 2nd ed., 1982. 314pp. illus. bibl.

    Detailed account of the Jameson Raid written in a popular readable style. Interesting descriptions are given of prominent people who participated in the planning and execution of the Raid and the author attempts to speculate on the degree of their involvement.

558. Pakenham, E. Jameson's Raid. London: Weidenfeld and Nicolson, 1960. 366pp. map. bibl.

    Investigates the mystery surrounding the Jameson Raid in order to determine how far the British government was involved, and how much encouragement Rhodes and Jameson had from the Colonial Secretary, Joseph Chamberlain.

559. Rhoodie, D. Conspirators in Conflict: A Study of the Johannesburg Reform Committee and its Role in the Conspiracy against the South African Republic. Cape Town: Tafelberg, 1967. 142pp. illus. bibl.

In describing the events of the Jameson Raid, the author makes use of hitherto unpublished documents belonging to the papers of Joseph Chamberlain, Sir Graham Bower and Charles Leonard. Bower, the Imperial Secretary, suppressed vital evidence in order to protect the High Commissioner, Sir Hercules Robinson. Leonard, chairman of the National Union, shielded Rhodes' conspirators in Johannesburg. The new evidence makes it clear that Rhodes and Chamberlain entered into conspiracy against the South African Republic and used the National Union of Uitlanders as an instrument for their conspiracy. The majority of the members of the Reform Committee had nothing to do with the conspiracy. Leonard was duped by false promises from Rhodes.

560. Van der Poel, J. The Jameson Raid. London: Oxford University Press, 1951. viii, 271pp. map. bibl.

An account of the Jameson Raid based on the papers of Sir Graham Bower, Sir James Rose Innes and Joseph Chamberlain.

CHAPTER IX
POLITICAL ASPECTS OF RAILWAY DEVELOPMENT INTO THE INTERIOR

Bibliographies

561. Buckland, M.V. South African Railways before 1910: A Bibliography. Cape Town: University of Cape Town, School of Librarianship, 1964. x, 79pp.

562. Pirie, G.H. Transport Development in Southern Africa. Monticello, Illinois: Vance Bibliographies, 1982. 19pp. (Public Administration Series Bibliography, p-953).

Monographs

563. Van der Poel, J. Railway and Customs Policies in South Africa, 1855-1910. London: Longmans Green, 1933. 151pp. map. bibl.

The author contends that the development of South African railways between 1885 and 1910 was closely linked with political developments of the period. The independent South African states regarded the railways as a source of revenue through the imposition of rates and as a means of furthering conflicting political aims. The railways were the only links between high-duty ports and valuable inland markets. As such they became an important factor in political inter-state rivalries, particularly in the case of the attempts of Rhodes, prime minister of the Cape, to isolate the Transvaal Republic from coastal ports.

564. Weinthal, E. The Story of the Cape to Cairo Railway and River Route, 1887-1922. London: Pioneer Publishing Co., 1932. 4v. illus. maps.

Covers many aspects of this monumental enterprise. Volumes 1 and 2 are relevant to South Africa. Vol. 1: Life and work of the founder of the route, C.J. Rhodes, the story of the Cape to Cairo Scheme, profiles of thirty-seven Cape to Cairo pioneers, story of the ox-wagon, old coaching days and motor cars, financial aspects and the influence of diamonds and gold discoveries on the route. Vol. 2: Describes route sections.

CHAPTER X
ANGLO-BOER WAR, 1899-1902
General History

Bibliographies

565. Kesting, J.G. The Anglo-Boer War, 1899-1902 [of overseas Magazine Contributions published January-December, 1899]: A Bibliography. Cape Town: University of Cape Town, School of Librarianship, 1956. xii, 51pp.

566. Male, D. South African War, 1899-1902: A Bibliography. F.L.A. Thesis. London: Library Association, 1974. Unpublished.

Monographs

567. Amery, L.S., ed. The Times History of the War in South Africa. 7v. London: Sampson Low, Marston, 1900-1909. illus. maps. bibl.

This was one of the first very detailed and comprehensive accounts to appear concerning the Anglo-Boer War. The editor admits that he is unable to be entirely impartial in describing events and that his sympathies are with the British. An attempt has been made to use reputable sources such as the writings of various pro-Transvaal writers, viz., Dr. Jorissen, J.F. van Oordt, as well as pro-British authors Flora Shaw, H. Rider Haggard and Percy Fitzpatrick. Blue Book material, correspondence, telegrams and material drawn from the press; e.g., the 'Staatscourant' of 1881 have been used. There are also various appendices and a detailed index.

568. Breytenbach, J.H., ed. Gedenkalbum van die Tweede Vryheidsoorlog. Cape Town: Nasionale Pers, 1949. xii, 604pp. illus.

Issued to commemorate the fiftieth anniversary of the outbreak of the Anglo-Boer War (1899-1902). Consists of fifty-one essays dealing with personalities connected with the war, events leading to the war, military campaigns, the Treaty of Vereeniging and foreign diplomacy during the war. Articles reflect the Afrikaner point of view. Interesting illustrations consisting of reproductions of photographs from archival sources.

Anglo-Boer War, 1899-1902 - General History

569. Breytenbach, J.H. Die Geskiedenis van die Tweede Vryheidsoorlog in Suid-Afrika, 1899-1902. Pretoria: Government Printer, 1969-1977. 4v. illus. maps. bibl.

   Important and comprehensive history of the Anglo-Boer War based on original sources drawn from state archives.

570. Creswicke, L. South Africa and the Transvaal War. Edinburgh: T.C. & E.C. Jack, 1900-1902. 7v. illus. maps.

   A very detailed history of the Anglo-Boer War, commencing with a brief description of the Cape Colony Boers, the Great Trek and the establishment of Boer Republics in Natal and subsequently in the Transvaal. The events leading up to the war of 1899 are described and finally the war itself. The writer represents the British point of view and shows intense dislike of the Boers. The descriptions of battles are very detailed but suffer from the author's patriotic prejudices and emotions.

571. Farwell, B. The Great Anglo-Boer War. New York: Harper & Row; London: Allen, 1976. 495pp. illus. maps. bibl.

   Traces the origins and events leading to the Anglo-Boer War. Describes the events of the war in great detail, the major battles, guerrilla warfare and the concentration camps. Credits Milner with effective post-war reconstruction, but his growing unpopularity among all sections of the post-war population led to his downfall. Concludes with the entry of South Africa into the 1914-1918 war.

572. Holt, E. The Boer War. London: Putnam, 1958. 319pp. illus. maps. bibl.

   A readable, concise and interesting account of the Boer War. The events covered are from the Battle of Majuba in 1881 to the end of the Boer War in 1902.

573. Judd, D. The Boer War. London: Hart-Davis, MacGibbon, 1977. 186pp. illus. maps. (British at War Series; ed. by Ludovic Kennedy).

   Brief, well-illustrated survey of the Boer War, designed for the non-specialist reader. Contains various extracts from diaries of the period; e.g., Sol Plaatje, Christiaan de Wet, and Dr. Alec Kay. Readable, interesting style.

574. Kriel, C. Rondom die Anglo-Boereoorlog, 1899-1902. Johannesburg: Perskor, 1979. 208pp. illus. bibl.

   A selection of photographs from the collection of Christofer Kriel, edited by J. de Villiers. These photographs are divided into sections, which are all annotated and illustrate the following themes: background and outbreak of the Anglo-Boer War, military campaigns, scenes from concentration camps, the British 'scorched earth' policy, the punishment of Boer prisoners-of-war, the peace treaty and its sequel, prominent people and tributes to the Boers.

Anglo-Boer War, 1899-1902 - General History

575. Kruger, R. Good-bye Dolly Gray: The Story of the Boer War. London: Cassell, 1959. xii, 540pp. illus. map. bibl.

Brief introduction giving the reasons for outbreak of the war. Very detailed account of battles, military engagements and participants in the war.

576. Maurice, F.M., and M.H. Grant, eds. History of the War in South Africa, 1899-1902. comp. by direction of H.M. Government. London: Hurst and Blackett, 1906-1910. 4v. + 4v. of maps.

Consists mainly of descriptions of military campaigns conducted during the war. No description of political events leading to the war or of the aftermath of the war. Has been edited so as to omit 'controversial matter' which might cause offence to either of the warring parties.

577. Meintjes, J. The Anglo-Boer War, 1899-1902: A Pictorial History. Cape Town: Struik, 1976. 192pp. illus.

Consists mainly of newspaper photographs (with captions) taken during the Boer War. Where photographs were not obtainable, sketches made by British 'special artists' of the period are provided.

578. Pakenham, T. The Boer War. Johannesburg: Jonathan Ball, 1979. xix, 659pp. illus. maps. bibl.

A comprehensive detailed account of the war, based on contemporary, largely unpublished accounts, both manuscript and oral. These include War Office files, the papers of Sir Redvers Buller, Lord Roberts, and members of Lord Salisbury's Cabinet, oral accounts of war survivors and letters and diaries of soldiers. Discusses the importance of the co-operation between Milner and the firm of Wernher-Beit, the disastrous results of the War Office feud between Buller and Lord Roberts, the part played by the Black peoples in the war and Kitchener's errors in pursuing a ruthless policy towards Boer farms, women and children.

579. Price, R. An Imperial War and the British Working Class: Working Class Attitudes and Reactions to the Boer War, 1899-1902. London: Routledge & Kegan Paul, 1972. xiii, 279pp. bibl.

Attempts to show that the working classes of England were largely indifferent to imperial sentiment and that 'jingoism' originated with the middle and upper classes of society.

580. Scholtz, G.D. Die Tweede Vryheidsoorlog, 1899-1902. Johannesburg: Voortrekkerpers, 1960. 150pp. illus. maps.

Written as a school text book at the request of the Suid-Afrikaanse Akademie vir Wetenskap en Kuns. A survey of the events leading to the Anglo-Boer War of 1899-1902 and of the war itself. The Peace negotiations at Vereeniging and the results of the war are discussed briefly.

Anglo-Boer War, 1899-1902 - General History

581. Warwick, P., ed. The South African War: the Anglo-Boer War 1899-1902. Harlow: Longman, 1980. 415pp. illus. bibl.

A detailed account of various aspects of the Anglo-Boer War by specialists on the subject. These aspects include the effects of the gold-mining industry and the British imperial policy on the advent of the war, military aspects of the war, women's roles in the war, Black people and the war, the attitude of British society to the war, the Anglican Church during the war, poetry of the war, and the United States and the war. Section 3 deals with the aftermath of the war, reconstruction of the Transvaal and the growth of Afrikaner nationalism 1902-1914.

582. Waters, W.H.H., and H. Du Cane. The German Official Account of the War in South Africa: Prepared in the Historical Section of the Great General Staff. London: John Murray, 1904-1906. 2v. illus. maps.

The object of this work, originally published in German in pamphlet form, was to describe campaigns of the Anglo-Boer War and to discuss and criticise the tactics employed in order that the German army could benefit from mistakes made during the campaigns.

ANGLO-BOER WAR, 1899-1902 - CAUSES AND EVENTS

583. Duminy, A.H. The Capitalists and the Outbreak of the Anglo-Boer War. Durban: University of Natal, 1977. 49pp. bibl.

The author attempts to disprove the belief first postulated by J.A. Hobson that the Anglo-Boer War was engineered by a small group of Rand financiers working through a kept press. Using original sources, the author examines the actions of the Rand financiers between 1897 and 1899. They were in a state of disunity and fear following the Jameson Raid and were further demoralised by the depressed state of the gold mining industry. They were concerned mainly with attempts to negotiate with Kruger's government. The composition of the Uitlander Council in June 1899 which was formed to articulate Uitlander demands consisted mainly of professional men and merchants. The mining magnates were poorly represented by three minor figures only.

584. Duminy, A.H. Sir Alfred Milner and the Outbreak of the Anglo-Boer War. Durban: University of Natal, 1976. 47pp. bibl.

The author re-examines the belief that Milner argued the need for war in South Africa long before it became apparent to other students of the South African or imperial problem. There is also doubt regarding Milner's insistence on franchise reform in the Transvaal as a means of luring Britain into war.

Milner believed that the Transvaal government would not go to war over the franchise question but would yield to British authority. He hoped that once the franchise question was conceded by the Transvaal, other reforms would follow, leading to peaceful settlement in South Africa.

585. Hobson, J.A. The War in South Africa, Its Causes and Effects. 2nd ed. London: Macmillan, 1900. viii, 324pp.

    An analysis of the political and economic causes of the Anglo-Boer War, the 'Outlander grievances' and the sentiments of Dutch and British South Africans on the eve of the conflict. The author also discusses essential factors which should be taken into account in order to achieve a peaceful settlement in South Africa; e.g., agricultural and industrial factors and future native policy.

586. Marais, J.S. The Fall of Kruger's Republic. London: Oxford University Press, 1961. xiv, 345pp. bibl.

    Describes how the discovery of gold on the Witwatersrand led to war between Britain and the Boer republics. Outlines how Kruger attempted to solve the problems arising from the mines and how he formulated a policy towards the 'Uitlanders' regarding internal government and education. The South African policy of Joseph Chamberlain, Colonial Secretary in 1895, and the events which led to war after the appointment of Sir Alfred Milner as High Commissioner are discussed. Milner considered Afrikaner nationalism a threat to British supremacy and determined to overcome it. This is a scholarly work which makes use of archival material and private papers of Joseph Chamberlain.

587. Porter, A.N. The Origins of the South African War; Joseph Chamberlain and the Diplomacy of Imperialism. Manchester: Manchester University Press, 1980. xiv, 321pp. bibl.

    Attempts to analyse the foreign policy of Chamberlain, the relations between Chamberlain and Milner and the Colonial Office and imperial officials in South Africa prior to the Anglo-Boer War. Chamberlain's efforts to win the British public's support in the pursuit of imperial interests in South Africa are described. The author maintains that Chamberlain abandoned the policy of secret diplomacy and publicised imperial affairs in order to further the values and aims of the Empire among the British electorate.

588. Scholtz, G.D. Die Oorsake van die Tweede Vryheids Oorlog, 1899-1902. Johannesburg: Voortrekkerpers, 1947. 2v. illus. bibl.

    Traces the development of the conflict between Britain and the Boer republics from 1836 to the outbreak of the Anglo-Boer War in 1899. Attempts to analyse Britain's motives in colonial policy in the late nineteenth century and to relate Britain's policy in South Africa to her rivalry with other European colonising powers. Concludes that the Uitlander grievances in the Transvaal were merely Britain's excuse for intervention in the affairs of the South African Republic. Britain's real motives were a fear of growing Afrikaner nationalism and a desire to uphold British international prestige.

589. Spies, S.B. The Origins of the Anglo-Boer War. London: Edward Arnold, 1972. 64pp. bibl.

Aims at providing primary source material on the topic of the Anglo-Boer War in a form suitable for high school students. Material includes extracts from newspapers, letters, speeches, diaries, treaties, novels, statutes and autobiographies. Extracts include the writings of the following notable people: Milner, Selborne, Kruger, Smuts, Balfour, Esselen and Rhodes. The background to the Anglo-Boer War and to each of the quotations is given so that all extracts can be understood in proper context.

590. Wilde, R.H. Joseph Chamberlain and the South African Republic, 1895-1899: A Study in the Formulation of Imperial Policy. Archives Yearbook for South African History. Vol. 19, Part 1, 1956. Pretoria: Government Printer, 1956. xiv, 158pp. map. bibl.

A study of the policy formulation of the British Colonial Office during the late nineteenth century. Assesses the roles played by Colonial Secretary Chamberlain and by members of the permanent civil service. Concludes that although Chamberlain played an active and continuous role in determining decisions on South African questions, he was often overridden by his subordinates in South Africa. Strong High Commissioners could control policy; e.g., Sir Hercules Robinson and Milner could control information reaching the Colonial Secretary. Rhodes used misleading information to commit Chamberlain to assisting the Jameson plan. The chances of misinformation were increased by the absence of British appointed on-the-spot observers free from local prejudice. Chamberlain also hampered by loyalty to his party, from considering the public interest in matters such as the parliamentary inquiry into the Jameson Raid. Chamberlain also biased in judgment by his conviction of the superiority of the British race and fear of foreign influence in South Africa. It is not clear that Chamberlain was very much won over by the arguments of the Uitlanders and would have pursued the war merely over the Uitlander question. Chamberlain had no long range plans for South African affairs but concentrated on day-to-day decisions. He did not clearly specify what he understood by British 'suzerainty', 'paramountcy' and 'supremacy' in South Africa. He lacked diplomacy, was unable to work out a compromise with Kruger, underestimated Boer fighting forces and distrusted Boer Republics so that no peaceful settlement was possible.

ANGLO-BOER WAR, 1899-1902 - MILITARY CAMPAIGNS

591. Atkins, J.B. The Relief of Ladysmith. London: Methuen, 1900. 320pp. illus. maps.

   An account by a reporter who accompanied the British troops at the Battles of Colenso, Venter's Spruit, Spion Kop, Railway Hill, Pieter's Hill and Relief of Ladysmith.

592. Bateman, P. Generals of the Anglo-Boer War. Cape Town: Purnell, 1977. 130pp. illus. map. bibl.

   The biographies of twelve important generals of the Anglo-Boer War are given. In addition, an introduction describes events leading up to the war, the war itself, and post-war reconstruction.

593. Belfield, E. The Boer War. London: Leo Cooper, 1975. xx, 181pp. illus. maps. bibl. (Concise Campaigns, 2).

   Concentrates on the military aspects of the war and demonstrates that at the commencement the British army was outdated and inefficient. The opening campaigns were fought according to the rules of nineteenth century operations; however, the war later demonstrated modern characteristics (such as the use of guerrilla tactics) and led to reforms in the British army which stood in good stead during the First World War.

594. [Botha, Louis] Barnard, C.J. Generaal Louis Botha op die Natalse Front, 1899-1900. Cape Town: Balkema, 1970. 329pp. illus. maps. bibl.

   Investigates aspects of the military contribution made by Botha during the early stages of the Boer War when regular warfare was carried out against the British.

595. [Botha, Louis] Moore, D.M. General Louis Botha's Second Expedition to Natal during the Anglo-Boer War, September-October, 1901. Cape Town: Historical Publication Society, 1979. (Originally submitted for degree of M.A. in the Department of History. University of South Africa). vi, 112pp. illus. maps. bibl.

   Discusses Botha's role in the guerrilla warfare carried out in Natal by the Boer forces subsequent to 1900. Analyses Botha's offensive on the towns of northern Natal which lasted from September to October 1901 and the manner in which Botha's successful escape from British forces boosted the morale of the Boer fighters still in the field.

596. Chisholm, R. Ladysmith. Johannesburg: Jonathan Ball; London: Osprey, 1979. 224pp. illus. maps. bibl.

   Attempts to describe not only the military campaigns which led to the siege of Ladysmith, but also studies the behaviour of Boer and British participants in the siege. Discusses briefly the causes of the Anglo-Boer War (1899-1902), the outbreak of hostilities and the battles leading to the encirclement of Ladysmith. The progress of the siege is described in detail and well-illustrated with photographs and maps. Concludes by analysing the results of the relief of Ladysmith on the progress of the war and by estimating the effects and errors made by both Boer and British in the conduct of the campaign. Is especially critical of Buller and Piet Joubert.

597. De Wet, C.R. Three Years' War (October 1899-June 1902). Westminster: Constable, 1902. 520pp. maps.

An account of the experiences of a burgher of the Orange Free State who fought against the British in the Anglo-Boer War.

598. Doyle, A.C. The Great Boer War. London: Smith Elder, 1900. x, 552pp. maps.

The causes of the war are briefly outlined. The military engagements of the war are described up to September 24, 1900, when the author mistakenly concludes that the war had ended.

599. Gardner, B. The Lion's Cage. London: Arthur Barker, 1969. 200pp. illus. maps. bibl.

A very detailed description of the siege of Kimberley during the Anglo-Boer War (1899) and of the strained relationship which arose between Cecil Rhodes and the military commander of Kimberley, Kekewich. Cecil Rhodes was able to use his influence at the end of the siege to discredit Kekewich, whom he felt had been indecisive in relieving the siege earlier and in refusing to accept instructions from Rhodes. A description is also given of the Battle of Magersfontein where the British suffered humiliating defeat.

600. Gardner, B. Mafeking: A Victorian Legend. London: Cassell, 1966. 246pp. illus. maps. bibl.

An attempt to reassess and re-examine the siege of Mafeking which led to Baden-Powell becoming a legendary hero in Victorian England. New research and new evidence tends to diminish the importance of the siege. Baden-Powell's conduct in military operations following the siege are presented in an unfavourable light. Africans were badly treated during the siege despite the active role which they played in the defence of Mafeking and many died of starvation. Baden-Powell exploited his prestige gained during the siege to further the boy scout movement and his literary career.

601. Grennell-Milne, D.W. Baden-Powell at Mafeking. London: Bodley Head, 1957. xi, 224pp. illus. maps.

Written to commemorate the centenary of the birth of Baden-Powell. Tends to be rather anti-Boer, intensely pro-British in style and to glorify Baden-Powell's exploits. Presents a very detailed account of the siege of Mafeking.

Anglo-Boer War, 1899-1902 - Military Campaigns

602. Griffith, K. Thank God We Kept the Flag Flying: The Siege and Relief of Ladysmith, 1899-1900. London: Hutchinson, 1974. xiii, 398pp. illus. maps. bibl.

   Popular account of military events leading to the British campaign in Natal, Boer siege and relief of Ladysmith during the Anglo-Boer War.

603. Gronum, M.A. Die Ontplooiing van die Engelse Oorlog, 1899-1900. Cape Town: Tafelberg, 1977. 207pp.

   A description of the early stages of the Anglo-Boer War. The successes and failures of these military campaigns are analysed.

604. Gronum, M.A. Die Engelse Oorlog, 1899-1902: Die Gevegs Metodes Waarmee die Boer-Republieke Verower is. Cape Town: Tafelberg, 1971. 244pp. illus. bibl.

   A study of the manner in which British military offensive tactics evolved during the course of the Anglo-Boer War. Finally Kitchener evolved the tactics of destruction of farms and establishment of concentration camps to force the surrender of Boer guerrilla forces still in the field.

605. Gronum, M.A. Die Bittereinders, Junie 1901-Mei 1902. Cape Town: Tafelberg, 1974. 150pp. illus. bibl.

   Account of the last year of the Anglo-Boer War. War was waged over a wide area, the west Transvaal, east Transvaal, north and north-east Transvaal, Orange Free State and Cape. Gronum describes the battles and skirmishes which took place and attempts to determine whether the Boers who fought to the bitter end gained any advantage from their hopeless struggle.

606. Hamilton, J.A. The Siege of Mafeking. London: Methuen, 1900. xi, 332pp. illus. maps.

   A diarised account of the siege of Mafeking by a British Colonel.

607. Hillegas, H.C. With the Boer Forces. 2nd ed. London: Methuen, 1901. 318pp. illus.

   A description by a correspondent of 'The New York World' of the military organisation and personality of the Boer soldiers, Boer generals, war presidents, foreign soldiers and Boer women during the Anglo-Boer War of 1899-1902.

608. [Kitchener, H.M.] Magnus, P. Kitchener: Portrait of an Imperialist. London: John Murray, 1958. 410pp. illus. maps.

   Chapters 9 and 10 (pp.160-191) contain a description of the part played by Kitchener in the Boer War between 1900 and 1901 and of the establishment of concentration camps for Boer women and children.

Anglo-Boer War, 1899-1902 - Military Campaigns

609. Kritzinger, P.M., and R.D. McDonald. In the Shadow of Death. London: Printed by William Clowes, 1904. 178pp. illus.

    Personal experiences of a Boer Commander fighting in the Cape Colony who was wounded, captured and brought to trial by the British.

610. Martin, C. The Boer War. London: Abelard-Schuman, 1969. 192pp. illus. maps. bibl.

    A simple account of the military progress of the Anglo-Boer War in which the author attempts to maintain an impartial attitude. Suitable for young readers.

611. Pemberton, W.B. Battles of the Boer War. London: Batsford, 1964. 216pp. illus. maps. bibl.

    The five battles of Belmont, Modder River, Magersfontein, Colenso and Spion Kop are discussed and analysed.

612. Ransford, O. The Battle of Spion Kop. London: John Murray, 1969. ix, 150pp. illus. maps. bibl.

    Detailed description of the Battle of Spion Kop (October 1899) and careful analysis of the Boer and British leaders and their military tactics.

613. Reitz, D. Commando: A Boer Journal of the Boer War. London: Faber & Faber, 1939. 331pp. maps.

    An autobiographical account of the experiences of a young Orange Free State soldier who participated in the Anglo-Boer War under Botha, De La Rey and Smuts.

614. Selby, J. The Boer War: A Study in Cowardice and Courage. London: Arthur Barker, 1969. 237pp. illus. maps. bibl.

    A description of the battles of the Anglo-Boer War (1899-1902). British and Boer strategy during these battles is analysed. The morale and fighting methods of both sides are discussed.

615. Sharp, G. The Siege of Ladysmith. Cape Town: Purnell, 1976. 164pp. illus. bibl.

    An account of the defence of Ladysmith in 1900 by a garrison of the Gordon Highlanders helped by Capt. Percy Scott of H.M.S. Terrible. Based on the siege log of Reynolds Sharp, Ian Forbes' diary and letters of Sir George White and Edward Chichester, all naval officers involved in the siege.

616. Smail, J.L. Monuments and Battlefields of the Transvaal War and the South African War, 1899. Cape Town: Timmins, 1966. 45pp. illus. maps.

    A graphic account by means of annotated photographs, maps, diagrams and pictures of the major battles and monuments of the Transvaal War (1881) and South African War (1899).

617. Smail, J.L. Those Restless Years: (Dealing with the Boer Wars and Bambata Rebellion). Cape Town: Timmins, 1971. 180pp. illus. maps. bibl.

Mainly pictorial account showing scenes and historical monuments dating from the Boer Wars and Bambata rebellion. There are also short descriptions of the various engagements. There is a list of forts, fortifications and laagers in Natal and Zululand dating from 1824 to 1906 and also a list of wars, rebellions and expeditions in Southern Africa from 1510 to 1953.

618. Symons, J. Buller's Campaign. London: Crescent Press, 1963. xvi, 312pp. illus. maps. bibl.

Describes the accession to power of Wolseley as Commander of the British army at a time when his mental powers were declining. Milner, anxious to promote British supremacy in South Africa, was urging Chamberlain into war with the Transvaal Republic. The British government was reluctant to embark on an expensive war and preparations were dilatory and inadequate. When war broke out, Buller was given command of the British army in South Africa. His failure in the Natal campaigns was due to lack of confidence, indecision and obstinacy. He was, however, not as foolish as he is often portrayed. He finally succeeded in raising the siege of Ladysmith, but was replaced by Roberts.

619. Wallace, R.I. The Australians at the Boer War. Canberra: Australian War Memorial and Australian Government Publishing Service, 1976. xv, 420pp. illus. bibl.

Describes the part played by Australians fighting against the Boers, on the imperial side, during the Anglo-Boer War of 1899-1902. Estimates that approximately 20,000 Australians participated in the war and describes various battles in which they took part particularly as members of mounted infantry and of scouting parties. This study is largely based on newspaper reports of the day and on soldiers' letters from the front.

ANGLO-BOER WAR, 1899-1902 - CONCENTRATION CAMPS

620. Hobhouse, E. The Brunt of the War and Where it Fell. London: Methuen, 1902. xvi, 356pp. illus. map. tabs.

Outlines the events of the period of destruction of Boer farms and sufferings of women and children in concentration camps (1900-1902). Many extracts given from letters of inmates of camps. Describes the authoress's visit to the camps in 1901 and the opposition aroused by her efforts to ameliorate conditions. Concludes with a description of improved conditions in the camps in 1902.

Anglo-Boer War, 1899-1902 - Concentration Camps

621. [Hobhouse, E.] Fisher, J. That Miss Hobhouse. London: Secker & Warling, 1971. 286pp. illus. bibl.

    Popular biography of Emily Hobhouse containing many extracts from her correspondence relating to her efforts at improving conditions in concentration camps during the Anglo-Boer War (1899-1902).

622. Martin, A.C. The Concentration Camps, 1900-1902: Facts, Figures and Fables. Cape Town: Timmins, 1957. 109pp. illus. bibl.

    Maintains that the British authorities were condemned unjustly for conditions in the camps. Admits that the mortality rate was high in the camps, but the British were hampered by a shortage of supplies and staff and the inhabitants of the camp themselves were insanitary and ignorant in their habits.

623. Otto, J.C. Die Konsentrasie Kampe. Cape Town: Nasionale Boekhandel, 1954. 187pp. illus. bibl.

    Author investigates and condemns the British policy of establishing concentration camps for Boer women and children. Concludes that these camps did irreparable harm to the prestige of the British and caused hatred and bitterness for the future.

624. Spies, S.B. Methods of Barbarism? Roberts and Kitchener and Civilians in the Boer Republics, January 1900 - May 1902. Cape Town: Human & Rousseau, 1977. 416pp. illus. bibl.

    Attempts to analyse the conditions which gave rise to and the motives which lay behind those measures of Roberts and Kitchener affecting civilians in the Boer Republics especially regarding the devastation of the countryside and establishment of concentration camps. Assesses the nature and efficiency of these measures and bases this analysis on a study of War Office Records, Roberts Papers and Kitchener Papers.

ANGLO-BOER WAR, 1899-1902 - INTERNATIONAL DIPLOMACY

625. Backeberg, H.E.W. Die Betrekkinge Tussen die Suid-Afrikaanse Republiek en Duitsland tot na die Jameson-Inval (1852-1896). M.A. Thesis. University of Pretoria. Archives Yearbook for South African History. Vol. 12, Part 1, 1949. pp.1-302. Pretoria: Government Printer, 1949.

    Detailed study of German influence on the affairs of the South African Republic from 1852 to 1896. This includes a discussion on German settlers in the Transvaal, trade, treaties, competition for concessions, particularly the banking and mint concessions, German capital invested in Transvaal gold mines and struggles for control over St. Lucia Bay and Delagoa Bay. The crisis came with the telegram of congratulations sent by the Kaiser to Kruger following the Jameson Raid. Germany was as yet unwilling to risk confrontation with Britain and gradually withdrew from the affairs of the Transvaal.

626. Cronwright-Schreiner, S.C. The Land of Free Speech; Record of a Campaign on Behalf of Peace in England and Scotland in 1900. London: New Age Press, 1906. xxxiv, 456pp. illus.

An account of a tour made by the author in England and Scotland in 1900 to endeavour to address the British public on the Boer War.

627. Davey, A. The British Pro-Boers, 1877-1902. Cape Town: Tafelberg, 1978. 220pp. illus. bibl.

A study of individuals and groups in Britain who from 1875 onwards identified themselves with the struggles for independence of the Boer Republics of South Africa. Sympathy for the Transvaal Republic first emerged during the Transvaal War of Independence, (1880). The sympathisers included Leonard Courtney, P.A. Molteno, Donald Currie, Dr. Gavin Clark and the London centred Transvaal Independence Committee. Gladstone was also said to have pro-Boer leanings. The movement reasserted itself during the Anglo-Boer War of 1899-1902. During this period the word 'Pro-Boer' became a term of condemnation. The Pro-Boers were an amorphous group consisting of left wing radicals, the emerging Labour Party, the liberal followers of Campbell-Bannerman, various Quaker groups and philanthropists such as Emily Hobhouse. Intermediaries at the Cape were J.X. Merriman and Samuel Cronwright-Schreiner. Various organisations were established but these lacked cohesive leadership. The most positive result of the movement was in countering imperial war propaganda and bringing relief to the Boer women and children who had suffered through the war.

628. Ferguson, J.H. American Diplomacy and the Boer War. Philadelphia: University of Pennsylvania, 1939. xi, 240pp. bibl.

An attempt to assess, by means of official sources, private collections of papers, secondary sources and newspapers, the extent and manner in which the American government was involved in the Boer War. The United States was officially neutral during the war, but had to assist American citizens in the Boer Republics and had to withstand pressure from Boers and their sympathizers to interfere actively in the conflict. In this many European powers who hoped for American pro-Boer interference, were disappointed. The American consular service in South Africa was at a disadvantage as it had inadequate and incompetent staff.

629. Kandyba-Foxcroft, E. Russia and the Anglo-Boer War. Roodepoort: Cum Books, 1981. 407pp. illus. bibl.

A survey of the attitude of the Tsarist government and Russian public to the events of the Anglo-Boer War of 1899-1902. Russia, although officially neutral, was intensely pro-Afrikaner due to Anglo-Russian rivalry in the East. Russian military attachés posted to Boer camps provided their government with regular despatches regarding events of the war. The Russian government attempted on several occasions to interfere on behalf of the Boers with offers of mediation. Other forms of assistance included Russian medical aid and Russian volunteers who joined the Boer armies. Interesting bibliography of original Russian sources.

630. Koss, S., ed. The Anatomy of an Antiwar Movement: The Pro-Boers. Chicago: University of Chicago Press, 1973. xl, 280pp. bibl.

A study of pro-Boer opinion in Great Britain during the South African War of 1899 to 1902 based on an analysis of public and private documents. Discusses the development and effects of pro-Boer sentiment in an introduction and links the documents by editorial passages which explain the events of the war and changing opinions within the pro-Boer camp.

631. Krige, J. American Sympathy in the Boer War. Pinedene, Transvaal: The Author, 1938. 256pp. illus.

Personal account of a Boer soldier who escaped in October, 1900 to Holland and the U.S.A. where he worked up support for the Boer cause by means of public lectures.

632. Kruger, D.W. Die Ander Oorlog: Die Stryd om die Openbare Mening in Engeland gedurende die Tweede Vryheidsoorlog. Cape Town: Tafelberg, 1974. 271pp. illus. bibl.

A study of fluctuations in British public opinion during the second Anglo-Boer War regarding the progress and outcome of the war. Analyses the growth of imperial sentiment in Britain, the desire to avenge the defeat at Majuba, disappointment at early British reverses, jubilation following the relief of Ladysmith, reaction to guerrilla warfare and Kitchener's scorched earth policy, growth of liberal opposition to concentration camps and the rise to power of the Liberal conciliatory party. Extracts from various newspapers of the period used extensively.

633. Omond, G.W.I. The Boers in Europe: A Sidelight on History. London: A. & C. Black, 1903. 278pp.

Describes the pro-Boer agitation in Belgium, Holland, France and Germany which was kept alive through the medium of certain continental newspapers issued during the Anglo-Boer War and immediately after the Peace of Vereeniging. This press agitation was said to be encouraged by Dr. Leyds. Germany in particular circulated anti-British propaganda because of her rivalry with Britain in the colonising of Africa.

634. Scholtz, G.D. Europa en die Tweede Vryheidsoorlog, 1899-1902. 2nd ed. Johannesburg: Voortrekkerpers, 1941. 224pp. bibl.

A study of the reactions of European states, particularly Holland and Germany, to the events of the Anglo-Boer War of 1899-1902.

ANGLO-BOER WAR, 1899-1902 - REMINISCENCES, BIOGRAPHIES

635. Burger, S.J. Oorlogs Joernaal van S.J. Burger, 1899-1902. ed. by T. van Rensburg. Pretoria: Institute for Historical Research, Human Sciences Research Council, 1977. 219pp. illus. maps. bibl.

    War diary of S.J. Burger, 1899-1902. He was an Orange Free State citizen who fought against the British on the western frontier and was taken prisoner of war during the surrender of General Cronje at Paardeberg. Diary written in Dutch. Describes the writer's deportation to Ceylon and return to South Africa at the end of 1902. Other reminiscences of those who fought against the British are: Ackerman, W.H. 'Opsaal; Herinneringe aan die Tweede Vryheidsoorlog'. Johannesburg: Voortrekkerpers, 1969. 403pp. illus.; Bredell, H.C. 'Dagboek van H.C. Bredell, 1900-1904'. ed. by A.G. Oberholster. Pretoria: Human Sciences Research Council, 1972. 105pp. illus. bibl.; Izedinova, S. 'A Few Months with the Boers: The War Reminiscences of a Russian Nursing Sister'. ed. and tr. by C. Moody. Johannesburg: Perskor, 1977. iv, 254pp. illus. bibl.; [Malan, W.] Pieterse, H.J.C. 'Oorlogs Avonture van Generaal Wynand Malan'. 2nd ed. Cape Town: Nasionale Pers, 1946. 373pp. illus.; Muller, C.H. 'Oorlogs-Herinneringe'. Cape Town: Nasionale Pers, 1936. ii, 212pp. illus. Reminiscences of a burgher of the Transvaal covering the years 1886 to 1925.

636. Churchill, W.S. London to Ladysmith via Pretoria. London: Longmans Green, 1900. xiv, 498pp. maps.

    Consists of a personal record of Churchill's adventures and impressions during the first five months of the Anglo-Boer War (October, 1899 to March, 1900). Contains descriptions of Churchill's capture and imprisonment at Pretoria, escape and of Buller's campaigns conducted to relieve the Siege of Ladysmith. Based on Churchill's reports to the 'Morning Post' newspaper.

637. Churchill, W.S. Ian Hamilton's March. London: Longmans Green, 1900. x, 409pp. illus. maps.

    A sequel to the account of the Anglo-Boer War contained in 'London to Ladysmith via Pretoria'. Describes the march of Lieutenant-General Ian Hamilton's column on the flank of Lord Roberts' main army from Bloemfontein to Pretoria. Based on letters submitted by Churchill to the 'Morning Post' newspaper.

638. Curtis, L. With Milner in South Africa. Oxford: Clarendon Press, 1951. xiv, 354pp. illus. map.

    Diary of Lionel Curtis, commencing in January, 1900 and ending in February, 1902. The period covered deals with Curtis' military career in the City Imperial Volunteers and the period of his service under Lord Milner as Town Clerk of Johannesburg.

Anglo-Boer War, 1899-1902 - Reminiscenses, Biographies   143

639. [De Wet, C.R.] Kestell, J.D. Christiaan de Wet: 'n Lewens-
      beskrywing. Cape Town: Nasionale Pers, 1920. 283pp. illus.

      Very patriotic and idealistic biography of De Wet. No bib-
      liography supplied. Author claims to have based information on
      records of parliamentary proceedings, journals, newspaper
      articles and personal information received from De Wet and his
      wife.

640. [De Wet, C.R.] Rosenthal, E. General De Wet: A Biography.
      Cape Town: Unie-Volkspers, 1946. viii, 229pp. illus. map.
      bibl.

      Very sympathetic study of De Wet's military and personal
      achievements, written in an interesting manner. Popular
      biography.

641. Marquard, M. Letters from a Boer Parsonage: Letters of
      Margaret Marquard during the Boer War. ed. by L. Marquard.
      Cape Town: Purnell, 1967. vii, 140pp. illus. map.

      Letters written by a Dutch Reformed Church Minister's wife
      at Winburg in the Orange Free State. Cover the period 16
      October, 1899 to 17 May, 1901. The first four chapters of the
      book provide historical and family background and the last
      chapter provides information on events subsequent to the
      letters.

642. May, H.J. Music of the Guns: Based on two Journals of the Boer
      War. London: Jarrolds, 1970. xii, 196pp. illus. maps.

      The journals in question are those of Freda Schlosberg, a
      fourteen-year old daughter of a Bronkhorstspruit farmer, and
      Dr. James Kay, who recorded his experiences of the Siege of
      Ladysmith and the occupation of Pretoria by Lord Roberts.

643. Philips, L.M. With Rimington. London: Arnold, 1902. x,
      219pp. map.

      Letters written from the field of action by a British soldier
      who fought in the Anglo-Boer War from November, 1899 to Decem-
      ber, 1900 under the command of Methuen.

644. Plaatje, S.T. The Boer War Diary of Sol. T. Plaatje: An
      African at Mafeking. ed. by J.L. Comaroff. Johannesburg:
      Macmillan, 1973. xii, 165pp. illus.

      Records the siege of Mafeking from a Barolong point of view.
      Plaatje later became a successful linguist, newspaper editor,
      author and leader of the emerging African national movement.
      This diary is considered to be one of his earliest literary
      works.

Anglo-Boer War, 1899-1902 - Reminiscences, Biographies

645. [Roberts, F.S.] James, D. Lord Roberts. London: Hollis & Carter, 1954. xv, 503pp. illus. maps.

Biography based on the personal papers of Lord Roberts. Part 4 is devoted to Roberts' career in South Africa as Commander-in-Chief of the British forces. The reforms introduced by Roberts into the British army and the campaigns carried out in South Africa are clearly described.

646. [Villebois-Mareuil, George] Macnab, R. The French Colonel: Villebois-Mareuil and the Boers, 1899-1900. Cape Town: Oxford University Press, 1975. 270pp. illus. maps. bibl.

Describes the part played by Villebois-Mareuil as commander of the International Legion fighting against the British during the second Anglo-Boer War (1899-1902) and the circumstances of his death in action in the Orange Free State (April, 1900).

CHAPTER XI
PEACE TREATY AND SETTLEMENT, 1902-1910

Bibliography

647. Van Heerden, J.F.G. Closer Union Movement, 1902-1910: A Bibliography. Cape Town, University of Cape Town, School of Librarianship, 1953. iv, 30pp.

Monographs

648. Beak, G.B. The Aftermath of War: An Account of the Repatriation of Boers and Natives in the Orange River Colony, 1902-1904. London: Edward Arnold, 1906. x, 296pp. illus. map.

   Account written by a former British Intelligence and Repatriation Officer. Attempts to describe the generosity and liberality of the repatriation scheme and the difficulties under which it was carried out in the Orange River Colony. Describes the campaign against animal diseases, the efforts to resettle farmers and supply them with temporary rations, seeds, implements and cattle. Also discusses the effects of the drought of 1903 and of the efforts of the administration to compensate the farmers for war losses.

649. Brand, R.H. The Union of South Africa. Oxford: Clarendon Press, 1909. 192pp.

   Attempts to give a brief description of the most important aspects of the South African constitution. The author acted as Secretary to the Transvaal delegates at the South African National Convention (1908). After outlining the constitution, the author expresses his own general reflections in such matters as the future of the party system in South Africa and the role of South Africa in the British Empire.

650. Campbell, P.C. Chinese Coolie Emigration to Countries Within the British Empire. London: P.S. King, 1923. 240pp.

   Chapter 4 is applicable to South Africa. Summarises the reasons for the labour crisis on the Witwatersrand mines after the Anglo-Boer War (1903). This crisis led to the introduction of Chinese mine workers under very strict conditions which emphasized the temporary nature of their employment. The experiment proved a failure and the system terminated in 1907.

651. Denoon, D. A Grand Illusion: The Failure of Imperial Policy in the Transvaal Colony During the Period of Reconstruction, 1900-1905. London: Longman, 1973. xviii, 275pp. bibl.

An examination of the reasons for the decline of imperial power in the Transvaal during the post-war reconstruction period 1902-1905. Analyses the limitations of Milner's administrative policy in the Transvaal, the antagonism caused by his appointment of non South Africans to important administrative positions and his reliance on the mining magnates. Afrikaner sections were excluded from local government. The problem of plural societies in the Transvaal increased imperial difficulties as neither imperial authorities nor Afrikaners were prepared to enfranchise the Black peoples and take the risk of gaining potential allies. Milner failed to contain Afrikaner nationalism which became a powerful force united under Smuts and Botha. The Transvaal administration caused great ill-will among industrial workers by the importation of cheap Chinese labour. An increasing difference of opinion appeared between mining magnates and workers and this led to divisions in the non-Afrikaner community.

652. Farrelly, M.J. The Settlement After the War in South Africa. Cape Town: Macmillan, 1900. 321pp.

Attempts to analyse the reasons for the war and to lay down certain principles which should be adhered to in the peace settlement. Bases conclusions on four years of examination of the political, racial, economical and legal problems of South Africa.

653. Hancock, W.K. Four Studies of War and Peace in This Century. Cambridge University Press, 1961. vii, 129pp.

Consists of four lectures delivered at Belfast under the terms of the Wiles benefaction. The second lecture is an analysis of the Treaty of Vereeniging which concluded the Anglo-Boer War of 1902 and of the Treaty of Versailles which concluded the First World War of 1914-1918. The role of Smuts is discussed in both these treaties. The third lecture is devoted to Gandhi and his belief in non-violent resistance which he formulated between 1894 and 1914 during his struggle against racially discriminating legislation in South Africa. Gandhi's campaign led to a compromise with Smuts in the passing of the Indian Relief Act of July, 1914.

654. Kestell, J.D., and D.E. Van Velden. The Peace Negotiations between the Governments of the South African Republic and the Orange Free State, and the Representatives of the British Government which Terminated in the Peace Concluded at Vereeniging on the 31st May, 1902. London: Richard Clay, 1912. xvii, 212pp. illus.

An official publication of all the preliminary correspondence and minutes of negotiations at Klerksdorp, Pretoria and Vereeniging which led to the peace concluded at Vereeniging on May 31, 1902.

655. Le May, G.H.L. British Supremacy in South Africa, 1899-1907. Oxford: Clarendon Press, 1965. 229pp.

Attempts to explain the far-reaching effects of the Anglo-Boer War on South African politics. Lord Milner's attempts to secure British supremacy in South Africa failed and a common unity was given to all Afrikaners under the leadership of vigorous, youthful leaders, Botha, Hertzog and Smuts. Attempts were made to reconcile South African Afrikaans and English speaking sections of the population but the price of reconciliation was the loss of the political and economic rights of the Black peoples.

656. Malan, F.S. Die Konvensie Dagboek van sy Edelagbare Francois Stephanus Malan, 1908-1909. ed. by J.F. Preller. English tr. by A.J. de Villiers. Cape Town: Van Riebeeck Society, 1951. 284pp. illus. (Van Riebeeck Society Publications, 32).

Introduction provides biographical details of the Malan family and of F.S. Malan. During the years in which the journal was written, Malan represented Malmesbury in the Cape parliament and was a member of the South African Party led by J.X. Merriman. The Convention was held in 1908 to 1909 to discuss union of the four provinces. The journal commences on October 7, 1908, and concludes on May 11, 1909. The only published record of the proceedings of the convention, apart from E. Walton's 'Inner History of the National Convention'. (See entry 667).

657. [Milner, A.] Gollin, A.M. Proconsul in Politics: A Study of Lord Milner in Opposition and in Power: With an Introductory Section, 1854-1905. London: Blond, 1964. xi, 627pp. illus. bibl.

Based upon a study of the private papers of Milner, Lloyd George, Leo Amery, Lionel Curtis, Geoffrey Dawson, Alfred Harmsworth and upon various other archival materials. Attempts to study Lord Milner's action in the political life of that time. Analyses the characters of Milner's contemporaries and describes the conditions under which he acted. Chapters 2 to 4 deal with Milner's career in South Africa from 1897 to 1905. Here his political ideals regarding the British Empire and his contempt for party politics became evident. He was highly regarded by Chamberlain and the Unionist Party but fiercely opposed by the Liberals. Due to his efficient administration, he acquired a tremendous public reputation. The Liberals used Milner's policy of introducing Chinese labour on the Rand as a weapon to attack Milner's administration and the Conservative government (1906).

658. [Milner, A.] Headlam, C., ed. The Milner Papers, v.II: South Africa, 1899-1905. London: Cassell, 1933. 592pp. map.

This volume deals with Milner's attempts to settle the problems of the Boer War, the peace negotiations and Milner's efforts at post-war reconstruction in South Africa. Each chapter opens with an explanatory account of events with references to Milner's despatches. This is then followed by relevant extracts from correspondence and diary entries obtained from the Milner papers. (For Volume I see entry 300).

659. [Milner, A.] Streak, M. Lord Milner's Immigration Policy for the Transvaal, 1897-1905. Johannesburg: Rand Afrikaans University, 1969. (M.A. Thesis. Rand Afrikaans University). 73pp. map. bibl.

Attempts to show how, through a policy of immigration aimed at anglicising the Transvaal, Lord Milner wished to secure South Africa's loyalty to the British Crown. All Milner's reconstruction work in the Transvaal in the period following the Anglo-Boer War, particularly in the sphere of economics, aimed at establishing British predominance. Attempts to illustrate the reasons for the failures of Milner's settlement policy and that of the British Conservative government which led to the victory of Afrikaner nationalism.

660. Nimocks, W. Milner's Young Men: The "Kindergarten" in Edwardian Imperial Affairs. Durham: Duke University Press, 1968. xi, 234pp. illus. bibl.

An account of the activities of the young Oxford followers of Lord Milner, who served under him in South Africa from 1900 to 1909, during the period of administrative reconstruction. Between 1909 and 1914 the Round Table movement was formed by Milner's followers in Britain to bring about the 'organic unity' of the British Empire, but the impetus for this movement was lost in the First World War. Individual members of Milner's 'kindergarten' however, achieved distinction in South Africa and elsewhere. These included Richard Feetham, Sir Patrick Duncan, Lionel Hichens, Lionel Curtis, Geoffrey Dawson and Philip Kerr. Of the original 'kindergarten' only three remained in South Africa after unification (1909). These were Hugh Wyndham, Richard Feetham and Patrick Duncan. The latter two rose to positions of prominence in South African politics.

661. Pyrah, G.B. Imperial Policy and South Africa, 1902-1910. Oxford: Clarendon Press, 1955. xvi, 272pp. bibl. Repr. Connecticut: Greenwood, 1975.

Attempts to analyse the colonial policy of the Liberal Party in Britain and the manner in which it was put into practice during the years 1902-1910. The Liberals under Campbell-Bannerman had condemned the Anglo-Boer War (1899-1902) but at its conclusion supported the annexation of the Boer Republics. They determined to introduce self-government as soon as possible. Responsible government was granted to the Boer colonies in 1906 and Union followed in 1910. The basis of this decision was the attempt to create a Dominion of autonomous Colonial States linked to the British Crown and co-operative in matters such as imperial defence. The Boer leader, Botha, responded to the policy of the Liberal government and attempted to create a government based on conciliation of Boer and British.

662. [Richardson, L.] Davey, A.M., ed. Lawrence Richardson: Selected Correspondence, 1902-1903. Cape Town: Van Riebeeck Society, 1977. 219pp. illus. map. (Van Riebeeck Society Publications, 2nd Series, 8).

Consists of the correspondence of Richardson, a member of the Society of Friends, or Quakers, who undertook two fact-finding and humanitarian missions to South Africa soon after the Anglo-Boer War (1899-1902). On the first mission (Sep.-Dec., 1902) Richardson was accompanied by W.H.F. Alexander. His colleague on the second mission was J. Butler (Sep.-Dec., 1903). The Richardson papers consisted of letterbooks and journals. Selections have been made from these to illuminate conditions in South Africa soon after the war and to show how humanitarian relief was provided by the Friends. In the annexures to this volume, the reports of Alexander and Richardson (Dec., 1902) and Butler and Richardson (Dec., 1903) are given.

663. Sacks, B. South Africa: An Imperial Dilemma: Non-Europeans and the British Nation, 1902-1914. Albuquerque: University of New Mexico, 1967. xii, 356pp. tabs. bibl.

A study based on extensive primary sources of the problems facing the non-white races after the Anglo-Boer War (1899-1902) and the manner in which the British government reacted to these problems. The experimental use of Chinese labour on the Rand Mines is described (1904-1907), the Zulu uprising in Natal (1906), the problem of integration of the Black population into the proposed federation and the Indian problem. The British government faced a dilemma in attempting to solve all these questions, as Britain desired to conciliate the White sections of the population and simultaneously uphold the fundamental rights of the Black peoples. The volume concludes with a survey of events since 1914. Maintains that Britain was largely unsuccessful in attempting to persuade South African Colonies to adopt a moral standard towards non-white peoples.

664. [Selborne, Earl of.] Williams, B., ed. The Selborne Memorandum: A Review of the Mutual Relations of the British South African Colonies in 1907. London: Oxford University Press, 1925. xxvii, 184pp. maps.

Part I consists of official documents relating to a proposed union of the British colonies and protectorates. These consist of a despatch from High Commissioner Lord Selborne to Secretary of State for the Colonies dated January 7, 1907, containing three enclosures. Enclosure I contains a despatch from the Governor of the Cape Colony, Enclosure II contains copies of despatches from the governments of Natal, Transvaal, Orange River Colony and Southern Rhodesia, and Enclosure III reviews present mutual relations of the British South African colonies. Part II consists of a despatch from Lord Selborne to the Secretary of State containing information on South African railway unification.

665. South Africa (Union). Minutes of Proceedings ... of the South African National Convention, 12th October 1908 to 11th May 1909. ed. by G.R. Hofmeyr. Cape Town: Government Printer, 1911. xxv, 451pp.

Official record of the proceedings of the South African National Convention which was held at Durban, Cape Town and Bloemfontein to discuss the union of the four provinces of South Africa. Consists of minutes of proceedings of the convention, resolutions passed, appointment of delegates to the convention, draft act and amendments and appointment of delegates to London in connection with the passage of the draft act through parliament of the United Kingdom.

666. Thompson, L.M. The Unification of South Africa, 1902-1910. Oxford: Clarendon Press, 1960. 549pp. map. bibl.

A detailed account of events leading to the National Convention and union of the provinces of South Africa. The author has made extensive use of the private papers of key politicians participating in these events to analyse motives. Thompson attempts to prove that the British government displayed unfounded optimism in permitting the introduction of a British type constitution into South Africa where Afrikaners would remain in a political majority to the detriment of the interests of other sections of the population. The Constitution of the United States of America would have served as a better model for South Africa.

667. Walton, E.H. The Inner History of the National Convention of South Africa. Cape Town: Maskew Miller, 1912. 346pp.

Detailed contemporary account of the proceedings of the National Convention which preceded the South African Act of 1909.

668. Worsfold, W.B. The Reconstruction of the New Colonies Under Lord Milner. London: Kegan Paul, 1913. 2v. map.

Volume 1: From the Vereeniging Agreement, May 31, 1902, to the introduction of Chinese labour, June, 1904. Volume 2: From the solution of the labour problem, June, 1904, to the departure of Lord Milner, April 2, 1905, with an epilogue covering the period 1905-1910. The author was permitted access to Milner's papers, private diaries and to other official papers, South African and imperial, in compiling these volumes, but was unable to disclose certain information still considered to be state secrets. A detailed account is given of Milner's achievements in regard to compensation for war losses, relationships with Delagoa Bay, administrative development, attempts to solve labour question by introducing Chinese labour, railway development, communications, education, agriculture, public works, police and native affairs. Discusses the personnel chosen for the new government, the attitude of the Transvaal Boers to Milner's rule and finally provides an analysis of the results of Milner's reforms.

CHAPTER XII
SOUTH AFRICA, 1910-1980

Bibliographies

669. Hoffman, M.W. Die Staking van 1922 op die Witwatersrand: 'n Bibliografie. Stellenbosch: University of Stellenbosch, Department of Librarianship, 1973. 20pp.

670. Quinn, G.D. The Rebellion of 1914-15: A Bibliography. Cape Town: University of Cape Town, School of Librarianship, 1959. v, 22p.

Monographs

671. Ballinger, M. From Union to Apartheid: A Trek to Isolation. Cape Town: Juta, 1969. 499pp.

The author describes how in 1936 the Representation of Natives Act removed the Africans in the Cape Province from the common roll vote. The Africans were subsequently entitled to elect three White representatives to the House of Assembly, of whom Mrs. Ballinger became one. Her period of office ended in 1960 when the Nationalist government abolished the 1936 Act. The author describes her experiences in the House of Assembly during the years 1936 to 1960.

672. Barber, J. South Africa's Foreign Policy, 1945-1970. London: Oxford University Press, 1973. 325pp. illus. maps. tabs. bibl.

A study of the manner in which South Africa's foreign policy during the era of Smuts, Malan, Verwoerd and Vorster was influenced by her internal political and social structure. During the immediate post-war era (1945), Smuts was the only South African leader to enjoy international prestige, but he was unable to propose any solution for South Africa's racial problems. Smuts played a large part in the formation of the United Nations, but from 1946 onwards, South Africa was attacked by opponents of the Union's racial policies, particularly in administration of South West Africa and regarding treatment of Indians within the Union. After the Nationalist rise to power in 1948, the emphasis in government policy was placed on defence of the White society and exclusion of the non-white majority from political participation. This led to increasing international isolation. Communism was seen as South Africa's greatest threat. The years 1960 to 1966 were characterised by internal crisis and doubt. From 1966 to 1970 South Africa gained confidence through economic prosperity. Slight signs of flexibility in South African internal policies appeared.

673. Bozzoli, B. The Political Nature of a Ruling Class: Capital and Ideology in South Africa, 1890-1933. London: Routledge & Kegan Paul, 1981. 384pp. bibl.

A study of the origin and characteristics of the South African capitalist class during the period 1890-1933, following the discovery of gold in the Transvaal. This class became powerful enough to influence social and political developments in South Africa according to the concepts of its own ideology. Capitalist ideology promoted racist tendencies in South African society.

674. Breitenbach, J.J., ed. South Africa in the Modern World (1910-1970): A Contemporary History. Pietermaritzburg: Shuter & Shooter, 1974. xi, 576pp. illus. bibl.

A history textbook for matriculation students. Section I covers the period 'general history' from 1910 to 1970. Section II deals with the same period of South African history.

675. Brookes, E.H. Apartheid: A Documentary Study of Modern South Africa. London: Routledge & Kegan Paul, 1968. xxxvii, 228pp. bibl.

In the introduction a historical survey is given of events in South Africa up to the year 1948 showing how the policy of 'apartheid' originated. The select documents on apartheid are divided into the following sections: Part 1: Definitions of apartheid. Part 2: Population Registration Act No. 30 of 1950 and its effects. Part 3: Opposition policies--The United Party, the Progressive Party, the Liberal Party. Part 4: Bantu education. Part 5: University education. Part 6: The Churches. Part 7: Apartheid in practice--work and voting. Part 8: The Group Areas Act. Part 9: Apartheid in practice--social consequences. Quotations are from official sources, the press and reputable monographs.

676. Brookes, E.H. South Africa in a Changing World. Cape Town: Oxford University Press, 1953. vii, 151pp.

Based on a series of public lectures given at the University of Natal in 1953. They deal with the decline of the British Empire, the passing of the white man's overlordship, nationalism and world unity, India in the new world, the importance of the United States of America, the credulity of liberals who accept dangerous doctrines and the fears that face South Africa and the modern world.

677. Callinicos, L. A People's History of South Africa. Volume 1: Gold and Workers. Johannesburg: Ravan Press, 1980. 112pp. illus.

A study of the part played by the African mine worker in the growth of the gold mining industry. The author describes the hardships endured by the Black mine worker and the various forms of Black protest which took place between the years 1886 to 1924.

678. Calpin, G.H. There Are No South Africans. London: Nelson, 1946. 412pp.

Attempts to demonstrate that there are no South Africans because of the deep divisions existing between the various racial groups. Outlines the arrival and history of the Dutch and English at the Cape and the emergence of Afrikanerdom during the time of the Great Trek. After the Boer War Hertzog was to keep alive the aims of Afrikaner nationalism while Smuts attempted to bring the English and Afrikaans sections together. The political history of the parliamentary parties is outlined from the Act of Union (1910) to World War II.

679. Carnegie Commission Report. The Poor White Problem in South Africa. Stellenbosch: Pro-Ecclesia, 1932.

An important source document reflecting a problem in contemporary South African society. Consists of the following sections, published separately: Part (1) Economic report: rural impoverishment and rural exodus, by J.F.W. Grosskopf. Part (2) Psychological report: the Poor White, by R.W. Wilcocks. Part (3) Educational report: education and the Poor White, by E.G. Malherbe. Part (4) Health report: health factors in the Poor White problem. Part (5) Sociological report: (a) The Poor White and society, by J.R. Albertyn; (b) The mother and daughter in the poor family, by M.E. Rothman.

680. Carter, G.M. The Politics of Inequality: South Africa since 1948. 2nd ed. New York: Praeger, 1962. 535pp. maps. bibl. First published in 1958.

A political study of South Africa after the National Party came to power in 1948. Analyses the political situation including the composition and aims of the various political parties; viz., the Nationalist Party, Afrikaner Party, United Party, Torch Commando, Labour, Liberal, Union Federalist and Conservative Party and also the Black political organisations. Studies the 1953 general election in order to determine the reasons for the Nationalist victory. The Nationalist racial policies are analysed in depth, and international reactions to South African race policies are discussed. The repercussions of these racial policies on the political, legislative, educational and economic systems of South Africa are assessed.

681. Herd, N. 1922: The Revolt on the Rand. Johannesburg: Blue Crane, 1966. 210pp. illus. maps. bibl.

The 1922 revolt on the Witwatersrand of the White mine labour force was complicated by the hatred of the White workers for the Black workers, whom they saw as a threat to their security. The events leading to the strike and the strike itself, are described. The steps taken by Smuts to suppress the strike and the consequences of these measures are discussed. An earlier account of the same event is: Urquhart, W. The Outbreak on the Witwatersrand, March 1922. Johannesburg: Horters, 1922. 100pp. illus. map. Brief discussion of the strike and its causes. A more significant recent study is:

681a. Oberholster, A.G. Die Mynwerkerstaking Witwatersrand, 1922. Pretoria: Human Sciences Research Council, 1982. 223pp. illus. bibl.

This study is based on a D.Phil. thesis submitted to the University of Pretoria. Includes primary archival evidence pertinent to Smuts' political and military handling of the strike. The author provides a detailed description of labour unrest leading to the 1922 revolt and of government intervention. The strike was a milestone in the development of labour relations in South Africa and also dramatically influenced future political, social and industrial developments. It was the culmination of events that had been building up over a long period, partly as a result of resentment against the domination of the British controlled Chamber of Mines, partly through the effort of the combined Labour and Nationalist parties to overthrow Smut's government.

682. [Hofmeyr, J.H.] Paton, A. Hofmeyr. London: Oxford University Press, 1964. 545pp. illus. bibl.

Biography of J.H. Hofmeyr, who from 1929 to 1948 played a decisive role in parliamentary affairs. He espoused Christian liberal convictions. During World War II he was acting Prime Minister on the occasion of Smuts' absence abroad and was regarded as Smuts' successor. He died in 1948, shortly after the defeat of the United Party in the general elections.

683. Hyam, R. The Failure of South African Expansion, 1908-1948. London: Macmillan, 1972. xiv, 219pp. illus. maps. bibl.

The Union of South Africa (1910) brought together the Cape Colony, Transvaal, Orange Free State and Natal. The schedule appended to the Act of Union provided for the eventual inclusion of Basutoland, Bechuanaland and Swaziland. Botha, the first prime minister, hoped also to include Southern Rhodesia with full British approval. Successive prime ministers failed to fulfil these goals. In 1922 Southern Rhodesia decided not to enter the Union, while thirty years of discussions aimed at including the High Commission Territories also proved futile. By 1960 it was clear that South Africa's expansionist hopes had failed completely.

684. Krüger, D.W. The Age of the Generals: A Short Political History of the Union of South Africa, 1910-1948. Johannesburg: Dagbreek, 1968. 229pp. bibl.

Attempts to evaluate the influence of Prime Ministers Botha, Smuts and Hertzog on the political development of South Africa during the period 1910-1948. Botha and Smuts both attempted to unite English and Afrikaans sections within the Union of South Africa, while Hertzog wanted the nation to develop on the basis of two parallel languages and cultures. These problems were further complicated by the problems of the Black, Coloured and Indian populations, especially in the area of labour relationships.

685. Krüger, D.W. The Making of a Nation: A History of the Union of South Africa, 1910-1961. Johannesburg: Macmillan, 1969. 348pp. illus. bibl.

Describes briefly the events leading to the Union of the four provinces in 1910. In outlining events from 1910 to the establishment of the South African Republic in 1961, emphasis is placed on the growth of Afrikaner nationalism and the achievements of the political leaders of South Africa. Up to 1945, these consisted of Boer-War generals Louis Botha, J.C. Smuts and J.B.M. Hertzog. From 1948 to 1961, control passed to Malan, Strijdom and Verwoerd. Racial problems, the socio-economic revolution brought about by increasing industrialization and urbanisation, and the cultural movement among the Afrikaners were decisive in influencing events during these years. After Smuts' fall, republican sentiment gained ground and eventually triumphed in 1961.

686. Krüger, D.W., ed. South African Parties and Policies, 1910-1960: A Select Source Book. Cape Town: Human & Rousseau, 1960. xix, 471pp.

In the introduction a survey is given of the origin and development of South African political parties since the beginning of the twentieth century. The collection of documents representing party principles and programmes of the various parties is divided into the following sections: Section 1: Leaders views in 1910. Section 2: Party principles and programmes. Section 3: Development of constitutional independence and symbols of nationhood. Section 4: Indian problem. Section 5: Cape Coloured representation. Section 6: The native problem. Except in the case of the Liberal Party, only the programmes of those parties represented in parliament were chosen.

687. Mansergh, N. South Africa, 1906-1961: The Price of Magnanimity. London: Allen & Unwin, 1962. 104pp.

Attempts to analyse the manner in which the South Africa Act, passed by the Liberal Party in 1910 as a gesture of goodwill towards the newly united South African states, influenced future events in South Africa. The Act failed to unite the English and Afrikaans speaking sections of the population in South Africa. The Act also disenfranchised the African population of Natal, Orange Free State and Transvaal and failed to protect the African vote in the Cape. Britain too paid a certain price for magnanimity in that she lost direct control over the policy, economy and wealth of South Africa. Other British colonies such as India demanded and received the same treatment. Ireland, India and various African states were granted the same independence, leading eventually to a British Commonwealth of Nations.

688. Marais, A.H., ed. Politieke Briewe. Bloemfontein: University of Orange Free State, Institute of Contemporary History, 1971-1973. 2v.

Each volume commences with an historical survey of important political events of the period under review. The selection of letters presented in each volume relates to key personalities of the period; e.g., President Steyn, Louis Botha, J.X. Merriman, J.C. Smuts and J.B.M. Hertzog. Volume 1 (1909-1910) deals with problems connected with unification, selection of a prime minister, efforts to establish a coalition government, the first elections after Union and establishment of the South African National Party. Volume 2 (1911-1912) deals with difficulties faced by the newly elected government, such as Hertzog's attitude towards the English speaking section of the population, which conflicted with Botha's policy of conciliation.

689. Marquard, D.L. The People and Policies of South Africa. 4th ed. Cape Town: Oxford University Press, 1969. 247pp. map.

First published in 1952. Briefly summarizes the history of South Africa to demonstrate how the race attitudes of the British, Afrikaners, Africans and Coloured people have arisen. The various racial policies of successive governments are discussed and evaluated, particularly in so far as these policies have influenced government, administration, education, religion and policy towards South West Africa, Basutoland, Swaziland and Bechuanaland. Out-of-date and of limited value.

690. Saker, H. The South African Flag Controversy, 1925-1928. Cape Town: Oxford University Press, 1980. xxiii, 316pp. illus. bibl.

Detailed account of the South African national flag controversy and of the political divisions caused by the controversy in the Nationalist, Labour and South African parties between the years 1925-1928.

691. Sampson, P.J. The Capture of de Wet: The South African Rebellion, 1914. London: Edward Arnold, 1915. xviii, 274pp. illus.

An account of the South African rebellion of 1914 by a former editor of the 'Transvaal Chronicle'. He bitterly denounces the rebels Beyers, De Wet, Martiz, Fourie, Muller and Kemp. The account is very detailed and written in readable style.

692. Scholtz, G.D. Die Rebellie, 1914-1915. Johannesburg: Voortrekkerpers, 1942. 312pp. bibl.

Describes the revolt of Boer officers (Generals C.F. Beyers, C.R. de Wet, S.G. Maritz, J.C.G. Kemp, A.P.O. Bezuidenhout and Commandant Kamfer) following the decision of the Prime Minister Louis Botha to enter World War I on the side of Britain. Discusses the effects of the rebellion and concludes that the rebellion stimulated the ideal of republicanism and the growth of the National Party in South Africa.

693. Stultz, N.M. Afrikaner Politics in South Africa, 1934-1948. Berkeley: University of California Press, 1974. x, 200pp. bibl.

A study of the period 1934 to 1948. Describes the establishment of the United Party based on the principle of political co-operation between English and Afrikaans speaking Whites. Maintains that the defeat of the United Party government in 1948 resulted not only from the 'apartheid' issue raised by the Nationalist Party but also from Smuts' decision in September 1939 to lead South Africa into World War II.

694. Van den Berghe, P.L. South Africa, a Study in Conflict. Middletown, Connecticut: Wesleyan University Press, 1965. x, 371pp. maps. bibl.

An attempt to analyse South African society from a broad sociological perspective. Maintains that the most important characteristic of this society is conflict between the four main racial groups and the two main European ethnic groups, English and Afrikaans. There is a brief historical introduction and succeeding chapters describe the culture, status groups, policy, economy, socio-political conflicts, value conflicts and external pressures existing in South Africa.

695. Van den Bosch, A. South Africa and the World: The Foreign Policy of Apartheid. Lexington, Kentucky: University Press of Kentucky, 1970. viii, 301pp. bibl.

Discusses the significance of South Africa in international affairs from 1652 onwards. Describes the development of an independent foreign policy by the South African government from the time of Union (1910). Analyses the effect of the 1926 Imperial Conference and subsequent Balfour Declaration on the Hertzog government's struggle for independent sovereign status. Describes the political conflict prior to World War II over the question of South Africa's participation in the war against Germany. Discusses the resurgence of Afrikaner nationalism during the years 1939 to 1948 and the development of the foreign policy of apartheid which led to South Africa's expulsion from the Commonwealth. Describes conflict with the United Nations regarding South West Africa and apartheid policy and subsequent political isolation of South Africa.

696. Walker, I.L., and B. Weinbren. 2000 Casualties: A History of
the Trade Unions and the Labour Movement in the Union of
South Africa. Johannesburg: South African Trade Union
Council, 1961. xxiii, 387pp. illus. bibl.

A detailed survey of the history of trade unions from the
second half of the nineteenth century onwards. Parts 2 to 10
cover the twentieth-century period in the history of white
trade unions. The strikes of the first half of the century,
particularly the 1922 strike, are dealt with in great detail.
Also describes methods used by the National Party to influence
free trade unions. Part 11 describes discriminating legislation affecting African workers. Part 12 contains descriptions of notable persons who furthered the case of the trade
unions. Part 13 is an account of the rise and decline of the
South African Labour Party. There are numerous other books on
industrial development and on the history of trade unions in
South Africa. For a full list see 'South African History and
Historians'. (Pretoria: University of South Africa, 1979).
Section 23 (entries 2586-2952).

CHAPTER XIII
BRITISH COLONIAL AND IMPERIAL POLICY

697. Austin, D. Britain and South Africa. London: Oxford University Press, 1966. viii, 191pp. illus. map. bibl. (Issued under the auspices of the Royal Institute of International Affairs).

    Attempts to assess the extent of British interests in South Africa and the degree to which they are likely to influence British policy towards the Republic. Investigates the disagreement between Britain and the Afro-Asian members of the Commonwealth over the question of sanctions against South Africa. Discusses British defence, trade, investment and gold interests in South Africa; the future of the High Commission territories of Basutoland, Bechuanaland and Swaziland as they move towards independence and finally the crisis in Rhodesia and the effectiveness of sanctions imposed against Rhodesia.

698. Bell, K.N., and W.P. Morrell, eds. Select Documents on British Colonial Policy, 1830-1860. Oxford: Clarendon Press, 1928. xlix, 610pp.

    Aims at covering whole field of colonial policy during the period. The dominant features of the period were the abolition of slavery and transportation, introduction of free trade and introduction of responsible government in the colonies. In the introduction the editors discuss the various officials in the Colonial Office. The documents themselves are chronologically arranged under the following headings: Section 1: Self government. Section 2: Colonization. Section 3: Transportation. Section 4: Commercial Policy. Section 5: Slavery and the Plantation System. Section 6: Native and Frontier Policy: A. South African; B. New Zealand.

699. Benyon, J. Proconsul and Paramountcy in South Africa: The High Commission, British Supremacy and the Sub-continent, 1806-1910. Pietermaritzburg: University of Natal Press, 1980. xv, 393pp. maps. bibl.

A study of the part played by successive high commissioners during the nineteenth century in the expansion of British supremacy in South Africa. The role of the high commissioner from 1846 onwards is defined as establishing frontier 'protectorates' beyond official colonial borders, co-ordinating the policies of colonial governments, chiefly the Cape and Natal, and watching over British interests in the interior. The study concludes with an examination of the policies of Rhodes and Milner together with the decline of the power of the High Commissioner after 1910.

700. Bixler, R.W. Anglo-German Imperialism in South Africa, 1880-1900. Baltimore: Warwick & York, 1932. x, 181pp. bibl.

A detailed, well-documented account of Anglo-German rivalry for Angra Pequena, Walfisch Bay and the interior and east coast of South Africa. The imperialistic rivalry resulted in trade rivalry and a struggle for economic concessions in the South African Republic. After the discovery of the Kimberley diamond fields and the gold mines of the Transvaal, the great powers of Europe became interested in Delagoa Bay as an important trading harbour. Lourenco Marques eventually was granted to Portugal (1875). Negotiations commenced for the building of a railway from Delagoa Bay to the Transvaal and Portugal attempted to raise a loan for the purpose. England and Germany were involved in the negotiations, but by 1898 Britain had succeeded in signing a treaty with Portugal which strengthened the British position in South Africa. In the Anglo-Boer War, the German government officially maintained a friendly neutrality to England, but German public opinion was hostile. Britain's victory in the war finally destroyed the influential position of Germany in the South African Republic and in the region generally.

701. Bodelson, C.A. Studies in Mid-Victorian Imperialism. Copenhagen: Grylendal Nordisk verlag, 1929; London: Heinemann, 1960. 226pp. bibl.

An attempt to describe the development of the imperialist spirit in England as reflected in contemporary literature, in public debate and in the press. Mid-Victorian imperialism was a reaction against the anti-colonial school of thought which regarded colonies as a liability. Discussion follows of the imperialist theories of Seeley and Froude and the formation of the Imperial Federation League.

702. Cell, J.W. British Colonial Administration in the Mid-nineteenth Century: The Policy-making Process. New Haven: Yale University Press, 1970. 344pp.

Covers the period 1830 to 1870. Describes the 'machinery' of the Colonial Office, the granting of responsible government to the colonies and the manner in which communications between Britain and the colonies developed.

703. De Kiewiet, C.W. British Colonial Policy and the South African Republics, 1848-1872. London: Longmans, 1929. xvi, 317pp. bibl.

The author asserts that the manner in which Britain dealt with local problems in South Africa was based on policies followed in other imperial colonies. The Secretary of State for the colonies was further influenced by decisions of the British Cabinet, parliament and public opinion in the formulation of a South African policy. Another important factor determining colonial policy was the proximity of a large black population which gradually became detribalized and formed a labouring class. The British Colonial Office was forced to attempt a solution of the 'native problem' which frequently resulted in an angry reaction from the white colonists. The author examines the relations betwen Great Britain and the South African Republics and the manner in which the Republics were affected by the successive developments of British Colonial Policy.

704. De Kiewiet, C.W. The Imperial Factor in South Africa: A Study in Politics and Economics. Cambridge: University Press, 1937. x, 341pp. bibl.

Deals mainly with the 'seventies and eighties' of the last century in order to trace the influence of this period on modern South African history. Discusses the racial, social and economic problems which confronted the British government in South Africa and analyses the reasons for the failure of British policy.

705. Egerton, H.E. A Short History of British Colonial Policy, 1606-1909. Revised by A.P. Newton. 12th ed. London: Methuen, 1950. xiii, 516pp. bibl.

First published in 1897. A history of the development of British colonial policy divided into the following sections: Book 1: The period of beginnings. Book 2: The period of trade ascendancy (1651-1830). This section includes a discussion on British colonial policy at the Cape. Book 3: The period of systematic colonization and the granting of responsible government (1831-1860). This section includes the Cape, Natal and Orange River Sovereignty and Transvaal Republic. Book 4: The period of the zenith and decline of laissez-aller principles (1861-1885). This section includes the British annexation of the Transvaal, the Zulu war, and the revolt of the Transvaal (1880-1881). The coming of the Empire-Commonwealth (1886-1909). The events of the Anglo-Boer War and unification of South Africa are very briefly described. In all sections South Africa is only briefly discussed as one of various British colonies and British colonial policy is seen as a unity.

706. Galbraith, J.S. Crown and Charter: The Early Years of the British South Africa Company. Berkeley: University of California Press, 1974. 354pp. front. bibl.

The early years of the British South Africa Company coincided with the period of Cecil Rhodes' rise to power. Rhodes dominated the Cape parliament and used his personal wealth to obtain the Rudd concession from Lobengula of Matabeleland. Between 1889, the date of its foundation and the Jameson Raid of 1896, the British South Africa Company was completely subservient to Rhodes. The directors in London imposed feeble and ineffective controls on Rhodes' authority and the British government did not restrain him provided his actions did not conflict with 'high policy'. It was because of this attitude of passivity that the directors and imperial government were implicated in errors of policy committed in Rhodesia.

707. Galbraith, J.S. Reluctant Empire: British Policy on the South African Frontier, 1834-1854. Berkeley: University of California Press, 1963. x, 293pp. maps. bibl.

Asserts that British policy on the South African frontier between 1834 and 1854 was a failure. This is due to the fact that British colonial policy was influenced by contradictory factors, a humanitarian desire to protect the frontier tribes and prevent constant border warfare, but at the same time to limit military expenditure.

708. Gann, L.H., and P. Duignan. Burden of Empire: An Appraisal of Western Colonialism in Africa South of the Sahara. New York: Praeger, 1967. xii, 435pp. bibl.

Asserts that European imperial rule in Africa is denigrated unfairly by modern political experts. Imperial rule did benefit African societies by bringing about social, economic and ideological changes which extended social opportunities for Africans. The books is divided into three sections: Section 1 deals with political theories concerning imperialism from the nineteenth century to the present day. Section 2 is a survey of the history of colonialism in Africa which attempts to prove that there were many different forms of imperialism. Section 3 deals with the period of 'decolonization'. This section is concluded with an account of the benefits brought to Africa by European colonizing powers and the difficulties faced by African states which have recently achieved independence.

709. Goodfellow, C.F. Great Britain and South African Confederation 1870-1881. Cape Town: Oxford University Press, 1966. 310pp. map. bibl.

A scholarly, detailed examination of the unsuccessful attempts of successive British governments to bring about the political unity of the South African sub-continent during the years 1870-1881. Throughout this study, the author is concerned with British imperial motives and methods. Confederation policies prior to 1870 are briefly discussed. The main emphasis is placed on the policies of Lord Kimberley 1870-1874, Lord Carnarvon 1874-1878 and Sir Bartle Frere 1878-1879. The author concludes that the chief motives influencing colonial policy makers were questions of national security, financial considerations, philanthropic sentiments towards Black peoples and notions of self-esteem and dreams of expansion.

710. Hall, H.L. The Colonial Office: A History. London: Longmans, 1937. xii, 296pp. illus. bibl.

Attempts to show the working of the Colonial Office from 1830 to 1835. Part 1 describes the administrative organization of the Colonial Office, the staff and their duties and the manner in which governors were chosen for the colonies. In colonies not possessing responsible government, the structure of the colonial civil service is described. Part 2 describes the policy of the Colonial Office and also the manner in which the Colonial Office dealt with constitutional problems and difficulties within the colonies. The Colonial Office made some attempt to promote the economic welfare of the colonies. In conclusion the difficulties faced by the Colonial Office and the reasons for its unpopularity among the colonists are described.

711. Harlow, V.T., and F. Madden. British Colonial Developments, 1774-1834: Select Documents. Oxford: Clarendon Press, 1953. xxi, 619pp.

Documents relating to the Cape are found in the following sections: 2: Constitutional Developments pp.111-15, 307-309, 313-15. 4: Emigration and Settlement; The '1820 Settlers' in the Cape Colony pp.466-76. 5: Frontier Problems. South Africa pp.503-18. 6: Humanitarian principles and Colonial policy: Treatment of Hottentots and Bushmen pp.593-614.

712. Hatch, J. The History of Britain in Africa From the Fifteenth Century to the Present. London: Deutsch, 1969. 320pp. maps. bibl.

Aims at showing the interaction of British and African cultures and economies. Prior to the nineteenth century, Britain was reluctant to incur the financial expenditure of colonies. European knowledge of Africa was largely limited to coastal areas where slaves were obtained. By the nineteenth century slavery had been abolished, and Africa was now important for raw materials and food. After 1870, competition from the U.S.A. and European powers forced Britain to pursue a more aggressive policy of colonial expansion and annexation. Because of the presence of diamonds and gold South Africa became of vital importance to Britain. After 1930, Britain abandoned a policy of free trade and adopted preferential treatment within the British dominions. After World War II Britain was compelled by pressure from the U.S.A. to relinquish overseas possessions and preferential treatment.

713. Hetherington, P. British Paternalism and Africa, 1920-1940. London: Frank Cass, 1978. xvi, 196pp. bibl.

A study of the theories and assumptions held by British intellectuals who concerned themselves with British African politics during the period 1920-1940. The most important authors and journals dealing with this theme are mentioned and discussed. The topics which chiefly preoccupied the intelligentsia were the meaning of colonial trusteeship, the problems of social change in societies disrupted by contact with the West, theories about race, Britain's role in applying Western knowledge and skills to the problems of Africa, the importance of educating African society and the importance of anthropological training for prospective White administrators of British colonies. In conclusion, the author argues that all these 'paternalistic' theories did not effectively prepare African states for self-government.

714. Hyam, R. Elgin and Churchill at the Colonial Office, 1905-1908: The Watershed of the Empire-Commonwealth. London: Macmillan, 1968. 574pp. illus. bibl.

A scholarly study of the period 1905 to 1908, when Lord Elgin served as Colonial Secretary and Winston Churchill as Under-Secretary of State for the Colonies in the Liberal government of Campbell-Bannerman. This period marked the end of the imperialistic phase in British colonial policy and the beginnings of the British Commonwealth of free nations. The Liberal government favoured the granting of responsible government to the Transvaal and Orange Free State and the establishment of a union of the South African provinces. Elgin desired to interfere as little as possible in matters such as the Chinese labour question, the Zulu uprising of 1906 and the Indian problem in the Transvaal. While expressing concern for the interests of the Black peoples, Elgin considered them inferior and favoured a policy of segregation under native councils and chiefs. He advocated that the Union of South African states should be left to solve the 'native problem' with minimal interference but refused to surrender the British protectorates to the South African states.

715. Hyam, R., and G. Martin. Reappraisals in British Imperial History. London: Macmillan, 1975. 234pp. bibl.

The chapters which deal specifically with South Africa are chapters 8 and 9, pp.167 to 199. Chapter 8 is entitled 'The Myth of the Magnanimous Gesture' and discusses the British Liberal government's grant of self-government to the Transvaal and Orange Free State in 1906. Chapter 9 deals with 'The Politics of Partition in Southern Africa, 1908-61'. An explanation is given of the reasons for Britain's refusal to allow the incorporation of the High Commission territories and Rhodesia into South Africa.

716. Keith, A.B., ed. Selected Speeches and Documents on British Colonial Policy, 1763-1917. Oxford: Clarendon Press, 1961. 381, 424pp. Part 2.

Section 6 contains two speeches relating to the Union of South Africa: (1) A speech by Winston Churchill on the Transvaal Constitution, December 17, 1906 and (2) Earl of Crewe's speech on the South Africa Bill, July 27, 1909.

717. Knaplund, P. James Stephen and the British Colonial System, 1813-1847. Madison: University of Wisconsin Press, 1953. ix, 315pp. bibl.

A study of James Stephen, Under-Secretary to the Colonial Office, in an effort to prove that he was unjustly accused of inefficiency. This study is based largely on Colonial Office material deposited at the Public Record Office in London. It is valuable in throwing new light on the policies and actions of the Colonial Office, as the Colonial Office tended to adopt the same basic policy towards all the colonies.

718. Knorr, K.E. British Colonial Theories, 1570-1850. Toronto: University of Toronto Press, 1944. xix, 429pp.

An examination of significant British colonial theories on the advantages and disadvantages of establishing British colonies overseas during the period 1570 to 1850.

719. Lovell, R.I. The Struggle for South Africa, 1875-1899: A Study in Economic Imperialism. New York: Macmillan, 1934. xv, 438pp. maps. bibl.

Attempts to analyse the history of 'interstate and international relations in South Africa' to the end of the nineteenth century. Describes the unsuccessful attempts to impose confederation on South African states between 1874 and 1881. The author analyses the Pretoria and London conventions and the division of Bechuanaland created in 1855. Anglo-German rivalry in Southern Africa is described. South African politics between 1885 and 1895 were largely influenced by Cecil Rhodes, Jan Hofmeyr and Paul Kruger. Rhodes' policy and ideals, and events of his rule to the time of the Jameson Raid are discussed. The intrigues of Germany in the Transvaal and in the construction of the railway from Delagoa Bay led to the 'Kruger telegram' which resulted in Anglo-German enstrangement. The concluding chapter analyses the diplomatic negotiations between Britain and the South African Republic (1896-1899) concerning the question of British suzerainty and the franchise question. The breakdown of this diplomacy led to war.

720. [Mackenzie, J.] Sillery, A. John Mackenzie of Bechuanaland/ 1835-1899: A Study in Humanitarian Imperialism. Cape Town: Balkema, 1971. 236pp. illus. maps. bibl.

A biography of John Mackenzie, missionary in Bechuanaland from 1875 to 1879 and Deputy Commissioner in Bechuanaland from April to August 1884. Mackenzie attempted desperately to persuade Britain to annex Bechuanaland. He deplored the practice of White settlers and adventurers moving into vulnerable borderlands and seizing tribal territories. He believed that Britain should be established as the ruling power in South Africa and that the government of native territories should not be relegated to self-governing communities of White colonists, particularly the Dutch. Rhodes opposed Mackenzie's plan of metropolitan rule as he wished to gain control over Bechuanaland through expansion of the Cape Colony. The opposition of Rhodes and the lack of support shown by High Commissioner Robinson brought about the dismissal of Mackenzie. In 1885 Britain annexed Southern Bechuanaland. In 1895 it was incorporated into the Cape.

721. Manning, H.T. British Colonial Government after the American Revolution, 1782-1820. London: Oxford University Press, 1938. New Haven: Yale University Press, 1933. xii, 568pp. bibl.

An attempt to study the important developments in British colonial government from the time of the loss of the American colonies to the end of the Napoleonic era. The effect of British colonial government on the Cape is discussed in Chapter 13. Britain considered the Cape as an important possession in view of its strategic position on the sea route to India. Even during the first British occupation of the Cape, Dundas, who was in charge of the colonies, attempted to introduce efficient colonial government and judicial system at the Cape and also remove restrictions on trade. Dutch civil servants played an important part in establishing British rule in South Africa but were not adequately paid. The Governor had autocratic power in the colony as he was responsible only to the distant Colonial Office. Britain was anxious to reduce colonial expenditure by making the Cape pay for its own military expenses. However, the only export which was profitable to the Cape was the wine trade. Britain finally consented in 1820 to allow 'friendly' foreign ships to trade at Cape Town.

722. Morrell, W.P. British Colonial Policy in the Age of Peel and Russell. Oxford: Clarendon Press, 1930. xii, 554pp. bibl.

Covers the period 1815 to 1841. The principles and tendencies of British colonial policy at this period were towards free trade between colonies. Emigration to colonies was encouraged. The Colonial Office under Peel and Stanley is described. The main problem of the Cape Colony in 1841 was continued unrest on the frontier. The Colonial Office was unable to solve the problem as official policy discouraged too much involvement and expenditure. During Lord Grey's period at the Colonial Office Sir Harry Smith extended British sovereignty as far as the Vaal River. This policy broke down and Britain favoured relinquishing the Orange River Sovereignty and granting the Cape responsible government so that the colonists could provide their own frontier defence. Lord Grey's policy towards Natal and the Zulus is also discussed.

723. Morrell, W.P. British Colonial Policy in the Mid-Victorian age: South Africa, New Zealand, the West Indies. Oxford: Clarendon Press, 1969. 507pp. maps.

The period covered is from 1853 to 1872. An introduction describes personalities influencing British government colonial policy during the period under discussion and the manner in which that policy was changing. The section on South Africa describes the frontier settlement of 1852, the withdrawal of Britain from the Orange River Sovereignty and recognition of the South African Republic. A representative form of government was introduced at the Cape. All this was an attempt on the part of Britain to reduce responsibilities in South Africa. Sir George Grey (1854-1858), despite Colonial Office reluctance, annexed British Kaffraria. Grey's policy towards Natal and his federation schemes are discussed. The British Colonial Office rejected Grey's policy. His successor, Wodehouse, made a further attempt to settle the frontier question and annexed Basutoland. The section concludes with the introduction of responsible government at the Cape, the dispute over the diamond fields and the introduction of Indian labour into Natal.

724. Newton, A.P., ed. Select Documents Relating to the Unification of South Africa. London: Longmans, 1924. 2v. Repr. London: Cass, 1968. 2v. in 1.

A selection of official documents (1857-1905) tracing the origin and development of support for the creation of a single South African state. Commences in the years 1858-1859 with extracts from Sir George Grey's correspondence with the Colonial Office regarding confederation. Continues with extracts from discussions by the responsible parliamentary government of the Cape from 1872 onwards regarding federation. Also contains extracts from Lord Carnarvon's speeches and addresses regarding the South African Confederation Bill and the Conference to discuss confederation. Statements by Rhodes on Union are included (1883 onwards). From 1902 onwards, documents include the establishment of a customs union and discussions on the 'native question' which led to the undermining of the Cape's non-racial franchise.

725. Nutting, A. Scramble for Africa: The Great Trek to the Boer War. London: Constable, 1970. 454pp. illus. maps. bibl.

A survey of South African history in the nineteenth century in which the emphasis is placed on British imperial policy and territorial expansion.

726. Robinson, R., J. Gallagher., and A. Denny. Africa and the Victorians: The Official Mind of Imperialism. London: Macmillan, 1961. xii, 491pp. maps. bibl.

A study of Victorian imperialism of the nineteenth century as a factor affecting colonial policy in Africa. Attempts to analyse the reasons for British colonization in Africa and discusses the concepts, prejudices and interests which lay in each case, behind British expansion in various regions of Africa. The regions discussed are Guinea, Zanzibar, Egypt, the Sudan, Uganda, West Africa and South Africa.

727. Schreuder, D.M. The Scramble for Southern Africa, 1877-1895: The Politics of Partition Reappraised. Cambridge: Cambridge University Press, 1980. (Cambridge Commonwealth Series). 384pp. map. bibl.

A scholarly study of the period of new imperialism in Southern Africa which commenced with the British annexation of the Transvaal in 1877 and ended with British annexation of the last frontier region, Thongaland, in 1895. The author maintains that British imperialism was influenced by diverse complicated factors such as racial conflict, frontier unrest, colonial trading and economic interest and the recommendations of colonial officials. Finally Anglo-German colonial rivalry forced Britain into playing an increasingly aggressive role in Southern Africa. By 1895 an uneasy stalemate existed in Southern Africa, with Britain attempting to control the aspirations of the independent Transvaal Republic by political encirclement, judicious capital investment and stringent railway and customs policies. This state of tension was shortly to explode into the events of the Jameson Raid and Anglo-Boer War of 1899 to 1902. Excellent bibliography.

728. Uys, C.J. In the Era of Shepstone: Being a Study of British Expansion in South Africa, 1842-1877. Lovedale: Lovedale Press, 1933. xv, 469pp. illus. map. bibl.

Describes the manner in which British economic and commercial interests influenced Shepstone's policy. The British annexation of Natal in 1843 was motivated by the discovery of coal in Natal and the ambitions of other European powers in South East Africa. Shepstone was appointed diplomatic agent in Natal. The Sand River Convention (1852) and Bloemfontein Convention (1854) conferred independence on the Orange River Sovereignty and South African Republic. Britain saw little advantage in administering these territories. Shepstone was plagued by conflicts between the Zulu chiefs and counselled the British Colonial Office on the advisability of a Confederation Policy of South African states, a move favoured by Lord Carnarvon. This proposal came to grief because of the Transvaal war with Sekukuni, quarrels with the South African Republic over a railway to Delagoa Bay and the intransigence of Shepstone. The only alternative was annexation of the South African Republic.

729. Vulliamy, C.E. Outlanders: A Study of Imperial Expansion in South Africa, 1877-1902. London: Jonathan Cape, 1938. 380pp. illus. map. bibl.

Covers the period 1870 to 1902, which marked the most important phase of British imperial expansion in South Africa. Commences with the appointment of Lord Carnarvon as Colonial Secretary and Carnarvon's unsuccessful effort to introduce a confederation scheme for the South African colonies. Shepstone, on Carnarvon's instructions, annexed the Transvaal (1877). Discusses the anti-British reaction which this produced in the Orange Free State, Transvaal and the Cape. Describes events leading to the First War of Independence of the Transvaal (1880-1881), the Pretoria Convention (1881) and the London Convention (1884) by which Britain gave up suzerainty over the Transvaal. In 1886, the Liberal Party was defeated in England and British imperial policy again prevailed. Describes the South African Republic's conflict with Rhodes and Britain over Bechuanaland, over St. Lucia Bay and Rhodes' British South Africa Company in Rhodesia. Discusses the 'Uitlander' problem in the South African Republic and British fear of German ambitions in South Africa. Describes the Jameson Raid and events leading to the Anglo-Boer War of 1899-1902.

730. Wilde, R.H. Joseph Chamberlain and the South African Republic, 1895-1899: A Study in the Formulation of Imperial Policy. Archives Yearbook for South African History, Vol. 19, Part I, 1956. Pretoria: Government Printer, 1956. xiv, 158pp. map. bibl.

A study of the workings of the Colonial Office during the late nineteenth century and the part played in policy formulation by Chamberlain, the Colonial Secretary, and by members of the permanent civil service. Analyses the problems of British relations with the South African Republic from 1895 to 1899 and ends with the outbreak of the Anglo-Boer War in 1899. Maintains that Chamberlain was often at the mercy of subordinates in South Africa, particularly the High Commissioner, who controlled the supply of information to the Colonial Office. Thus Rhodes committed Chamberlain to assisting the Jameson plan and Milner encouraged the Uitlanders to petition. Chamberlain also was hampered by party politics within the British parliament. Chamberlain feared foreign intervention, e.g. Germany, in South Africa. He favoured a policy of 'suzerainty' over the South African Republic but it was not clear how far this control was intended to go, or how far he sincerely believed in the Uitlander grievances. Chamberlain falsely believed that the British Uitlanders outnumbered the Afrikaners on the Rand and hoped to 'swamp' the South African Republic with 'loyal Anglo-Saxons'. Led on by Milner, Chamberlain hoped in 1899 for a short successful war and the subsequent flooding of South Africa with loyal British settlers. Subsequent events proved him wrong.

CHAPTER XIV
POLITICAL PARTIES

National Party

731. Goosen, D.P. Die Triomf van Nasionalisme in Suid-Afrika. Johannesburg: Impala, 1953. 736pp. illus.

Issued to commemorate the successful achievements of the National Party in the 1953 elections. Provides a history of the Party from 1903 onwards, short biographies of prominent Nationalist leaders, descriptions of Nationalist youth movements and women's associations and detailed descriptions of the 1953 general election.

732. Institute for Contemporary History. Die Nasionale Party, Agtergrond, Stigting en Konsolidasie. Bloemfontein: Institute for Contemporary History, University of the Orange Free State, 1975-.

Two volumes have appeared todate. Vol. 1 is edited by O. Geyser and A.H. Marais. Vol. 2 is edited by J.H. le Roux and P.W. Coetzer. They contain a detailed history of the National Party of South Africa covering the years 1914 to 1961. Aims at covering a wider background than mere party history, as there is also an attempt to describe the cultural and political struggles of the Afrikaner people.

733. Mulder, C.P., and W.A. Cruywagen, eds. Die Eerste Skof van die Nasionale Party in Transvaal, 1914-1964. Pretoria: National Party, 1965. 256pp. illus.

Issued on the occasion of the fiftieth anniversary of the National Party in the Transvaal. Contains articles on the formation of the Party in 1914 and on events immediately preceding this formation. Records the growth of the Party and pays tribute to various Party leaders. Provides brief descriptions of the history of the Party in the various constituencies of the Transvaal.

734. Reitz, H., and H. Oost, eds. Die Nasionale Boek; 'n Geskiedenis van die Ontstaan en Groei van die Nasionale Party van Suid-Afrika. Johannesburg: Commercial Printers, 1931. 714pp. illus.

Consists of articles describing the history of the National Party, biographies of Nationalist supporters and leaders and government achievements.

Political Parties - National Party   171

735. Roberts, M., and A.F.G. Trollip. The South African Opposition,
      1939-1945: An Essay in Contemporary History. London: Long-
      mans, 1947. x, 240pp.

      A history of the Nationalist Opposition party from September,
      1939 to the end of World War II. Malan's Nationalist Party was
      strengthened by the Hertzog faction, who opposed South Africa's
      entry into the war. There was further opposition from organi-
      zations such as the Handhawersbond and Ossewa-Brandwag. Malan
      eventually triumphed over these organizations. The aims and
      objectives of Malan's party and the reasons for the success of
      the party are analysed.

736. Van Rooyen, J.J. Die Nasionale Party, Sy Opkoms en Oorwinning
      - Kaapland se Aandeel. Cape Town: Nasionale Party, 1956.
      329pp. illus.

      The emphasis in this work falls on the history of the Cape
      branch of the National Party, established in 1915. The polit-
      ical career of Dr. D.F. Malan was largely bound up with the
      Cape National Party, especially during the years 1934 to 1954.
      In the latter year he resigned as prime minister. This
      internal structure and functioning of the National Party are
      also described. Appendices give lists of the names of National
      Party members elected from 1915 to 1954.

737. Van Schoor, A.M., ed. Die Nasionale Boek: Gewy aan 25 Jaar van
      Nasionale Bewind (1948-1973). Braamfontein: Edupress, 1973.
      208pp. illus.

      Commemorates the twenty-fifth anniversary of the Nationalist
      Party's accession to power. Describes the history of the
      Nationalist Party from 1903 onwards; provides biographies of
      leaders D.F. Malan, J.G. Strijdom, H.F. Verwoerd, B.J. Vorster
      and B. Schoeman; discusses Nationalist achievements in the four
      provinces and South West Africa; the policy of separate
      development and South Africa's international status.

738. Vatcher, W.H. White Laager: The Rise of Afrikaner Nationalism.
      London: Pall Mall, 1965. x, 309pp. illus. bibl.

      A study of the growth of Afrikaner nationalism from the mid-
      nineteenth century onwards. Part 1 consists of a summary of
      events covering the establishment of the Boer Republics and the
      two Wars of Independence (1881-83) and (1899-1902). Part 2
      entitled 'The Struggle for Supremacy', discusses the growth of
      nationalism in the first half of the twentieth century.
      Afrikaner nationalism was influenced by the suppression of the
      Afrikaner Rebellion (1914); the strikes of 1913, 1914 and 1922;
      the postwar depression, the establishment of the Afrikaner
      Broederbond (1918); the rise of national socialism in Germany,
      World War II; the decline of Britain as a world power and the
      rise of nationalism in Asia and Africa. Part 3 summarises the
      progress of extreme nationalism after 1948. South Africa was
      proclaimed a Republic and the policy of apartheid was
      entrenched.

Liberal Parties

739. Robertson, J. Liberalism in South Africa, 1948-1963. Oxford: Clarendon Press, 1971. viii, 252pp. bibl. (Oxford Studies in African Affairs).

    Describes the activities and fate of the Black and White groups formed after World War II to oppose racial discrimination and extend equal rights to non-whites within the existing parliamentary system. These groups included the Liberal Party, Progressive Party, Torch Commando, Black Sash and African National Congress.

740. Strangwayes-Booth, J. A Cricket in the Thorn Bush: Helen Suzman and the Progressive Party. Johannesburg: Hutchinson, 1976. 320pp. illus. bibl.

    Popular biography in which the history of the Progressive Party between the years 1959 to 1974 is outlined, and the important role of Helen Suzman in attempting to keep alive the policies of the Party is described.

Black Sash

741. Michelman, C. The Black Sash of South Africa: a Case Study in Liberalism. London: Oxford University Press, 1975. x, 198pp.

    Published under the auspices of the Institute of Race Relations. Analyses the structure, aims, membership and achievements of the Black Sash and related bodies which form part of the 'Liberal Establishment' in South Africa. Outlines the background of the Liberal struggle which commenced in 1955 with the passing of the Senate Act, and describes the setbacks and achievements of the movement up to the year 1973.

742. Rogers, M. The Black Sash: The Story of the South African Women's Defence of the Constitution League. Johannesburg: Rotonews, 1956. xvi, 273pp. illus.

    An outline of events which took place in 1956, when the Black Sash movement was formed in response to the Senate Act of 1955. The author is a member of the Black Sash movement. Many extracts from newspapers and political cartoons are included in descriptions of events.

Afrikaner Broederbond

743. Pelzer, A.N. Die Afrikaner-Broederbond: Eerste 50 Jaar. Cape Town: Tafelberg, 1979. (Uitgegee in opdrag van die Uitvoerende Raad van die Afrikaner Broederbond). 193pp. illus.

An account of the history, aims and achievements of the Broederbond based on the files of the organization. Aims at counteracting the unfavourable publicity which has been attached to the work of the Organization by political opponents. Covers the years 1918 to 1968. Discusses the achievement of members in the economic, industrial, cultural and political spheres, the reasons for secrecy of membership and the manner in which secret documents fell into the hands of political opponents.

The following publications all adopt a critical approach in discussing the history, rise to power and influence of the Broederbond in the political, economic, cultural and social life of South Africa. Much use is made of secret documents which were leaked to the press by recalcitrant Broederbond members during the 1960s and 1970s. Schoeman, B.M. Die Broederbond in die Afrikaner-politiek. Pretoria: Aktuele publikasies, 1982. 218pp.; Serfontein, J.H.P. Brotherhood of Power: An Exposé of the Secret Afrikaner Broederbond. London: Rex Collins, 1979. 278pp. illus.; Wilkins, I., and H. Strydom. The Super-Afrikaners. Johannesburg: Jonathan Ball, 1978. 458,139pp.

CHAPTER XV
PRIME MINISTERS SINCE UNION
Collective Studies

744. Scholtz, G.D. Hertzog en Smuts en die Britse Ryk. Cape Town: Tafelberg, 1975. vii, 158pp.

    A study of the conflicting ideas of Smuts and Hertzog regarding the influence of Britain over South African affairs and the triumph of the republican ideal over Smuts' philosophy of holistic imperialism. Covers the period 1910 to 1950.

745. Williams, B. Botha, Smuts and South Africa. London: Hodder & Stoughton, 1946. xi, 216pp. illus. maps. bibl.

    A simply written account of the careers of Botha and Smuts which would be suitable for young readers.

Individual Prime Ministers

BOTHA, L.

Bibliography

746. Clark, E.M.M. Louis Botha. Cape Town: University of Cape Town, School of Librarianship, 1959. iv, 30pp.

Monographs

747. Buxton, Earl. General Botha. London: John Murray, 1924. ix, 347pp. illus. maps.

    Biography of Botha dealing with the period August, 1914 to August, 1919. The author worked closely with Botha during this period, as Buxton became Governor-General of the Union and High Commissioner for South Africa.

748. Engelenburg, F.V. General Louis Botha. Pretoria: Van Schaik, 1929. 352pp. illus. maps.

    English translation of a biography of Botha published in 1928 in Afrikaans. The author was unable to have access to all official documents relating to Botha's period of administration and many statements are based on individual recollections of the author's close personal relationship with Botha.

749. Strydom, C.J. Scheepers. Held van Colenso: Die Verhaal van Generaal Louis Botha. Cape Town: Tafelberg, 1972. 95pp.

Popular biography of Louis Botha suitable for young people.

HERTZOG, J.B.M.

Bibliography

750. Burger, M.J. Generaal J.B.M. Hertzog: 'n Bibliografie. Cape Town: University of Cape Town, School of Librarianship, 1953. iv, 31pp.

Monographs

751. Naudé, J.D. Generaal J.B.M. Hertzog en die Ontstaan van die Nasionale Party, 1913-1914. Johannesburg: Voortrekkerpers, 1970. 194pp. bibl.

A study of the conditions leading to Hertzog's exclusion from Louis Botha's second cabinet in 1912 and Hertzog's subsequent formation of the National Party in 1914. Well-documented account of a critical period in South African history.

752. Neame, L.E. General Hertzog: Prime Minister of the Union of South Africa Since 1924. London: Hurst and Blackett, 1930. 288pp. illus.

Interesting and unbiased biography of General Hertzog.

753. Nienaber, P.J., and others, eds. Gedenkboek Generaal J.B.M. Hertzog. Johannesburg: Afrikaanse Pers-Boekhandel vir Suid-Afrikaanse Akademie vir Wetenskap en Kuns, 1965. 392pp. front. bibl.

Memorial volume issued to commemorate Hertzog's achievements as a soldier, cultural leader, educational leader, legal expert, statesman, arbiter in racial affairs and founder of South Africa's steel industry. Each section of the volume consists of articles enumerating Hertzog's achievements. There are also extracts from his speeches.

754. Pirow, O. James Barry Munnik Hertzog. Cape Town: Timmins, n.d. 288pp. front.

Popular biography of Hertzog written by a supporter and former cabinet minister in Hertzog's Nationalist government of the 1930s.

755. Van den Heever, C.M. General J.B.M. Hertzog. Johannesburg: Afrikaanse Pers, 1946. 298pp. illus.

Abridged from the original Afrikaans version published in 1943. Presents the policies of Hertzog in a favourable light.

MALAN, D.F.

Bibliography

756. Williams, L.E. Dr. Daniel Francois Malan, 1874-1959: A Bibliography. Pretoria: University of South Africa, Department of Bibliography and Library Science, 1967. 27pp.

Monographs

757. Booysens, B. Die Lewe van D.F. Malan: Die Eerste Veertig Jaar. Cape Town: Tafelberg, 1969. 329pp. bibl.

    A study of Malan in his early formative years from 1875 to 1915, before he embarked on his political career. Describes his student years at Stellenbosch, his four and a half year study period overseas and his career as minister of the Dutch Reformed congregations at Heidelberg (Transvaal), Montagu and Graaff-Reinet. During this period, certain ideals became apparent; viz., greater church unity, the education of teachers for the Afrikaans speaking child, the struggle for an Afrikaans university, the provision for the spiritual and material needs of Afrikaners in Rhodesia and the advancement of Afrikaans language and literature. He was passionately interested in education, the acceptance of the Dutch language in the school curriculum and the poor white problem and its amelioration.

758. Robins, E. This Man Malan. Cape Town: South African Scientific Publishing Co., 1953. 116pp. illus.

    A description of Malan by a British journalist based on material obtained from personal contact over a five-year period. A popular biography.

SMUTS, J.C.

Bibliographies

759. Greenwald, D.J. Jan Christiaan Smuts. A Bibliography. Cape Town: University of Cape Town School of Librarianship, 1951. vii, 21pp. Unpublished.

760. Ratcliffe, U.M. A Bibliography of Books and Speeches by the Late General J.C. Smuts. Cape Town: University of Cape Town, School of Librarianship, 1953. 47pp. Unpublished.

761. Scott, J.A. Sinclair. Jan Christiaan Smuts; A Bibliography of prefaces, forewords and introductions by Smuts, and biographical data about him. Cape Town: University of Cape Town, School of Librarianship, 1954. vi, 46pp.

Monographs

762. Smuts, J.C. Africa and Some World Problems, Including the Rhodes Memorial Lectures, Delivered in Michaelmas Term, 1929. Oxford: Clarendon Press, 1930. xiv, 184pp. illus. map.

    Consists of various lectures: 1. Livingstone and after. 2. African settlement (advocates White settlement in Africa as a means of improving the lot of the Black man). 3. Native policy in Africa (emphasizes the importance of preserving 'native system of organization and social discipline' and advocates territorial segregation). 4. World peace (defends the League of Nations). 5. Future tasks of the League (disarmament, justice, punishment of aggressors). 6. Democracy (advocates the replacement of aggressive nationalism by international committees and experts. Political democracy, though admirable, has certain weaknesses because power is concentrated in the hands of the civil service).

763. Smuts, J.C. Plans for a Better World: Speeches of Field-Marshal the Right Hon. J.C. Smuts. London: Hodder & Stoughton, 1942. xiv, 288pp. illus.

    A selection of Smuts' speeches covering the period May, 1917 to May, 1941 in which he discusses native policy in Africa and South Africa, the British Commonwealth concept, the Statute of Westminster, the growth of fear and Nazi tyranny in Europe, the philosophical theory of holism, the advance of South African science, war speeches and a plea for a post-war Association of Nations.

764. Armstrong, H.C. Grey Steel: J.C. Smuts. London: Methuen, 1937. xi, 333pp. illus. maps. bibl.

    Biography covering Smuts' career from 1870 to 1933. The author attempts to present an honest appraisal of Smuts' character including his ruthless methods against the 1922 strikers. Popular, readable style.

765. Blanckenberg, P.B. The Thoughts of General Smuts. Cape Town: Juta, 1951. 230pp. illus.

    Consists of extracts from Smuts' private correspondence and public speeches recorded by his private secretary between the years 1933-1939. They cover topics such as national unity, the Christian mission, a changing world, education, holism, racial intolerance, war memories, the native in South Africa, plant life in South Africa, democracy, the British Commonwealth of Nations, soil conservation, the African continent and religion.

766. Crafford, F.S. Jan Smuts: A Biography. Cape Town: Timmins, 1945. x, 369pp. illus. maps. bibl.

    A popular biography of Smuts, written by a contemporary and therefore not fully evaluative of Smuts' achievements and failures.

767. Friedlander, Z., ed. Jan Smuts Remembered: A Centennial Tribute. Cape Town: Timmins, 1970. 104pp. illus.

Consists of short articles by well-known personalities paying tribute to various aspects of Smuts' personality.

768. Friedman, B. Smuts: A Reappraisal. London: Allen and Unwin; New York: St. Martins, 1976. 222pp.

Deals with three aspects of Smuts' career: (1) the manner in which he influenced the drawing up of the South African Constitution in 1908-1910 so that a flexible, unitary constitution was adopted, (2) the formation of the fusion government with Hertzog in 1933 and (3) an analysis of the reasons for Smuts' political defeat in the elections of 1948.

769. Haarhoff, T.J. Smuts the Humanist. Oxford: Basil Blackwell, 1970. 113pp. bibl.

Pays tribute to Smuts' political philosophy and ideals, especially as expressed in Smuts' belief in holism and evolution. Discusses the influence of ancient Greek philosophy on Smuts' political concepts. Analyses Smuts' attitude towards the non-white people of South Africa, his relationship with Kruger and certain English friends such as Emily Hobhouse and the influence of Oxford scholars on Smuts' philosophical development. Concludes with a description of the dilemma Smuts faced in attempting to reconcile his theories of holism with political expediency in guiding South Africa's destiny.

770. Hancock, W.K., and J. van der Poel, eds. Selections from the Smuts Papers. Cambridge: University Press, 1966-1973. 5v.

Covers the period June, 1886 to August, 1945. Consists of Smuts' documents, chosen mainly for historical importance. Personal and private letters only given in selected cases. Key speeches, letters and memoranda are also included. The correspondence of certain notable figures to Smuts is included. Material has also been selected from public papers, especially that relating to the Anglo-Boer War, from the States Attorney series in the Pretoria State Archives and from Cape Town newspapers. Dutch and Afrikaans papers have been translated into English. Annotations are provided.

771. Hancock, W.K. Smuts: The Sanguine Years, 1870-1919. Cambridge: University Press, 1962. xii, 619pp. illus. maps. bibl.

Volume 1 of a biography of Smuts based on primary sources obtained from the Smuts Archives. This biography was written at the same time as Hancock and Van der Poel's first four volumes of selections from the Smuts Archives. (see entry 770).

772. Hancock, W.K. Smuts: The Fields of Force, 1919-1950. Cambridge: University Press, 1968. 590pp. illus. bibl.

Vol. 2 of an authoritative biography based on authentic documentation.

773. Meiring, P. Smuts: The Patriot. Cape Town: Tafelberg, 1975. 215pp. illus. bibl.

Popular biography of Smuts in which the author attempts to show that Smuts, despite the fact that he never promoted the Afrikaans language cause or republicanism after 1910, was a true patriot in promoting the political future of South Africa. The author analyses the motivation behind Smuts' pro-British policy and the reasons for the eventual estrangement of Smuts from the Afrikaners.

774. Millin, S.G. General Smuts. London: Faber, 1936. 2v. illus. bibl.

Popular, interesting biography written with the co-operation of General Smuts and covering his career up to the year 1936.

775. Smuts, J.C. Jan Christian Smuts. Cape Town: Heinemann & Cassell, 1952. xvi, 568pp. illus. map. bibl.

Biography of J.C. Smuts written by his son. A popular biography written in an interesting manner. Is not entirely impartial in judgment because of the author's strong admiration for his father.

STRIJDOM, J.G.

776. Basson, J.L. J.G. Strijdom: Sy Politieke Loopbaan van 1929 tot 1948. Pretoria: Wonderboom, 1980. 622pp. bibl.

Traces the political career of Strijdom during the years when he was a member of the opposition Nationalist party. He was responsible for the creation of a strong party structure, particularly in the Transvaal and was an uncompromising supporter of Christian National Republicanism. He was a staunch upholder of the doctrine of apartheid. At times his views conflicted with those of Nationalist contemporaries such as Hertzog and Malan whom he considered inclined to compromise.

VERWOERD, H.F.

777. Verwoerd, H.F. Verwoerd aan die Woord: Toesprake, 1948-1962. ed. by A.N. Pelzer. Johannesburg: Afrikaanse Pers, 1963. 676pp.

A selection of Verwoerd's speeches arranged in chronological order and followed by a subject index to assist readers who are anxious to study Verwoerd's views on various policies of importance. All the speeches are provided in their Afrikaans version, even in cases where the speech was actually delivered in English.

778. Kenny, H. Architect of Apartheid: H.F. Verwoerd - an Appraisal. Johannesburg: Ball, 1980. 278pp.

An attempt to present an unbiased assessment of Verwoerd's career aims and achievements in the context of the times in which he lived. The author analyses the policy of 'separate freedom' which was rigidly systematised by Verwoerd in an attempt to uphold White supremacy. The author also attempts to explain the reasons for the long-term failure of Verwoerd's racial policy.

779. Scholtz, G.D. Dr. Hendrik Frensch Verwoerd, 1901-1966. 2v. Johannesburg: Perskor, 1974. illus. bibl.

Lengthy Afrikaans biography in which the author pays tribute to Verwoerd's achievements.

780. Strydom, C.J. Scheepers. Black and White Africans: A Factual Account of South African Race Policies in the Verwoerd Era. Cape Town: Tafelberg, 1967, 200pp. bibl.

A discussion of Dr. H.F. Verwoerd's policy of separate development between the period 1950 to 1966 in which the author assumes a very sympathetic attitude towards Dr. Verwoerd's aims and achievements.

VORSTER, B.J.

781. Cockram, G.M. Vorster's Foreign Policy. Pretoria: Academica, 1972. 222pp. illus. map.

Outlines the difficulties facing the South African Republic from May, 1961, onwards. Stresses the positive aspects of Vorster's foreign policy in attempting to solve these difficulties. Deals with the problems of South West Africa and relationships with Israel, Latin America, Portugal, Rhodesia and neighbouring states and the U.S.A. Also deals with Vorster's immigration, monetary, defence and sports policies.

782. D'Oliveira, J. Vorster: The Man. Johannesburg: Stanton, 1977. 292pp. illus.

Popular, readable biography of Vorster by a journalist.

CHAPTER XVI
RACE CONTACTS, RACE POLICY, RACE RELATIONS

Bibliographies

783. Blum, P. Union Native Policy as reflected in Government Legislation and Publications, 1910-1948. A Bibliography. Cape Town: University of Cape Town, School of Librarianship, 1951. 2nd ed., 1963. 21, v, 21pp.

784. Kaplan, B.B. Race Relations in South Africa: A Bibliography. Johannesburg: University of the Witwatersrand, Department of Bibliography, Librarianship and Typography, 1971. 67pp.

785. Potgieter, P.J.J.S. Index to Literature on Race Relations in South Africa, 1910-1975. Boston: Hall, 1979. 555pp. Coverage is confined to periodicals.

786. Scholtz, P.L., and others. Race Relations at the Cape of Good Hope, 1652-1795: A Select Bibliography. Boston: Hall, 1981. 124pp.

787. South African Institute of Race Relations. Survey of Race Relations in South Africa. Johannesburg: The Institute, 1954-. Annual.

Monographs

788. Benson, M. The African Patriots: The Story of the African National Congress. London: Faber, 1963. 310pp. illus. map. bibl.

    A history of the African National Congress from its foundation in 1910 to 1961. The author shows a strong sympathy towards the aims and struggles of the organization.

789. Bozzoli, B., ed. Labour, Townships and Protest: Studies in the Social History of the Witwatersrand. Johannesburg: Ravan, 1979. 342pp.

    A selection of research papers presented at the history workshop held at the University of the Witwatersrand in February, 1978. The papers are divided into three sections, as follows: Part 1: Township life and patterns of protest. Part 2:

Cultural alternatives to hegemony. Part 3: Worker experience and action. The papers are predominantly concerned with the Black workers and Black proletariat.

790. Brookes, E.H. The Colour Problems of South Africa. Lovedale: Lovedale Press, 1934. viii, 237pp.

Attempts to cover the Union's native policy from 1910 to 1934. Discusses the effects of nationalism and segregation on the Coloured and Black peoples of South Africa. Maintains that the liberal tradition and the rule of law has been weakened in twentieth century South Africa. Points out the dangers of a purely 'economic approach' to South Africa's colour problem. Also evaluates the 'anthropological approach'. Discusses the effects of Christianity on Bantu thought and practice and also on Bantu education. Concludes with a plea for abolition of racial prejudices and inequality.

791. Brookes, E.H., and J.B. Macaulay. Civil Liberty in South Africa. Cape Town: Oxford University Press, 1958. viii, 175pp.

Analyses the manner in which legislation in South Africa has restricted civil liberty, especially in regard to the Black man. Discusses the special powers of the police force, racial discrimination, legal restraints on freedom of movement, freedom of speech and on economic and educational freedom. Concludes with a discussion of the franchise and the administration of native affairs with special reference to the Reserves.

792. Brookes, E.H. The History of Native Policy in South Africa from 1830 to the Present Day. 2nd rev. ed. Pretoria: Van Schaik, 1927. xii, 524pp. bibl.

The first section, which deals with the history of South Africa's policy towards the non-white races from 1830 onwards, is still of value. The analytical section of the book which attempts to discuss administration, native law, the political question of black participation in government and native agriculture, native labour, and to make suggestions for future policy, has become rather out-of-date.

793. Brookes, E.H. White Rule in South Africa, 1830-1910: Varieties in Government Policies Affecting Africans. Pietermaritzburg: University of Natal, 1974. 223pp.

An extensive revision of 'The History of Native Policy in South Africa', which appeared in 1924. Attempts to study the history of the period from 1830, when Africans first came under the rule of the Cape government, to 1910, when the Union of South Africa came into existence. Discusses the manner in which 'native policy' evolved in the four provinces of South Africa. Also analyses the recognition and codification of African customary law, the system of land distribution and land tenure, the development of African agriculture, particularly in the Cape Colony, and the influence of Christian religion and education on African tribes.

794. Calpin, G.H., ed. The South African Way of Life: Values and Ideals of a Multi-racial Society. London: Heinemann, 1953. ix, 200pp. illus. tabs.

Demonstrates how the conflict between the White and Black men arose in South Africa by describing the history of the six different race groups of the country. Also analyses education, political institutions, political parties and trends and economic factors in South Africa. Each chapter of the book is written by a specialist on the particular field under discussion.

795. Carter, G.M., ed. South Africa's Transkei: The Politics of Domestic Colonialism. London: Heinemann, 1967. 200pp. bibl.

Analyses the reasons for the establishment of the Transkei as a semi-autonomous territory in December, 1963. Maintains that the 'Bantustan program' is a response of appeasement to hostile domestic and external pressures resulting from the South African government's policies of white supremacy and separate development. Investigates the legislative, administrative, political and economic conditions prevailing in the Transkei prior to and after independence. Concludes that for the first time, black peoples have been given the opportunity to undertake political and administrative responsibilities. However, the economic situation within the Transkei is critical due to lack of industry and opportunities for employment and inadequate harbour facilities. The policy of separate territorial development cannot succeed unless it is based on full co-operation and consultation between Blacks and Whites and equal rights and opportunities for all.

796. Chilvers, H.A. The Yellow Man Looks on: Being the Story of the Anglo-Dutch Conflict in Southern Africa and its Interest for the Peoples of Asia. London: Cassell, 1953. 240pp.

Attempts to trace the origin of Anglo-Dutch conflict in South Africa. Covers the Slagters Nek Rebellion, the Great Trek, the disputes concerning ownership of the diamond fields in the 1860s, the first and second Anglo-Boer Wars and racial conflicts resulting from discovery of the Rand goldfields. Uses an anecdotal style in tracing these events. Discusses the 1922 Rand revolt and General Hertzog's anti-sterling policy of 1932 which had catastrophic results on the South African economy in 1933. Author concludes that South Africa must abandon racial conflicts because of the threat of attack by Japan.

797. Davenport, T.R.H. The Beginnings of Urban Segregation in South Africa: The Natives (Urban Areas) Act of 1923 and its Background. Grahamstown: Institute of Social and Economic Research, Rhodes University, 1971. 23pp. bibl.

The author describes the colonial origins of urban segregation prior to union (1910). The governments of Botha and Smuts were anxious to establish a uniform urban segregation

policy in all four provinces. In 1918 the Department of
Native Affairs released proposals for urban areas. In 1921
the Native Affairs Commission and Transvaal Local Government
Commission jointly drew up a memorandum for the proposed new
act for approval by municipal associations and a Native Conference in Bloemfontein. The Urban Areas Bill was substan-
tially altered in the committee stage. The proposal that
Blacks should have tenure in their areas of urban settlement
was thrown out. Pass law provisions and registration of service contracts were introduced. The Urban Areas Act succeeded
in regulating slum clearance, in the financial control of
locations and in establishing advisory boards for townships.
Its greatest flaw was the abolition of the right of the Black
man to own property in the segregated urban areas, despite the
recommendations of the Native Affairs Commission.

798. Davies, R.H. Capital, State and White Labour in South Africa,
1900-1960: An Historical Materialist Analysis of Class Formation and Class Relations. Brighton: Harvester Press,
1979. 414pp. bibl.

A study of South African state intervention during the
period 1900-1960 to ensure that a privileged white class was
created within the wage earning classes. This caused a division of labour on a racist basis between white and black
workers. The book is divided into the following sections:
Part 1: 'White Wage-Earners and the Hegemony of Mining
Capital'. Part 2: 'White Wage-Earners and the Hegemony of
National Capital 1924-1939'. Part 3: 'Afrikaner Nationalism,
White Wage-Earners and the Apartheid State 1934-1960'.

799. De Kiewiet, C.W. Anatomy of South African Misery. London:
Oxford University Press, 1956. 88pp. Widden lecture
delivered at McMaster University, Hamilton, in January,
1956.

Discusses the problems of nationalism and racialism and
presents a summary of their historical origins. Analyses the
policy of apartheid, the reasons for the adoption of this
policy in South Africa and the weaknesses inherent in apartheid. Pleads for a policy of greater co-operation between
White and Black to solve South Africa's problems.

800. Feit, E. African Opposition in South Africa: The Failure of
Passive Resistance. Stanford: Hoover Institution on War,
Revolution and Peace, 1967. 223pp. bibl.

Describes the structure and organization of the African
National Congress and analyses the weakness and vulnerability
of its leadership. From 1949 onwards the Congress became more
militant in action and attempted to mobilize the African majority. From 1953 to 1956 an alliance was formed of African,
White, Asian and Coloured Congresses. The plan was formulated
to promote passive resistance to government laws considered un-
just and restrictive. The author describes how the Congress
attempted to apply the system of passive resistance to the

Western Areas Removal scheme (1949) and to the provisions of the Bantu Education Act (1953). In both cases the Congress was unable to organize public opinion sufficiently behind it. The failure of passive resistance led to a loss of prestige and further disunity among the leaders of the movement.

801. Feit, E. South Africa: The Dynamics of the African National Congress. London: Oxford University Press, 1962. 73pp.

Uses the material of the 'Treason Trial' (December, 1956 to March, 1961) to analyse the failure of the African National Congress to gain mass support. Discusses briefly the history of the A.N.C. from 1912 onwards, the reaction of the government to the movement, the organization and campaign methods of the A.N.C. and lack of popular support for the movement.

802. Feit, E. Workers without Weapons: The South African Congress of Trade Unions and the Organization of the African workers. Connecticut: Archon, 1975. 230pp.

Traces the development of the Black Trade Union movement from 1918 onwards, with the formation of the Industrial and Commercial Union (I.C.U.) and Industrial and Commercial Workers' Union (I.C.W.U.). By 1930 these two unions had disintegrated and were replaced by the communist inspired Trade Unions. By 1950 there were approximately fifty-two non-white trade unions in existence, but these were not officially recognized and strikes by black members were illegal. These trade unions suffered from lack of funds and effective leadership. The South African Congress of Trade Unions was founded in 1954 in an attempt to change both the political and economic situation within South Africa. By 1964 SACTU had virtually ceased to function. The aims of SACTU and the work which it attempted to carry out in organizing workers, controlling industrial unions, heavy industry and agriculture and in obtaining higher wages for workers is discussed.

803. Fredrickson, G.M. White Supremacy: A Comparative Study in American and South African History. New York: Oxford University Press, 1981. 356pp. maps. bibl.

An attempt to compare the evolution of race patterns in the United States and South Africa. A thematic approach has been chosen, associated with specific periods of history and sometimes with individual areas or provinces. The first theme deals with frontier expansion at the Cape compared with the dispossession of the coastal Indians of America. The author discusses the origin and effects of racial slavery, race mixture and the colour line, the emergence of independent white-dominated states, industrialisation and labour discrimination and finally the comparison of segregation policies in South Africa and the southern states of the United States of America.

804. Gerhart, G.M. Black Power in South Africa: The Evolution of an Ideology. Berkeley: University of California Press, 1978. xi, 364pp. illus. maps. bibl. (Perspectives on Southern Africa, 19).

Examines the development of Black nationalism in South Africa since World War II (1945-1975). Concentrates mainly on tracing the evolution of the orthodox nationalist or Black power school of African politics. Examines the role of the Black urban intelligentsia, particularly that played by Robert Sobukwe, Anton Lembede, Ashby Peter Mda and Steve Biko. Most information in the volume is based on interviews with South Africans between the years 1968 and 1973, on interviews conducted by Carter, Karis and Johns (1963-1964) and examination of documentary materials, Black political pamphlets, newspapers and periodicals. The Black associations discussed include the African National Congress, the Africanist Movement of 1951-1958, the Pan-Africanist Congress of 1959-1960 and the Black Consciousness Movement of the 1970s.

805. Gibson, R. African Liberation Movements: Contemporary Struggles Against White Minority Rule. London: Oxford University Press, 1972. xiii, 350pp. map. tabs. bibl.

A study of African liberation movements based on ten years travel and research throughout Africa. Areas covered include South Africa (Azania), South West Africa (Namibia), Zimbabwe (Rhodesia), the former Portuguese colonies of Angola and Mozambique, Guinéa and the Cape Verde Islands, the Horn of Africa and some islands. In each case, the history of the liberation movements are outlined, the difficulties and internal dissensions facing the movements are discussed and also the problems presented by the neo-colonial ambitions of foreign backers enumerated.

806. Hare, A.P., G. Wienbieck and M. Von Broembsen, eds. South Africa: Sociological Analyses. Cape Town: Oxford University Press, 1979. 430pp. bibl.

Designed as an introduction to the sociological study of South African society. Discusses the cultural values, religion, family structure, education, labour relations, legal system, social stratification, political sociology and social changes prevalent in modern South Africa.

807. Hellmann, E., and L. Abrahams, eds. Handbook on Race Relations in South Africa. Cape Town: Oxford University Press, 1949. xii, 778pp. map.

Aims at assembling all relevant information on racial relations within one volume. Consists of articles written by experts in that particular field. Relevant statistics are included where possible. Covers aspects such as population of various races, administration, laws, labour, trade unions, agriculture within the reserves, pass laws, education, social welfare, sport and recreation, religion, the press, the arts and inter-racial co-operation. Now considerably out-of-date.

Race Contacts, Race Policy, Race Relations 187

808. Hellmann, E., and H. Lever, eds. Conflict and Progress: Fifty Years of Race Relations in South Africa. Johannesburg: Macmillan, 1979. x, 278pp.

Ten specialist articles presenting an overview of the racial situation in South Africa. The contributions survey analytically African nationalism and Black consciousness, politics, education, the economy, legislation and civil rights, urbanization, racial attitudes, South African literature and international relations. The introductory chapter by Ellen Hellmann deals with the history of the South African Institute of Race Relations. The book commemorates the fiftieth anniversary of the Institute.

809. Hoernlé, R.F.A. Race and Reason, Being Mainly a Selection of Contributions to the Race Problem in South Africa. Edited with a memoir by Professor I.D. MacCrone. Johannesburg: Witwatersrand University Press, 1945. xxxvi, 182pp.

A compilation of Professor Hoernlé's writings covering the years 1927 to 1938, which originally appeared in various journals. These articles all illustrate the liberal approach of the author to adjustment of relations between White and Black. The work forms a memorial volume to Hoernlé and the articles are preceded by a biographical tribute to Hoernlé by I.D. MacCrone.

810. Hoernlé, R.F.A. South African Policy and the Liberal Spirit. 2nd ed. Johannesburg: Witwatersrand University Press, 1945. xiv, 190pp. (Phelps-Stokes lectures, 1939).

Lectures 1 and 2 analyse native policy in the Union during the 1930s as one of White domination tempered by 'trusteeship' of the non-white races. Lecture 3 attempts to analyse the 'liberal spirit' and meaning of 'liberty'. Lecture 4 contains the assertion that only total parallelism, or inter-racial assimilation are compatible with liberal ideals. Half measures are unacceptable.

811. Hudson, W., G.F. Jacobs., and S. Biesheuval. Anatomy of South Africa: A Scientific Study of Present-day Attitudes. Cape Town: Purnell, 1966. 140pp. illus. maps. tabs.

A scientific study made by three leading South African social psychologists into the attitudes of white South Africans concerning certain social, political, racial and international topics. A cross-section of the population was selected, interviewed and required to complete a questionnaire. The results are analysed and interpreted in the book and the authors attempt some sort of proposals for solution of South Africa's problems.

812. Jabavu, D.D.T. The Life of John Tengo Jabavu. Lovedale: Lovedale Press, 1922. 154pp. illus.

Describes the life and achievements of Jabavu in the fields of politics, education, religion and journalism.

813. Jabavu, D.D.T. The Segregation Fallacy and Other Papers: A Native View of Some South African Inter-racial Problems. Lovedale: Lovedale Press, 1928. vii, 137pp.

Consists of essays and addresses initially published in various journals and books which deal with the Black man's view of the policy of segregation in South Africa. These articles are entitled: 'The Segregation Fallacy', 'Hertzogian Segregation Versus the Cape Native Policy', 'White Students and Black Students', 'The Disfranchisement of the Cape Native', 'Some Aspects of the Native Bills', 'The Financial Strangulation of Native Education', 'Native Unrest', 'Cross-roads of Native Policy', 'The Bantu and the Gospel' and 'Christian Missions and the Bantu'.

814. Johnstone, F.A. Class, Race and Gold: A Study of Class Relations and Racial Discrimination in South Africa. London: Routledge & Kegan Paul, 1976. 298pp.

A sociological study of racial discrimination in the gold mines and of historical developments regarding this system during the period 1914 to 1922. The historical section of the book occurs in Part 2. The post-war crisis in the mining industry is described. The mining companies attempted to overcome this crisis by making more use of cheaper Black labour in the mines and reducing White labour costs. This led to the strike and uprising of White workers in 1922. The alliance of White Labour Party and Nationalist Party won the general election of 1924. The 'Colour Bar Act' of 1926 legalised the job colour bar. African mine workers became increasingly dissatisfied during the period 1913 to 1918 because of low wages and the employers' system of forced labour. Their forms of protest were doomed to failure. The author adopts a Marxist structuralist explanation of the system of racial discrimination.

815. Jones, J.D.R., and A.L. Saffery. Social and Economic Conditions of Native Life in the Union of South Africa: Findings of the Native Economic Commission, 1930-1932, Collated and Summarised. Johannesburg: University of the Witwatersrand, 1933-34. Repr. from 'Bantu Studies', Vol. 7, no. 3, Sept. 1933, pp.235-55; Vol. 7, no. 4, Dec. 1933, pp.317-40; Vol. 8, no. 1, Mar. 1934, pp.61-94; Vol. 8, no. 2, June 1934, pp.193-211.

Defines the basis of the native problem in South Africa as the conflict between the 'primitive subsistence economy' of the native and the 'advanced money economy' of the Europeans. Examines the social and economic condition of the Black peoples in tribal reserves, on land in rural areas and in urban areas. Makes recommendations regarding centralised control of native education, the taxation of natives, improvements of race relations, partial segregation of races, the labolo system, operation of pass laws and the control of liquor through state or municipal beer shops. Also makes recommendations concerning health, trading rights and housing of Black peoples. Concludes with a discussion of labour conditions and problems in industry, agriculture, and the mines. The majority view of the Commission favoured retention of the 'Colour Bar' and the absence of wage regulation for Black workers.

816. Karis, T., and G.M. Carter. From Protest to Challenge: A Documentary History of African Politics in South Africa, 1882-1964. Stanford: Hoover Institution Press, 1972-1977. 4v.

The documents included in each volume are selected to trace the main developments in Black politics in South Africa from 1882 to recent times. Includes documents of political activities in which Whites, traders and Coloureds were closely involved with Blacks. Each volume is divided into sections. The documents in each section are preceded by an introductory essay explaining the background to the documents and commenting on their significance. At the end of the volume there is a helpful bibliographical note. The titles of the volumes are as follows: Volume 1: 'Protest and Hope, 1882-1934'. Volume 2: 'Hope and Challenge, 1935-1952'. Volume 3: 'Challenge and Violence, 1953-1964'. Volume 4: 'Political Profiles, 1882-1964'.

817. Kotzè, D.A. African Politics in South Africa, 1964-1974: Parties and Issues. London: Hurst, 1975. xi, 276pp. front. bibl.

An intensive study of contemporary Black participation in South African politics following the banning of organizations such as the African National Congress and the Pan-African Congress. Traces and analyses the creation of new political organization and their attitudes to South African government's policy of separate development. Discusses Black consciousness as a reaction to government policy.

818. Kuper, L. An African Bourgeoisie: Race, Class and Politics in South Africa. New Haven: Yale University Press, 1965. xviii, 452pp. illus. bibl.

A study of the professional people and traders who make up the 'upper' occupational strata of African society and the way in which they are affected socially and politically by racial segregation. The area of research for this study was mainly Durban with its largely Zulu-speaking Black population.

819. Kuper, L. Passive Resistance in South Africa. London: Jonathan Cape, 1956. 256pp. illus.

Analysis of the 1952 passive resistance campaign organized jointly by the African National and South African Indian Congresses. Discusses the ideological background to passive resistance, apartheid legislation and its effect on non-whites, and the sociological nature of passive resistance. Provides a detailed historical account of the 1952 campaign.

820. Lamar, H., and L. Thompson, eds. The Frontier in History: North America and Southern Africa Compared. New Haven: Yale University Press, 1981. 360pp. maps. bibl+

The essays contained in this book are based on papers delivered at seminars on comparative frontier history held between 1971 and 1979 at Yale University. The aim of the editors is to promote the study of comparative frontier historiography. This is done by firstly defining the concept of a frontier in universal terms and arriving at some general conclusions regarding the nature of interaction of the conflicting frontier societies. Individual frontier zones in different areas of the world can then be compared and contrasted once these generalizations have been established. The first section of the work consists of an introduction by the editors to North American and Southern African frontier history. The rest of the book consists of comparative essays under the following headings: Part 2: Phases and Processes. Parallel essays on North American and South African frontiers by R.F. Berkhofer and H. Giliomee. Part 3: Political Processes on the Frontiers by C.A. Milner II and C. Saunders. Part 4: Social and Economic Processes by R. Cook and R. Ross. Part 5: Christianity on the Frontier by J. Axtell and R. Elphick. There is a valuable bibliography of publications pertaining to comparative frontier history compiled by G. Miles, pp.317 to 333.

821. Le May, G.H.L. Black and White in South Africa: The Politics of Survival. London: Macdonald, 1971. (Library of the Twentieth Century Series). 127pp. illus. bibl.

A survey of South African political history in which the author describes the origins and growth of Afrikaner nationalism, the genesis of Afrikaner supremacy in the twentieth century and the conflict between the apartheid movement and the Black and Coloured people's congress movement. Under the premiership of Verwoerd (1958-1966), South Africa became a republic (1960) and the policy of apartheid was put into practice with the creation of national units for the Black people. The author concludes with the observation that he sees no prospects for change in South Africa.

822. Lewin, J. Politics and Law in South Africa: Essays on Race Relations. London: Merlin Press, 1963. 116pp.

This book comprises eight essays which have as central theme the 'relative power of Afrikaner nationalism, African nationalism and Englich economic interests'. The author discusses the rise of Afrikaner and African nationalism, the indifference of the English-speaking South Africans to any matters except their own economic interests, the use of political machinery to further Afrikaner interests, the vindication of the nineteenth-century missionary, Dr. John Philip, the Immorality Act, the rigidity of South African racial policy, and the unlikelihood of immediate revolution in South Africa.

823. Lewin, J. The Struggle for Racial Equality. London: Longmans, 1967. xii, 191pp. bibl.

Attempts to demonstrate how racial discrimination began and why this policy persists. The roots of colour prejudice are found in British imperialism and in American history and also existed in South Africa before the Nationalist party rose to power. Law plays an important part in regulating race relations. The position of racial minorities in various countries and international progress regarding racial minorities are considered. Extracts from thirty documents relating to race relations are given covering the years 1833 to 1964.

824. MacCrone, I.D. Race Attitudes in South Africa: Historical, Experimental and Psychological Studies. 2nd ed. Johannesburg: Witwatersrand University Press, 1957. xiv, 328pp. bibl. Repr. 1965.

An attempt to study and analyse the origin and development of social attitudes on the part of the White people of South Africa which underline race contacts and race relations in modern times. The book is divided into three sections -- historical, experimental and psychological. The latter two sections are concerned with the scientific approach to and measurement of race attitudes. Part 1 (historical) deals with European expansion at the Cape and contacts with Hottentots and slaves in the sixteenth and seventeenth centuries. Analyses colonist's attitude of growing intransigence towards Hottentots and acceptance of certain baptized freed slaves into the community. Describes and analyses race attitudes of frontier society of the eighteenth and nineteenth centuries. Insecurity of the frontier society led to development of a sense of racial, social and religious supremacy with distinctions based on creed and colour. In the older established districts of the Cape, freed slaves of dark complexion could no longer be easily assimilated into the community despite being baptized. Thus by the early nineteenth century racial prejudice had become established.

825. Moodie, T. Dunbar. The Rise of Afrikanerdom: Power, Apartheid and the Afrikaner Civil Religion. Berkeley: University of California, 1975. xii, 328pp. bibl.

A study of the ideological sources underlying the moral commitment of the Afrikaner to separate development. Assesses the importance of the 'Christian-Nationalist Afrikaner civil religion' in the 1948 Nationalist election victory. Commences with a description of the so-called 'Afrikaner civil religion' and its origins in the political philosophy of Paul Kruger and the Afrikaans language movement. Also evident in Dutch Reformed theology. By the 1930s the Afrikaner Broederbond and purified National Party had adopted this civil faith to generate mass support. After 1944 Afrikaner leaders united by concentrating on the tenets of this civil faith and mobilized the Afrikaner electorate for victory in 1948. Concludes with a description of the ideological and historical connections between the

Christian-Nationalist ideology and the policy of separate development and also provides a brief account of current controversies within Afrikanerdom.

826. Munger, E.S. Afrikaner and African Nationalism: South African Parallels and Parameters. London: Oxford University Press, 1967. xviii, 142pp. maps.

Briefly summarizes the origins of Afrikaner and African nationalism. Maintains that the concept of a common nationalism is absent in South Africa. Defines groups such as the English, Jewish, Indian and Coloured sections as being 'outsiders' to Afrikaner nationalism. Discusses subordination of class distinctions to nationalism, the influence of radio and the press in South Africa, and the result of press censorship. Reviews the development of Afrikaner nationalism to the final stages and also does the same for African nationalism. Concludes with a discussion of the relationships of Afrikaner and African nationalisms with other forces on the African continent and with the world at large.

827. Neame, L.E. The History of Apartheid: The Story of the Colour Bar in South Africa. London: Pall Mall Press, 1962. 200pp. maps.

Attempts to explain how the crisis situation of racial conflict has arisen in South Africa. Traces the development of the colour bar from the beginning of the nineteenth century until the era of Verwoerd's government, explaining how racial discrimination became embodied in law. Sets out the arguments of those who uphold the colour bar and of those who denounce it.

828. Oliver, S.H. Anatomy of African Misery. London: Hogarth Press, 1927. 234pp.

This book has become rather out-of-date. It was written to voice the author's indignation against the passing of the Colour Bar Law in the Union Legislature in 1926. The author feels that racial discrimination is a relic of the Cape Colony's former attitude to slaves and this discrimination was reinforced by the growth of capitalist industry, particularly the mining industry. The Black man, forced off his land, is compelled to seek unremunative employment with the farmer or work in the towns. The author fears that these evils will spread through Rhodesia and Kenya. Attributes the 'Poor white' problem in South Africa to the prevalent contemptuous attitude towards certain types of labour as being only fit for the Black man.

829. Paton, A. The Long View. ed. by E. Callan. London: Pall Mall Press, 1968. xiii, 295pp. bibl.

A selection from the writings of Alan Paton, former President of the South African Liberal Party. These are divided into three parts, each with an introduction by the editor. Part 1: Into deep waters, 1958-1959. Part 2: After Sharpeville, 1960. Part 3: With bell, book and candle, 1963-1967.

830. Patterson, S. Colour and Culture in South Africa: A Study of the Status of the Cape Coloured People within the Social Structure of the Union of South Africa. London: Routledge, 1953. vi, 402pp. bibl.

Describes the origins and early history of the Coloured people. Outlines the political, legal, economic, educational and social status of the Coloured people, which subordinates them to the White ruling group. Finally, concludes with an account of the internal social structure of the present-day Cape Coloured people, of the development of European attitudes to the Coloured peoples and of Coloured responses to their status.

831. Rhoodie, N.J. Apartheid and Partnership. Pretoria: Academica, 1966. 395pp. bibl.

An attempt to justify the principle of 'separate development' as opposed to partnership of races within South Africa. Attempts to prove that partnership failed in the Federation of Rhodesia, analyses the causes of this failure, and concludes that separate development is preferable for South Africa.

832. Rhoodie, N.J., ed. South African Dialogue: Contrasts in South African Thinking on Basic Race Issues. Johannesburg: McGraw-Hill, 1972. 309pp. map.

Presents the viewpoints of distinguished South Africans both for and against certain contentious aspects of racial policies. The issues discussed are: apartheid, Bantu homelands; alternatives to apartheid, racial issues in the South African economy, the urban African, the Coloured and Asian South Africans, church and education in an apartheid society, verkramp/verlig dichotomy and apartheid and international relations.

833. Rogers, H. Native Administration in the Union of South Africa. 1st ed. Johannesburg: University of the Witwatersrand Press, 1933. 2nd ed. rev. by P.A. Linington. Pretoria: Government Printer, 1949. xi, 267pp. map. bibl.

Prepared on behalf of the Department of Native Affairs. Attempts to supply information on the functions and powers of the Department. Describes systems of local government in native areas, native land administration, native agricultural development and taxation, natives in urban and industrial centres, and recognition of native law and allied topics.

834. Rotberg, R.I., and A.A. Mazrui, eds. Protest and Power in Black Africa. New York: Oxford University Press, 1970. 1274pp. maps. bibl.

Consists of numerous essays divided into sections according to theme. The essays relevant to South Africa are as follows: Part 2: 'Rebellions against Alien Rule', Marks, S. The Zulu Disturbances in Natal. pp.213-257. Part 5: 'The Economic Expression of Discontent', Johns, S.W. Trade Union, Political

Pressure Group or Mass Movement? The Industrial and Commercial Workers Union of Africa. pp.695-754. Kuper, L., 'Non-violence Revisited'. pp.788-802. Part 6: 'The Literary Expression of Protest in the African Novel in English'. pp.823-853.

835. Roux, E. Time Longer than Rope: A History of the Black Man's Struggle for Freedom in South Africa. 2nd ed. Madison: Wisconsin University Press, 1964. 424pp.

First published in 1948. Discusses the political history of the Black population from the nineteenth century onwards. The AmaXosa gradually became detribalized at the Cape, while in the interior various tribes suffered as a result of inter-tribal warfare and the expansion of the Voortrekkers and British. Discusses the career and betrayal of John Tengo Jabavu at the Cape, the Ethiopian movement which aimed at establishing independent African churches, and the influence of Gandhi's theory of passive resistance in the early twentieth century. Describes the abortive struggle of the urban Blacks to achieve recognition in the South African Labour Party. The South African Native National Congress and Industrial and Commercial Workers Union of Africa failed to achieve emancipation for the Black workers. From 1921 the Communist Party of South Africa was active among the Black peoples under the leadership of Bunting. The Nationalists were swept to power in 1929 and were active against leaders and agitators of the Communist Party. In the 1930s unemployment was rife and various demonstrations and unrest occurred before World War II.

836. Sachs, E.S. The Anatomy of Apartheid. London: Colletts, 1965. 424pp.

Traces the historical development of apartheid from the seventeenth century onwards particularly its operation in the mining and manufacturing industry. Discusses South African labour legislation and the injustices and repressive laws perpetrated by the South African government. Concludes with a discussion of the Sharpeville massacre. The author is inclined to be biased against the South African government for personal reasons and his descriptions lack objectivity.

837. Saunders, C., ed. Black Leaders in Southern African History. London: Heinemann, 1979. 160pp. illus. maps. bibl.

Nine leaders have been selected who were essentially nineteenth-century figures. The response of these leaders to white intrusion is an important theme of this volume. The biographical sketches cover: Ngqika (1779-1829); Mzilikazi (1795-1868); Mpanda (1798-1872); Mswati II (1826-65); Cetshwayo (1832-34); Masupha (1820-99); Adam Kok III (1811-75); Tiyo Soga (1829-71) and John Tengo Jabavu (1859-1921).

838. Simons, H.J., and R.E. Simons. Class and Colour in South Africa, 1850-1950. Harmondsworth, Middlesex: Penguin, 1968. 702pp. bibl.

A survey of radical movements from 1850 to 1950 in which two main streams of resistance to White domination were discernable: the national movements of Africans, Indians and Coloureds; and the class struggles of socialists and communists. The year 1850 is taken as the starting point because by this period Britain was preparing to grant representative government to the Cape Colony. The 1853 constitution effectively debarred the majority of the Coloured people from the franchise through the introduction of a high property and wage qualification. The Cape franchise was further loaded against Africans in 1887 and 1892. The discovery of diamonds and gold was a prelude to the industrialization of South Africa and the rise of the urban proletariat, many of whom were mine workers. Black mine workers were subjected to unfair discriminatory practices. White labour parties were interested only in securing employment for White miners and artisans. The Black workers were unable to improve their position because the Act of Union (1909-1910) and the removal of Cape Africans from the Common Voters Role (1936) led to the establishment of exclusive white power. The conservative branch of the Labour Party entered into a coalition with Afrikaner nationalism. The Labour Left wing formed the Communist Party to defend African and Coloured interests.

839. Tatz, C.M. Shadow and Substance in South Africa: A Study in Land and Franchise Policies affecting Africans, 1910-1960. Pietermaritzburg: University of Natal Press, 1962. 238pp. bibl.

The author discusses legislation dealing with land provision for Blacks and the Black franchise passed in South Africa between the years 1910 to 1960. He concludes that there is a close connection between franchise and land policies throughout this period. Prior to Union (1910) the Cape Province favoured a national franchise for all citizens based on an income or property qualification. The opposing view of the northern provinces denied equality of rights and privileges to the African. The basis of the Union's policy towards non-whites was laid down in the recommendations of the South African Native Affairs Commission, 1903-1905. The principles of White domination, territorial segregation and separate representation were formulated by the Commission and formed the basis of all subsequent government legislation. The author analyses the Natives Land Act of 1913, the Native Affairs Act, 1920 and the Native Trust and Land Act 1936, which established separate areas for Black settlement. The Representation of Natives Act of 1936, which abolished the Cape African franchise is discussed. In June 1960, African representation in the Senate and House of Assembly finally ended. A system of local tribal authorities was introduced with limited power and no right of criticism. Africans surrendered land and franchise rights for unfulfilled promises of compensation.

840. University of London. Institute of Commonwealth Studies.
Seminar Papers on the Societies of Southern Africa in the
19th and 20th Centuries. Vol. 1. October 1969-April 1970.
London: University of London, 1969-70. 151pp. bibl.

The seminar was called to co-ordinate correct research in
the Southern African field at different university centres
and in different disciplines in the United Kingdom, North
America, and in Southern Africa itself. In volume 1, most
papers deal with the influence of White pressure and colonial
rule on the political, economic and cultural structure of
African societies. The following papers were presented:
1. Race relations in Southern Africa at the turn of the nineteenth century: the Cape Colony in the Batavian era, 1803-6
by W. Freund. 2. Enter the British legal machine: law and
administration at the Cape 1806-1910 by A. Sachs. 3. The new
African elite in the Eastern Cape and some late nineteenth
century origins of African nationalism by C.C. Saunders. 4.
Independency and Ethiopianism among the Tswana in the late
nineteenth and early twentieth centuries by Q.N. Parsons.
5. The Cape Liberal tradition -- myth or reality? by P. Lewsen.
6. The origin and development of the African political organization by S. Trapido. 7. Class conflict and colour bars in the
South African gold mining industry, 1910-26 by F.A. Johnstone.
8. Party politics and the plural society: South Africa 1910-29
by N. Garson. 9. The I.C.U. and British Imperialism by
S. Neame.

841. Van Biljon, P. Grensbakens tussen Blank en Swart in Suid-
Afrika: 'n Historiese Ontwikkeling van Grensbeleid en Beleid
van Grond Toekenning aan die Naturel in Suid-Afrika. Cape
Town: Juta, 1947. xiii, 490pp. maps. bibl.

Describes the development of the policy of territorial
separation of Black and White races, a policy much influenced
by economic factors both before and after Union. The author
maintains that the policy originated as early as the eighteenth century and during the British era of colonial government and was much influenced by the intervention of philanthropists. The development of territorial segregation is described to the year 1936.

842. Van der Horst, S.T. Native Labour in South Africa. Cape Town:
Oxford University Press, 1942. xii, 239pp. bibl.

Traces the growth of the use of Black labour from the beginning of the nineteenth century and analyses the economic
significance of the measures imposed by law and custom relating
to contact between various races of South Africa. Commences
with a discussion of the growth of economic co-operation between White employer and Black agricultural labourer in the
Cape Colony, Natal and Voortrekker Republics between 1806 and
1870. Describes the effect of the gold and diamond discoveries
upon the market for Black labour, 1870-1899. Labour also became increasingly necessary for transport development, coal
production and urban development. Discusses the problem of the

twentieth century as one of competition between White and Black workers. This led to the introduction of legislative measures protecting the interests of the White workers in the mining and industrial sectors. Discusses the present-day opportunities existing for employment of Black workers, the increasing demand for agricultural workers and the effect of native reserves on the labour force.

843. Walshe, P. Black Nationalism in South Africa: A Short History. Johannesburg: Ravan Press, 1973. 40pp. illus. (Spro-cas publications).

Describes the growth of Black nationalism in South Africa from the formation of the African National Congress (1912) to the Black Peoples' Convention of 1972.

844. Walshe, P. The Rise of African Nationalism in South Africa: The African National Congress, 1912-1952. London: Hurst, 1970. xvi, 480pp. illus. bibl.

Traces the origin of African political consciousness in the nineteenth century, particularly Black participation in Cape politics and missionary and Christian influence. The African National Congress was formed in 1912 as a result of concern among Black leaders regarding discriminatory legislation being passed by the newly constituted Union parliament. The A.N.C. became a movement of protest against official native policy as it slowly developed after Union. There are three chronological periods of developments. From 1912 to 1924 covers the years prior to Hertzog's premiership. During the period 1921 to 1939, Hertzog established a policy of segregation. From 1939 to 1952, Dr. A.B. Xuma led the revival of Congress. The rejection of General Smuts' trusteeship was followed by deep resentment of apartheid policies of the Nationalist Party. During each of these periods, the Congress reactions became generally more radical, changing from consultation to non-collaboration and passive resistance. Discusses Congress policy towards socio-economic issues and ideological influence such as Christianity and the Communist Party of South Africa. Also analyses the organization of Congress and the weaknesses within its structure and its political ineffectiveness.

845. Wilson, F., and D. Perrot, eds. Outlook on a Century: South Africa, 1870-1970. Lovedale: Lovedale Press; Johannesburg: Spro-cas, 1973. xix, 746pp. illus.

Consists of a collection of articles from the journal 'South African Outlook' founded in 1870 at Lovedale missionary institution. Contains contributions by twenty-five Black contributors from 1870 onwards. Other contributors consist of experts who studied African affairs and race relations. The articles are divided into three periods: 1870-1900, 1901-1931 and 1932-1970. Within these period divisions, articles are divided into subject divisions, such as people, land and labour, education, politics, industrial relations, indigenous churches, socio-economic conditions, rule of law and apartheid.

CHAPTER XVII
MISSIONARIES

Bibliographies

846. Brownlee, M. The Lives and Work of South African Missionaries: [excluding Livingstone]. A Bibliography. Cape Town: University of Cape Town, School of Librarianship, 1952. 32pp.

847. Cowie, M.J. The London Missionary Society in South Africa: A Bibliography. Cape Town: University of Cape Town, School of Librarianship, 1969. vi, 81pp.

848. Frost, P.J. A Bibliography of Missions and Missionaries in Natal. Cape Town: University of Cape Town, School of Librarianship, 1969. v, 29pp.

849. Hinchliff, P.B. Calendar of Cape Missionary Correspondence, 1800-1850. Pretoria: National Council for Social Research, 1967. 255pp.

850. Meyer, P.M. The Roman Catholic Church in South Africa: A Bibliography. Cape Town: University of Cape Town, School of Librarianship, 1979. iv, 54pp.

851. Tait, E.C. Dr. John Philip, 1775-1851: A Bibliography. Johannesburg: University of the Witwatersrand, Department of Bibliography, Librarianship and Typography, 1972. 70pp.

852. Turnbull, C.E.P. The Work of the Missionaries of Die Nederduitse Gereformeerde Kerk up to the Year 1910. Johannesburg: University of the Witwatersrand, Department of Bibliography, Librarianship and Typography, 1965. 90pp.

Monographs

853. Briggs, D.R., and J. Wing. The Harvest and the Hope: The Story of Congregationalism in Southern Africa. Johannesburg: Congregational Church of Southern Africa, 1970. 344pp. illus. map. bibl.

A comprehensive history of the London Missionary Society and American Board Missions is provided for Southern Africa from

1801 onwards. The areas covered are the Cape Colony, Kaffraria, Natal, Zululand, Kuruman and Rhodesia.

854. Brown, W.E. The Catholic Church in South Africa. London: Burns & Oates, 1960. 384pp. illus. bibl.

Chapter 9 of this book, entitled 'The Church and the Africans' provides a summary of missionary activities and attitudes to the African tribes in the Cape, Zululand, Basutoland and Natal in the nineteenth century. Chapter 10 discusses the work of the Trappist monks at Marianhill from 1882 to 1910.

855. Calderwood, H. Caffres and Caffre Missions: With Preliminary Chapters on the Cape Colony as a Field for Emigration and a Basis of Missionary Activity. London: James Nisbet, 1858. vii, 234pp.

An account of the author's experiences among the Gaikas and Fingos, first as missionary and later as civil commissioner. His first post was Gaika commissioner under Sir Peregrine Maitland. Sir Harry Smith appointed him civil commissioner of Victoria.

856. Callaway, G. Pioneers in Pondoland. Lovedale: Lovedale Press, n.d. ix, 199pp. illus. map.

Records the beginning of the Anglican Church in western and eastern Pondoland. Descriptions of the chief Faku, of the events leading to the annexation of Pondoland, of the tribal way of life and of the establishment of the Holy Cross Mission.

857. Campbell, J. Travels in South Africa, Undertaken at the Request of the Missionary Society. London: Black, Parry, 1815. xv, 400pp. illus. map.

Describes a tour of inspection made by the author at the request of the London Missionary Society. The areas covered included Stellenbosch, Caledon, Genadendal, Bethelsdorp, Graaff-Reinet and Lattakoo. After a journey of nine months the author reached Cape Town in November 1813. A very poor impression is formed of the mission station at Bethelsdorp.

858. Campbell, J. Travels in South Africa, Undertaken at the Request of the Missionary Society, being a Narrative of the Second Journey in the Interior of that Country. London: London Missionary Society, 1822. 2v. illus. map.

The author, accompanied by Dr. Philip and Messrs. Evans and Moffat visited mission stations in the Cape Colony and Kaffraria. He returned to Cape Town in November 1819. The second journey was started in January 1820 and covered Lattakoo (Kuruman), Mashow and Griqua country. Various observations are made on the Griquas, Bushmen and Bechuanas.

859. Casalis, E. The Basutos; or Twenty-three Years in South Africa. London: James Nisbet, 1861. xix, 355pp.

The volume is divided into two parts entitled: 1. 'Journeys of Exploration -- Labours' and 2. 'Manners and Customs of the Basuto'. There is an account of the foundation of the French Protestant Mission at Thaba Bosigo in 1833 by Casalis, Arbousset and Gosselin. This mission was considered a great success due to the support of Moshesh. The author describes the social customs and culture of the Basuto.

860. Clinton, D.K. The South African Melting Pot; a Vindication of Missionary Policy, 1799-1836. London: Longmans Green, 1937. xvi, 158pp. illus. map. bibl.

Describes from original records of missionaries and the government, the work, policy and difficulties of the London Missionary Society during the first half of the nineteenth century. The methods, motives, ideas and attitudes of the missionaries are evaluated. The author deals with the formation of the Society, the Bethelsdorp mission, the spread of missionary activity and the work of Dr. John Philip, the most important missionary.

861. Davies, H., and R.H.W. Shepherd, comps., South African Missions, 1800-1950: An Anthology. London: Thomas Nelson, 1954. 232pp. illus.

The introductory chapter of the book provides a brief survey of the indigenous people of South Africa, a description of the various missionary movements and an estimate of missionary achievements. The rest of the work is devoted to extracts from the writings of numerous missionaries which provide the reader with a description of the environmental conditions under which the missionaries laboured. Some idea is given of the clash of culture between the white man and the tribal people.

862. Davies, H. Great South African Christians. Cape Town: Oxford University Press, 1951. 190pp. bibl.

The author has selected eighteen biographies of leading Christians who influenced the course of history in South Africa. Most of the biographies deal with missionaries and include Georg Schmidt, John Philip, Robert Moffat, William Shaw, Daniel Lindley, Eugene Casalis, David Livingstone and Francis Pfanner.

863. Du Plessis, J. A History of Christian Missions in South Africa. London: Longmans Green, 1911. 393pp. map. bibl. Repr. Cape Town: Struik, 1965.

A history of Christian missions covering the period from the seventeenth to the end of the nineteenth century in South Africa. The period up to 1850 is described in great detail and the work of all Christian missions is included.

Missionaries

864. Edmunds, A. A Great Adventure: The Story of the Founding of Methodism in Southern Africa. Palmerton: Mission Printing Press, 1936. 144pp.

Discusses the work and achievements of the missionaries Barnabas Shaw, William Shaw and Thomas Jenkins, who laboured among the tribes of Namaqualand and of the eastern Cape.

865. Gerdener, G.B.A. Recent Developments in the South African Mission Field. London: Marshall Morgan & Scott, 1958. 286pp.

The author intends this work to be a follow-up to 'A History of Christian Missions in South Africa' by J. du Plessis (see entry 863). There are very comprehensive accounts of all Christian denominations.

866. Groves, C.P. The Planting of Christianity in Africa. London: Lutterworth Press, 1954. 4v.

This is regarded as the standard work on mission history in Africa. There are various references to South African missions in these volumes.

867. Grubb, K.G. Christian Handbook of South Africa. Lovedale: Lovedale Press for Christian Council of South Africa, 1938. viii, 290pp.

Lists Christian workers of all denominations in South Africa and gives various statistics on the missions and churches in 1938.

868. Hinchliff, P. The Church in South Africa. London: S.P.C.K. for the Church Historical Society, 1968. 116pp. map. bibl. (Church History Outlines ed. by V.H.H. Green).

This book consists of various essays, chronologically arranged, which provide interesting interpretations of aspects of Church history in South Africa. These essays include discussions of the Moravian Mission, the achievements of Vanderkemp, Philip and Shaw, frontier and mission, missionary conflict and growth in the north, Scottish missions and Ethiopianism.

869. Holden, W.C. A Brief History of Methodism and of Methodist Missions in South Africa: Wesleyan Methodist Book Room, 1877. viii, 519pp. illus.

Part 2 of this volume deals with Methodist missions in South Africa particularly contemporary accounts of missions in Natal, the Eastern Cape, Orange Free State, Transvaal and Swaziland. Author a missionary in Natal, who describes conditions in mission stations at the time he was resident in South Africa.

870. Jordaan, B. Splintered Crucifix: Early Pioneers for Christendom on Madagascar and the Cape of Good Hope. Cape Town: Struik, 1969. 276pp. illus. bibl.

A readable biography of the Scottish missionary artisan James Cameron, who spent twenty-eight years at the Cape (1835-1863), after fleeing from Madagascar. Although Cameron no longer practised as a missionary at the Cape, he continued to correspond with the London Missionary Society regarding events in the Colony. He was also in close contact with missionaries Dr. John Philip, Dr. John Campbell, Robert Moffat, J.J. Freeman and William Ellis and thus played a part in the pioneer nineteenth century missionary movement. Cameron is also remembered as a builder, city engineer and photographer of Cape Town.

871. Kellerman, A.G. Profetisme in Suid-Afrika in Akkulturasie Perspektief: 'n Studie van die Impakt van die Christendom en die Westerse Kultuur op die Bantoe, soos Gemanifesteer in Profetiese Bewegings. Prophetism in South Africa in Acculturation Perspective: A Study of the Impact of Christianity and Western Culture on the Bantu as Manifested in Prophetic Movements. Voorburg: Zanoni-Offset, 1964. 282pp. bibl.

A scholarly study of African prophetic or separatist movements, in which the author maintains that the movements must be explained in the culture-historical perspective of the comprehensive acculturation situation in South Africa. The first part of the dissertation describes the historical contact between African and Westerner and the resultant acculturation process. The second chapter surveys the infra-structure of tribal culture. Missionary effort, education, governmental administrative action and a new economic structure have affected traditional tribal society. The prophetic movements are a form of protest against cultural disintegration and an attempt to reconcile tribal and Christian beliefs.

872. Kitchingman, J. The Kitchingman Papers: Missionary Letters and Journals, 1817 to 1848 from the Brenthurst Collection, Johannesburg. ed., by B. Le Cordeur and C. Saunders. Johannesburg: Brenthurst Press, 1976. 274pp. illus.

Correspondence and journal of Kitchingman, who was a representative of the London Missionary Society at Bethelsdorp for most of the period between 1821 and 1848.

873. Kotze, D.J., ed. Letters of the American Missionaries, 1835-1838. Cape Town: Van Riebeeck Society, 1950. (Van Riebeeck Society Publications, 30). 294pp. illus. map.

The American Board of Commissioners for Foreign Missions sent out its first party of missionaries to South Africa in February 1835. On the recommendation of Dr. John Philip, the Board decided to establish missions among the Zulu and Matabele. The missionaries chosen were H.I. Venable, A.E. Wilson, D. Lindley, G. Champion, A. Grout and N. Adams. In the Transvaal, Lindley, Wilson and Venable attempted to establish a mission station among the Matabele. This station was abandoned after a clash between Moselekatse and the voortrekkers. The missionaries subsequently attempted to establish mission stations in Natal. Their efforts were again disrupted by Dingaan's massacre of Retief's party and the battles of Bloukrans and Weenen. The letters of the missionaries during the period 1835-1838 relate the misfortunes which befell them. These letters were sent to the Prudential Committee of the Missionary Board and published in the Missionary Herald.

874. [Lindley, D.] Smith, E.W. The Life and Times of Daniel Lindley, 1801-1890. London: Epworth Press, 1949. xxx, 456pp. illus. maps.

The above biography also throws light on the work of the American missionaries.

875. Kruger, B. The Pear Tree Blossoms: A History of Moravian Mission Stations in South Africa, 1737-1869. Genadendal: Moravian Church in South Africa, 1966. 335pp. illus. maps.

Describes the history of the Moravian mission stations at the Cape from their beginning until the division of the work into two provinces. Research is based on archival sources at Genadendal. Discusses Moravian missionary work among the Hottentots in the eighteen century, under the leadership of Georg Schmidt, the establishment of Genadendal, and further mission stations at Hemel en Aarde, Elim and Clarkson in the nineteenth century. The effects on the missions of the liberation of the slaves, transfer of lepers to Robben Island and frontier wars are discussed.

876. Lewis, C., and G.E. Edwards. Historical Records of the Church of the Province of South Africa. London: Society for Promoting Christian Knowledge, 1934. xviii, 821pp. illus. map.

Covers the history of this Church in the Cape Province, Natal, Orange Free State, Kaffraria, Transvaal, Zululand, Southern Rhodesia, Lebombo and Damaraland. Important in showing the educational work of the Church mission, particularly in tribal areas.

877. Lovett, R. The History of the London Missionary Society, 1795-1895. London: Henry Frowde, 1899. 2v. illus. maps.

A detailed history of the London Missionary Society describing the work of the society in all parts of the world where it is active. Volume 1 deals with the London Missionary Society in South Africa.

878. Majeke, N. The Role of the Missionaries in Conquest. Johannesburg: Society of Young Africa, 1952. 140pp.

The author attempts to prove that the missionary in Southern Africa was an agent of British imperialism in the subjugation of the tribal inhabitants. He discusses the imperialistic motives of missionaries Philip, Ayliff, Moffat and Livingstone.

Missionaries

879. Moffat, R. Missionary Labours and Scenes in Southern Africa ... London: John Snow, 1842. viii, 624pp. illus.

Preliminary chapters deal with the early work of the London Missionary Society in South Africa, including the achievements of van der Kemp and Philip. There is a valuable account of mission work among the Bechuanas and a description of Moselekatse and the Matabele. The author also describes the work of various mission stations among the Bechuanas, Matabele, Basutos and other tribes.

880. Orr, J.E. Evangelical Awakenings in Africa. 2nd ed. Minneapolis: Bethany Fellowship, 1975. 245pp. bibl.

This book provides a good summary of the evangelical revival which took place in Europe and North America in the nineteenth century. The revival resulted in the establishment of denominational mission societies, Sunday schools and Bible societies. In South Africa, missionaries from abroad and certain colonists commenced work among the indigenous population. By the mid-nineteenth century, the evangelical movement had affected both Dutch Reformed and English-speaking churches and the missionary movement received an added impetus. Many missionaries of this period were university trained. They were able to reduce the languages of the Africans to writing, educate the indigenous population and establish hospitals. Missionaries often fought exploitation of the native population by colonists and encouraged their charges to become self-reliant. As native cultures disintegrated, many secessionist churches arose such as Zionism and Pentecostalism. Many leaders of the African movements for political independence from White rule were mission trained.

881. Philip, J. Researches in South Africa: Illustrating the Civil, Moral and Religious Condition of the Native Tribes; Including Journals of the Author's Travels in the Interior; Together with Detailed Accounts of the Progress of the Christian Missions, Exhibiting the Influence of Christianity in Promoting Civilization. London: James Duncan, 1828. Repr. New York: Negro Universities Press, 1969. 2v.

This work caused bitter controversy at the time of publication because it severely criticised the policy of the colonial government and the colonists towards the tribal peoples of the Cape. Despite the biased views of Dr. Philip, the volumes contain considerable information regarding the inhabitants of the Cape Colony and the progress of missionary work in the first quarter of the nineteenth century.

882. [Philip, J.] Schutte, C.E.G. Dr. John Philip's Observations Regarding the Hottentots of South Africa. Archives Yearbook for South African History. Vol. 3, Part 1, 1940. Pretoria: Government Printer, 1940. pp.89-256. bibl. (M.A. Thesis. University of Stellenbosch, 1937).

Attempts to prove that Dr. Philip's assertions, contained in his 'Researches in South Africa' published in 1828, were highly

Missionaries

prejudiced and biased against the colonial government and Cape farmers. Maintains that Philip had an ulterior motive in condemning the so-called oppressive policies of the colonists towards the Black and Coloured peoples, as he wished to increase his own prestige and influence with the British government.

883. Sales, J.M. Mission Stations and the Coloured Communities of the Eastern Cape, 1800-1852. Cape Town: Balkema, 1975. 176pp. illus. bibl.

Discusses the history of the London Missionary Society at the Cape from its commencement in 1800, when Vanderkemp established a mission station among the Hottentots at Bethelsdorp. By 1851, the Coloured settlement at Kat River had been adversely affected by the Frontier Wars of 1835, 1846 and 1851. Theopolis ceased to exist as a mission station. Missionary interest in the Coloured community waned with the deaths of Dr. John Philip (1851) and James Read, senior (1852).

884. Sales, J.M. The Planting of the Churches in South Africa. Michigan: Eerdmans, 1971. 170pp. maps. bibl.

This book provides a comprehensive account of missionary work and achievements in South Africa from the seventeenth century onwards. The author devotes much attention to the London Missionary Society and its expansion in the Cape Colony and Botswana throughout the nineteenth century. The sections on missions in the Orange Free State, Lesotho, Natal, the Transvaal and Swaziland, are briefer. There are two short concluding chapters on separatist churches and the state of the churches after the Anglo-Boer War (1899-1902).

885. Schimlek, F. Mariannhill: A Study in Bantu Life and Missionary Effort. Mariannhill: Mariannhill Mission Press, 1953. 352pp. illus.

A description of the founding and growth of the Mariannhill Mission Station in Natal from 1882 onwards. The mission station was founded by Trappist monks and spread to Umtata, Southern Rhodesia and Bechuanaland. The order was responsible for the establishment of schools, seminaries, hospitals, clinics, orphanages, workshops and printing presses which operate for the benefit of African, Coloured and Indian inhabitants.

886. Shaw, B. Memorials of South Africa. London: Hamilton Adams, 1840. 371pp.

The author established the first Wesleyan Mission Station in the interior of South Africa at Lily Fountain. Valuable descriptions are given of pioneer missionaries and of Hottentots, Bushmen, Korannas, Namaquas and various Black tribes.

887. [Shaw, W.] Boyce, W.B. Memoir of the Rev. William Shaw, late General Superintendent of the Wesleyan Missions in South-Eastern Africa ... London: Wesleyan Conference Office, 1874. vi, 463pp. illus. map.

An account of the missionary labours of Shaw. Describes the Albany settlements, frontier wars and the condition of the frontier settlements in the mid-nineteenth century.

888. [Shaw, W.] Hammond-Tooke, W.D., ed. The Journal of William Shaw. Cape Town: Balkema, 1972. 220pp.

The journal of William Shaw covers two periods. The period 1820 to 1821 deals with Shaw's period of service among the settlers at Salem. The second period, 1827 to 1829, describes his work at Wesleyville, a mission station. The editor has provided a biographical introduction, attended to matters of punctuation and added various explanatory notes at the end of the text.

889. [Shaw, W.] Sadler, C., ed. Never a Young Man: Extracts From the Letters and Journals of the Rev. William Shaw. Cape Town: HAUM, 1967. 189pp. illus.

Shaw was an 1820 British settler minister appointed as Methodist chaplain to Sephton's party on the Aurora. In 1823 he established the first of a series of mission stations at Wesleyville, across the eastern frontier of the Cape. His journal commences with the departure of the settlers in 1819. The last entries contained in this volume date from the year 1856, when he returned to England, following the death of his wife. The journal provides a vivid account of the difficulties encountered by the 1820 settlers, the departure of the Dutch trekkers, the customs of the Xhosa, Fingoes, slaves and Hottentots and the progress of missionary work on the eastern frontier.

890. Shaw, W. The Story of my Mission in South-Eastern Africa: Comprising some Account of the European Colonists, with Extended Notices of the Kafir and other Native Tribes ... London: Hamilton, Adams, 1860. ix, 576pp. illus. map.

Describes Shaw's arrival at the Cape as a member of Sephton's Party in 1820. Details the progress, grievances and misfortunes of the settlers. The misunderstandings between Dr. Philip and the Wesleyan missionaries are mentioned. There is considerable information on Kaffraria and the various tribes. The progress of the various missionary institutions of South-East Africa is described.

891. Strassberger, E. The Rhenish Mission Society in South Africa, 1830-1950. Cape Town: Struik, 1969. xvi, 109pp. illus. bibl.

Discusses the achievements and work of the Rhenish Mission Society, which was active at the southern stations of Stellenbosch, Tulbagh and Worcester, at the institutes Wupperthal and

Ebenhaezer, in Namaqualand and in the Karree Mountains. Laboured mainly among the Coloured peoples during the nineteenth century. The Dutch Reformed Church eventually took over the Rhenish mission stations.

892. Sundkler, B.G.M. Bantu Prophets in South Africa. 2nd ed. London: Oxford University Press, 1961. 381pp. illus. bibl.

First published in 1948. This work was published under the auspices of the International African Institute. The author describes the rise of the African Separatist or Independent Church Movement, which was formed partly by secession from White mission churches and partly by spontaneous growth. African leaders of the movement have attempted to find some synthesis between their own tribal religion and Christianity. The organization of the different Independent Churches, the forms of worship and the personalities of the leaders are described.

893. Taylor, J. Dexter, ed. Christianity and the Natives of South Africa: A Year-Book of South African Missions. Lovedale: Lovedale Institution Press, 1927. 500pp.

This year-book was published under the auspices of the General Missionary Conference of South Africa (1927). Commences with a series of special articles setting forward the political, economic, social and racial background of missionary effort. The second section surveys the work of all missionary bodies in Southern Africa. There are directories of European missionaries and ordained native clergy. Reports are given on educational institutions throughout Southern Africa, including Southern Rhodesia.

894. Van der Merwe, W.J. The Development of Missionary Attitudes in the Dutch Reformed Church in South Africa. Cape Town: Nasionale Pers, 1936. 279pp. maps. bibl.

The Dutch did little towards the conversion of Hottentots at the Cape during the seventeenth, eighteenth and early nineteenth century. Slaves who professed Christianity and who could speak Dutch were freed and the Dutch East India Company made some effort to convert their slaves. Colonists were reluctant to do so and most slaves became Mohammedans. The Moravians were the first to establish a mission station among the Hottentots in the eighteenth century. During the nineteenth century, the efforts of the London Missionary Society representatives such as Dr. John Philip, aroused resentment among the Cape frontier farmers and certain officials. At the same time the work of the missionaries stimulated some fervour within the Dutch Reformed Church. The South African Missionary Society began some mission work at the Cape, despite the opposition of the Dutch Reformed Church to its interdenominational character. In the second half of the nineteenth century more ministers were available for the Dutch Reformed Church and the training of missionaries was undertaken at Wellington. Missionaries were sent to the Transvaal,

Bechuanaland and Mashonaland. One of the best known of these missionaries was Stephanus Hofmeyr, who worked among the Bakhatla tribe.

895. Van Heerde, G.L. Twee Eeue van Sendingwerk: 'n Oorsig oor ons Kerk se Sendingwerk in Suid-Afrika, 1652-1857. Cape Town: N.G. Kerk-Uitgewers, 1951. 139pp.

This work covers much the same ground as the book mentioned in entry 894.

896. Warren, M. The Missionary Movement from Britain in Modern History. London: SCM Press, 1965. 192pp. bibl.

Discusses the political, economic and social factors which influenced the missionary movement in Britain from the eighteenth century onwards. Describes the interaction between Christianity, commerce and imperialism. The missionary may unintentionally have been the agent of colonial expansion as the missionary movement openly rejected government supervision and interference and had separate financial resources. The main areas of communication through which the missionaries were able to make contact with tribal peoples were the mission hospitals and mission schools. Indigenous cultures gradually disintegrated under Western influence but traces of primitive religions remained and gave rise to various sects in Africa. The author terms these sects 'crisis-religion'. There has also been a revolt in Africa against White domination in the form of nationalism.

897. Whiteside, J. History of the Wesleyan Methodist Church of South Africa. London: Elliot Stock, 1906. viii, 479pp. illus. bibl.

Detailed history of the establishment of the Wesleyan Methodist Church at the Cape, and of the work of the various mission stations on the eastern frontier. Briefer descriptions of Methodism in the Orange River Colony, Transvaal and Natal and of the mission among the Barolongs and in Rhodesia. Interesting account of the frontier wars as seen from the missionaries' point of view. Author displays certain bias e.g., against Dr. John Philip.

898. [Williams, J.] Holt, B. Joseph Williams and the Pioneer Mission to the South-Eastern Bantu. Lovedale: Lovedale Press, 1954. 186pp. illus. bibl.

Williams was one of the pioneer missionaries among the Xhosa (1816-1818), and established the Kat River Mission. He is regarded as the forerunner of the Methodist, Presbyterian and Anglican missionaries who laboured in the Ciskeian and Transkeian territories.

CHAPTER XVIII
SOUTH AFRICAN POPULATION

Black Peoples

Bibliographies

899. Schapera, I. Select Bibliography of South African Native Life and Problems. London: Oxford University Press, 1941. 249pp.

This work was first compiled for the Inter-University Committee for African Studies. The section entitled 'Modern Status and Conditions' (pp.110-203) was of particular value historically. In order to keep this section up-to-date, the University of Cape Town, School of Librarianship has published the following four supplements which appear in entry 900.

900. Schapera, I. Select Bibliography of South African Native Life and Problems. [Supplements to Section on Modern Status and Conditions]. Cape Town: University of Cape Town, School of Librarianship, 1950-1974.

First Supplement (1939-1949). Compiled by M.A. Holden and A.J. Jacoby. Published in 1950. 25,34pp.

Second Supplement (1950-1958). Compiled by J. Back and R. Giffen. Published in 1960. 31,31pp.

Third Supplement (1958-1963). Compiled by C. Solomon. Published in 1964. 51pp.

Fourth Supplement (1964-1974). Compiled by S.B. Alman. Published in 1974. 39pp.

Monographs

901. Alberti, L. Ludwig Alberti's Account of the Tribal Life and Customs of the Xhosa in 1807. Cape Town: Balkema, 1968. xiv, 117pp. illus.

Ethnographic account by Alberti, military officer in the service of the Batavian Republic at the Cape and landdrost of Uitenhage from 1804 to 1806. Describes the tribal life and customs of the Xhosa and relations between the Xhosa and colonists.

902. Angas, G.F. The Kafirs Illustrated in a Series of Drawings taken among the Amazulu, Amaponda, and Amakosa Tribes: Also Portraits of the Hottentot, Malay, Fingo and other Races inhabiting Southern Africa; Together with Sketches of Landscape Scenery in the Zulu Country, Natal and the Cape Colony. London: Hogarth, 1849. Facs. repr. Cape Town: Balkema, 1974. 133pp. illus.

Angas, an English traveller and natural history artist, visited South Africa in 1847 and spent a year in the western and eastern Cape and Natal. 'The Kafirs Illustrated' was published in an unusually large folio size and contains a valuable pictorial record of the landscape of the period and the costume and customs of various tribes, particularly the Zulus. The text accompanying the illustrations is reasonably accurate, but rather verbose and sentimental.

903. Ayliff, J., and J. Whiteside. History of the Abambo, Generally Known as "Fingos". Butterworth: Gazette Printers, 1912. 101pp. Facs. repr. Cape Town: Struik, 1962.

Relates the history of the Abambo in the nineteenth century. Concludes with an account of the effects of the Glen Grey Act, passed by the Cape parliament, on the Fingos. Lists the various Fingo clans, chiefs and places of residence. Provides a genealogical table of the ancestry of Fingo chiefs and also supplies the names of chiefs and councillors in various districts during 1910.

904. Brownlee, C. Reminiscences of Kaffir Life and History. Lovedale: Lovedale Mission Press, 1896. vii, 402pp. Repr. ed. by C.C. Saunders. Pietermaritzburg: University of Natal Press, 1977. xliv, 475pp. (Killie Campbell African Reprint Series).

An introductory memoir by Mrs. Brownlee describes the events of Brownlee's life. The rest of the volume is divided into various sections: Personal incidents; i.e., personal encounters with Xhosa tribes described by Brownlee and others. Historical chapters recounting events which occurred in Brownlee's lifetime at the Cape and Natal. Superstitions and customs among the Native races. Biographical sketches of various chiefs; e.g., Sandile, Xoxo, Tola, Eno, Tyala. Addresses of missions.

905. Bruwer, J.P. Die Bantoe van Suid-Afrika. Johannesburg: Afrikaanse Pers, 1963. 220pp. illus. maps. bibl.

Attempts to describe the cultural, political, religious, social and legal organization of the various tribes of South Africa and the manner in which tribal culture has been affected by western civilization. Provides a rather outdated description of state administration of Black peoples of South Africa.

South African Population - Black Peoples 211

906. Bryant, A.T. Bantu Origins; the People and Their Language.
Cape Town: Struik, 1963. 340pp. front. bibl.

Discusses the various anthropological theories regarding origin of the 'African negroes', 'Negrillos' of the Congo forests and 'Bushmen'. Discusses and compares various theories on origins of 'Bantu Language' giving examples from the various languages to show similarities and variations. Also attempts to explain the mystery of Zimbabwe as being of Phoenician and Arabic origins.

907. Bryant, A.T. History of the Zulu and Neighbouring Tribes.
Cape Town: Struik, 1964. 157pp. Repr. of work first published in 1913.

This book is divided into various sections. Part 1 deals with the history of the Swazi, Ndwandwe Clan, Mashaband Clan, Abasembo Tribal Family, Myeni Clan, Zikali Clan, Mngomezulu Clan, Nyawa Clan, Matenjwa Clan, Emanlutjini, Emazizini, Emabheleni, and Dlamini Clan. Parts 2-5 deal with Shaka's Natal campaigns against various clans. Part 6 deals with the history of the Tembe Tongas. Part 7 covers the Great Nguni Trek (- 700 B.C. to 100 A.D.). Part 8 describes early Zululand and its people.

908. Bundy, C. The Rise and Fall of the South African Peasantry.
London: Heinemann, 1979. 275pp. bibl.

A study of African agriculture in South Africa between the years 1870 to 1913. Commences with a description of tribal agricultural practices before conquest by the White settlers. By the final third of the nineteenth century three types of African peasants existed. Firstly, in the African reserves, peasants still lived in tribal organization and used traditional production methods. Secondly, peasants lived on land owned by Whites and paid rent in return for the right to cultivate the land for their own needs. A third type of peasant were commercial farmers holding land on individual tenure. In the twentieth century mine-owners and White farmers were anxious to dislodge African labour from rural areas. White farmers feared competition from Black peasants and mine-owners needed a cheap source of labour. Legislative measures, culminating in the Natives Land Act of 1913 undermined the prosperity of the Black peasantry and promoted the system of migrant labour to the towns. This work is based on a D.Phil. thesis, submitted to Oxford University in 1976 and entitled 'African Peasants and Economic Change in South Africa, 1870-1913, with particular reference to the Cape'.

909. Ellenberger, D.F., and J.C. MacGregor. History of the Basuto, Ancient and Modern. London: Caxton, 1912. xxii, 396pp.

Very detailed history of the Basuto up to the time of Moshesh's rise to power. The origins of the Basuto are discussed including evidence derived from oral tradition. The Basuto people are shown to originate from various tribes whose history is given. Moshesh is lauded as the promoter of

Christianity among his people. An appendix contains notes on the religion, superstitions, law, customs and social, civil and political life of the Basuto. There is also a history of Sebetoane and genealogical tables of tribes mentioned in the book.

910. Hammond-Tooke, W.D., ed. The Bantu-speaking Peoples of Southern Africa. London: Routledge & Kegan Paul, 1974. xxii, 525pp. illus. bibl.

Successor to Schapera's survey of the Bantu-speaking tribes of South Africa (published 1937). (See entry no.931). Various contributors record physical characteristics, traditional cultures and important social, cultural and economic changes that have occurred since the coming of the White man.

911. Hodgson, T.L. The Journals of the Rev. T.L. Hodgson. ed. by R.L. Cope. Johannesburg: Witwatersrand University Press, 1977. xvii, 435pp. illus.

Covers the period July, 1821 to December, 1830. Recounts Hodgson's experiences as member of the Methodist Missionary Society among the Tswana of the Transvaal.

912. Holden, W.C. The Past and Future of the Kaffir Races. London: The Author, 1866. Facs. repr. Cape Town: Struik, 1963. xii, 576pp. illus. maps.

This work is divided into three sections: 1. History. 2. Manners and customs. 3. Means needful for preservation and improvement. Author was a Wesleyan missionary whose duties brought him into frequent contact with ministers, colonists, magistrates and tribes. Observations on tribal manners and customs of interest form most informative section of the work. Various digressions exist on Christian duties of the White man to the various tribes.

913. Hunter, M. Reaction to Conquest: Effects of Contact with Europeans on the Pondo of South Africa. 2nd ed. London: Oxford University Press, 1961. 582pp. illus. maps.

Detailed account of the Pondo in the process of change from cattle-raising tribesmen to wage-earners in a modern economic system. Divided into three sections. The first section studies the effects of culture contact upon the Pondo living in the reserves. The second section discusses urbanization and the third describes the position of Black people living on White men's farms.

914. Lagden, Sir G. The Basutos; the Mountaineers and Their Country: Being a Narrative of Events Relating to the Tribe from its Formation early in the Nineteenth Century to the Present Day. London: Hutchinson, 1909. 2v. illus. maps.

Comprehensive and detailed history of the Basuto by a former resident Commissioner in Basutoland. Use has been made of official Basutoland records from the archives at Cape Town,

South African Population - Black Peoples   213

   journals and publications of the Paris Evangelical Mission
   Society and the memoirs of missionaries Casalis, Mabille and
   Coillard, as well as material loaned from the Colonial Office
   and Royal Colonial Institute.

915. MacLean, J., comp. A Compendium of Kafir Laws and Customs,
   Including Genealogical Tables of Kafir Chiefs and Various
   Tribal Census Returns. Mount Coke: Wesleyan Mission Press
   for the government of British Kaffraria, 1858. vii, 168pp.

   Consists of extracts from the writings of various White
   officials and missionaries who were in close contact with the
   tribes of Kaffraria and who provide descriptions of their
   social customs and tribal laws. These writers include Rev.
   H.H. Dugmore, J.C. Warner (Tambookie agent), Charles Brownlee
   (Gaika Commissioner), and John Ayliff. The compiler himself
   acted as Chief Commissioner in British Kaffraria and has
   supplied a description of chiefs in British Kaffraria in the
   mid-nineteenth century and also answers to certain queries
   regarding the supposed alliance between the Xhosa and Fingoes
   in 1855.

916. Macmillan, W.M. Bantu, Boer and Briton: The Making of the
   South African Native Problem. Rev. ed. Oxford: Clarendon
   Press, 1963. xviii, 382pp. maps. bibl.

   This study evolved from new information supplied by the
   private papers of Dr. John Philip and shows how he influenced
   Cape Colonial government policy of mid-nineteenth century.
   A new interpretation of the economic and political aspects of
   the 'native problem' is attempted. The 'problem' arose from
   the disintegration of the Amaxosa as a result of the frontier
   wars and the dispossession of tribes of the interior by the
   Great Trek. The British government failed to prevent this
   process, particularly after the abandonment of the Orange
   River Sovereignty and Sand River Convention when economic
   considerations made Britain reluctant to accept responsibility
   for affairs of the interior.

917. Marquard, L., and T.G. Standing. The Southern Bantu. London:
   Oxford University Press, 1939. 262pp. maps. bibl.

   Rather outdated description of social customs and life of
   the Black peoples. Contains various prejudiced ideas.

918. Meintjes, J. Sandile: The Fall of the Xhosa Nation. Cape
   Town: Bulpin, 1971. 312pp. illus. bibl.

   Popular biography based mainly on secondary sources.

919. Molema, S.M. The Bantu, Past and Present: An Ethnological and
   Historical Study of the Native Races of South Africa. Edinburgh: W. Green, 1920. Facs. repr. Cape Town: Struik,
   1963. 398pp. bibl.

   Written by a Black author in an attempt to acquaint English
   speaking people with South African affairs and to inspire Black

people to record their history. The book is divided into three sections: Part 1. The Revelation; i.e., prehistoric African and primitive races. Part 2. The Past; i.e., history of the Bantu races. Part 3. The Present; i.e., missionary influence, civilization and education of the Bantu, South African government and the Bantu, Bantu and labour supply, Bantu in South African War, 1899-1902, in European War, 1914-1918, Bantu National Congress: Bantu Press, present social condition. Part 4. Possibilities and Impossibilities: intellectual, religious, social and economic prospects.

920. Moodie, D., ed. The Record: Or a Series of Official Papers Relative to the Condition and Treatment of the Native Tribes of South Africa, 1838-1841. Repr. Amsterdam: Balkema, 1960. [657]p.

This Record was compiled on the instruction of the Governor of the Cape, Sir Benjamin D'Urban, and an attempt was made to compile and translate from the Dutch, official Cape records from the earliest times to 1834, as far as they dealt with the relations between the colonists and various tribes. The work, which covers the years 1651-1690 and 1769-1809, was not completed due to lack of funds. The value of this work lies in the fact that it contains important archival material and was one of the first attempts in this direction. It served as the basis of most historical writing about South Africa before the time of Theal. The work comprises three separate parts, 1, 3 and 5. Parts 2 and 4 were not published. The original copies were issued in a fragmentary and erratic manner and are extremely rare today.

921. [Moshesh.] Becker, P. Hill of Destiny: The Life and Times of Moshesh, Founder of the Basotho. London: Longman, 1969. xx, 294pp. illus. maps. bibl.

Readable account of Moshesh's life and career.

922. [Moshesh.] Sanders, P. Moshoeshoe: Chief of the Sotho. London: Heinemann, 1975. xviii, 350pp. illus. maps. tabs. bibl.

Detailed, well-documented biography in which the author seeks to establish the connection between the politics and social structure of Moshesh's kingdom on the one hand, and Moshesh's reactions to European pressures on the other.

923. [Moshesh.] Thompson, L.M. Survival in Two Worlds: Moshoeshoe of Lesotho, 1786-1870. Oxford: Clarendon Press, 1975. xx, 389pp. illus. maps. bibl.

Well-documented and interesting biography in which the changing conditions in south-eastern Africa during Moshesh's career, are described. The effects of Shaka's depredations, the teaching of Christian missionaries, and White secular pressure on Sesotho society are discussed as factors influencing Shaka's policy. Shaka is presented as humane, intelligent and patriotic and devoted to his people.

South African Population - Black Peoples

924. [Moshesh.] Tylden, G. The Rise of the Basuto. Cape Town: Juta, 1950. 270pp. illus. maps. bibl.

    History of the Basuto nation from 1824 onwards, commencing with the foundation of the nation by Moshesh. (Chapters 1-7).

925. [Moshesh.] Williams, J.G. Moshesh: The Man on the Mountain. London: Oxford University Press, 1959. 148pp. illus.

    Biography of Moshesh suitable for young readers.

926. [Mzilikazi.] Becker, P. Path of Blood: The Rise and Conquests of Mzilikazi, Founder of the Matabele. London: Panther, 1972. 282pp. bibl.

    First published London: Longmans Green, 1962. Authoritative biography of Mzilikazi.

927. Omer-Cooper, J.D. The Zulu Aftermath: A Nineteenth-century Revolution in Bantu Africa. London: Longmans, 1966. xiv, 208pp. illus. maps. bibl.

    By the nineteenth century, the slow period of expansion and colonization of the African tribes in the area south of the Sahara, gave way to military conflict and pressure originating in the Zulu kingdom under Shaka. Inter-tribal warfare led to the decimation of weaker tribes, and the rise of large centralized kingdoms consisting of the fragments of formerly independent tribes banded together under one king. These kingdoms have survived to this day and often came into conflict with the White settlers.

928. Peires, J.B. The House of Phalo: A History of the Xhosa People in the Days of their Independence. Johannesburg: Ravan Press, 1981. 281pp. illus. bibl.

    A history of the amaGcaleka and amaRharhabe peoples, who in the period 1700 to 1850 lived in the coastal area between the Sundays and Mbashe rivers. Discusses the origins of the Xhosa, their social and political structure and the rivalries of their chiefs. Describes the frontier wars against the colonists from the Xhosa point of view. The Xhosa evolved their own military tactics to counteract the superior weapons of their enemies. They were finally defeated not by battle, but by the usurption of their land and destruction of their homes, crops and cattle. The author is particularly condemnatory of Sir Harry Smith's administration of British Kaffraria which forced the Xhosa into final poverty (1847).

929. Plaatje, S.T. Native Life in South Africa, Before and Since the European War and the Boer Rebellion. 3rd ed. London: P.S. King, 1917. 382pp. illus. map.

    Attempts to describe the adverse effects the Natives Land Act of 1913 had on the Black peoples of South Africa. Outlines the history of the Land Act from its commencement and quotes from official speeches and documents. Describes the Native Congress held at Johannesburg in July, 1913 and the

Kimberley Conference, both held to protest against the Act. A deputation was sent to London to protest against the Act. A Lands Commission was established and reported on the Act in 1916. The findings of this commission did nothing to alleviate the injustices meted out to Black landowners.

930. Saunders, C., and R. Derricourt, eds. Beyond the Cape Frontier: Studies in the History of the Transkei and Ciskei. London: Longman, 1974. 228pp. illus. maps. bibl.

    A collection of edited papers presented at a conference held at Rhodes University, Grahamstown in 1973 to discuss aspects of the history of the Transkei and Ciskei. Topics discussed include prose poems as historical sources, settlement in the Transkei and Ciskei before the Mfecane, self-defence in the Cape frontier wars, the role of the Wesleyan missionaries and the annexation of the Transkei.

931. Schapera, I., ed. The Bantu Speaking Tribes of South Africa: An Ethnographical Survey. London: Routledge, 1937. xv, 453pp. illus. map. bibl.

    A collection of essays by various experts in the field of ethnology and social anthropology describing the tribes as they were before the intrusion of western civilization. Chapters are included on racial origins, habitat, ethnic history, social organization, individual development, domestic and communal life, economic activities, government and law, religion and magic, music, traditional literature, and language. In conclusion, the effect of European control and the subsequent changes in tribal culture are considered. (For the successor to this volume see entry no. 900).

932. Schapera, I., ed. Western Civilization and the Natives of South Africa: Studies in Culture Contact. London: Routledge, 1934. xiv, 312pp. illus. map.

    A collection of essays by prominent scholars on the effect of various aspects of White culture on tribal civilization; viz., Christianity, education, influence on the development of Black language, literature and music, economic condition of the rural Blacks, social and economic condition of the urban Black people, the effect of 'native administration' and 'native policy' in South Africa and grievances of the Black man, as well as the attitude of the White community to the Black peoples.

933. Soga, J.H. The Ama-Xosa: Life and Customs. Lovedale: Lovedale Press, 1931. xvii, 431pp. illus.

    Part 1 consists of a brief historical sketch of the Ama Xosa tribe. Part 2 covers a description of the customs and life of the Xhosa. The author feels that these customs are fast disappearing under the influence of the White man.

934. Soga, J.H. The South-Eastern Bantu (Abe-Nguni, Aba-Mbo, Ama-Lala). Johannesburg: Witwatersrand University Press, 1930. xxxi, 490pp. illus. tabs.

Translation from the isi-Xhosa of a work originally intended for Black scholars, and written by an historian of mixed Xhosa Scottish descent. The origins of the 'South-Eastern Bantu' are traced and the circumstances of their migration into southeast Africa are described. Details of tribal history are given, including genealogy of chiefs and details of various tribal wars. The emphasis is mainly on tribal constitution and movements. There are detailed genealogical tables of the more important tribes. The contact between White and Black peoples is described very briefly.

935. South Africa (Union). Summary of the Report of the Commission for the Socio-Economic Development of the Bantu Areas within the Union of South Africa. Chairman: F.R. Tomlinson. Pretoria: Government Printer, 1955. 214pp. 64 maps. (U.G. 61 of 1955).

Discusses the origin of the Black peoples of South Africa, historical survey of contacts between Black and White peoples in the political, religious, educational and economic spheres and the result of these contacts. Describes the pattern of race relations in South Africa in the first half of the twentieth century, including the effect of Christian missions and education on the Black peoples. Analyses the population problem and position of the Black people in the present political and economic structure. In Part 2 the economy, administration, social problems, agriculture and industry of the Bantu areas are described in great detail. Part 3 discusses development of the Bantu areas. Parts 4 and 5 describe execution of development proposals and certain recommendations are made in regard to these proposals.

936. South African Native Affairs Commission. Report, 1903-1905. Chairman: Sir G. Lagden. Cape Town: Government Printer, 1904-1905. 6v. (Cd. 2399 of 1905).

This report concerns the following matters connected with native affairs: status and condition of the natives, suggestions for education, industrial training and labour, land tenure; native law and administration, prohibition of sale of liquor to natives; native marriages, extent and effect of polygamy.

937. South African Native Races Committee. The Natives of South Africa: Their Economic and Social Conditions. London: John Murray, 1901. xiii, 359pp. maps.

Attempts to supply accurate information regarding the social and economic conditions of the native as existing at the end of the nineteenth century. Report supplies information regarding non-white races and population in each of the southern African territories, native laws and customs, administration of native territory, labour supply, occupations and salary, labour conditions, pass laws, education, taxation, savings banks and labour agencies.

938. South African Native Races Committee. The South African Natives: Their Progress and Present Condition. London: John Murray, 1909. xii, 247pp.

   A supplement to the 1901 report of the Committee, in which the changes achieved in the social and economic status of the natives regarding labour employment, land tenure, administration, legal status, education and religious organization, are discussed.

939. Stanford, Sir W. The Reminiscences of Sir Walter Stanford. ed. by J.W. Macquarrie. Cape Town: Van Riebeeck Society, 1958-1962. 2v. illus. maps. bibl. (Van Riebeeck Society Publications, 39,43).

   Volume 1 covers the period of Stanford's life from 1850 to 1885, when he became Chief magistrate of east Griqualand. Volume 2 covers the period 1885 to 1929. Describes various events in the territories of Pondoland and east Griqualand as well as Stanford's promotion to Chief magistrate of Transkeian terrotories in 1902 and his membership of the Senate (1910-1929).

940. Stockenstrom, A. The Autobiography of the Late Sir Andries Stockenstrom, Bart. ed. by C.E. Hutton. Cape Town: Juta, 1887. Facs. repr. Cape Town: Struik, 1964. 2v. illus. map.

   This autobiography was compiled from Stockenstrom's correspondence, papers, and notes written in 1856-1858 and partly in 1862-1863, and also from journals and memoranda. These were incomplete at the time of Stockenstrom's death and were edited by C.W. Hutton to form a complete biography covering the period 1792 to 1864.

941. [Stockenstrom, A.] Dracopoli, J.L. Sir Andries Stockenstrom, 1792-1864: The Origins of the Racial Conflict in South Africa. Cape Town: Balkema: 1969. xii, 211pp.

   Maintains that the study of the life of Stockenstrom is also a study of the problems of the Cape eastern frontier in the first half of the nineteenth century, when bigotry and injustice towards the Xhosa influenced the actions of the eastern frontier farmers. Compares the modern race policies of South Africa with those of the nineteenth century Cape colony and finds the same mistaken policies are being pursued.

South African Population - Black Peoples

942. Stow, G.W. The Native Races of South Africa: A History of the Intrusion of the Hottentots and Bantu into the Hunting Grounds of the Bushmen, the Aborigines of the Country. ed. by George McCall Theal. London: Swan Sonnenschein, 1910. 618pp. illus. map.

Comprehensive material on the history and customs of Bushmen was collected by the author from 1843 onwards in order to show that these were the earliest inhabitants of the Cape colony and of South Africa. He also attempted to collect evidence of the early migrations of the Hottentot and Black tribes of the interior, with the assistance of various officials and missionaries stationed within the native reserves. Inaccuracies occur in descriptions of the Hottentot tribes at the time of the early Dutch settlement as Stow was unable to consult colonial archives and was dependent upon secondary sources for information.

943. Summers, R., and C.W. Pagden. The Warriors: The Story of the Matabele Army. Cape Town: Books of Africa, 1970. 181pp. plates.

Describes the Matabele nation between 1822 and 1893 when it reached its zenith of military power. Sources of information include oral accounts of former Matabele warriors, accounts by native commissioners, missionary reports, military intelligence reports, war diaries and accounts of battles, descriptions by travellers and modern accounts by social anthropologists. Discusses the origins, military life, training and history of the Matabele under chiefs Mzilikazi and Lobengula.

944. Theal, G. McCall. The Yellow and Dark-skinned People of Africa South of the Zambesi: A Description of the Bushmen, the Hottentots and Particularly the Bantu. London: Swan Sonnenschein, 1910. xiv, 397pp. illus.

An attempt to collect various chapters on ethnography contained in the author's 'History of South Africa' and present these in a volume dealing solely with the indigenous tribes of South Africa. In each case, the history and origins of the tribe are given and their social customs, daily life, and political institutions described.

945. Thompson, L.M., ed. African Societies in Southern Africa. London: Heinemann, 1969. 336pp. maps.

Based on papers read at a conference at the University of Zambia, 1968, dealing with African societies in southern Africa before subordination to White control. Two chapters cover archaeological evidence of early societies. Four chapters are devoted to tribal history before the nineteenth century, three deal with Zulu expansion under Shaka, and the final four chapters cover Mpondomise, Ndebele, southern Sotho and Zulu politics in the last years' of these nations' independence.

946. Tyrrell, B. Tribal Peoples of Southern Africa. Cape Town: Books of Africa, 1968. 206pp. illus. bibl.

   A lavishly illustrated work which deals with the customs, traditions and tribal dress of the tribal people of southern Africa.

947. Tyrrell, B. Suspicion Is My Name. Cape Town: Books of Africa, 1971. 191pp. illus.

   A companion volume to 'Tribal Peoples of Southern Africa' (see entry no. 946) in which the author concentrates on the religious beliefs and superstitions of primitive African cultures.

Bushmen and Hottentots

Bibliography

948. Willet, S.M. The Bushman, 1652-1962. Johannesburg: University of the Witwatersrand, Department of Bibliography, Librarianship and Typography, 1965. 40pp.

Monographs

949. Dornan, S.S. Pygmies and Bushmen of the Kalahari. London: Seeley, Service, 1925. 318pp. map.

   Provides a very full description of the Bushmen, their origin, customs, family organization, food gathering, religion, and language. The descriptions of the Hottentots, Namaquas, Koranas, Griquas, Damaras, Bakalahari, and Bechuanas are briefer. The birth, invitation, marriage, death, and religious customs of the Bechuana are described. There is a brief chapter on the Sechuana language.

950. Elphick, R. Kraal and Castle: Khoikhoi and the Founding of White South Africa. New Haven: Yale University Press, 1977. 266pp. maps. bibl.

   A study of the Cape Khoikhoi or Hottentots living in the Cape south of the Orange River valley in the seventeenth century. Sixty years after the arrival of the White settlers in 1652, the traditional Khoikhoi economy, social structure and political system collapsed. The author analyses the reasons for this disintegration. The Khoikhoi were never a politically strong people and in times of stress reverted easily to a more primitive stage of hunting and food gathering. Pressure from the White settlers caused the Khoikhoi to surrender cattle, their only source of wealth. Dispossessed Khoikhoi in turn robbed other tribes resulting in further depredations and warfare. Drought and the outbreak of smallpox caused the final decimation of the Khoikhoi tribes.

South African Population - Bushmen and Hottentots

951. Ross, R. Adam Kok's Griquas: A Study in the Development of Stratification in South Africa. Cambridge: University Press, 1976. xiii, 194pp. (African Studies Series, 21).

A detailed description of the history of the Griqua group of peoples in the Philippolis and Kokstad regions of South Africa. These people, of mixed origins, played an important part in South African history in the nineteenth century. For detailed description see entry no. 975.

952. Schapera, I., and B. Farrington, eds. The Early Cape Hottentots Described in the Writings of Olfort Dapper (1668), Willem Ten Rhyne (1686) and Johannes Gulielmus de Grevenbroek (1695). Cape Town: Van Riebeeck Society, 1933. xv, 309pp. illus. bibl. (Van Riebeeck Society Publications, 14).

The work of Dapper is translated by Schapera and the works of Ten Rhyne and de Grevenbroek by Farrington. Each of the three sections is preceded by an explanatory preface giving details regarding the author. The actual text is given both in the original language and in English translation. The descriptions provided by the three authors are fairly comprehensive in portraying the tribal structure, appearance, and customs of the Hottentots.

953. Schapera, I. The Khoisan Peoples of South Africa: Bushmen and Hottentots. London: Routledge, 1930. xi, 450pp. illus. map. bibl.

A description of the ethno-geography, history, social organization, economic and political life, religion and magic, art and knowledge of the Hottentots and Bushmen. There is also a concluding section on the Khoisan languages, discussing grammar, syntax and vocabulary.

954. Tobias, P.V., ed. The Bushmen: San Hunters and Herders of Southern Africa. Cape Town: Human & Rousseau, 1978. 206pp. illus. bibl.

A comprehensive work, by various authorities, on all aspects of Bushmen life and culture. Chapter 5 deals with the role of the Bushmen in history (pp.76-87). There is an extensive bibliography at the end of the work, which contains a section entitled 'Historical writings'.

955. Wannenburgh, A. Forgotten Frontiersmen. Cape Town: Timmins, 1980. 194pp. illus.

Brief popular biographies of notable personalities who were of Khoikhoi and Coloured origin, and who helped shape the destiny of the Coloured people from the end of the seventeenth to the end of the nineteenth century. These include leaders such as Adam Kok and his descendants and the Waterboer dynasty of Griquatown.

956. Wright, J.B. Bushman Raiders of the Drakensberg, 1804-1870: A Study of Their Conflict with Stock-keeping Peoples in Natal. Pietermaritzburg: Natal University Press, 1971. ix, 235pp. illus. maps. bibl.

A study of the relationship between the Bushmen living in east Griqualand and the Drakensberg and Maluti mountains on the one hand, and the White and Bantu-speaking peoples in Natal on the other, during the period 1840 to the 1970s. These conflicts eventually led to the disappearance of the Bushmen from the Drakensberg-Maluti area. The last Bushman raid into Natal took place in 1872. This study originally was accepted for a M.A. degree in history by the University of Natal and is based upon documentary evidence present in the Natal archives, Pietermaritzburg.

Chinese Peoples

957. Imperial South African Association. Chinese Labour Question: Handy Notes. Westminster: The Association, 1905. 56pp.

Pamphlet attempting to justify the introduction of Chinese labour on the Transvaal mines.

958. Payne, E.C. An Experiment in Alien Labour. Chicago: University of Chicago, 1912. v, 72pp. bibl.

A study in immigration presented as a doctoral thesis. Aims primarily at discussing the reasons for the employment of Chinese in South Africa and the economic significance of that employment. Describes the special restrictions under which the Chinese were employed, the relation of the Chinese to the other races in Africa, and the comparison of their introduction and employment in South Africa with their immigration to, and labour in, other lands. The method of indenture used for employment of Chinese in the Transvaal was experimental. The reasons for the failure of the experimental introduction of Chinese labour are analysed. The most serious cause of the failure is defined as the problem of control.

959. Richardson, P. Chinese Mine Labour in the Transvaal. London: Macmillan, 1982. 287pp. maps. bibl.

A detailed study of conditions in the Transvaal gold mining industry between 1901 and 1910 which led to the importation and repatriation of Chinese mine labourers. The role of British state intervention in the scheme is examined. The author stresses that the scheme was made possible because of the extending world circulation of labour power in the twentieth century and also because of the development of the system of indentured labour.

960. Schumacher, R.W. A Transvaal View of the Chinese Labour Question. Westminster: Imperial South African Association, 1906. 60pp.

   Pamphlet expressing the views of the Transvaal Chamber of Mines regarding the introduction of Chinese labour, and justifying the use of Chinese labour.

961. Smedley, L. The Chinese Community in South Africa. Pretoria: Human Sciences Research Council, 1976-1978. 2v. bibl. (Reports Nos. S-44, S-50).

   Phase 1: Background and attitudes of the White population group towards the Chinese minority group. Phase 2: A sociological study. The first volume contains a chapter on the history of the South African Chinese and the circumstances under which Chinese labour was introduced into the mines in 1904. The rest of volume 1 is devoted to a study of present-day White attitudes to the Chinese population of South Africa. Volume 2 has a brief historical introduction and is mainly concerned with a study of Chinese culture, professional occupations, income, religion and social adjustment to conditions in South Africa, as compared to Chinese adjustment to conditions in other countries such as Britain and the United States.

Coloured Peoples

Bibliographies

962. Jacobson, E. The Cape Coloured: A Bibliography. Cape Town: University of Cape Town, School of Librarianship, 1950. 43pp.

963. Manuel, G.A. The Coloured People: A Bibliography. Cape Town: University of Cape Town, School of Librarianship, 1950. ii, 18pp.

964. South Africa (Union). Department of Coloured Affairs. General Bibliography: The Coloured People of South Africa. Cape Town: The Department, 1960. iv, 79pp.

Monographs

965. Arnott, D., and F.H.S. Orpen. The Land Question of Griqualand West: An Inquiry into the Various Claims to Land in that Territory: Together with a Brief History of the Griqua Nation. Cape Town: Saul Solomon, 1875. 351pp. map.

   Consists of extracts from official records covering the years 1837 to 1874, compiled by two government officials of Griqualand West who were attempting to disprove rumours that the

British government was guilty of unfair practices in disposing of vacant land in Griqualand West. A short historical account of the Griquas and of Griqualand West is given, including circumstances leading to British annexation up to 1868. Also refutes the claims of the Orange Free State, the South African Republic and individuals such as Thomas Holden Bowker, P.L. Buyskes, Rev. W.A. Robinson, and W.B. Sampson to land within Griqualand West.

966. Bradlow, F.R., and M. Cairns. The Early Cape Muslims: A Study of Their Mosques, Genealogy and Origins. Cape Town: Balkema, 1978. 144pp.

Deals essentially with the history of the Auwal Mosque in Dorp Street, Cape Town, built in the first half of the nineteenth century, and constituting the oldest mosque in South Africa. The second part of the book deals with the history of a Muslim family connected with the mosque, the descendants of Saartjie van de Kaap and Achmat van Bengalen, who acted as priest to the Muslim community. The third section of the book deals with the origins of the Cape Muslim community.

967. Cilliers, S.P. The Coloureds of South Africa: A Factual Survey. Cape Town: Banier, 1963. 65pp.

A factual survey of some of the salient features of the position of the Coloured population. Discusses briefly, origin and development, demographic characteristics, social conditions, economic conditions and education and religion. Statistics are given throughout.

968. Cruse, H.P. Die Opheffing van die Kleurling Bevolking. Stellenbosch: Christen Studentevereniging, 1947. 292pp.

This work has no bibliography but contains footnotes. Volume 1 covers the period 1652-1795, and deals with the origins of the Bushmen and Hottentots, the first contacts between these races and the White colonists and the arrival of slaves at the Cape. Describes attempts to educate the Hottentots and slaves and the way in which education was affected by de Chavonnes' ordinance of 1714. Discusses Moravian missionary work among the Hottentots, and the impressions of various travellers such as Lieut. Beutler, van Plettenberg, Thunberg, Sparrman and Le Vaillant, Jacobus Coetsé and Wikar. Describes the conflict between the Bushmen and colonists in the eighteenth century, the emancipation of slaves in the seventeenth and eighteenth centuries and the education of non-whites during the second half of the eighteenth century.

969. Du Plessis, I.D. The Cape Malays. 2nd ed. Cape Town: Maskew Miller, 1947. 93pp. illus. bibl.

Deals with the origin and history of the Malays. Describes religion, customs and traditions, superstitions and the 'Malay Quarter' of Cape Town. Concludes with a plea for better living conditions for the Coloured section of the population.

970. Du Plessis, I.D., and L.C. Lückhoff. The Malay Quarter and its People. Cape Town: Maskew Miller, 1955. 91pp. illus. bibl.

There is a description of the Malay quarter and its inhabitants. The religion and customs and traditions of the Malay are described in detail. The impact of modern western society and mechanisation of the Malay social system is discussed. There are numerous photographs of the Malays and their dwellings.

971. Engelbrecht, J.A. The Korana: An Account of Their Customs and Their History. Cape Town: Maskew Miller, 1936. 239pp. illus. bibl.

Consists of Part 1: Origin, migration and history of the Korana. Part 2: Culture. Part 3: Language. Use is made of written historical references to the origin and migrations of the Kora clans and tribes and of unwritten records. The section on culture includes aspects such as hunting, transportation, clothing, food and drink, family relationships, music, dancing, religion and social offences. The third section, on language, contains vocabulary collected at random from various tribal members.

972. Halford, S.J. The Griquas of Griqualand: An Historical Narration of the Griqua People and Their Rise, Progress and Decline. Cape Town: Juta, 1949. ix, 209pp. illus.

Covers the history of the Griquas from the late fifteenth to the first half of the twentieth century. Describes the racial origin of the Griquas, their progress under missionary influence and under the leadership of chiefs such as Adam Kok I, II, III and Cornelius Waterboer. Their relationships with the British government, the trekkers, republic of the Orange Free State and also with tribes such as the Basuto and Bacas are described. The author concludes by outlining the legal and political condition of the Griquas at the beginning of the twentieth century. The author is sympathetically inclined towards the Griquas, having served as mayor of Kokstad and resided in Griqualand East for over thirty years.

973. Macmillan, W.M. The Cape Colour Question: A Historical Survey. London: Faber, 1927. Facs. repr. Cape Town: Balkema, 1968. xvi, 304pp. portrait. maps.

Discusses the origin and history of the Coloured races showing how racial prejudice arose. Describes the influence of missionary activity on Coloured policy of the British colonial government, with particular emphasis on the role played by Dr. John Philip. By the mid-nineteenth century the Coloured people had been granted certain political rights in the Cape colony but economically and socially were reduced to poverty and landlessness. Contends in modern times these 'Eurafricans' are accepted as a more highly civilized section of the population than the Black peoples.

South African Population - Coloured Peoples

974. Marais, J.S. The Cape Coloured People, 1652-1937. 2nd ed. Johannesburg: Witwatersrand University Press, 1957. xxiv, 296pp. map. bibl.

Traces the origins and early history of the Cape Coloured peoples and the rise and decline of the Griquas and Bastards of the north west Cape. Describes the position of the Hottentots in the service of the frontier farmers and in the army. Discusses the influence of the missionaries as well as the failure of the Kat River settlement, which was established after the repeal of Ordinance 50 of 1828. Concludes with a survey of the social and political status of the Coloureds in the twentieth century.

975. Ross, R. Adam Kok's Griquas: A Study in the Development of Stratification in South Africa. Cambridge: University Press, 1976. xiii, 194pp. maps. bibl.

Describes the early history and origin of the Griquas, descendants of early Boer frontiersmen, remnants of Khoisan tribes, escaped slaves, free Blacks and tribesmen detached from their tribes. The Griquas established a state in the southern Orange Free State with a capital at Philippolis and also established themselves in Griqualand West with a centre at Griquatown. Many Griquas of the nineteenth century were literate and Christianized and established a prosperous state under Adam Kok. This state disintegrated under pressure from the White settlers and farmers of the Orange Free State. In 1861-62 the Griquas trekked over the Drakensberg and established themselves in Nomansland which became Griqualand East. In 1879 Griqualand East was annexed to the Cape and the Griqua political and social structure collapsed. The main reason for the disintegration of the Griquas was the existence of racial domination on the part of the White inhabitants of South Africa which prevented any Black or Coloured community from advancing.

976. Theron, E., and M.J. Swart, eds. Die Kleurling Bevolking van Suid-Afrika. Stellenbosch: Universiteits uitgewers, 1964. xi, 234pp. bibl.

Consists of a report of a Committee of the South African Bureau of Race Relations. Each section of the report drawn up by specialist contributors. The following aspects are discussed: Origin of the Coloured population, demographic aspects (largely statistical), geographical distribution, labour and economy, family life, health services, housing, sociological problems, religion, education, cultural activities and recreation, influence on Afrikaans literature, Department of Coloured Affairs, local administration, constitutional rights, differentiated legislation and the Coloureds of South West Africa.

977. Theron, E., and J.B. du Toit. Kort Begrip van die Theron-Verslag. Cape Town: Tafelberg, 1977. 114pp.

A summary of the Theron report laid before parliament on 18 June, 1976. The most important aspects of the report and its recommendations concerning the Coloured people are summarised. Discusses the demographic and statutory position of the Coloured people, education, living and recreation conditions, health and health services, sociological problems and welfare services, cultural and spiritual life, socio-political and administrative conditions regarding the Coloured people. Analyses the attitudes and reactions of the Coloured people towards their socio-political conditions. Makes certain recommendations for the amelioration of the living conditions of the Coloured people.

Indian Peoples

Bibliographies

978. Currie, J.C. A Bibliography of Material Published during the Period 1946-1956 on the Indian Question in South Africa. Cape Town: University of Cape Town, School of Librarianship, 1959. 28pp.

979. Greyling, J.J.C., and J. Miskin. Bibliography on Indians in South Africa. Durban: Institute for Social and Economic Research, University of Durban-Westville, 1976. 51pp.

980. Kovalsky, S.J. Mahatma Gandhi and his Political Influence in South Africa, 1892-1914. Johannesburg: University of the Witwatersrand, Department of Bibliography, Librarianship and Typography, 1971. 33pp.

981. Morris, G.R. A Bibliography of the Indian Question in South Africa. Cape Town: University of Cape Town, School of Librarianship, 1950. 17pp.

Monographs

982. Beyers, C.J. Die Indiërvraagstuk in Natal, 1870-1910. (D.Litt. Thesis. Potchefstroom University for Christian Higher Education, May 1969). Archives Yearbook for South African History. Vol. 34, part 2, 1971. Pretoria: Government Printer, 1976. 272pp. illus. maps. bibl.

Detailed account of the Indian problem in Natal during the second half of the nineteenth century especially as regards the second immigration scheme of 1874 to 1910. Research based upon archival sources obtained from the Natal archives, upon a study of the Natal Hansards and upon material obtained from newspapers, particularly 'The Natal Mercury'. Describes the origin of the Indian immigrants, the circumstances under which emigration took place, the development of the Indian problem during the first and second periods of immigration up to the year 1887, the Wragg Commission, and the development of the Indian problem following the grant of responsible government to Natal. Natal authorities attempted to control Indian immigration and restrict Indian traders towards the end of the nineteenth century. From 1870 to 1910, an attempt was made to protect legally contract workers, and medical services for Indians were introduced. An analysis is given of social life, customs and education of Indians at this period. The influence of Indians on economic, agricultural and military development is assessed.

983. Calpin, G.H. Indians in South Africa. Pietermaritzburg: Shuter & Shooter, 1949. 310pp.

A history of the Indians in South Africa from 1860, when indentured Indians were brought into Natal as labourers on the sugar plantations, to the year 1949, when African riots against Indians occurred in Durban.

984. Huttenback, R.A. Gandhi in South Africa: British Imperialism and the Indian Question, 1860-1914. Ithaca: Cornell University Press, 1971. 368pp. illus. bibl.

Describes the reasons for the introduction of Indian labour into Natal during the second half of the nineteenth century and the growth of racial prejudices towards the Indians in South Africa. After 1893, Natal was granted self-government and was determined to prevent further Indian immigration or the acquisition of the vote by Indians and attempted to limit Indian trading rights. From 1893 to 1914, Gandhi became the champion of Indian rights, firstly in Natal and after 1903, in the Transvaal and Orange River Colony. The British imperial authorities were placed in a predicament as Britain had guaranteed equal rights for all subjects of British dominions. However, Britain was unable to prevent discriminatory laws being passed in Natal, the Cape, Transvaal and Orange Free State. Gandhi initiated the policy of passive resistance (satyagraha), which led to the Indian Inquiry Commission of April 19 and the redress of certain grievances (Act 22 of 1914). Gandhi left South Africa, but the Indian community continued to suffer certain disadvantages.

985. Kuper, H. Indian People in Natal. Pietermaritzburg: Natal University Press, 1960. xx, 305pp. illus. bibl.

A study of the Indian people of Natal based on field work done at Merebank, Springfield, and Newlands in association with the Family Research Unit of the Institute of Family and Community Health. Part 1 deals with the background of South African Indians and the way in which the caste system became modified by the conditions of emigration to Natal in the nineteenth century. Part 2 discusses the kinship among Durban

Hindu. Part 3 deals with the practice of the Hindu religion in Natal, religious ceremonies and health cults. The conclusion discusses the social and political status of the Indians in South Africa and compares this with the status of the Black people.

986. Narain, I. Politics of Racialism: A Study of the Indian Minority in South Africa down to the Gandhi-Smuts Agreement. Delhi: Shiva Lal Agarwala, 1962. xv, 304pp. bibl.

Based on material originally submitted for a Ph.D. degree. Describes emigration of Indians to Natal in nineteenth century, discusses daily life and problems of the early emigrants, the curtailment of their rights and liberties till the Gandhi-Smuts agreement, and the manner in which the imperial government behaved as guardian of the interest of its Indian subjects.

987. Pachai, B. The International Aspects of the South African Indian Question, 1860-1971. Cape Town: Struik, 1971. xi, 318pp. bibl.

This study is based on material submitted for a Ph.D. degree at the University of Natal. Deals mainly with the Indian question as an inter-governmental matter between states and countries (e.g., between the South African Republic and Natal before 1910, and India and Great Britain) and international aspects of the question, involving institutions such as the League of Nations and the United Nations. Local and domestic issues are only briefly dealt with in order to elucidate the international problems. Discusses the arrival of the first Indians in South Africa as a result of a tripartite pact between the governments of Natal, India, and Great Britain. Descendants of the first indentured labourers and traders encountered considerable opposition in different parts of South Africa. Their plight led to lengthy intergovernmental negotiations, imperial conferences, and discussions in the League of Nations and United Nations between 1860 and 1961. The author discusses the reasons for the anti-Indian attitude of the South African governments and the social, economic, and political status of the Indians of South Africa.

988. Palmer, M. The History of the Indians in Natal. Cape Town: Oxford University Press, 1957. x, 197pp. illus. map. (Natal Regional Survey, vol. 10).

Discusses the role of Gandhi in South Africa and the evolution of the technique of passive resistance as a political weapon. Analyses legislation affecting Indians and Indian political organization. Discusses development of Indian education, culture and charitable activities. No bibliography given; various footnotes throughout the text.

South African Population - Indian Peoples

989. Pather, S.R., ed. Centenary of Indians, 1860-1960. Durban: Cavalier publishers, 1960. 215pp. illus.

   Contains articles describing the arrival of the Indians in Natal from 1860 onwards, the contributions of the Indians to agriculture and commerce, and the struggles of the Indian community against political, social, and commercial disabilities.

990. Pillay, B. British Indians in the Transvaal: Trade, Politics and Imperial Relations, 1885-1906. London: Longmans, 1976. xviii, 259pp. bibl.

   Indian traders entered the Transvaal in the 1880s and encountered opposition from the White inhabitants. The Afrikaners already had certain established race attitudes and the British traders in the Transvaal feared competition from their Indian rivals. The author studies the growth of White hostility from the passing of the discriminatory Law 3 of 1885 to the granting of responsible government to the Transvaal in 1906. The part played by Gandhi in organizing Indian political expression and protest from 1893 to 1914, is outlined. At the close of the nineteenth century the Indian community of the Transvaal appealed to Britain for assistance by virtue of their status as British subjects. From 1884 to 1899 Britain attempted to protect Indian interests in the South African Republic. However, in 1902, after the Anglo-Boer War, a British administration in the Transvaal rigorously enforced the South African Republic's anti-Indian laws. Milner and Selbourne were anxious to reconcile the Boer and British in South Africa and sacrificed the rights of the Indians for the sake of political expediency. When the Transvaal received responsible government, Act 2 of 1907 and Act 15 of 1907, both discriminatory against Indian population, were passed.

991. Thompson, L.M. Indian Immigration into Natal: 1860-1872. (M.A. Thesis. University of South Africa). Archives Yearbook for South African History. Vol. 15, Part 2, 1952. Pretoria: Government Printer, 1952. 168pp. bibl.

   Discusses the circumstances leading to the introduction of Indian labour into Natal to be used on the sugar plantations (Indian Act of 1860). Describes in detail the methods used in recruiting Indian labour, the assignment of indentured immigrants, financial provisions, and the treatment of indentured immigrants. Complaints by Indians who had returned to India in 1871, regarding treatment at the hands of Natal plantation owners, led to legal amendments in 1874 and creation of an Indian Immigration Trust Board. Concludes with discussion of Indian problems after 1872 and the contribution of the Indians to Natal's agriculture.

WHITE PEOPLES
Afrikaners

992. Coetzee, J.A. Politieke Groepering in die Wording van die Afrikanernasie met Besondere Verwysing na die Tydperk van die Eerste tot die Tweede Vryheidsoorlog. Johannesburg: Voortrekkerpers, 1941. 383pp. bibl.

    A detailed examination of the growth of Afrikaner nationalism from the time of the Dutch East India Company rule at the Cape (seventeenth and eighteenth centuries) to the end of the nineteenth century. The development of the Afrikaner Bond in the Cape Colony is studied between the years 1878 to 1899, as is the development of political parties in the Orange Free State and Transvaal during the same period. The effect of the Anglo-Boer War (1899-1902) on the various political parties is discussed and post-war political reconstruction under General Botha is examined.

993. Colenbrander, H.T. De Afkomst der Boeren. Repr. Cape Town: Struik, 1964. 127pp. (Algemeen Nederlandsch Verbond No. 9, 1902).

    Discusses the genealogy of the Afrikaner nation. Based partly on information contained in 'Geslacht Register der Oude Kaapsche Familiën', but also contains new information. Contains valuable tables showing ancestors of the Afrikaners between the years 1657 to 1807.

994. De Klerk, W.A. The Puritans in Africa: A History of Afrikanerdom. Harmondsworth: Penguin in association with Rex Collings, 1975. 376pp. bibl.

    Traces the history of the Afrikaans people from the seventeenth to the twentieth century and attempts to show that the Calvinist-Puritan tradition which influenced South Africa was similar to the Anglo-Saxon Puritan spirit, especially in New England. Calvinism has undergone certain subtle changes to justify the political ideals and creeds of Afrikanerdom. The author finally examines other aspects of Afrikaner ideals in the sphere of cultural, religious, economic, and social matters to demonstrate how calvinistic creeds influenced progress in the twentieth century.

995. De Villiers, C.C., comp. Geslachtsregister den Oude Kaapsche Familien. 3v. Cape Town, 1893-1894. Rev. ed. entitled 'Geslagsregister Van die Ou Kaapse Families' rev. by C. Pama. Cape Town: Balkema, 1966.

    The genealogies of old Cape families alphabetically arranged are tabulated mostly up to the time of the Great Trek, although many exceptions extend into the twentieth century. Many errors and omissions present in de Villiers' original work have been eliminated in the revised edition, which pays tribute to de Villiers as 'the father of South African genealogy'.

996. Du Plessis, A.P. Die Nederlandse Emigrasie na Suid-Afrika: Sekere Aspekte Rakende Voorbereiding tot Aanpassing. Amsterdam: Teerhuis and Klinkerberg, 1956. 250pp. bibl.

Contains a summary at the end of the work in English. Deals firstly with an historical survey of Dutch emigration from 1602 to the post Second World War period. The remainder of the work is devoted to the integration and adjustment of the Dutch immigrant to South African conditions.

997. Fisher, J. The Afrikaners. London: Cassell, 1969. xviii, 380pp. illus. maps. bibl.

Describes the origin and history of the Afrikaners, factors influencing their development and the qualities of famous Afrikaner leaders. The author has attempted to place emphasis on the role of the Afrikaners in South African history rather than emphasising the role of personalities such as Rhodes, Milner, and Chamberlain.

998. Heese, J.A. Die Herkoms van die Afrikaner, 1657-1867. Cape Town: Balkema, 1971. 335pp. bibl.

Part 1 discusses the genealogical history of the Afrikaners during the periods 1657-1807, 1808-1837 and 1838-1867 respectively. Part 2 provides lists of Afrikaans forefathers during the period 1657 to 1867. This period of 200 years is subdivided into thirty-year periods and has an alphabetical arrangement by surname.

999. Hexham, I. The Irony of Apartheid: The Struggle for National Independence of Afrikaner Calvinism against British Imperialism. New York: Edwin Mellen, 1981. 237pp. bibl.

Maintains that Afrikaner nationalism and the mythology of apartheid developed in the period after the Anglo-Boer War of 1899 to 1902. The poet Totius (J.D. du Toit) and the writer Willem Postma had a decisive influence in the development of nationalism. The Gereformeerde Kerk (Reformed Church), an offshoot of the State Church of the Netherlands, gained ascendency among the Afrikaner Calvinists providing a religious background to nationalistic sentiments. The author discusses the development of the Afrikaans language, the establishment of Christian-National education and the growth of the National Party and Broederbond as further instruments in the strengthening of Afrikaner nationalism.

1000. Hoge, J. Bydraes tot die Genealogie van ou Afrikaanse Families: Verbeterings en Aanvullings op die 'Geslacht-Register der oude Kaapsche familien' deur C.G. de Villiers. Cape Town: Balkema, 1955. 224pp.

Contains corrections and additions to information supplied in the 'Geslacht-Register der Oude Kaapsche Familien', (see entry 995).

South African Population - Afrikaners

1001. Krige, J.D.A. Oorsprong en Betekenis van Nederlandse ou Duitse Familiename in die 'Geslacht-Register den Oude Kaapsche Familien'. Pretoria: Van Schaik, 1934. 109pp. bibl.

Attempts to provide the origin and meaning of Dutch and German surnames found in the Geslacht-Register.

1002. Malherbe, D.F. du T. Driehonderd Jaar Nasiebou: Stamouers van die Afrikaner Volk. Stellenbosch: Tegniek, 1959. xxv, 267pp.

Attempts to provide genealogical information concerning families not mentioned by de Villiers in the 'Geslacht-Register den Oude Kaapsche Familien'. Also provides information about families who arrived in South Africa at a later date than those dealt with in the Geslacht-Register.

1003. Munger, E.S., ed. The Afrikaners. Cape Town: Tafelberg, 1979. 183pp.

A wide range of views on Afrikanerdom seen through the contributions of fourteen well-known South Africans. Includes many historical reflections.

1004. Nienaber, G.S. Afrikaanse Familie Name: 'n Geselsie vir Belangstellende Leke oor die Betekenis van Ouer Afrikaanse Vanne. Cape Town: Balkema, 1955. 108pp.

Discusses the origin and meaning of various common surnames found among the Afrikaner nation.

1005. Patterson, S. The Last Trek: A Study of the Boer People and the Afrikaner Nation. London: Routledge and Kegan Paul, 1957. viii, 336pp. bibl.

Attempts to trace objectively the growth of the Afrikaner nation and nationalism. Summarizes South African history to the post-Boer War period and maintains that the Great Trek and the Wars of Independence have been used as a means of stimulating racial antagonism in recent times. Discusses the growth and recognition of the Afrikaans language, the political dominance of the Nationalist Party, the role of the Afrikaner in agriculture, industry, mining and commerce, the influence of the Dutch Reformed Church, upbringing and education of Afrikaans youth and social and cultural life of the Afrikaner. Analyses modern Afrikaner nationalism and attempts to predict the future of the Afrikaner nation.

1006. Pienaar, P. de V., ed. Kultuurgeskiedenis van die Afrikaner. Cape Town: Nasionale Boekhandel, 1968. 419pp. illus.

Consists of articles which deal with every aspect of the cultural and spiritual achievements of the Afrikaner nation. These include Afrikaner history, the effects of Dutch, French, British, Cape Malay, and tribal influences on Afrikaner culture, economic and social development, the growth of Afrikaans language and literature, the influence of the Dutch Reformed Church, development of Afrikaner constitutional concepts, art, music, architecture, science, and librarianship.

1007. Redelinghuys, J.H., comp. Die Afrikaner-Familie Naamboek: Sketse en Besonderhede omtrent die Voorgeslagte van Bekende Afrikaner-families. Cape Town: Publisitas, 1954. 311pp.

Discusses the genealogical details and brief family history of Afrikaner families which have made contributions to the history of the nation. These families are alphabetically arranged and are of Dutch, German, French, and other extraction.

1008. Scholtz, G.D. Die Ontwikkeling van die Politieke Denke van die Afrikaner. Johannesburg: Voortrekkerpers, 1967-1974.

Volume 1: 1652-1806. Volume 2: 1806-1854. Volume 3: 1854-1881. This work is intended to be issued in ten volumes covering the political development of the Afrikaner people from 1652 to 1961. Three volumes have appeared to date. The author analyses the history of South Africa in order to determine which factors influenced and shaped modern political doctrines.

1009. Streak, M. The Afrikaner as Viewed by the English, 1795-1854. Cape Town: Struik, 1974. xvi, 231pp. bibl.

Attempts to trace the development of the prejudiced attitude towards the Afrikaners, which exists within South Africa and abroad, in modern times. These unfavourable opinions of the Afrikaners already evident at the beginning of the nineteenth century when travellers such as John Barrow described the indolent lives of the Cape Dutch and their reliance on slave, Hottentot, and Black labour. The philanthropic movement in England also led to criticisms of Boer cruelty towards the Black population of the frontier. The frontier Boer was depicted as rebellious towards government authority. The Great Trek was viewed by anti-Boer opinion as an attempt by the frontier farmers to escape government control and continue cruel practices towards the tribes of the interior. By 1854, however, the philanthropic movement in Britain was on the wane and for reasons of economy Britain decided on a policy of non-interference in matters beyond the Cape boundaries.

1010. Van Jaarsveld, F.A. The Awakening of Afrikaner Nationalism, 1868-1881. Cape Town: Human & Rousseau, 1961. 259pp.

Maintains that Afrikaner nationalism developed after 1868 as a reaction to British imperialism. Summarizes the development of the Afrikaner nation up to 1868 by which time the Afrikaner language had developed. The struggle of the voortrekkers to establish their Republics had resulted in a potential sense of national independence and consciousness. Afrikaner nationalism was slower to develop in the Cape. Patriotism in the Orange Free State developed after the British annexation of Basutoland in 1868 and the annexation of the diamond fields in 1871, both of which were felt to be acts of great injustice. The Afrikaners of the Cape were also stirred to greater feelings of sympathy with the Republics and between 1868-1877 developed national and cultural consciousness. The South African Republic was economically weak and politically divided until its annexation by Britain in 1877. This resulted in the growth of anti-British sentiment, national pride and an awareness of Afrikaner historical traditions. The First Transvaal War of Independence 1881 roused Afrikaner consciousness throughout southern Africa. The following two works by the same author are important for an assessment of Afrikaners in South African history:

1011. Van Jaarsveld, F.A. Die Afrikaner en sy Geskiedenis. Cape Town: Nasionale Boekhandel, 1959. 124pp. bibl.

Attempts to define and analyse the meaning of history, historical writing, critical research in history, the value of historical writing, and dangers inherent in historical writing. Examines historical writing between the period 1836 to 1881. Maintains that Afrikaner awareness and historical writing commences with the Great Trek and quotes various early historical documents connected with the Trek (1842 to 1854). Traces the development of historical writing in the Orange Free State (1868-1881), the Cape (1868 onwards), and the Transvaal (1880 onwards). Maintains that the development of interest in historical writing was closely linked to the development of Afrikaner nationalism and a sense of national unity which did not occur until the late nineteenth century. For this reason, historical writing lacked objectivity, was emotional, and tended to glorify the deeds of forefathers.

1012. Van Jaarsveld, F.A. The Afrikaner's Interpretation of South African History. Cape Town: Simondium, 1964. 199pp.

A series of lectures in Afrikaans in various periodicals, books and brochures. Attempts to analyse the traditional approach to South African history and how this approach influences the present day field of race relations, political and human relations. Covers topics such as the widespread awakening of historical interest among Afrikaners in the second half of the nineteenth century, the traditional historical image of the Afrikaner emphasizing the Trek and Anglo-Boer War, the influence of Dr. W.J. Leyds' historical writings, the relationship of history and politics, various interpretations in nineteenth and twentieth century historical writing, the teaching of history, and the methods used in teaching 'general' and 'national' history in South African schools.

Americans

1013. Clendenen, C.C., and P. Duignan. Americans in Black Africa up to 1865. Stanford: Stanford University, 1964. (Hoover Institution Studies, 51). 109pp. bibl.

   Consists of three sections entitled: 'American Traders', 'Missionaries and Colonization Societies', and 'Explorers and Frontiersmen'. Each of these sections contain a sub-section on American contributions to South Africa, although the monograph deals mostly with American contributions to Africa as a whole continent.

1014. Clendenen, C.C. Americans in Africa, 1865-1900. Stanford: Stanford University, 1966. 130pp. bibl.

   Chapters 6 and 7 contain accounts of the role played by American miners, adventurers and capitalists in South Africa in the second half of the nineteenth century after the discovery of gold and diamonds. Colonel Edward McMurdo was involved in the building of a railroad from Lourenco Marques to the Transvaal frontier. The American Board of Commissioners for Foreign Missions was active in South Africa from 1835 onwards.

1015. Rosenthal, E. Stars and Stripes in Africa: Being a History of American Achievements in Africa. Cape Town: Nasionale Pers: 1968. 256pp. illus. bibl.

   Covers the evidences of United States influence on South Africa from the period of Columbus to the modern period of American investment in South Africa. This influence is evident in the history of engineering, exploration, missionary endeavour, mining, commerce, science, and military affairs in South Africa.

English

1016. Stone, J. Colonist or Uitlander? A Study of the British Immigrant in South Africa. Oxford: Clarendon Press, 1973. 313pp. bibl.

   A sociological study of the rapid integration of the British immigrant into the structure of South African society and his acceptance of its norms and values, e.g., racial attitudes. Part 1 contains a comparison of race relations in Britain and South Africa. Part 2 outlines the historical background and development of British immigration to South Africa between 1820 and 1960. Part 3 consists of an analysis and interpretation of data from a sample survey of post-war British immigrants interviewed in South Africa in 1967 and 1968. See also the sections (1) 'Cape Settlers of British Origin, 1820 onwards' entries 193 to 226. (2) 'Natal History and Description' entries 337 to 386.

Germans

Bibliography

1017. Nicholson, G. German Settlers in South Africa: A Bibliography. Cape Town: University of Cape Town, School of Librarianship, 1962. vii, 52pp.

Monographs

1018. Ffolliott, P. From Moscow to the Cape: The Story of the Wienands of Waldeck. Cape Town: Timmins, 1963. 191pp. illus.

    Primarily a biography of Ernst Daniel Wienand who came to South Africa in 1818 from Waldeck, Germany. Also attempts to pay tribute to German settlers who came to the Cape from 1750 to 1820.

1019. Schnell, E.L.C. For Men Must Work: An Account of German Immigration to the Cape with Special Reference to the German Military Settlers of 1857 and the German Immigrants of 1858. Cape Town: Maskew Miller, 1954. 298pp. illus. map. bibl.

    Commences with an explanation of Sir George Grey's frontier policy of establishing immigrants among the Xhosa. This led to the establishment of the German military settlers of 1857 and the emigration of parties of German settlers to the Cape in 1858-9 and 1859-62. Later immigrants arrived in 1877 and 1883. The role of German missionaries, German churches, and schools is discussed. Appendices supply official documents connected with the German immigrants, lists of immigrant ships, statistical tables, and lists of the name of German immigrants.

Huguenots

Bibliography

1020. Verner, B.A. Huguenots in South Africa: A Bibliography. Cape Town: University of Cape Town, School of Librarianship, 1967. vii, 44pp.

Monographs

1021. Botha, C.G. The French Refugees at the Cape. Cape Town: Cape Times, 1919. viii, 171pp. illus. maps. bibl.

    A brief account of the arrival and settlement of the Huguenots at the Cape in the seventeenth century, showing the benefits which they brought to the colony. A list of the French refugees who arrived between 1688 and 1700 is given, also a list of baptisms between 1694 and 1713, and a table of lands granted to the Huguenots. Finally, there are extracts from the principal official documents relating to the Huguenots.

1022. Boucher, M. French Speakers at the Cape in the First Hundred Years of Dutch East India Company Rule: The European Background. Pretoria: University of South Africa, 1981. 446pp. bibl.

A detailed description of the places of origin of French speakers who visited the Cape or settled there temporarily or permanently during the period of the late sixteenth century to the year 1685.

1023. Kannemeyer, A.J. Hugenote-Familie Boek. Cape Town: Unie-Volkspers, 1940. 282pp. illus. bibl.

An alphabetically arranged biographical dictionary of South African families of Huguenot descent. Where possible, family coat-of-arms is supplied and photographs of ancestors who settled at the Cape. The family history of each family is given from the time of arrival in South Africa.

1024. Nathan, M. Huguenots in South Africa. Johannesburg: Central News Agency, 1924. xii, 159pp. illus. maps. bibl.

Recounts the history of the Huguenots from the sixteenth century to their settlement at the Cape. Attempts to assess the value which the Huguenot settlement brought to the Cape. Appendix I lists the names of Huguenot immigrants and settlers. Appendix II deals with the subsequent family history and lineage of noteworthy Huguenots.

Jews

1025. Abrahams, I. The Birth of a Community: A History of Western Province Jewry from Earliest Times to the End of the South African War, 1902. Cape Town: Cape Town Hebrew Congregation, 1955. xvi, 166pp. illus.

During the nineteenth century the Cape Town Hebrew community was the focal point of South African Jewish life. The first Jewish settlers are described together with the growth of the Cape Town and Kimberley communities, and the work of Joel Rabinowitz, Rev. A.F. Ornstein, and Rev. A.P. Bender.

1026. Herrman, L. A History of the Jews in South Africa from the Earliest Times to 1895. Johannesburg: South African Jewish Board of Deputies, 1935. 288pp. illus. bibl.

A history of the part played by the Jews in the European colonization of South Africa from the fifteenth century voyages of the Portuguese explorers to the end of the nineteenth century.

South African Population - Jews

1027. Saron, G., and L. Hotz, eds. The Jews in South Africa: A History. Cape Town: Oxford University Press, 1956. xvii, 422pp. illus. map.

A history of the Jews in South Africa from the early nineteenth century to modern times. Each essay is written by a specialist contributor and discusses circumstances bringing Jewish immigrants to South Africa, how they adapted to South African conditions, their influence on South Africa, how they built up their group life, and their contact with Jewish institutions and communities abroad.

Scandinavians

1028. Winquist, A.H. Scandinavians and South Africa: Their Impact on the Cultural, Social and Economic Development of pre-1902 South Africa. Cape Town: Balkema, 1978. ix, 268pp. maps. bibl.

An account of the influence of Scandinavians, particularly Swedes and Norwegians, on the development of South Africa in their capacity as explorers, naturalists, missionaries, pioneer settlers, fishermen, miners, engineers, and businessmen. The Scandinavian influence was evident already in the period of the Dutch East India Company, and natural scientists, such as Linnaeus, Sparrman, and Thunberg, visited the Cape prior to 1815. After 1850, Scandinavian missionaries, explorers, and scientists were attracted to Namibia. Between 1815-1911, immigration in general increased and Scandinavians were rapidly assimilated into South African society. Scandinavian missionaries played an important part in opening up Zululand and recording Zulu history. The Scandinavians participated in the Anglo-Boer War, those in the Transvaal were pro-Boer, those in the Cape were pro-British.

AUTHOR/TITLE INDEX

Numbers refer to item numbers, not pages
'n' denotes a subsidiary entry.

Abantu Abamnyama, 394
About the Bechuanas, 100
Abrahams, I., 1025
Abrahams, L., 807
Ackerman, W.H., 635n
Adam Kok's Griquas, 951, 975
Adamantia: the Truth about the South African Diamond Fields, 455
Adams, W.J., 255
Adventure at the Cape of Good Hope in December 1672, 073
Afkomst der Boeren, 993
Africa and Some World Problems, 762
Africa and the Victorians, 726
African Bourgeoisie, 818
African Hunting and Adventures from Natal to the Zambesi, 107
African Liberation Movements, 805
African Opposition in South Africa, 800
African Patriots, 788
African Peasants and Economic Change in South Africa, 908
African Politics in South Africa 1964-1974, 817
African Societies in Southern Africa, 945
Afrikaanse Familie Name, 1004
Afrikaner and African Nationalism, 826
Afrikaner as Viewed by the English 1795-1854, 1009
Afrikaner Bond, 273
Afrikaner-Broederbond: Eerste 50 Jaar, 743
Afrikaner en sy Geskiedenis, 1011
Afrikaner-Familie Naamboek, 1007
Afrikaner Politics in South Africa 1934-1948, 693
Afrikaners (Fisher), 997
Afrikaners (Munger), 1003
Afrikaners in die Goudstad, 514
Afrikaners in die Vreemde, 331
Afrikaner's Interpretation of South African History, 1012
Aftermath of War, 648
Agar-Hamilton, J.A.I., 001, 228, 464
Age of the Generals, 684
Agriculture in Natal 1860-1950, 358
Alberti, L., 901
Alexander, J.E., 091
Alfonso de Albuquerque, Governor of India, 061

Author/Title Index

Alfred Lord Milner: The Man of no Illusions, 305
All Sir Garnet: A Life of Field-Marshal Lord Wolseley, 383
Allen, V., 465
Alman, S.B., 900
Ama-Xosa: Life and Customs, 933
American Diplomacy and the Boer War, 628
American Sympathy in the Boer War, 631
Americans in Africa 1865-1900, 1014
Americans in Black Africa up to 1865, 1013
Amery, L.S., 567
Anatomy of African Misery, 828
Anatomy of an Antiwar Movement: The Pro-Boers, 630
Anatomy of Apartheid, 836
Anatomy of South Africa, 811
Anatomy of South African Misery, 799
Ander Oorlog, 632
Anderson, H.J., 156
Andrew Smith and Natal, 378
Andrew Smith's Journal of His Expedition... 102, 189
Andries Pretorius... 239
Andries Pretorius in Natal, 370
Angas, G.F., 902
Anglo-Boer War 1899-1902: A Pictorial History, 577
Anglo-German Imperialism in South Africa 1880-1900, 700
Anglo-Zulu Relations, 424
Anglo-Zulu War: New Perspectives, 424
Anglo-Zulu War of 1879, 422
Angove, J., 256
Annals of Natal 1495-1845, 337
Anti-slavery Agitation Against the Transvaal Republic, 490
Apartheid, 675
Apartheid and Partnership, 831
Appelgryn, M.S., 472
Appleyard, J.W., 257
Arbousset, T., 092
Architect of Apartheid: H.F. Verwoerd, 778
Argonauts of the Rand, 547
Arkin, M., 172
Armstrong, H.C., 764
Arnott, D., 965
Arthur, G., 384
Ashe, W., 410
Assegai Over the Hills, 296
Atkins, J.B., 591
Atmore, A., 025
Attree, E.M., 446
Austin, D., 697
Australians at the Boer War, 619
Autobiography of Lieutenant-General Sir Harry Smith, 326
Autobiography of the Late Sir Andries Stockenstrom, 940
Awakening of Afrikaner Nationalism 1868-1881, 1010
Axelson, E., 047, 048, 049
Axtell, J., 820
Ayliff, J., 194, 195, 903
Aylward, A., 466

Back, J., 900
Backeberg, H.E.W., 625
Baden-Powell at Mafeking, 601
Bain, A.G., 093
Baines, T., 094
Baker, Sir H., 313
Baldwin, W.C., 107
Ballard, C., 424
Ballinger, M., 671
Bantoe van Suid-Afrika, 905
Bantoebeleid van Theophilus Shepstone, 372
Bantu, Boer and Briton, 916
Bantu Origins, 906
Bantu Past and Present, 919
Bantu Prophets in South Africa, 892
Bantu Speaking Peoples of Southern Africa, 910
Bantu Speaking Tribes of South Africa, 931
Barber, J., 672
Barker, M., 251
Barlow, T.B., 447
Barnard, A., 154-157
Barnard, C.J., 594
Barthorpe, M., 411
Basson, J.L., 776
Basutos, 914
Basutos; or Twenty-three Years in South Africa, 859
Bateman, P., 592
Battle of Majuba Hill: The First Boer War, 529
Battle of Spion Kop, 612
Battles of the Boer War, 611
Beak, G.B., 648
Beazley, R., 050
Becker, P., 392, 921, 926
Before and after Shaka, 402
Before Van Riebeeck, 063
Beginnings of Urban Segregation in South Africa, 797
Belfield, E., 593
Bell, K.N., 698
Bell, M., 196
Bellairs, B. St. J., 522
Benson, M., 788
Bent Pine: the Trial of Chief Langalibalele, 362
Benyon, J., 699
Bergh, O., 075
Berning, J.M., 193
Betrekkinge Tussen die Suid-Afrikaanse Republiek en Duitsland... 625
Bevan, D., 259
Beyers, C., 123
Beyers, C.J., 982
Beyond the Cape Frontier, 930
Bibliografie van Werke oor die Oranje-Vrystaat, 445
Bibliography of Books and Speeches by General J.C. Smuts, 761
Bibliography of Cecil John Rhodes, 314
Bibliography of Missions and Missionaries in Natal, 848
Bibliography of Personal Accounts of the Cape of Good Hope... 045

Author/Title Index

Bibliography on Indians in South Africa, 979
Bibliography on the Indian Question in South Africa, 978, 981
Biesheuvel, S., 811
Binns, C.T., 412, 438
Bird, J., 337
Bird, W., 173
Birth and Development of the Natal Railway, 344
Birth of a Community, 1025
Bischoff, L.R., 532
Bittereinders Junie 1901 - Mei 1902, 605
Bixler, R.W., 700
Black and White Africans, 780
Black and White in South Africa, 821
Black Leaders in Southern African History, 837
Black Nationalism in South Africa, 843
Black People and Whence They Came, 394
Black Power in South Africa, 804
Black Sash, 742
Black Sash of South Africa, 741
Blanckenberg, P.B., 765
Bleek, W.H.I., 338
Blommaert, W., 124, 171
Blum, P., 783
Bodelson, C.A., 701
Boer War (Belfield), 593
Boer War (Holt), 572
Boer War (Judd), 573
Boer War (Martin), 610
Boer War (Pakenham), 578
Boer War: A Study in Cowardice and Courage, 614
Boer War Diary of Sol. T. Plaatje, 644
Boers in Europe, 633
Böeseken, A.J., 002, 125, 126, 148n
Bond, G., 404
Booth, A.R., 391
Booysens, B., 757
Bosch, D.W., 339
Botha, C.G., 111, 127-128, 1021
Botha, P.R., 467
Botha, Smuts and South Africa, 745
Boucher, M., 1022
Bowler's Cape Town, 311
Boyle, F., 260
Boxer, C.R., 051, 052, 129
Boyce, W.B., 887
Bozzoli, B., 673, 789
Bradlow, E., 087, 267
Bradlow, F.R., 087, 267, 966
Brand, R.H., 649
Bredell, H.C., 636n
Breitenbach, J.J., 674
Breytenbach, J.H., 513, 523, 568-569
Brief History of Methodism, 869
Briggs, D.R., 853
Bringing Forth Light, 421

Brink, C.F., 080
Brinton, W., 268
Britain and South Africa, 697
British Colonial Administration in the Mid-Nineteenth Century, 702
British Colonial Developments 1774-1834, 711
British Colonial Government after the American Revolution, 721
British Colonial Policy and the South African Republics, 703
British Colonial Policy in the Age of Peel and Russell, 722
British Colonial Policy in the Mid-Victorian Age, 723
British Colonial Theories 1570-1850, 718
British Indians in the Transvaal, 990
British Land Policy at the Cape 1795-1844, 183
British Paternalism and Africa 1920-1940, 713
British Policy Towards the Boers, 524
British Pro-Boers, 627
British Residents at the Cape 1795-1819, 188
British Rule in South Africa, 397
British Settlement of Natal, 351
British Settlers in Natal, 379
British South Africa, 174
British Supremacy in South Africa 1899-1907, 655
British to Southern Africa, 200
Britse Owerheid en die Groot Trek, 233
Broederbond in die Afrikaner-politiek, 743n
Brookes, E.H., 340, 437, 675-676, 790-793
Brotherhood of Power, 743n
Brown, W.E., 854
Brownlee, C., 904
Brownlee, F., 269
Brownlee, M., 846
Brunt of the War and Where it Fell, 620
Bruwer, J.P., 905
Bryant, A.T., 341, 389, 906-907
Buckland, M.V., 561
Buller's Campaign, 618
Bulpin, T.V., 229, 342-343, 390, 468-471
Bundy, C., 908
Burchell, W.J., 095, 158
Burden of Empire, 708
Burger, M.J., 750
Burger, S.J., 635
Burke, E.E., 314
Burman, J., 053, 112, 130
Burrows, E.H., 159, 197
Burton, A.W., 270
Bushman 1652-1962, 948
Bushman Raiders of the Drakensberg 1804-1870, 956
Bushmen: San Hunters and Herders of Southern Africa, 954
Butler, G., 198-199
Butler, J., 552
Buxton, S.C., Earl, 747
By Strength of Heart, 057
Bydraes tot die Genealogie van Ou Afrikaanse Families, 1000

Author/Title Index

Caffres and Caffre Missions, 855
Caffrey, K., 200
Cairns, M., 966
Calderwood, H., 855
Calendar of Cape Missionary Correspondence, 849
Callan, E., 829
Callaway, G., 856
Callinicos, L., 677
Calpin, G.H., 678, 794, 983
Cambridge History of Africa, 003
Cambridge History of the British Empire, 004
Camera on Old Natal, 352
Campbell, C.T., 174
Campbell, E.D., 344
Campbell, J., 857-858
Campbell, P.C., 650
Campbell, W.B., 271
Cape Colour Question: A Historical Survey, 973
Cape Coloured: A Bibliography, 962
Cape Coloured People 1652-1937, 974
Cape Epic, 121
Cape Frontier: A Study of Native Policy... 278
Cape Journals of Archdeacon N.J. Merriman 1848-1855, 295
Cape Malays, 969
Cape of Adventure, 054
Cape of Good Hope. Archives, 175-177
Cape of Good Hope and the Eastern Province of Algoa Bay, 178
Cape of Good Hope at the Turn of the Eighteenth Century, 165
Cape of Good Hope 1652-1702, 076
Cape of Good Hope under the Batavian Republic, 152
Cape of Good Intent, 130
Cape Parliament 1854-1910, 290
Capital, State and White Labour, 798
Capitalists and the Outbreak of the Anglo-Boer War, 583
Capture of de Wet: The South African Rebellion 1914, 691
Carnegie Commission Report, 679
Carter, G.M., 680, 795, 816
Carter, T.F., 474
Cartwright, A.P., 475, 481, 534-538
Casalis, E., 859
Catholic Church in South Africa, 854
Cecil Rhodes (Flint), 315
Cecil Rhodes (Williams), 323
Cecil Rhodes: A Study of a Career, 317
Cecil Rhodes by His Architect, 313
Cecil Rhodes: His Political Life and Speeches, 322
Cell, J.W., 702
Centenary of Indians 1860-1960, 989
Cetshwayo's Dutchman, 413
Chadwick, G.A., 433
Chaka: An Historical Romance, 405
Chaka the Terrible, 404
Champion, G., 391
Changuion, L., 493
Chapman, J., 108

Chase, J.C., 178, 345
Chavonnes, M.P. de, 131
Child, D., 346
Chilvers, H.A., 261-262, 796
Chinese Community in South Africa, 961
Chinese Coolie Emigration to Countries Within the British Empire, 650
Chinese Labour Question, 957
Chinese Mine Labour in the Transvaal, 959
Chisholm, R., 596
Christiaan de Wet: 'n Lewensbeskrywing, 639
Christian Handbook of South Africa, 867
Christianity and the Natives of South Africa, 893
Christopher, A.J., 005
Chronicle of Jeremiah Goldswain, Albany Settler of 1820, 213
Chronicles of Cape Commanders, 144
Church in South Africa, 868
Churchill, J., 346
Churchill, M., 346
Churchill, W.S., 636-637
Cilliers, S.P., 967
Civil Liberty in South Africa, 791
Clammer, D.G., 415
Clark, E.M.M., 746
Clark, G.B., 524
Clark, J., 367
Clarke, S., 416
Class and Colour in South Africa, 838
Class, Race and Gold, 814
Clear Description of the Cape of Good Hope, 074
Clements, W.H., 417
Clendenen, C.C., 1013-1014
Clinton, D.K., 860
Closer Union Movement, 647
Closer Union Movements... 446
Coates, P.R., 113
Cockram, G.M., 781
Coetzee, D.J., 477
Coetzee, J.A., 992
Coetzer, P.W., 732
Cole, G.S., 179
Cole, M.L., 179
Colenbrander, H.T., 993
Colenbrander, P.J., 424
Colenso, F., 347
Colenso, F.E., 418-419
Colenso, J.W., 347
Colenso Letters from Natal, 347
Collectanea, 127
Collier, J., 478
Collins, J.A., 449
Collins, W.W., 450
Colonial Office, 710
Colonist or Uitlander, 1016
Colony of Natal to the Zulu War, 333
Colour and Culture in South Africa, 830

Author/Title Index

Colour Problems of South Africa, 790
Coloured People: A Bibliography, 963
Coloured People of South Africa, 964
Coloureds of South Africa, 967
Colvin, I.D., 054, 556
Comaroff, J.L., 644
Commando: A Boer Journal of the Boer War, 613
Company's Men, 139
Compendium of Kafir Laws and Customs, 915
Complete Story of the Transvaal, 510
Concentration Camps 1900-1902, 622
Conflict and Progress: Fifty Years of Race Relations... 808
Confronting Imperialism, 424
Conquests and Discoveries of Henry the Navigator, 056
Consolidated Gold Fields of South Africa Ltd., 539
Conspirators in Conflict, 559
Convict Crisis and the Growth of Unity, 285
Cook, R., 820
Cope, A.T., 387, 394
Cope, J., 006, 021, 055
Cope, R.L., 422, 911
Corner House: The Early History of Johannesburg, 534
Cornish Immigrants to South Africa, 201
Correspondence of... Sir George Cathcart, 272
Cortemunde, J., 073
Cory, Sir G.E., 004, 007, 401
Coupland, R., 423
Cowan, N., 475
Cowie, M.S., 847
Cox, G.W., 420
Cradle Days of Natal, 365
Crafford, F.S., 766
Crankshaw, E., 298
Creswicke, L., 570
Cricket in the Thorn Bush: Helen Suzman... Progressive Party, 740
Crisp, R., 479
Croft, E.L.H., 206
Cronwright-Schreiner, S.C., 626
Crown and Charter, 706
Cruse, H.P., 968
Cruywagen, W.A., 733
Cunynghame, A.T., 181
Currey, R.N., 369
Currie, J.C., 978
Curtis, L., 638

Dagboek van H.A.L. Hamelberg 1855-1871, 451
Dagboek van H.C. Bredell 1900-1904, 635
Dagboek van Louis Trichardt, 242-243
Dagut, J., 022
Danziger, C., 008, 553
Dark Bright Land, 208
Daumas, F., 092
Davenport, T.R.H., 009, 010, 273, 797
Davey, A.M., 525, 627, 662

David and Goliath, 526
David Livingstone: South African Papers 1849-1853, 507
Davies, H., 861-862
Davies, J.H., 274
Davies, R.H., 798
Dear Louisa: History of A Pioneer Family in Natal, 366
De Castro e Almeida, V., 056
De Kiewiet, C.W., 011, 703-704, 799
De Klerk, W.A., 994
De Kock, V., 018, 057, 132
De Kock, W.J., 058, 275
De La Caille, N.L., 081
De Mist, A.U., 159
De Mist, J.A., 160-161
Denny, A., 726
Denoon, D., 012, 651
Derricourt, E., 930
Descriptions of the Cape of Good Hope... 145
Destruction of the Zulu Kingdom, 439
Detained in Simon's Bay, 164
De Villiers, C.C., 995, 1000-1001
De Villiers, J., 574
De Villiers, S.A., 117
Development of Missionary Attitudes, 894
De Wet, C.R., 597
De Wet, G.C., 079, 138
Diamonds and Gold in South Africa, 264, 548
Diary of a Journey to the Cape of Good Hope... 159
Diary of Adam Tas, 142-143
Diary of Dr. Andrew Smith, 103
Diary of Henry Francis Fynn, 349
Diary of the Rev. Francis Owen, 401
Dickason, G.B., 201-202
Dinuzulu: The Death of the House of Shaka, 438
Dobie, J.S., 348
Dr. Daniel Francois Malan, 756
Dr. Hendrik Frensch Verwoerd, 779
Dr. John Philip, 851
Dr. John Philip's Observations regarding the Hottentots, 882
Documents relating to the Kaffir War of 1835, 175
D'Oliveira, J., 782
Dominion of Afrikanerdom, 306
Donkin, Sir R.S., 182
Dornan, S.S., 949
Doughty, O., 263
Doyle, A.C., 598
Dracopoli, J.L., 276, 941
Dreyer, A., 230
Drie Eeue: Die Verhaal van ons Vaderland, 002
Driehonderd Jaar Nasiebou, 1002
Drums of the Birkenhead, 259
Du Cane, H., 582
Duckitt, W., 162
Duff-Gordon, L., 277
Duignan, P., 708, 1013

Author/Title Index

Duly, L.C., 183
Duminy, A.H., 332, 424, 583-584
Duminy, F.R., 163
Duminy-dagboeke, 163
Duminy Diaries, 163
Du Plessis, A.P., 996
Du Plessis, I.D., 969-970
Du Plessis, J., 863
Du Plessis, J.S., 494
Durnford, E., 418
Dutch Seaborne Empire 1600-1800, 129
Du Toit, A.E., 278
Du Toit, J.B., 977
Dutton, F.H., 405
Duvenhage, G.D.J., 488
Duxbury, G.R., 526

Eales, M., 443
Early Cape Hottentots, 952
Early Cape Muslims, 966
Early Diamond Days: The Opening of the Diamond Fields... 263
Early French Callers at the Cape, 077
Economic Influences on the South African Frontier... 136
Economic Imperialism in Theory and Practice, 545
Economy and Society in Pre-Industrial South Africa, 025
Edgecombe, R., 421
Edgell, E.V.W., 410
Edges of War, 120a
Edmunds, A., 864
Edwards, E.J., 554
Edwards, G.E., 870
Edwards, I., 184
Edwards, I.E., 204
Eenheidstrewe van die Republikeinse Afrikaners, 248
Eerste Skof van die Nasionale Party in Transvaal, 733
Eerste Vryheidsoorlog, 530
Egerton, H.E., 705
1820 Settlers: An Illustrated Commentary, 198
1820 Settlers in South Africa, 204
Eighth Kaffir War, 253
Eilande in die Vaal Rivier, 487
Elgin and Churchill at the Colonial Office, 714
Ellenberger, D.F., 909
Elphick, R., 013, 820, 950
Emden, P.H., 540
Emery, F., 425
Engelbrecht, J.A., 971
Engelbrecht, S.P., 473, 495
Engelenburg, F.V., 748
Engels, L.J., 043
Engelse Oorlog 1899-1902, 604
Englishman's Inn, 376
Etherington, N.A., 424
Europa en die Tweede Vryheidsoorlog 1899-1902, 634
European Immigration into Natal, 334

Europe's Discovery of South Africa, 068
Evangelical Awakenings in Africa, 880
Eveleigh, W., 205
Ewart, J., 096
Expedition of Discovery into the Interior of Africa, 091
Experiment in Alien Labour, 958
Eybers, G.W., 014

Failure of South African Expansion 1908-1948, 683
Fairbridge, D., 133, 157, 277
Fall of Kruger's Republic, 586
Farrelly, M.J., 652
Farrer, J.A., 393
Farrington, B., 952
Farwell, B., 571
Feit, E., 800-802
Ferguson, J.H., 628
Few Months with the Boers, 635
Ffolliott, P., 098, 206, 1018
Fifty Golden Years of the Rand 1886-1936, 543
Fifty Years of the History of the Republic in South Africa... 036
Findlay, J., 207
Findlay Letters 1806-1870, 207
First Annexation of the Transvaal, 505
First Boer War, 527
First British Occupation of the Cape of Good Hope, 153
First-Hand Accounts of Johannesburg, 463
First South African... Life and Times of Sir Percy Fitzpatrick, 481
First South Africans and the Laws Which Governed Them, 140
Fisher, J., 496, 621, 997
Fitz: The Story of Sir Percy Fitzpatrick, 482
Fitzpatrick, J.P., 480
Fitzroy, V.M., 208
Five Hundred Years: A History of South Africa, 028
Flint, J., 315
For Men Must Work: An Account of German Immigration... 1019
Forbes, V.S., 082, 086, 088, 106
Forgotten Frontiersmen, 955
Forsaken Idea: A Study of Viscount Milner, 298
Foto Biografie: Paul Kruger 1825-1904, 493
Fouche, L., 142-143
Foundation of the Cape, 100
Four Centuries of Portuguese Expansion 1415-1825, 051
Four Studies of War and Peace in This Century, 653
Fourie, J.J., 514
Franken, J.L.M., 163, 171
Frederickson, G.M., 803
Free Statia, 450
French, G., 426
French Colonel: Villebois-Mareuil and the Boers, 646
French Refugees at the Cape, 1021
French Speakers at the Cape, 1022
Freund, W., 840
Friedlander, Z., 767
Friedman, B., 768

Author/Title Index 251

From Dias to Vorster: Source Material on South African History, 017
From Moscow to the Cape: The Story of the Wienands of Waldeck, 1018
From Protest to Challenge, 816
From the Land of the Zulu Kings, 408
From Union to Apartheid, 671
From Van Riebeeck to Vorster 1652-1974, 034
Frontier Flames, 214
Frontier in History, 820
Frost, P.J., 848
Frye, S., 257
Fryer, A.K., 281
Fuller, C., 244
Fun They Had: The Pastimes of Our Forefathers, 018n
Furneaux, R., 427
Further South African Recollections, 307
Fuze, M.M., 394
Fynn, H.F., 349

Galbraith, J.S., 706-707
Gallagher, J., 726
Galloway, M.H., 388
Game and Gold: Memories of over 50 Years... 485
Gandhi in South Africa, 984
Gann, L.H., 708
Gardiner, A.F., 350
Gardner, B., 599-600
Garrett, E., 554
Garson, N.G., 484, 840
Gedenkalbum van die Tweede Vryheidsoorlog, 568
Gedenkboek Generaal J.B.M. Hertzog, 753
Geen, M.S., 015
Generaal J.B.M. Hertzog, 750
Generaal J.B.M. Hertzog en die Ontstaan van die Nasionale Party, 751
Generaal Louis Botha op die Natalse Front 1899-1900, 594
General Botha, 747
General De Wet: A Biography, 640
General Hertzog, 752
General J.B.M. Hertzog, 755
General Louis Botha, 748
General Louis Botha's Second Expedition to Natal... 595
General Remarks on the Cape of Good Hope 1803, 170
General Smuts, 774
Generals of the Anglo-Boer War, 592
Geographical and Topographical Description of the Cape... 085
Gerdener, G.B.A., 865
Gerhart, G.M., 804
German Official Account of the War in South Africa, 582
German Settlers in South Africa, 1017
Geschiedenis van de Slavernij aan de Kaap, 124
Geskiedenis van die Tweede Vryheidsoorlog in Suid-Afrika, 569
Geskiedenis van Suid-Afrika (Gie), 016
Geskiedenis van Suid-Afrika (Van der Walt), 033
Geslachtsregister den Oude Kaapsche Familien, 995
Geslagsregister Van die Ou Kaapse Families, 995
Geyser, O., 372, 732

Gibson, J.Y., 395
Gibson, R., 805
Gie, S.F.N., 016, 160
Giffen, R., 900
Giliomee, H., 013, 820
Gladstone and Kruger: Liberal Government and Colonial Home Rule, 512
Glamour and Tragedy of the Zulu War, 417
Glover, M., 428
Glynn, M.T., 485
Godlonton, R., 185, 209, 282
Gold, Bricks and Mortar: 60 Years of Johannesburg History, 549
Gold Fields 1887-1937, 539
Gold! Gold! Gold!: The Johannesburg Gold Rush, 550
Gold Miners, 535
Gold Mines of Southern Africa, 546
Gold Mining in the Eastern Transvaal, 533
Gold Mining on the Witwatersrand, 544
Gold Paved the Way: The Story of the Gold Fields Group, 536
Golden Age: The Story of the Industrialization of South Africa...537
Golden Republic, 469
Goldswain, J., 213
Gollin, A.M., 657
Golovnin, V.M., 164
Gon, P., 429
Good-bye Dolly Gray: The Story of the Boer War, 575
Goodfellow, C.F., 709
Goosen, D.P., 731
Gordon, C.T., 486
Gordon, R.E., 017, 366, 375
Gordon-Brown, A., 255
Government Finance and Political Development in Natal, 363
Government of the Cape of Good Hope 1825-1854, 281
Grand Illusion, 651
Grant, M.H., 576
Gray, E., 542
Gray, J., 541-542
Great Adventure, 864
Great Anglo-Boer War, 571
Great Boer War, 598
Great Britain and South African Confederation, 709
Great South African Christians, 862
Great Trek (Bulpin), 229
Great Trek (Walker), 250
Greatheart of the Border, 211
Greenlees, M., 135
Greenwald, D.J., 759
Grennell-Milne, D.W., 601
Grensbakens Tussen Blank en Swart in Suid-Afrika, 841
Grey, P.C., 487
Grey Steel: J.C. Smuts, 764
Greyling, J.J.C., 979
Griffith, K., 602
Griquas of Griqualand, 972
Grivainis, I., 227
Grobler-moord: Historiese Rekonstruksie... Matabele Dinastie, 511

Author/Title Index

Gronum, M.A., 603-605
Gross, F., 316
Grout, L., 396
Groves, C.P., 866
Growth of Boer Opposition to Kruger 1890-1895, 486
Growth of Johannesburg, 462
Grubb, K.G., 867
Guest, W.R., 361, 424
Guide to Official Records of the Colony of Natal, 336
Guide to Unofficial Sources Relating to the History of Natal, 332
Gutsche, T., 118
Guy, J.J., 422, 424, 439

Haarhoff, T.J., 769
Halford, S.J., 972
Hall, H.L., 710
Halperin, V., 299
Hamelberg, H.A.L., 451
Hamilton, J.A., 606
Hammond-Tooke, W.D., 888, 910
Hancock, W.K., 653, 770-772
Handbook on Race Relations in South Africa, 807
Hardman, S., 024
Hare, A.P., 806
Harford, H., 430
Harington, A.L., 327
Harlow, V.T., 711
Hart, H.H., 059
Harvest and the Hope, 853
Hatch, J., 712
Hattersley, A.F., 004, 018, 019, 283, 285, 348, 351-356
Hawk's Eye, 191
Headlam, C., 300, 658
Heathcote, E.K., 216
Heese, J.A., 186, 998
Held van Colenso: Die Verhaal van Generaal Louis Botha, 749
Hellmann, E., 807-808
Hennings, N.H.P., 073
Hensman, H., 317
Hepple, A., 020
Herd, N., 362, 681
Here Comes the Alabama: The Career of a Confederate Raider, 267
Herkoms van die Afrikaner 1657-1867, 998
Herrman, L., 360, 1026
Hertzog en Smuts en die Britse Ryk, 744
Hetherington, P., 713
Hewson, L.A., 195, 203
Hexham, I., 999
Hill of Destiny: The Life and Times of Moshesh, 921
Hillegas, H.C., 607
Hinchliff, P.B., 194, 849, 868
Historia Trágico-Marítima, 052
Historic Farms of South Africa, 133
Historic Natal and Zululand, 364
Historical Records of the Church of the Province of South Africa, 876

History of Apartheid, 827
History of Britain in Africa, 712
History of Christian Missions in South Africa, 863
History of Johannesburg: The Early Years, 504
History of Natal, 340
History of Native Policy in South Africa... 792
History of South Africa (Lacour-Gayet), 024
History of South Africa (Theal), 031
History of South Africa (Were), 038
History of South Africa: Social and Economic (De Kiewiet), 011
History of South and Central Africa (Wilson), 040
History of Southern Africa (Walker), 037
History of the Abambo... 903
History of the Basuto Ancient and Modern, 909
History of the British Regiments in South Africa 1795-1895, 268
History of the Colony of Natal, 357
History of the Discovery of the Witwatersrand Goldfields, 542
History of the Indians in Natal, 988
History of the Jews in South Africa... 1026
History of the London Missionary Society, 877
History of the War in South Africa 1899-1902, 576
History of the Wesleyan Methodist Church, 897
History of the Zulu and Neighbouring Tribes, 907
History of the Zulu Rebellion, 442
History of the Zulu War, 435
Hobhouse, E., 620-621
Hobson, E.G., 433
Hobson, J.A., 585
Hockly, H.E., 210
Hodgson, T.L., 911
Hoernlé, R.F.A., 809-810
Hoffman, M.W., 669
Hofmeyr, J.H., 021, 682
Hoge, J., 1000
Holden, M.A., 900
Holden, W.C., 357, 397, 869, 912
Hole, H.M,, 555
Holt, B., 211, 898
Holt, E., 572
Hondius, J., 074
Hopper, M.J., 122
Hotz, L., 1027
Houghton, D.H., 022
House of Phalo, 928
Hudson, W., 811
Hugenote-Familie Boek, 1023
Hughes, E.B., 461
Huguenots in South Africa, 1024
Hunt, K.S., 009, 180
Hunter, M., 913
Hurwitz, N., 358, 437
Huttenback, R.A., 984
Hutton, C.E., 940
Hyam, R., 683, 714-715
Hyatt, S.P., 286

Author/Title Index

Ian Hamilton's March, 637
Idenburg, P.J., 165
Illustrated Social History of South Africa, 018
Imperial Factor in South Africa, 704
Imperial Policy and South Africa 1902-1910, 661
Imperial South African Association, 957
Imperial War and the British Working Class, 579
In Mid-Victorian Cape Town, 324
In the Era of Shepstone, 728
In the Era of Shepstone: Being a Study of British Expansion... 374
In the Early Days: The Reminiscences of Pioneer Life... 256
In the Land of the Settlers, 218
In the Shadow of Death, 609
In Zululand with the British Throughout the War of 1879, 434
Indaba My Children, 400
Index to Literature on Race Relations, 785
Indian Immigration into Natal 1860-1872, 991
Indian People in Natal, 985
Indians in South Africa, 983
Indiërvraagstuk in Natal 1870-1910, 982
Ingram, J.F., 359
Inner History of the National Convention of South Africa, 667
Innes, Sir J.R., 287
Inscriptions left by Early European Navigators... 060
Institute for Contemporary History, 732
International Aspects of the South African Indian Question, 987
Invasion of Zululand 1879, 416
Invoeren van die Slavernij aan de Kaap, 124
Irish Settlers to the Cape, 202
Irony of Apartheid, 999
Irving, E., 282
Izedinova, S., 635n

Jabavu, D.D.T., 812-813
Jacob van Reenen and the Grosvenor Expedition... 089
Jacobs, G.F,, 811
Jacobson, D., 543
Jacobson, E., 962
Jacoby, A.J., 900
Jaff, F., 212
Jaffe, E.L., 409
James Barry Munnik Hertzog, 754
James, D., 645
James Ewart's Journal Covering his Stay at the Cape... 096
James Stephen and the British Colonial System 1813-1847, 717
Jameson Raid (Danziger), 553
Jameson Raid (Hole), 555
Jameson Raid (Moggridge), 551
Jameson Raid (Van der Poel), 560
Jameson's Raid (Longford), 557
Jameson's Raid (Pakenham), 558
Jan Christiaan Smuts (Greenwald), 759
Jan Christiaan Smuts (Scott), 761
Jan Christian Smuts (Smuts), 775
Jan Smuts: A Biography, 766

Jan Smuts Remembered, 767
Jan van Riebeeck: A Bibliographical Study, 148
Jan van Riebeeck en sy Gesin, 148n
Jan van Riebeeck en sy Tyd, 149
Jansen, E.G., 231
Jansz, J.C., 090
Jeffreys, K.M., 138, 160
Jennings, B., 252
Jeppe, C., 489
Jeppe, C.B., 544
Jews in South Africa: A History, 1027
Joernaal van Dirk Gysbert van Reenen 1803, 171
John Mackenzie of Bechuanaland, 720
John Sheddon Dobie: South African Journal 1862-1866, 348
John X. Merriman: Paradoxical South African Statesman, 293
Johns, S.W., 834
Johnson, J., 517
Johnstone, F.A., 814
Johnstone, F.N., 840
Jones, J.D.R., 815
Jordaan, B., 870
Jordan, R.A., 521
Joseph Chamberlain and the South African Republic, 590, 730
Joseph Williams and the Pioneer Mission... 898
Joubert, D.C., 513
Journal Historique du Voyage Fait au Cap de Bonne Esperance, 081
Journal of a Visit to South Africa in 1815 and 1816, 099
Journal of 'Harry Hastings', Albany Settler, 195
Journal of Hendrik Jacob Wikar, 090
Journal of His [Van der Stel's] Expedition to Namaqualand, 078
Journal of Jan van Riebeeck, 147
Journal of John Ayliff, 194
Journal of Residence in Africa 1842-1853 (Baines), 094
Journal of the First Voyage of Vasco da Gama 1497-1499, 067
Journal of the Reverend George Champion... 1835-1839, 391
Journal of William Shaw, 888
Journals of Andrew Geddes Bain, 093
Journals of Brink and Rhenius, 080
Journals of Sophia Pigot 1819-1821, 217
Journals of the Expeditions of... Olof Bergh and Isaq Schrijver, 075
Journals of the Rev. T.L. Hodgson, 911
Judd, D., 573
Juta, M., 497

Kaap onder die Bataafse Republiek, 169
Kaapse Argiefstukke, 138
Kaapse Kerk en die Groot Trek, 230
Kaapse Patriotte... 123
Kaatje Kekkelbek, 093
Kaffer Oorlog van 1793, 168
Kafirs Illustrated, 902
Kafirs of Natal and the Zulu Country, 407
Kaleidoscopic Transvaal, 489
Kandyba-Foxcroft, E., 629
Kannemeyer, A.J., 1023

Kaplan, B.B., 784
Karis, T., 816
Kay, J.A., 642
Kaye, H., 509
Keith, A.B., 716
Kellerman, A.G., 871
Kennedy, R.F., 094
Kenny, H., 778
Keppel-Jones, A., 023, 216
Kestell, J.D., 639, 654
Kesting, J.G., 565
Khoikhoi Rebellion in the Eastern Cape, 166
Khoisan Peoples of South Africa, 953
Kieser, A., 453
Kilpin, R., 119-120
Kimberley and the Diamond Fields of Griqualand West, 254
Kimberley: Turbulent City, 265
King of the Hottentots, 055
Kirby, P.R., 083, 089, 104, 378
Kistner, W., 490
Kitchener: Portrait of an Imperialist, 608
Kitchingman, J., 872
Kitchingman Papers: Missionary Letters and Journals, 872
Klare Besgryving van Cabo de Bona Esperanca, 074
Kleurling Bevolking van Suid-Afrika, 976
Knaplund, P., 717
Knorr, K.E., 718
Konsentrasie Kampe, 623
Konvensie Dagboek van... Francois Stephanus Malan, 656
Korana, 971
Kort Begrip van die Theron-Verslag, 977
Koss, S., 630
Kotzé, D.A., 817
Kotzé, D.J., 873
Kovalsky, S.J., 980
Kraal and Castle, 950
Krauss, F., 097
Krebs, L., 098
Kriel, C., 574
Krige, J., 631
Krige, J.D.A., 1001
Kritzinger, P.M., 609
Kruger, B., 875
Kruger, D.W., 033, 491, 632, 684-686
Kruger, R., 575
Kruger, S.J.P., 492
Kruger's Pretoria, 465
Kultuurgeskiedenis van die Afrikaner, 1006
Kultuurskatte uit die Voortrekker-tydperk, 249
Kubicek, R.V., 545
Kuper, H., 985
Kuper, L., 818-819, 834

Labour, Townships and Protest, 789
Lacour-Gayet, R., 024
Lady Anne Barnard at the Cape of Good Hope 1797-1802, 157
Ladysmith, 596
Lagden, Sir G., 914, 936
Lamar, H., 820
Lamb, D., 454
Land of Free Speech, 626
Land Question of Griqualand West, 965
Land They Left, 225
Landdros en Heemrade, 192
Langalibalele: The Crisis in Natal 1873-1875, 361
Last Trek: A Study of the Boer People and the Afrikaner Nation, 1005
Last Zulu King: The Life and Death of Cetshwayo, 412
Later Annals of Natal, 354
Latrobe, C.I., 099
Laurence, P., 292
Le Cordeur, B., 288-289, 872
Lehmann, J.H., 328, 383, 527
Leibbrandt, H.C.V., 176
Leiers na die Noorde: Studies oor die Groot Trek, 234
Leighton, S., 109
Leipoldt, C.L., 148
Le May, G.H.L., 655, 821
Leonard, C., 503
Le Roux, J.H., 732
Le Roux, T.H., 243
Letcher, O., 546
Letterbook of Sir Rufane Shaw Donkin, 182
Letters and Other Writings of a Natal Sheriff, Thomas Phipson, 369
Letters from a Boer Parsonage: Letters of Margaret Marquard, 641
Letters from the Cape, 277
Letters of Lady Anne Barnard to Henry Dundas... 1797-1803, 154
Letters of the American Missionaries, 873
Lever, H., 808
Leverton, B.J., 363
Lewe van D.F. Malan, 757
Lewe van President S.J.P. Kruger... 501
Lewin, J., 822-823
Lewis, C., 876
Lewsen, P., 293-294, 840
Leyds, G.A., 504
Leyds, W.J., 505, 506
Liberal Party and the Jameson Raid, 552
Liberalism in South Africa 1948-1963, 739
Lichtenstein, W.H.C., 100, 101
Liebenberg, B.J., 370
Life and Correspondence of Sir Bartle Frere, 279
Life and Times of Daniel Lindley, 874
Life and Times of Sir John Charles Molteno, 308
Life and Times of Sir Richard Southey, 329
Life at the Cape in Mid-Eighteenth Century, 135
Life of Jameson, 556
Life of John Tengo Jabavu, 812
Life of John William Colenso, 420

Life of John Xavier Merriman, 292
Life of Lieutenant-General Sir Henry Evelyn Wood, 531
Life of Lord Wolseley, 384
Life of the Rt. Hon. Cecil John Rhodes, 321
Lindley, A.F., 455
Linington, P.A., 833
Lion's Cage, 599
Lister, M.H., 093
Liversidge, R., 098
Lives and Work of South African Missionaries, 846
Livingstone, D., 507
Lloyd, A., 398, 431
Lloyd, A.C.G., 156
Lockhart, J.G., 318
London Missionary Society in South Africa, 847
London to Ladysmith via Pretoria, 636
Long, I., 213
Long View, 829
Longford, E., 557
Lord Chelmsford and the Zulu War, 426
Lord Milner and South Africa, 303
Lord Milner and the Empire, 299
Lord Milner's Immigration Policy for the Transvaal, 659
Lord Milner's Work in South Africa, 304
Lord Roberts, 645
Lords of Stalplein, 312
Lost Trails of the Low Veld, 468
Lost Trails of the Transvaal, 468
Louis Botha, 746
Louis Trigardt's Trek across the Drakensberg, 244
Lovell, R.I., 719
Lovett, R., 877
Low Veld Trails, 470
Lucas, T.S., 432
Luckhoff, L.C., 970
Ludwig Alberti's Account of the... Xhosa, 901
Lugg, H.C., 364
Lye, W.F., 102, 189

Macaulay, J.B., 791
McCracken, J.L., 290
MacCrone, I.C., 809, 824
McDonald, J.G., 319
McDonald, R.D., 609
MacDonald, T., 508
McGeogh, R.T., 226
MacGregor, J.C., 909
McKay, J., 291
Mackenzie, N.M., 044
Mackeurtan, G., 365
MacLean, J., 915
MacLeod, E., 366
MacLeod, L., 110
Macmillan, M., 258
Macmillan, W.M., 004, 916, 973

Macnab, R., 646
Macquarrie, J.W., 939
Madden, F., 711
Mafeking: A Victorian Legend, 600
Magnus, P., 608
Mahatma Gandhi, 980
Majeka, N., 878
Majuba Gedenkboek, 523
Making of a Nation, 685
Making of South Africa, 015
Malan, F.S., 656
Malan, J.H., 456
Malan, S.F., 457
Malan, S.I., 445
Malay Quarter and its People, 970
Malcolm, D.M., 349
Male, D., 566
Malherbe, D.F. du T., 1002
Malherbe, V.C., 166
Mandelbrote, J.H., 085
Manning, H.T., 721
Mansergh, N., 687
Manuel, G.A., 963
Marais, A.H., 688, 732
Marais, J.S., 134, 586, 974
Marks, S., 025, 440, 834
Marlowe, J., 301
Marquard, D.L., 689
Marquard, L., 026, 917
Marquard, M., 641
Marsh, J.W., 350
Martin, A.C., 622
Martin, C., 610
Martin, G., 715
Martineau, J., 279
Masters of the Castle, 137
Material Published after 1925 on the Great Trek, 227
Matthew, H.M., 295
Maurice, F.B., 384
Maurice, F.M., 576
Maxwell, W.A., 226
May, H.J., 642
Maynier and the First Boer Republic, 134
Mazrui, A.A., 834
Meintjes, J., 232, 498, 577, 918
Meiring, J., 084
Meiring, P., 773
Memoir of Allen F. Gardiner, 350
Memoir of the Rev. William Shaw, 887
Memoirs of Paul Kruger, 492
Memoirs of Sir Lowry Cole, 179
Memorandum of Commissary J.A. de Mist, 160
Memorials of South Africa, 886
Memorials of the British Settlers of South Africa, 209
Mentzel, O.F., 085, 135

Author/Title Index

Merchant Family in Early Natal, 346
Merriman, J.X., 294
Merriman, N.J., 295
Methods of Barbarism? Roberts and Kitchener... 624
Metrowich, F.C., 214, 296-297
Meyer, P.M., 850
Michelman, C., 741
Microcosm, 118
Midgley, J.F., 458
Miles, C., 820
Millar, A.K., 190
Millin, S.G., 027, 320, 774
Milner, C.A., 820
Milner: Apostle of Empire, 301
Milner: Viscount Milner of St. James's and Cape Town, 302
Milner Papers, 300, 658
Milner's Young Men, 660
Milton, J., 120a
Miskin, J., 979
Mission Stations and the Coloured Communities, 883
Missionary Labours and Scenes in Southern Africa, 879
Missionary Movement from Britain, 896
Mitchell, L., 321
Moffat, R., 879
Mofolo, T., 405
Moggridge, C.A., 551
Molema, S.M., 919
Molsbergen, E.C.G., 090, 149
Molteno, Sir J.T., 306-307
Molteno, P.A., 308
Monuments and Battlefields of Transvaal War and South African War, 616
Monuments and Trails of the Voortrekkers, 241
Moodie, A.D., 252
Moodie, D., 920
Moodie, T.D., 825
Moodies of Melsetter, 197
Moody, C., 635n
Moore, D.M., 595
Moore, G.C., 326
More Annals of Natal, 353
Morrell, W.P., 698, 722-723
Morris, D.R., 399
Morris, G.R., 981
Morse-Jones, E., 215
Moshesh: The Man of The Mountain, 925
Moshoeshoe: Chief of the Sotho, 922
Mossop, E.E., 075, 080, 090, 114
Mulder, C.P., 733
Muller, C.F.J., 028, 233-236
Muller, C.H., 635n
Muller, D.J., 444
Muller, H.P.N., 452, 460
Munger, E.S., 826, 1003
Murray, A.H., 161
Murray, I.M., 171

Murray, J., 324
Murray, M., 115-116
Music of the Guns: Based on Two Journals of the Boer War, 642
Mutwa, V.C., 400
My Command in South Africa, 181
Mynwerkstaking Witwatersrand 1922, 681a

Narain, I., 986
Narrative of a Residence in South Africa, 220
Narrative of an Exploratory Tour to the North-East... Cape, 092
Narrative of Private Buck Adams, 255
Narrative of the Boer War, 474
Narrative of the Eighth Frontier War of 1851-1853, 330
Narrative of the Irruption of the Kaffir Hordes, 185
Narrative of the Kaffir War of 1850-51-52, 282
Nasionale Party (Institute for Contemporary History), 732
Nasionale Boek (Van Schoor), 737
Nasionale Party (Goosen), 731
Nasionale Party (Van Rooyen), 736
Natal and the Boers: The Birth of a Colony, 371
Natal and the Zulu Country, 342
Natal Diaries of Dr. W.H.I. Bleek 1855-1856, 338
Natal, 1881-1911: A Bibliography, 335
Natal Papers 1498-1843, 345
Natal Past and Present, 386
Natal Provincial Museum Advisory Board, 433
Natal Settler-Agent: The Career of John Moreland, 367
Natalia, 359
Natalians: Further Annals of Natal, 355
Nathan, M., 237, 499, 1024
Native Administration in the Union of South Africa, 833
Native Labour in South Africa, 842
Native Life in South Africa, 929
Native Policy of Sir Theophilus Shepstone, 373
Native Policy of the Voortrekkers, 228
Native Races of South Africa, 942
Native Reserves of Natal, 437
Natives of South Africa, 937
Naudé, J.D., 751
Naude, S.D., 138
Neame, L.E., 752, 827, 840
'n Nederlander in Diens van die Oranje Vrystaat, 460
Nederlandse Emigrasie na Suid-Afrika, 996
Nederlandse Kommissarisse... 125
Neumark, S.D., 136
Never a Young Man, 889
Newton, A.P., 705, 724
Newton-King, S., 166
Nicholson, G., 1017
Nienaber, G.S., 1004
Nienaber, P.J., 753
Nimocks, W., 660
1922: The Revolt on the Rand, 681
Nixon, J., 510
Nobbs, E.A., 162

Noble, J., 310
Noordwaartse Beweging van die Boere voor die Groot Trek, 245
Norris-Newman, C.L., 434, 528
Northward Trek, 286
Notes on a Visit to South Africa 1889, 109
Notule van die Volksraad van die Suid-Afrikaanse Republiek, 513
Nutting, A., 725

Oberholster, A.G., 635n, 681a
O'Brien, T.H., 302
O'Byrne, S.P.M., 333
Old Cape Highways, 114
Old Cape House, 119
Old Transvaal 1834-1899, 475
Olden Times in Zululand and Natal, 341
Oliver, S.H., 828
Omer-Cooper, J.D., 927
Omond, G.W.I., 633
One Titan at a Time, 206
Ontplooiing van die Engelse Oorlog 1899-1900, 603
Ontwikkeling van die Politieke Denke van die Afrikaner, 1008
Oorlogs Avonture van Generaal Wynand Malan, 635n
Oorlogs-Herinneringe, 635n
Oorlogs Joernaal van S.J. Burger 1899-1902, 635
Oorsake van die Tweede Vryheidsoorlog 1899-1902, 588
Oorsprong en Betekenis van Nederlandse ou Duitse Familiename, 1001
Oorsprong van die Groot Trek, 235
Oost, H., 734
Opheffing van die Kleurling Bevolking, 968
Opkoms van 'n Republiek, 456
Opsaal: Herinneringe aan die Tweede Vryheidsoorlog, 635n
Orange River: A Bibliography, 444
Orange River Sovereignty 1848-1854, 458
Origins of the Anglo-Boer War, 589
Origins of the South African War, 587
Origins of the War, 424
Orpen, F.H.S., 965
Orpen, J.M., 459
Orr, J.E., 880
Otto, J.C., 623
Oude Tyden in den Oranje-Vrystaat, 452
Our Colony of Natal, 368
Out of the Crucible, 476
Outbreak on the Witwatersrand March 1922, 681n
Outlanders: A Study of Imperial Expansion in South Africa, 729
Outlanders: The Men who Made Johannesburg, 479
Outlook on a Century: South Africa 1870-1970, 845
Owen, F., 401
Oxford History of South Africa, 041

Pace of the Ox: The Life of Paul Kruger, 497
Pachai, B., 987
Pagden, C.W., 943
Pakenham, E., 558
Pakenham, T., 578

Palgrave and Damaraland, 274
Palmer, M., 988
Pama, C., 187, 311, 995
Papers on the Political Situation in South Africa 1885-1895, 503
Parsons, Q.N., 840
Passive Resistance in South Africa, 819
Past and Future of the Kaffir Races, 912
Paterson, A.C., 142
Paterson, W., 086
Paterson's Cape Travels 1777 to 1779, 086
Path of Blood: The Rise and Conquests of Mzilikazi, 926
Pather, S.R., 989
Paton, A., 682, 829
Patterson, S., 830, 1005
Paul Kruger: His Life and Times (Fisher), 496
Paul Kruger: His Life and Times (Nathan), 499
Paul Kruger: Van die Wieg tot die Graf, 502
Paul Kruger's Amptelike Briewe 1851-1877, 495
Payable Gold, 541
Payne, E.C., 958
Peace, W., 368
Peace Negotiations, 654
Pear Tree Blossoms, 875
Peires, J.B., 402, 928
Pelzer, A.N., 743
Pemberton, W.B., 611
People and Policies of South Africa, 689
People of South Africa, 027
People's History of South Africa, 677
Peringuey, L., 060
Perrot, D., 845
Personal Accounts of the Cape of Good Hope, 043
Personal Reminiscences of Early Johannesburg, 461
Perspectives on the South African Past, 029
Pheiffer, R.H., 079
Philip, J., 881
Philip, P., 188
Philipps, T., 216
Philipps 1820 Settler: His Letters, 216
Philips, L.M., 643
Phipson, T., 369
Picard, H.W.J., 121, 137, 312
Pictorial History of the Great Trek, 236
Pienaar, P. de V., 1006
Piet Retief: Lewensgeskiedenis... 240
Pieterse, H.J.C., 635n
Pigot, S., 217
Pillay, B., 990
Pioneer Travellers of South Africa, 082
Pioneers, B.C. - 1795, 008
Pioneers in Pondoland, 856
Pioneers of Natal and Southeastern Africa 1552-1878, 380
Pirie, G.H., 562
Pirow, O., 754
Plaatje, S.T., 644, 929

Plans for a Better World, 763
Plant, Sir A., 004
Plantagenet in South Africa: Lord Charles Somerset, 190
Planting of Christianity in Africa, 866
Planting of the Churches in South Africa, 884
Political Nature of a Ruling Class, 673
Political Philosophy of J.A. de Mist, 161
Politics and Law in South Africa, 822
Politics of Eastern Cape Separatism, 289
Politics of Inequality: South Africa Since 1948, 680
Politics of Racialism, 986
Politieke Briewe, 688
Politieke Groepering in die Wording van die Afrikanernasie, 992
Politieke Strominge... Afrikaners van die Vrystaatse Republiek, 457
Poor White Problem in South Africa, 679
Porter, A.N., 587
Portrait of a Colony: The Story of Natal, 356
Portugese Ontdekkers om die Kaap, 058
Portuguese and Dutch in South Africa 1641-1806, 151
Portuguese Colonization in the Sixteenth Century, 064
Portuguese in South Africa, 066
Portuguese in South-East Africa 1480-1600, 047
Portuguese Pioneers, 062
Portuguese Rule and Spanish Crown in South Africa, 072
Potgieter, P.J.J.S., 785
Povey, J., 834
Preller, G.S., 238-240, 242, 511, 547
Preller, J.F., 656
President Brand and His Times, 447
President Johannes Henricus Brand, 448
President Kruger aan die Woord, 494
President Paul Kruger: A Biography, 498
President Steyn en die Krisisjare 1896-1899, 453
Prestage, E., 061, 062
Preston, A., 385, 436
Pretorius, D.J., 218
Pretorius, H.S., 513
Price, R., 579
Prince Henry the Navigator, 050
Pringle, E., 219
Pringle, T., 220
Pringles of the Valleys, 219
Proconsul and Paramountcy in South Africa, 699
Proconsul in Politics: A Study of Lord Milner... 657
Profetisme in Suid-Afrika, 871
Protesbeweging van die Transvaalse Afrikaners, 519
Protest and Power in Black Africa, 834
Puritans in Africa: A History of Afrikanerdom, 994
Purple and the Gold: The Story of Pretoria and Johannesburg, 478
Pygmies and Bushmen of the Kalahari, 949
Pyrah, G.B., 661

Quinn, G.D., 670

Race and Reason, 809
Race Attitudes in South Africa, 824
Race Relations at the Cape of Good Hope, 786
Race Relations in South Africa, 784
Railway and Customs Policies in South Africa 1885-1910, 563
Rainier, M., 217
Randlords, 540
Ransford, O., 529, 612
Ratcliffe, U.M., 760
Raven-Hart, R., 063, 076, 081
Ravenstein, E.G., 067
Reaction to Conquest, 913
Reappraisals in British Imperial History, 715
Rebellie 1914-1915, 692
Rebellion of 1815, 176
Rebellion of 1914-15, 670
Recent Developments in the South African Mission Field, 865
Recollections of Adventures, 516
Reconstruction of the New Colonies under Lord Milner, 668
Record (Moodie), 920
Records of the Cape Colony 1806-1834, 177
Records of the Cape Colony 1793-1806, 167
Red Soldier : Letters from the Zulu War 1879, 425
Redelinghuys, J.H., 1007
Rees, W., 347
Reference Guide to the Literature of Travel, 042
Regency Cape Town, 187
Rego, A. Da Silva, 064
Reitz, D., 613
Reitz, H., 734
Reizens in Zuid Afrika, 090
Relief of Ladysmith, 591
Reluctant Empire: British Policy on the South African Frontier, 707
Reluctant Rebellion: The 1906-1908 Disturbance in Natal, 440
Remember You Are an Englishman: A Biography of Sir Harry Smith, 328
Reminiscences of an Albany Settler, 203
Reminiscences of Kaffir Life and History, 904
Reminiscences of Life in South Africa... 459
Reminiscences of Sir Walter Stanford, 939
Reminiscences of the Last Kafir War, 291
Reminiscences of Thomas Stubbs, 226
Reports of Chavonnes and his Council of van Imhoff, 131
Republic of Natal: The Origin of the Present Pondo Tribe, 381
Republican Presidents, 454
Republiek van Suid-Afrika, 035
Researches in South Africa, 881
Reunert, T., 264, 548
Rev. John Brownlee: A Veteran Missionary, 211n
Revolt on the Rand, 681
Rhenish Mission Society, 891
Rhenius, J.T., 080
Rhodes (Lockhart and Woodhouse), 318
Rhodes (McDonald), 319
Rhodes (Millin), 320
Rhodes of Africa, 316

Rhoodie, D., 559
Rhoodie, N.J., 831, 832
Richardson, L., 662
Richardson, P., 959
Right to the Land: Documents on Southern African History, 009
Rise and Fall of the South African Peasantry, 908
Rise of African Nationalism in South Africa, 844
Rise of Afrikanerdom, 825
Rise of South Africa, 007
Rise of the Basuto, 924
Ritter, E.A., 406
River of Diamonds, 266
Rivett-Carnac, D.E., 191, 222
Road to Isandlwana, 429
Road to the North, 464
Robben Island: Out of Reach, Out of Mind, 117
Roberts, B., 265, 403
Roberts, M., 735
Robertson, J., 739
Robins, E., 758
Robinson, A.M.L., 109, 154
Robinson, E.F., 065
Robinson, R., 726
Rogers, H., 833
Rogers, M., 742
Role of Colonial Officials in Destruction of Zulu Kingdom, 424
Role of the Missionaries in Conquest, 878
Roll of the British Settlers in South Africa, 215
Roman Catholic Church in South Africa, 850
Romance of a Colonial Parliament, 120
Rondom die Anglo-Boeroorlog 1899-1902, 574
Roots of Segregation: Native Policy in Colonial Natal, 382
Rorke's Drift: A Victorian Epic, 428
Rose-Innes, R.W., 211n
Rosenthal, E., 266, 549-550, 640, 1015
Ross, R., 820, 951, 975
Rotberg, R.I., 834
Rourke, J., 086
Roux, E., 835
Rowell, T., 371
Ruin of Zululand: An Account of British Doings in Zululand, 419
Rule of Fear: The Life and Times of Dingane, 392
Russia and the Anglo-Boer War, 629
Rutherfoord, E., 324
Rutherford, J., 284

Sachs, A., 840
Sachs, E.S., 836
Sacks, B., 663
Sadler, C., 889
Saffery, A.L., 815
Saker, H., 690
Sales, J.M., 883-884
Sampson, P.J., 691
Sanders, P., 922

Sandile: The Fall of the Xhosa Nation, 918
Saron, G., 1027
Saunders, C.C., 288, 820, 837, 840, 872, 930
Scandinavians and South Africa, 1028
Schapera, I., 004, 158, 507, 899-900, 931-932, 952-953
Schimlek, F., 885
Scholsberg, F., 642
Schmidt, K.L.M., 045
Schnell, E.L.C., 1019
Schoeman, B.M., 743n
Scholtz, G.B., 035
Scholtz, G.D., 448, 580, 588, 634, 692, 744, 779, 1008
Scholtz, P.L., 786
Schreuder, D.M., 512, 727
Schrijver, I., 075
Schumacher, R.W., 960
Schutte, C.E.G., 882
Scott, J.A., 761
Scott, J.B., 182
Scramble for Africa, 725
Scramble for Southern Africa, 727
Sea Road to the Indies, 059
Search for Gold in South Africa from 1842-1872, 532
Segregation Fallacy and Other Papers, 813
Selborne Memorandum, 664
Selby, J., 441, 614
Select Bibliography of South African Native Life and Problems, 899, 900
Select Bibliography on the 1820 Settlers and Settlement, 193
Select Bibliography Relating to the Zulu People of Natal, 387
Select Constitutional Documents Illustrating South African History, 014
Select Documents on British Colonial Policy 1830-1860, 698
Select Documents Relating to the Unification of South Africa, 724
Selected Speeches and Documents on British Colonial Policy, 716
Selections from the Correspondence of J.X. Merriman, 294
Selections from the Correspondence of Percy Alport Molteno, 309
Selections from the Smuts Papers, 770
Seminar Papers on the Societies of Southern Africa, 840
Serfontein, J.H.P., 743n
Serton, P., 074, 145
Settlement After the War in South Africa, 652
Settlers and Methodism 1820-1920, 205
Settler's Heritage, 224
Seven Lost Trails of Africa, 262
Seventh Kaffir War; or, The War of the Axe, 252
Shadow and Substance in South Africa, 839
Shaka Zulu: The Rise of the Zulu Empire, 406
Shaka's Country: A Book of Zululand, 390
Shaka's Heirs, 441
Shaping of South African Society 1652-1820, 013
Sharp, G., 615
Shaw, B., 886
Shaw, T.R., 462
Shaw, W., 890
Sheffield, T., 223
Shepherd, R.H.W., 861

Author/Title Index 269

Shepstone: The Role of the Family in the History of South Africa, 375
Ships and South Africa, 115
Short History of British Colonial Policy 1606-1909, 705
Shooter, J., 407
Shuter, C.F., 376
Siege of Ladysmith, 615
Siege of Mafeking, 606
Siege of Pretoria 1880-1881, 525
Sillery, A., 720
Simmonds, H.A., 334
Simon van der Stel's Journal of his Expedition to Namaqualand, 146
Simon van der Stel's Journey to Namaqualand in 1683, 079
Simons, H.J., 838
Simons, R.E., 838
Sir Alfred Milner and the Outbreak of the Anglo-Boer War, 584
Sir Andrew Smith: His Life, Letters and Works, 104
Sir Andries Stockenstrom 1792-1864, 276, 941
Sir Bartle Frere: A Footnote to the History of the British Empire,280
Sir Benjamin D'Urban's Administration of the Eastern Frontier, 251
Sir George Grey: A Study in Colonial Government, 284
Sir Harry Smith: Bungling Hero, 327
Sir Henry Barkly: Mediator and Moderator, 258
Sir James Rose Innes: Selected Correspondence, 287
Sir Lowry Cole, 180
Slagtersnek en sy Mense, 186
Slater, F.C., 224
Slavery at the Cape 1652-1834, 122
Slaves and Free Blacks at the Cape 1658-1700, 126
Smail, J.L., 241, 377, 408, 616-617
Smedley, L., 961
Smit, F.P., 500
Smith, Sir A., 102-104, 189
Smith, E.W., 874
Smith, Sir H., 326
Smuts, J.C., 762-763, 775
Smuts: A Reappraisal, 768
Smuts: The Fields of Force 1919-1950, 772
Smuts: The Humanist, 769
Smuts: The Patriot, 773
Smuts: The Sanguine Years 1870-1919, 771
So High the Road: Mountain Passes of the Western Cape, 112
Social and Economic Conditions of Native Life, 815
Social Life in the Cape Colony in the 18th Century, 128
Soga, J.H., 933-934
Solomon, C., 900
Solomon, V., 309
Somerville, W., 087
Source Material on the South African Economy, 022
South Africa (Agar-Hamilton), 001
South Africa (Cope), 006
South Africa (Hofmeyr), 021
South Africa (Union). Commission for Socio-Economic Development...935
South Africa (Union). Department of Coloured Affairs, 964
South Africa (Union). State Archives, 138
South Africa a Century Ago, 154-156

South Africa: A Modern History, 010
South Africa: A Political and Economic History, 020
South Africa: A Short History, 023
South Africa: A Study in Conflict, 694
South Africa: An Historical Introduction, 032
South Africa: An Imperial Dilemma, 663
South Africa and the Transvaal War, 570
South Africa and the World, 695
South Africa in a Changing World, 676
South Africa in the Modern World 1910-1970, 674
South Africa in the Making 1652-1806, 141
South Africa 1906-1961, 687
South Africa 1652-1933, 019
South Africa of To-day, 520
South Africa Past and Present, 310
South Africa: Sociological Analyses, 806
South Africa: The Dynamics of the African National Congress, 801
South Africa under John III 1521-1557, 070
South Africa under King Manuel 1495-1521, 069
South Africa under King Sebastian and the Cardinal 1557-1580, 071
South African Archival Records, 513
South African Dialogue, 832
South African Diaries of Sir Garnet Wolseley, 385
South African Explorers, 048
South African Flag Controversy, 690
South African Frontier, 1865-1885: A Study in Expansion, 271
South African Institute of Race Relations, 787
South African Journal of Sir Garnet Wolseley 1879-1880, 436
South African Melting Pot, 860
South African Memories, 483
South African Missions, 861
South African Native Affairs Commission, 936
South African Native Policy and the Liberal Spirit, 810
South African Native Races Committee, 937-938
South African Natives, 938
South African Opposition 1939-1945, 735
South African Parties and Policies 1910-1960, 686
South African Policy and the Liberal Spirit, 810
South African Railways before 1910, 561
South African Travel Literature, 044
South African War 1899-1902, 566
South African War: the Anglo-Boer War 1899-1902, 581
South African Way of Life, 794
South Africa's Foreign Policy 1945-1970, 672
South Africa's Transkei, 795
South Africa's Yesterdays, 030
South-East Africa 1488-1530, 049
South-Eastern Bantu, 934
Southern Africa, 005
Southern Africa Since 1800, 012
Southern Bantu, 917
Southern Land: The Prehistory and History of Southern Africa, 039
Southey, N.M., 254
Sparks from the Border Anvil, 270
Sparrman, A., 088

Author/Title Index 271

Spencer, S. O'Byrne, 379
Spies, F.J. du Toit, 451, 460
Spies, S.B., 589, 624
Spilhaus, M.W., 139-141, 225
Splintered Crucifix, 870
Spohr, O.H., 097, 100, 164, 338
Spoorwegontwikkeling in die Suid-Afrikaanse Republiek, 477
Staatkundige Ontwikkeling van die Suid Afrikaanse Republiek, 467
Staatsopvattinge van Paul Kruger, 500
Staking van 1922, 669
Stals, E.L.P., 514
Stals, W.A., 530
Standing, T.G., 917
Stanford, Sir W., 939
Staples, I., 330
Stars and Stripes in Africa, 1015
State of the Cape of Good Hope in 1822, 173
Steedman, A., 105
Steenkamp, A.J., 501
Stephen, R.G., 046
Stockenstrom, Sir A., 940
Stone, J., 1016
Storm in a Teacup: The Later Years of John Company at the Cape, 172
Storm over the Transvaal, 471
Story of an African Crisis, 554
Story of De Beers, 261
Story of my Mission in South-Eastern Africa, 890
Story of South Africa, 026
Story of the British Settlers of 1820 in South Africa, 210
Story of the Cape to Cairo Railway and River Route, 564
Story of the Settlement, 223
Story of the Zulu Campaign, 410
Story of the Zulus, 395
Stow, G.W., 942
Strangman, E., 077
Strangwayes-Booth, J., 740
Strassberger, E., 891
Streak, M., 659, 1009
Struben, C., 515
Struben, H.W., 516
Struggle for Racial Equality, 823
Struggle for South Africa 1875-1899, 719
Struggles of an Infant State, 449
Strydom, C.J.S., 331, 749, 780
Strydom, H., 743n
Stuart, J., 349, 442
Stubbs, T., 226
Studies in Mid-Victorian Imperialism, 701
Studies in the Social and Economic History of the Witwatersrand, 517a
Stultz, N.M., 693
Suid-Afrikaanse Argiefstukke: Kaap, 138
Sullivan, J.R., 373
Summers, R., 943
Sumner, J.A., 335
Sundkler, B.G.M., 892

Super Afrikaners, 743n
Survey of Race Relations, 787
Survival in Two Worlds: Moshoeshoe of Lesotho 1786-1870, 923
Suspicion is My Name, 947
Swart, M.J., 976
Swaziland Question and the Road to the Sea, 484
Symons, J., 618

Tabler, E.C., 108, 380
Tait, C., 851
Talbot, C.J., 017
Tas, A., 142-143
Tatz, C.M., 839
Taylor, J.D., 893
Thank God We Kept the Flag Flying: Siege... of Ladysmith, 602
That Miss Hobhouse, 621
Theal, G. McCall, 031, 066, 144, 167, 175, 177, 381, 944
There are No South Africans, 678
Theron, E., 976-977
They Came from a Far Land, 196
They Came to South Africa, 212
This Man Malan, 758
Thom, H.B., 147
Thomas Francois Burgers: A Biography, 473
Thomas Francois Burgers: Staatspresident 1872-1877, 472
Thomas Pringle in South Africa 1820-1826, 221
Thompson, G., 106
Thompson, L.M., 041, 666, 820, 923, 945, 991
Those in Bondage, 132
Those Restless Years, 617
Thoughts of General Smuts, 765
Three Years' War, 597
Thus Came the English 1820, 222
Time Longer than Rope: A History of the Black Man's Struggle, 835
Times History of the War in South Africa, 567
Tingay, P., 517
To the Cape for Diamonds, 260
To the Shores of Natal, 343
Tobias, P.V., 954
Tomlinson, F.R., 935
Towards Emancipation: A Study in South African Slavery, 184
Track and Trackless: Omnibuses and Trams in the Western Cape, 113
Tragic History of the Sea 1589-1622, 052
Transkeian Native Territories: Historical Records, 269
Transport Development in Southern Africa, 562
Transvaal Epic, 517
Transvaal From Within, 480
Transvaal of Today, 466
Transvaal Story, 508
Transvaal Surrounded, 506
Transvaal View of the Chinese Labour Question, 960
Transvaal War 1880-1881 (Bellairs), 522
Transvaal War 1880-1881 (Jordan), 521
Trapido, S., 840
Travel Journal Cape to Zululand... 1838-1840, 097

Author/Title Index 273

Travellers in South Africa in the Eighteenth Centry, 046
Travels and Adventures in Eastern Africa, 360
Travels and Adventures in Southern Africa, 106
Travels at the Cape 1751-1753, 081
Travels from the Cape of Good Hope into the Interior, 084
Travels in Eastern Africa, 110
Travels in South Africa, 857-858
Travels in Southern Africa in the Years 1803-1806, 101
Travels in the Interior of South Africa, 108
Travels in the Interior of Southern Africa, 095, 158
Trek: Studies oor die Mobiliteit van die Pioniers, 247
Trekboer in die Geskiedenis van die Kaapkolonie, 246
Tribal Peoples of Southern Africa, 946
Trichardt, L., 242-244
Triomf van Nasionalisme in Suid-Afrika, 731
Trollip, A.F.G., 735
Troup, F., 032
True Story of the Grosvenor East Indiaman, 083
Truth in Masquerade: The Adventures of Francois le Vaillant, 084
Turnbull, C.E.P., 852
Twee Eeue van Sendingwerk, 895
Tweede Vryheidsoorlog 1899-1902, 580
2000 Casualties, 696
Tycoon and the President, 509
Tylden, G., 924
Tyrrell, B., 946-947

Unification of South Africa 1902-1910, 666
Union of South Africa. See South Africa (Union).
Union-Castle Chronicle 1853-1953, 116
Union Native Policy, 783
University of London. Institute of Commonwealth Studies, 840
Unterhalter, E., 424
Urquhart, W., 681n
Uys, C.J., 374, 502, 728

Valentyn, F., 145
Valiant but Once, 297
Valley of Gold, 538
Van Biljon, P., 841
Van den Berghe, P.L., 694
Van den Bosch, A., 695
Van den Heever, C.M., 755
Van der Horst, 842
Van der Merwe, J.P., 169
Van der Merwe, P.J., 168, 245-247
Van der Merwe, W.J., 894
Van der Poel, J., 560, 563, 770
Van der Riet, F.G., 195, 203
Van der Stel, S., 078, 079, 146
Van der Walt, A.J.H., 033
Van Heerde, G.L., 895
Van Heerden, J.F.G., 647
Van Jaarsveld, F.A., 034, 035, 248, 530, 1010-1012
Van Onselen, C., 517a

Van Oordt, L.C., 074
Van Pallandt, A., 170
Van Reenen, D.G., 171
Van Reenen, J., 089
Van Reenen, W., 090
Van Rensburg, A.P.J., 530
Van Rensburg, E.E.J., 152
Van Rensburg, T., 635
Van Riebeeck, J., 147
Van Rooyen, G.H., 249
Van Rooyen, J.J., 736
Van Rooyen, T.S., 518
Van Schoor, A.M., 737
Van Schoor, M.C.E., 445
Van Velden, D.E., 654
Van Zyl, M.C., 519
Varley, D.H., 073, 295
Varley, V., 073
Vatcher, W.H., 738
Vein of Gold, 515
Velho, A., 067
Venter, P.J., 192
Verhoudinge Tussen die Boere, Engelse en Naturelle, 518
Verner, B.A., 1020
Verwoerd, H.F., 777
Verwoerd aan die Woord, 777
Victorian Lady at the Cape 1849-1851, 283
Vijn, C., 413
Vindex, pseud., 322
Voight, J.C., 036
Von Broembsen, M., 806
Voortrekker Mense, 238
Voortrekkers, 232
Voortrekkers en Hul Kerk, 230n
Voortrekkers in Natal, 231
Voortrekkers of South Africa, 237
Vorster The Man, 782
Vorster's Foreign Policy, 781
Voyage to the Cape of Good Hope 1772-1776, 088
Vulliamy, C.E., 729

W.P. Schreiner, 325
Wagner, M. St. Clair, 153
Wagner, Z., 150
Wahl, J.R., 221
Walker, E., 325
Walker, E.A., 004, 037, 250, 303
Walker, I.L., 696
Wallace, R.I., 619
Wallis, J.P.R., 482
Walshe, P., 843-844
Walton, E.H., 667
Wanderings and Adventures in the Interior of Southern Africa, 105
Wannenburgh, A., 955
War in South Africa, 585

Author/Title Index

War, Natal and Confederation, 424
War of the Axe 1847, 288
War of the Axe and the Xosa Bible, 257
Warren, M., 896
Warriors: The Story of the Matabele Army, 943
Warwick, P., 581
Washing of the Spears: A History of the Zulu Nation, 399
Waterhouse, G., 078, 079, 146
Waters, W.H.H., 582
Watts, B.H., 533
Webb, C. de B., 336, 340, 414, 424
Weg na die See, 491
Weinbren, B., 696
Weinthal, E., 564
Welch, S.R., 068-072, 151
Welsh, D., 382
Were, G.S., 038
Western Civilization and the Natives of South Africa, 932
When Boys Were Men, 199
White Laager: The Rise of Afrikaner Nationalism, 738
White Rule in South Africa 1830-1910, 793
Whiteside, J., 897, 903
White Supremacy, 803
Who Really Discovered South Africa?, 053
Wienbieck, G., 806
Wiid, J.A., 171
Wikar, H.J., 090
Wilde, R.H., 590, 730
Wilgefontein Settlement 1880, 339
Wilkins, I., 743n
Wilkins, W.H., 155, 156
Willcox, A.R., 039
Willem Hendrik Jacobsz, 488
Willet, S.M., 948
William Duckitt Diary, 162
William Somerville's Narrative of his Journeys... 087
Williams, B., 323, 664, 745
Williams, C., 531
Williams, J.G., 925
Williams, L.E., 756
Wilmot, A., 329, 435
Wilson, D., 040
Wilson, F., 845
Wilson, G.M., 483
Wilson, M., 041
Wing, S., 853
Winquist, A.H., 1028
Winter, J.S., 463
With Milner in South Africa, 638
With Rimington, 643
With Shield and Assegai, 377
With the Boer Forces, 607
With the Boers in the Transvaal and Orange Free State, 528
With the Da Gamas in 1497, 065
Wolseley, Sir G., 385, 436

Wood, A.A., 386
Woodhouse, C.M., 318
Work of the Missionaries of Die Nederduitse Gereformeerde Kerk, 852
Workers Without Weapons, 802
Worsfold, B., 280
Worsfold, W.B., 304, 668
Wrench, J.E.L., 305
Wright, H.M., 287
Wright, J.B., 414, 956

Yellow and Dark-skinned People of Africa South, 944
Yellow Man Looks On, 796
Younghusband, F., 520

Zacharias Wagner: Second Commander of the Cape, 150
Ziervogel, D., 028
Zulu Aftermath: A Nineteenth Century Revolution, 927
Zulu Battle Piece: Isandhlwana, 423
Zulu King Speaks, 414
Zulu Kings, 403
Zulu Peoples as They Were Before the White Man Came, 389
Zulu Political Economy on the Eve of War, 424
Zulu War (Clammer), 415
Zulu War (Lloyd), 431
Zulu War: A Pictorial History, 411
Zulu War and the Colony of Natal, 433
Zulu War 1879, 398
Zulu War: Isandhlwana and Rorke's Drift, 427
Zulu War Journal of Colonel Henry Harford, C.B., 430
Zulu War of 1879, 409
Zululand, 396
Zululand and the Zulus, 393
Zululand and the Zulus: A Bibliography, 388
Zulus and the British Frontiers, 432

SUBJECT/TOPOGRAPHICAL INDEX

Numbers refer to item numbers, not pages

Abambo Tribe, 903
Adams, B., 255
Adams, N., 873
African National Congress, 739, 788, 800-801, 804, 817, 819, 835, 838, 843-844
Afrikaans-speaking Peoples
  emigrants to other lands, 331,
  genealogy, 993, 995, 1000-1002, 1004, 1007
  historiography, 1011-1012
  history and cultural development, 992-1012
  language, 999, 1005-1006
  nationalism, 731-738, 822, 825-826, 999, 1005, 1010-1012
  of the Witwatersrand, 514
  political parties, 680, 686
Afrikaner Bond, 273, 275, 457, 512, 992
Afrikaner Broederbond, 738, 743, 999
Afrikaner Party, 680
Afrikaner Protest Movement, 519
Agriculture
  Black Reserves, 908
  Cape, 133, 162, 173
  Natal, 358
Alabama, raider ship, 267
Algoa Bay, 195, 221
Allemann, R.S., 135
Amabaca Tribe, 269
Amacqua Tribe, 145
Amaxesibe Tribe, 269
Amaxosa Tribe. See Xhosa Tribe
American Board of Commissioners for Foreign Missions, 365, 391, 396, 853, 873, 1013-1015
Americans. See United States of America
Andersson, C., 048
Anglo-Boer War (1880-1881). See Transvaal War of Independence
Anglo-Boer War (1899-1902)
  concentration camps, 620-624
  causes and events, 583-590
  general history, 565-582
  international diplomacy, 625-634
  military campaigns, 591-619
  peace treaty and settlement, 647-668
  public attitudes, 626-634
  reminiscences, biographies, 635-646

Anglo-German Rivalry, 625, 700
Anglo-Portuguese Treaty, 286
Anti-Convict Agitation (1849), 285
Anti-Slavery Agitation, 490, 507
Apartheid Policy. See Separate Development
Appleyard, J.W., 257
Arbousset, T., 092
Armstrong, A.B., 175
Atherstone, G., 296
Aubertin, J.J., 354
Auret, W.H., 503
Austen, H., 297
Australia, soldiers in the Boer War, 619
Auwal Mosque, 966
Ayliff, J., 175, 194-195, 205, 915
Azurara Chronicles, 056

Baden-Powell, R.S.S., 212, 601
Bain, A.G., 093, 105, 212, 296
Bain's Kloof, 114
Baines, T., 094, 212, 354
Baker, H., 212
Baldwin, W.C., 107
Balfour, A.J., 1st Earl, 483, 589
Bambata Rebellion, 390, 617
Bapedi Tribe, 466
Barberton, 294
Barkly, Sir H., 258
Barnard, A., 154-157, 212
Barnato, B., 265
Barrow, J., 048, 082, 133, 1009
Barry, J., 212
Basuto Wars, 446-447, 450, 459
Basutoland, history, 909, 914, 921-925
Batavian Republic, rule at the Cape, 152, 159-166, 168-171
Bathurst, 195, 296
Battle sites, 241, 616
Battles. See names of individual battles
Baviaans River, 221
Bax, J., 144
Beach, Sir M.H., 280
Beacons, 060
Beaconsfield, Lord, 280
Bechuana Tribes, 100-101, 106, 949
Bechuanaland
  annexation, 275, 464, 720
  history, 464, 511, 683, 720, 729
Beeckman, D., 127
Beit, A., 483, 540
Belgium, pro-Boer agitation during Anglo-Boer War, 633
Bell, C.D., 189
Bell, J., 175
Belmont, Battle of (1899), 611
Bender, A.P., 1025
Bergh, O., 075

Subject/Topographical Index

Berlin Missionary Society, 518
Berning, J.M., 193
Bethelsdorp, 857, 883
Beutler, A.F., 082, 968
Beyers, C.F., 691-692
Bezuidenhout, A.P.O., 692
Bigge, J.T., 192
Biko, S., 804
Bird, C., 353
Birkenhead, shipwreck (1852), 259
Bisset, J.J., 297
Black Consciousness Movement, 804
Black Peoples
  churches, 835, 871, 880, 892
  civil liberty, 835, 839
  history, description, 899-947
  nationalism, 804-805, 826
  peasants, 908
  political organizations, 680, 804-805, 838
  politics, 804-805, 816-817, 839
  prophetic movements, 871, 892
  race contacts, race policy, 228, 788-845
  representation in parliament, 839
  reserves, 382
  working classes, 677, 789, 798, 835, 842
Black Sash Movement, 739, 741-742
Bleek, W.H.I., 338
Bloemfontein, 450, 451
Bloemfontein Convention, 446, 728
Borghorst, J., 144
Boshof, J.N., 454
Botha, L.
  role in Anglo-Boer War, 594-595
  rise to power after War, 273, 688, 992
  failure to extend boundaries, 683
  influence on South African development, 684-685
  biographies of, 745-749
Bower, G., 559-560
Bowker, T.H., 965
Bowler, T., 311
Boyce, W.B., 175
Brand, J.H., 446-448, 454, 457
Brink, C.F., 048, 080
British South Africa Company, 706, 729
Broederbond. See Afrikaner Broederbond
Brown, G., 297
Brownlee, C., 915
Brownlee, J., 211
Buffalo River, 270
Buller, R.H., 618
Bultfontein, 260
Bulwer, Sir H., 416
Burchell, W.J., 048, 095, 158, 212
Burgers, T.F., 374, 454, 464, 472-473, 491
Burnett, B., 297

Bushmen, 088, 092, 095, 101, 106, 942, 944, 948-956
Butterworth, 194
Buys Family, 242
Buyskes, P.L., 965
Byrne Emigration Scheme, 355, 366-367
Byrne Valley, 366

Caledon, 277
Calvinism, 994, 999, 1005-1006
Cameron, J., 870
Campbell, D., 175
Campbell, J., 048
Cape of Good Hope
  administration, 173, 192, 281
  agriculture, 133, 162, 173
  archives, 111, 127-128, 138, 144, 175-177
  banking system, 173
  constitutional history, 119-120, 258
  courts, 192
  fauna and flora, 081, 086, 088, 091, 095, 097-099, 101-102
  governors, 137, 281, 312
  history
    general, 111-121
    1652-1795, 122-151
    1795-1806, 152-171
    1806-1836, 172-192
    1836-1899, 251-331
  land policy, 183
  legal history, 173
  medical history, 111
  mountain passes, 112, 114
  parliament, 119-120, 290
  shipping, 115-116
  social and cultural history, 128, 187
  trade, 172, 173, 180
  transport, 113-116
Cape Patriots, 123
Cape Town
  eighteenth century, 128
  nineteenth century, 187, 221, 277, 283, 311, 324
Capitalism, 673
Carnarvon, 4th Earl (H.H.M. Herbert), 280, 709, 724, 728-729
Cartography, 062
Casalis, E., 859, 914
Castle, Cape Town, 085, 130, 135
Cathcart, Sir G., 272
Catholic Church, 854
Cattle farming, 245-247
Central Mining and Investment Corporation, 534, 537
Cetewayo (Cetshwayo), 393, 412-414, 425, 430, 837
Chaka. See Shaka
Chamberlain, J.,
  and Jameson Raid, 552, 554, 558-560, 730
  and Anglo-Boer War, 586-587, 590, 730
Champion, G., 391, 873

Subject/Topographical Index 281

Chapman, J., 048, 108
Chase, J.C., 289
Chavonnes, M.P. de, 131, 133
Chelmsford, Lord (F.A. Thesiger), 426
Chichester, E., 615
China, immigration to the Transvaal, 650, 663, 668, 957-961
Christian, W., 053
Christian National Education, 999
Chronicles of Azurara, 056
Church of the Province of South Africa, 876
Churchill, W., 636-637, 714
Ciskei, 930
Civil Liberty, 791
Cloete, E., 256
Coetse, J., 053, 968
Coillard, P., 914
Cole, Sir L., 179-180
Colebrooke, W.M.G., 192
Colenbrander, P.J., 424
Colenso, F., 347
Colenso, J.W., 340, 361, 394, 413, 420-421, 439
Colenso, Battle of (1899), 483, 611
Colonial Office, Britain, 698, 702, 710, 717
Colonial policy
  Britain, 697-730
  Germany, 700
Colonial Secretary, 281, 730
Colour Bar Law (1926), 814, 828
Coloured Peoples, 092, 830, 955, 962-977
Communist Party, 835, 838
Concentration Camps, Anglo-Boer War (1899-1902), 620-624
Confederation policy, 284, 310, 374, 424, 709, 719, 724
Conservative Party, 680
Consolidated Gold Fields, 539
Constitution Ordinance, 281
Constitutional history, 014, 281
Corner House Mining Companies, 534, 537
Cornwall, immigrants to South Africa, 201
Cortemunde, J., 073
Cox, W., 175
Cradock, J., 096, 183
Crewe, Lord, 716
Cruse, H., 053
Cultural history, 018, 030
Curtis, L., 660
Customs Union, 563
Cuyler, J.G., 175, 297

Da Gama, V., 048, 057, 059, 065, 067, 069
Damara Peoples, 949
Damaraland, 090, 274-275
Dampier, W., 127
D'Anaya, P., 066
Dapper, O., 952
Daumas, F., 092

Davis, W.J., 175
Dawson, G., 660
De Albuquerque, A., 061
De Beaulieu, A., 077
De Beers' Diamond Company, 261, 540
De Brito, B.G., 052
De Chaumont, Chevalier, 077
De Choisy, F.T., 077
De Flacourt, E., 077
De Forbin, C., 077
De Gonneville, B.P., 077
Degrandpré, L.M., 082
De Grevenbroek, J.G., 952
De La Caille, N.L., 081
Delagoa Bay, 244, 374, 491, 625, 668, 700
De La Rey, J.H., 483
De Mist, A.U., 159
De Mist, J.A., 101, 133, 159-161, 165, 169
Denmark, early exploration of Cape, 063
De Vis, shipwreck (1740), 135
De Wet, C.R., 573, 639-640, 691-692
Diamond Fields, 181, 254, 256, 260-266, 450, 455, 464
Diana (Russion sloop), 164
Diaz, B., 057
Dingane (Dingaan) (Zulu chief), 360, 365, 391-393, 401-403
Dingiswayo (Zulu chief), 399
Dinuzulu (Zulu chief), 394, 438, 442
Dobie, J.S., 348
Donkin, R.S., 182
Dos Santos, J., 048
D'Oyly, C., 187
Drège, C.F., 378
Duckitt, W., 162
Dugmore, H.H., 203, 205, 915
Duminy Family, 163
Duncan, Sir P., 660
Dundas, H., 154-156
Dunn, J., 413, 424
D'Urban, Sir B., 175, 251, 920
Durban, history, 356-357, 359, 365
Dutch East India Company, 057, 060, 071, 078, 085, 122-151
Dutch Reformed Church, 894-895, 999, 1005-1006
Du Toit, J.D., 999
Dutoitspan, diamond diggings, 260, 263

Eastern Cape
 administration, 281
 description, 178, 216
 expeditions, 093, 094, 101, 105-106
 separatist movement, 289
Eastern Frontier
 bibliographies, 251-253
 frontier wars, 120a, 185
 in the eighteenth and early nineteenth centuries, 087, 095, 099

in the period of the 1820 settlers, 198, 210, 214, 220-221, 226
in the second half of the nineteenth century, 271, 278, 283, 296-297, 329
Eastern Nguni Tribe, 341
Eastern Transvaal, history, 518, 533, 538
Economic history, 011, 020, 022, 025
Edgell, E.V.W., 410
1820 Settlers. See Britain, Settlers of 1820
Elgin, Lord, 714
Elliott, A., 212
Empire League, 503
England. See Great Britain
English East India Company, 172
Eno (Xhosa chief), 175
Escombe, H., 354
Esselen, E.W., 589
Ethiopian Movement, 835, 880
Ewart, J., 096
Expansion of South Africa, failure of (1908-1948), 683
Expeditions
  1800-1850, 091-106
  1850-1900, 107-110
Exploration and explorers
  early (to 1652), 047-072
  seventeenth century, 073-074
  1800-1850, 091-106
  1850-1900, 107-110

Fadani (Xhosa chief), 175
Fairbridge, W.E., 264
Faku (Pondo chief), 269
Farewell, F.G., 378, 403
Farming. See Agriculture
Federation scheme. See Confederation policy
Feetham, R., 660
Findlay, J., 207
Fingo Peoples, 194, 903, 915
Fitzpatrick, J.P., 480-483
Flag controversy (1925-1928), 690
Frontier
  Eastern Cape. See Eastern Frontier
  economy, 136, 245-247
  history, North America and South Africa compared, 820
  policy of Britain (1834-1854), 698, 707
  Wars
    general descriptions, 094, 105, 120a, 141, 268, 271
    1793, 168
    1799-1803, 166
    1834-1835,   175, 185, 198, 203, 210, 213-215, 223, 226, 329
    1846-1847 (War of the Axe), 094, 223, 226, 252, 255, 257, 288
    1850-1853, 094, 223, 226, 253, 272, 282, 291, 327-328, 330
    1870-1878, 181, 429
Frykenius, S.H., 165
Fuller, C., 244

Furniture, Voortrekkers, 249
Fynn, H.F., 048, 349, 378, 403

Galton, F., 048
Gandhi, M.K., 653, 835, 984, 988, 990
Gardiner, A.F., 048, 350
Gcaleka Tribe, 327
Genadendal Mission Station, 099, 277, 875
Genealogy, Afrikaner families, 993, 995, 1001-1002, 1004, 1007
Germany
  account of Anglo-Boer War (1899-1902), 582
  immigrants to South Africa, 1019
  influence on South African Republic (1852-1896), 512, 625
  missionaries, 1019
  pro-Boer sentiment, 633-634
  rivalry with Britain, 512, 700
Gill, D., 212
Gillespie, E., 346
Gillespie, H., 346
Gladstone, W.E., 512
Glen-Lynden, 220-221
Godlonton, R., 282, 289
Gold, discovery of, 516, 532-550
Gold Fields Company, 536, 539
Gold Fields Deep Mine, 539
Gold Mining Industry
  class conflict, 677, 814
  history, 534-550
  role of Afrikaners, 514
Goldswain, J., 213, 296
Gordon, R.J., 082
Goshen, 464
Goske, I., 144
Graaff-Reinet, 101, 123, 136, 289
Graham, J., 223, 297
Grahamstown, 136, 214, 223, 289, 296
Grahamstown Journal, 282
Gray, L., 283
Gray, S., 283
Great Britain
  Anglo-Boer War (1880-1881), causes and events, 522-531
  Anglo-Boer War (1899-1902). See Anglo-Boer War (1899-1902)
  Anglo-Zulu War (1879), causes and events, 410, 415-419, 422-436
  attitude towards Afrikaners (1795-1854), 1009
  colonial policy
    Great Trek, 233
    South Africa, 661, 663, 697-730
  early attempts at colonization of the Cape, 055, 057, 063
  imperial policy, 512, 661, 663, 697-730
  occupation of the Cape
    1795-1803, 153-158, 167
    1806-1836, 172-192
    1836-1899, 251-331
  regiments, 188, 268

Subject/Topographical Index

settlers in South Africa
  prior to 1820, 188
  1820, 173-174, 178, 182, 193-226, 329-330
  1820-1960, 1016
  Natal, 351, 355-358, 366-369, 376, 379
  Transvaal, first British occupation, 505, 518-519, 524
  warships, 188
Great Trek, 136, 227-250
Grey, Lord (H. Grey, 3rd Earl), Colonial policy, 278, 722
Grey, Sir G.
  Federation schemes, 278, 284, 374, 446, 723-724
Griqua Peoples, 092, 103, 189, 949, 951, 965, 972, 974-975
Griqualand East, 269, 939, 956
Griqualand West, 105, 294, 329, 965
Grobler, P., 511
Groene Kloof Mission Station, 099
Groenkloof, agriculture, 162
Grosvenor, shipwreck (1782), 083, 089, 105, 262
Grout, L., 396, 873
Guanya (Xhosa chief), 175
Gush, R., 296

Haarlem, shipwreck, 074
Hamelberg, H.A.L., 451-452
Hamilton, I., 637
Harcourt, W., 552
Harford, H., 430
Harness, A., 416
Harris, W.C., 048
Harrison, G., 542
Hastings, H., 195
Heemraden, 192
Henry the Navigator, 050, 056-057
Hertzog, J.B.M.
  rise to power after Anglo-Boer War, 688
  failure to extend South African boundaries, 683
  influence on South African development, 684-685
  biographies of, 744, 751-755
Heuningvlei, 095
Hichens, L., 660
High Commission Territories. See under the names of individual
  territories: Basutoland, Bechuanaland, Swaziland
High Commissioner, role, 281, 699, 730
Hintsa (Gcaleka chief), 327
Hobhouse, E., 212, 620-621
Hoffman, J.P., 454
Hofmeyr, J.H. (1894-1948), 682
Hofmeyr, J.H. (1845-1909), 719
Holden, W.C., 397
Holland
  colonial power, 129, 151
  early exploration at the Cape, 063, 074
  immigrants to the Cape, 996
  pro-Boer agitation in Anglo-Boer War, 633-634
Hoole Family, 196

Hop, H., 080
Hopetown, 260
Horse breeding, 162
Hot Springs, Caledon, 127
Hottentot Holland Pass, 114
Hottentot Peoples, 055, 073, 081, 088, 095, 101, 127, 166, 282, 942, 944, 948-956
Houtman, C. de, 074
Hubner, H., 053
Huguenots, 223, 1020-1024
Hulley, R.B., 401

Imperial policy
  Britain, 587, 704, 713-715, 719
  European Powers, 708
  Germany, 700
Indian Inquiry Commission, 984
Indian Peoples in South Africa, 653, 978-991
Industrial and Commercial Workers Union of Africa, 834-835
Innes, Sir J.R., 287, 560
Ireland, immigrants to South Africa, 202
Isaacs, N., 360, 403
Isandhlwana, Battle of (1879), 423, 425, 427, 429-432, 441
Italy, early exploration of the Cape, 063, 074

Jabavu, J.T., 835, 837
Jacobsz, W.H., 488
Jameson, L.S., 551-560
Jameson Raid, 480-481, 483, 503, 551-560, 729
Janssens, H., 101
Janssens, J.W., 165, 169-171
Jansz, J.C., 090
Jenkins, T., 205
Jeppe, C., 489
Jervis, J., 416
Jewish immigrants to South Africa, 1025-1027
Johannesburg, history, 294, 461-463, 471, 476, 478, 504, 514
John III, King of Portugal, 070
Jojo (Amaxesibe chief), 269
Jordan, G., 297
Joubert, P.J., 486

Kaffir Wars. See Frontier Wars
Kaffraria, 105, 110, 181, 185, 272, 278, 915
Kalahari, 102-103, 107
Kama (Zulu chief), 397
Kat River Settlement, 105, 974
Kay, A., 573
Kay, J.A., 642
Kayser, F.G., 175
Kekewich, R.G., 599
Kemp, J.C.G., 691-692
Kerr, P., 660
Khoisan Peoples, 166, 948-956
Kimberley, Earl of (J. Wodehouse), 709

Subject/Topographical Index   287

Kimberley
  Diamond Fields, 181, 254, 256, 260-266
  Siege, 599
Kirkman, J., 401
Kitchener, H.M., 608, 624
Kitchingman, J., 872
Klapmuts Agricultural Station, 162
Knights Deep Mine, 539
Knyvett, F., 187
Kok, A., 951, 955, 975
Kok, A. III, 837
Kok, C., 102
Kokstad, 951
Kolbes, P., 081
Korana Tribes, 092, 106, 949, 971
Krauss, F., 097
Krebs, L., 098
Kreli (Xhosa chief), 295
Kruger, S.J.P.
  administrative policy, 500
  correspondence, 494-495
  political opposition to, 486
  relations with Britain, 512, 719
  role in War with Britain, 586, 589
  treasure, 262
  biographies of, 492-502
Kuruman, 102, 189
Kusia (Xhosa chief), 175

Labour
  Black, 835-836, 838, 842, 845
  Revolt, Witwatersrand (1922), 669, 681, 681a
Labour Party, 680, 838
Ladysmith, Siege of (1899-1900), 591, 596, 602, 615, 642
Land Acts (1910-1936), 839
Land and Immigration Board, Natal, 339
Land Tenure, 009, 183
Landdrosts, 192
Langalibalele (Amahlubi chief), 361-362
Latrobe, C.I., 099
Lattakoo (or Lattakoe), 087
Legaut, F., 077
Leighton, S., 109
Lembede, A., 804
Leonard, C., 503, 559
Le Vaillant, F., 054, 082, 084, 968
Leyds, W.J., 467, 505-506, 1012
Liberal Party
  in Britain, 512, 661
  in South Africa, 552, 680, 739, 829
Liberation Movements, 805
Lichtenstein, H., 054, 100-101
Liddle Expedition, 094
Lindley, D., 873-874
Linnaeus (Von Linne), 1028

Literary and Scientific Institution, 102
Livingstone, D., 048, 507
Lobengula (Matabele chief), 262, 286, 441, 511
London Convention (1884), 512, 719, 729
London Missionary Society, 853, 857-858, 860, 872, 877, 879, 883-884
Lovedale Institute, 181
Luipaards Vlei Estate and Gold Mining Company, 539
Lydenburg, 466, 485
Lyell, G., 347
Lyell, M., 347

Mabasa (Pondo chief), 269
Mabille, A., 914
Macarthur, J.S., 264
Macartney, G., Earl, 157
McCabe, J., 094
Mackenzie, J., 286, 720
MacLeod, L., 110
MacLeod Family, 366
McMurdo, E., 1014
Mafeking, Siege of (1899/1900), 600-601, 644
Magaliesberg, 102
Magersfontein, Battle of (1899), 599, 611
Mail Steamers, 115
Maitland Treaty (1884), 269
Majuba Hill, Battle of (1881), 475, 523, 528-529
Makana (Xhosa chief), 296
Makaula (Amabaca chief), 269
Makoma (Xhosa chief), 175
Makwassieberg, 098
Malan, D.F., 685, 735-737, 756-758
Malan, W., 635n
Malay Peoples, 969-970
Maluti Mountains, 956
Manuel I, King of Portugal, 069
Marais, P.J., 547
Mariannhill Mission Stations, 885
Marico River, 102
Maritz, S.G., 691-692
Masson, F., 082
Masupha (Basuto chief), 837
Matabele Tribe, 511, 943
Maxwell, J., 127
Maynier, H.C.D., 123, 134, 168
Mda, A.P., 804
Merriman, J.X., 292-294, 309, 688
Merriman, N.J., 295
Methodist Church, 205, 864, 869, 911
Military History, 268
Milner, A., Viscount
  reconstruction policy (1902-1905), 657-660, 668
  role in South Africa, 584, 586, 589, 638, 699, 730
  biographies of, 298-305, 657-659
Mine Labour Revolt, Witwatersrand (1922), 669, 681, 681a
Mission Stations, 092, 099, 257

Subject/Topographical Index 289

Missions and Missionaries
  American, 350, 365, 873-874, 1013, 1015
  Basutoland, 859
  bibliographies, 846-852
  Catholic, 854, 885
  Dutch Reformed Church, 894, 895
  Eastern Cape, 194, 205, 220, 228, 257, 278, 855, 875, 896, 911, 968
  general works, 861-869, 876, 878, 880, 893, 896
  German, 1019
  London Missionary Society, 853, 857-858, 860, 872, 877, 879, 881-884
  Methodist Missions, 205, 896
  Moravian, 875, 968
  Natal, 350, 365, 873, 874
  Pondoland, 856
  Scandinavian, 1028
  Separatist Churches, 871, 892
  Transvaal, 507
  Zululand, 391, 396-397
Mkhosana, M., 439
Mocquet, J., 077
Modder River, Battle of (1900), 611
Moffat, R., 048
Molopo River, 093
Molteno, J.C., 275, 293, 308
Molteno, J.T., 306-307
Molteno, P.A., 309
Moluccas, 061
Moodie, B., 197
Moodie, D., 217
Moodie Family, 197, 208
Moreland, J., 367
Moravian Mission Stations, 875, 968
Moroko (Matabele chief), 103
Moselikatze (Mzilikaze) (Matabele chief), 103, 189, 234, 469, 511, 926
Moshesh (Basuto chief), 103, 189, 921-925
Mosques, 966
Motor Buses, Cape, 113
Mount Ayliff, 269
Mozambique, 047, 069, 070, 110
Mpanda (Zulu chief), 393, 837
Mpondomise Tribe, 945
Mswati II (chief), 837
Muller, C.H., 691
Muller, H.P.N., 460
Muslims, 966
Mzilikazi (Matabele chief). See Moselikatze

Namaqua Tribes, 106, 274-275
Namaqualand, 078, 079, 080, 104, 106, 247
Napoleon, Eugene Louis Joseph, Prince Imperial of France, 410, 433, 435

Natal
  agricultural development, 348
  British settlers (1849-1891), 346, 351, 356, 366-369, 376, 379
  constitutional development, 363
  history and description, 061, 105, 108, 110, 181
  immigration, 334, 339, 357
  Indians, treatment of, 982-989
  police, 386
  railways, 344
  segregation policy, 437
  tribal reserves, 437
  Voortrekkers, 231, 370
Natal Native Corps, 433
National Convention (1908-1909), 656, 665-667
National Party, history, 731-738, 999, 1005
National Union of Uitlanders, 559
Nationalism. See Afrikaner Peoples, Nationalism; Black Peoples, Nationalism
Native Affairs Act (1920), 839
Natives. See Black Peoples
Natives Land Act (1913), 839, 908, 929
Navigation, 062
Nederburgh, S.C., 165
Nellmapius, A.H., 509
Neptune (convict ship), 285
Netherlands. See Holland
Ngqika (Xhosa chief), 837
Nguni Tribe, 402
Niven, R., 297
Nonquase, Prophecy of (1856/1857), 270
Norton, J., 296
Norway, immigrants to South Africa, 1028

Oldenborg (ship), 073
Omnibuses, Cape, 113
Oppenheimer, Sir E., 261
Orange Free State, history, 248, 443-460, 648, 992
Orange River, 090-091
Orange River Sovereignty (1848-1854), 278, 327, 458-459
Ornstein, A.F., 1025
Orpen, J.M., 269
Oswell, W.C., 048
Outlanders. See Uitlanders
Ovington, J., 127
Owen, F., 401
Ox wagons, description, 113, 249

Padroes, description, 060
Palgrave, W.C., 274-275
Pan-African Congress, 804, 817, 838
Panda (Mpanda) (Zulu chief), 393, 837
Paris Evangelical Mission, 092, 914
Parliament, Cape, 119-120
Parmentier, J., 077

Passenger liners, 115-116
Passive Resistance, 819, 835, 984, 988
Paterson, J., 206
Paterson, W., 082, 086
Pearson, C.K., 425
Pedi Tribe, 518
Peel, R., 722
Pereira, N.V., 053
Philip, J., 206, 278, 822, 860, 881-882, 916, 973
Phillipolis, 102, 951
Philipps, T., 216
Phillips, L., 540
Phipson, T., 369
Pictorial histories, 018, 030, 236
Pienaar, P., 053
Pietermaritzburg, description, 352, 359, 365
Pigot, S., 217
Pigot Family, 208, 217
Pilgrim's Rest, 485, 538
Pine, B.C.C., 340, 361-362
Plakkaaten, 140
Plaatje, S., 573
Political
  history, 020, 688
  parties, 686
    See also names of individual parties
Pondo Tribe, 269, 381, 913, 939
Poor White Problem, 294, 679
Port Elizabeth, 136, 289
Port St. Johns, 269
Portugal, in Africa, 047-072, 074, 151, 491, 700
Postma, W., 999
Potgieter, A.H., 469, 491
Press, Freedom, 220-221
Pretoria
  in nineteenth century, 465, 478, 515
  siege of (1880-1881), 475, 525, 642
Pretoria Convention (1881), 512, 719, 729
Pretorius, A., 234, 239, 327, 370
Pretorius, M.W., 446, 454, 464, 488, 491
Pringle, T., 219, 220-221, 297
Pringle Family, 219
Progressive Party, 739-740
Pyrard, F., 077

Quitrent Tenure, 183

Rabinowitz, J., 1025
Race
  policy, 680, 689, 788-843
  relations, 276, 694, 783-843
Railways
  political aspects, 561-564
  South African Republic (1872-1899), 477, 484, 491, 700, 1014
  South Africa, 344, 664, 668

Rand Mines Company, 534, 537
Rand Revolt (1922), 669, 681
Rebellion (1914-1915), 670, 691-692
Reform Committee, 480-481
Regimental histories, 188
Reitz, F.W., 454
Representation of Natives Act (1936), 839
Reserves, Natal, 437
Responsible Government, Cape, 258, 698
Retief, P., 240, 400-401
Rhenish Mission Stations, 891
Rhenius, J.T., 080
Rhodes, C.J.
  and Jameson Raid, 719
  and diamond mining, 261, 265
  and gold mining, 536, 539, 540
  and siege of Kimberley, 599
  imperialistic policies, 286, 511, 589, 699, 719
  prime minister of Cape, 293-294
  statements on Union, 724
  biographies, 313-323
Richardson, C., 216
Richardson, L., 662
Rietfontein Consolidated Mining Co., 539
Rimington, M.F., 643
Riou, E., 089
Robben Island, 117
Roberts, F.S., Earl, 624, 645
Robinson, H.G.R. (Lord Rosmead), 414, 559
Robinson, J.B., 265, 540
Robinson, W.A., 965
Robinson Deep Gold Mine, 539
Rorke's Drift, Battle of (1879), 425, 427-428, 430
Royal Ordinances of Portugal, 064
Russell, J., 1st Earl, 722
Russia, and Anglo-Boer War (1899-1902), 629

Saint Lucia Bay, 374, 625, 729
Salem, 194, 214, 296
Sampson, W.B., 965
Sand River Convention, 446, 728
Sandile (Xhosa chief), 918
Santo Alberto, shipwreck, 052
Sào Thoma, shipwreck, 052
Sao Joao Baptista, shipwreck, 052
Sauer, J.W., 309
Scandinavia, immigrants to South Africa, 1028
Scanlen, T.C., 275, 293
Schlosberg, F., 642
Schoeman, B., 737
Schreiner, C., 207
Schmidt, G., 875
Schreiner, W.P., 293, 325
Schrijver, I., 075
Scoon, R., 234

Subject/Topographical Index   293

Scott, P., 615
Sebastian, King of Portugal, 071
Secessionist Church Movement, 871, 880, 892
Segregation. See Separate Development
Sekukuni (Sekhukuni) (Bapedi chief), 374, 429, 475
Sekonyela (Tlokwa chief), 103, 189
Selborne, Lord (W.W. Palmer), 589
Selborne Memorandum (1907), 664
Selous, F., 048
Semi-Nomadic Farmers, 245-247
Separate Development, 675, 695, 798-799, 813, 818, 827-828, 831-832, 836, 841, 999
Sernigi, G., 067
Settlers of 1820. See Britain, Settlers of 1820
Shaka (Chaka) (Zulu chief), 360, 365, 390, 393-394, 403-406
Sharp, R., 615
Shaw, W., 205, 886-890
Shepstone, J.W., 175, 375
Shepstone, T., 340, 354, 361-362, 372, 375, 382, 728-729
Shippard, Sir S., 511
Ships, 115-116
Shipwrecks, 052, 054, 057, 115
    See also names of individual shipwrecks
Sikonyela. See Sekonyela (Tlokwa chief)
Simmer and Jack Mines, 539
Simons, C.J., 127
Slagtersnek Rebellion, 176, 186
Slater, A.W., 224
Slater, S.C., 224
Slavery
    Cape, 122, 124, 126, 132, 173, 180, 184, 698
    Transvaal Republic, anti-slavery agitation, 490, 507
Sluysken, A.J., 165
Smith, Sir A., 102-104, 189, 378
Smith, Sir H.G.W., 120a, 175, 278, 297, 326-328, 458, 722
Smith, J.H., 264
Smuts, J.C.
    role in Anglo-Boer War, 589
    rise to power after Anglo-Boer War, 684
    and Gandhi, 984, 986
    role in Treaty of Vereeniging, 653
    failure to extend South African boundaries, 683
    influence on South African development, 685, 688
    biographies, 759-775
Sobukwe, R., 804
Social and cultural history, 013, 018, 025, 027, 030
Soga, T., 837
Somerset, C.H., Lord, 190, 204
Somerset, F., 175
Somerset, H., 175, 191
Somerville, W., 087
Source Books, 017, 022
South Africa Act (1910), 687
South African Congress of Trade Unions, 802
South African Indian Congress, 819

South African Institute of Race Relations, 808
South African Land and Immigration Association, 378
South African National Convention, 649, 656, 667
South African Native Affairs Commission (1903-1905), 797, 839
South African Native National Congress (1912), 440
South African Outlook (Journal), 845
South African Party, 273
South African Rebellion (1914), 691-692
South African Republic. See Transvaal (before Union)
South African War (1899-1902). See Anglo-Boer War, 1899-1902
Southern Rhodesia, failure to enter Union of South Africa, 683
Southey, Sir R., 329
Sparrman, A., 048, 082, 968, 1028
Spion Kop, Battle of (1899), 611-612
Sprigg, G., 275
Staples, I., 330
Staples, J.B., 330
Starrenburg, J., 145
Statues of Voortrekkers, 241
Steamships, 115-116
Steedman, A., 105
Stefler, J., 053
Stellaland, 464
Stephen, J., 717
Stewart, J., 439
Steyn, M.T., 294, 453-454, 457, 688
Stockenstrom, Sir A., 276, 940-941
Strike of 1922, Witwatersrand, 669, 681, 681a
Strijdom, J.G., 685, 737, 776
Struben, C., 515
Struben, E., 516
Struben, H.W., 264, 516, 542
Stuart Family, 208
Stubbs, T., 226
Sub Nigel Mine, 539
Sundays River Settlement, 482
Suzman, H., 740
Swaziland, 484, 511, 683
Sweden, immigrants to South Africa, 1028
Swellendam, 101, 123, 329
Swellengrebel, H., 082

Table Mountain, 085
Tachard, G., 077
Takoon, 095
Tas, A., 140, 142-143
Tavernier, J., 077
Taylor Family, 208
Tea trade, 172
Tembuland, 269
Ten Rhyne, W., 952
Territorial Segregation. See Separate Development
Theiler, A., 212
Thlaping Tribe, 087, 189
Thompson, G., 106

Subject/Topographical Index 295

Thunberg, C.P., 082, 968, 1028
Tlokwa Tribe, 189
Tombstones, 060
Tools of Voortrekkers, 249
Torch Commando, 680, 739
Toverberg, 118
Trade Unions, 696, 800-802
Tram cars, 113
Transkei
  description, 795, 939
  historical records, 269, 920
  history, 930
Transport, 113, 115-116
Transvaal (before Union)
  anti-slavery agitation (1852-1868), 490, 507
  1852-1899, 248, 374, 464-510, 992
  annexation (1877), 181, 374, 491, 505-506, 519
  War of Independence (1880-1881), 268, 474-475, 510, 519, 521-531
  Jameson Raid (1896), 551-560
  Anglo-Boer War (1899-1902), 565-646
  post-war reconstruction, 648-668
  treatment of Indians (1885-1906), 990
  Volksraad, 513
Travel and Exploration, Bibliographies, 042-046
Travellers
  seventeenth century, 073-079
  eighteenth century, 080-090
  1800-1850, 091-106
  1850-1900, 107-110
Treaty of Vereeniging (1902), 653-654
Treaty System, 278
Trekboers, 245-247
Trichardt, L. (Trigardt), 048, 242-244, 491
Trolley buses, Cape, 113
Tshangane Tribe, 270
Tswana Tribe, description, 911
Tulbagh, R., 139
Tulbagh Kloof, 114
Tulbagh (Town), 101
Tyali (Xhosa chief), 175

Uitenhage, 289
Uitlanders, 480, 503, 729
Ulundi, Battle of (1879), 415
Umhala (Xhosa chief), 295
Umqikela (Pondo chief), 269
Umzimvubu River, 093
Unification of South Africa (1910-1912), 649, 654-656, 661, 663-667
Union Castle Shipping Company, 116, 309
Union Federalist Party, 680
United Brethren, 099
United Party, 680, 686, 693
United States of America
  American Board Missions in South Africa, 853, 873-874
  Americans in Anglo-Boer War (1899-1902), 628, 631

United States of America (cont.)
  and South Africa, 853, 873-874, 1013-1015
  missionaries in Natal, 365
  race contacts, South Africa and United States compared, 803
Urban Areas Act (1928), 797
Uys, P., 234

Vaal River
  diamond diggings, 261, 263, 266
  expedition, 094
Vaal River Island Treaty (1895), 487
Valentyn, F., 145
Van Bengalen, A., 966
Van Breugel, A., 144
Van de Kaap, S., 966
Van der Kemp, J.T., 171
Van der Stel, S., 048, 078-079, 127, 139, 141, 144-146
Van der Stel, W.A., 127, 133, 140-143
Van Dieden, W., 053
Van Imhoff, G.W., 131
Van Linschoten, J.H., 071
Van Meerhoff, P., 053
Van Pallandt, A., 170
Van Plettenberg, J., 082, 968
Van Quaelberg, C., 144
Van Reenen, D.G., 171
Van Reenen, J., 082, 089
Van Reenen, S.V., 163
Van Reenen, W., 090
Van Riebeeck, J., 057, 139-141, 144, 147-149
Van Spilberger, J., 074
Van Wouw, A., 212
Van Wyk, S., 175
Venable, H.I., 873
Vergelegen, 133
Verwoerd, H.F.
  policy of separate development, 778, 780, 821
  biographies of, 737, 777-780
Viervoet, Battle of (1851), 458
Vijn, C., 413
Villebois-Mareuil, G., 646
Volks Vereniging, 273
Voorspoed Diamond Mine, 261
Voortrekkers, 227-250
Vorster, B.J., biographies of, 737, 781-782

Wagner, Z., 150
Wagons. See Ox wagons
Walker, G., 542
Walvis (Walvisch) Bay, 108, 163
War of the Axe. See Frontier War of 1846-1847
Warden, H.D., 458
Warner, J.C., 915
Warships, 188
Waterboer dynasty, 955

Waterboer, N., 955
Wesleyan missionaries, 886-890, 897, 912
Wessels, J.W., 503
West, M., 340
White, Sir G., 615
Whiteside, J., 903
Wienand, E.D., 1018
Wikar, H.J., 090, 968
Wilgefontein Settlement, 339
Williams, J., 898
Wilmot, A., 224
Wilson, A.E., 873
Winburg, 459
Witwatersrand
  goldfields, 532-550
  mine labour revolt, 669, 681-681a
Wodehouse, Sir P.E., 278, 723
Wolseley, Sir G., 383-385, 424, 436
Wood, H.E., 425, 531
Wood family, 196
Working classes, 798
Wragg Commission, 982
Wyndham, H., 660

Xhoré (Hottentot chief), 055
Xhosa Bible, 257
Xhosa Tribe, 120a, 223, 270, 278, 282, 901, 903, 915-916, 918, 928, 933-934

Zulu Rebellion (1906-1908), 438, 440, 442, 663, 834
Zululand
  description, 097, 107, 356, 359, 902, 907
  history to 1879, 341-342, 349, 360-362, 370, 372-375, 377, 389-408, 927
  War of 1879, 268, 383, 385, 397-398, 409-436
  after 1879, 382, 437-442